Wahhabi Islam

Wahhabi Islam

From Revival and Reform to Global Jihad

NATANA J. DELONG-BAS

OXFORD
UNIVERSITY PRESS

2004

OXFORD
UNIVERSITY PRESS

Oxford   New York
Auckland   Bangkok   Buenos Aires   Cape Town   Chennai
Dar es Salaam   Delhi   Hong Kong   Istanbul   Karachi   Kolkata
Kuala Lumpur   Madrid   Melbourne   Mexico City   Mumbai   Nairobi
São Paulo   Shanghai   Taipei   Tokyo   Toronto

Copyright © 2004 by Oxford University Press, Inc.

Published by Oxford University Press, Inc.
198 Madison Avenue, New York, New York 10016

www.oup.com

Oxford is a registered trademark of Oxford University Press

Published in the UK and Commonwealth by I.B. Tauris & Co. Publishers
6 Salem Road, London W2 4BU

www.ibtauris.com

Library of Congress Cataloging-in-Publication Data
DeLong-Bas, Natana J.
Wahhabi Islam: from revival and reform to global Jihad /
Natana J. DeLong-Bas.
    p.   cm.
Includes bibliographical references and index.
ISBN 0-19-516991-3
1. Wahhābīyah.   2. Islamic fundamentalism—History.
3. Islam—Doctrines.   4. Muhammud ibn 'Abd al-Wahhāb, 1703 or 4-1792.
I. Title.
BP195.W2 D45 2004
297.8'14—dc22   2003016382

9 8 7 6 5 4 3 2 1

Printed in the United States of America
on acid-free paper

To the glory of God

and in loving memory of two remarkable women

my mother
Grace Ann Toothaker DeLong
(1945–1998)

and my grandmother
Florence Margaret Rohe Toothaker
(1913–2003)

Preface

The poet John Donne once wrote that "No man is an island." Similarly, no book is ever the product of a single person. This work has been influenced not only by the scholars and activists about whom it is written, but also by a variety of scholars, both American and Saudi, who have read, commented on, and critiqued it. I would like to particularly acknowledge the seminal roles of John O. Voll and John L. Esposito in shaping my thought and for their encouragement and support as I have sought to shatter the stereotypes of Wahhabi Islam. John L. Esposito has been instrumental in keeping me focused on the relevance of my historical research on contemporary issues and expanding my vision to encompass a more global understanding of the phenomenon of political Islam. John O. Voll has proven endlessly resourceful, knowledgeable, and enthusiastic in appreciating the value of a study of Ibn Abd al-Wahhab's thought within the various contexts of eighteenth-century Islamic intellectual history, world history, and Islamic activism in the contemporary era. Thanks are due to Judith E. Tucker for her insightful comments on and suggestions for providing a broader framework for the chapters on Islamic law and women and gender in order to appreciate better Ibn Abd al-Wahhab's contributions to these fields. Thanks are due to David Commins and William Ochsenwald for their careful reviews of the chapters on theology and jihad. I am indebted to the late George Makdisi for his research on Hanbali law and Ibn Taymiyya. I am grateful to Ira Lapidus for discussions of eighteenth-century *hadith* criticism. Thanks are due to Hala Fattah for discussions of Gulf history over the years. I am grateful to Amira El-Azhary Sonbol for sparking my initial interest in this topic. I am also grateful to my Saudi friends and colleagues for their insights into and discussions of both Ibn Abd al-Wahhab and Osama bin Laden.

The in-depth study of Ibn Abd al-Wahhab and his writings has been made possible by the generosity and support of many people. Thanks are due to Faisal bin Salman, Abd Allah S. al-Uthaymin, and Dr. Fahd al-Semmari, Director of the King Abd al-Aziz Foundation for Research and Archives, in Riyadh, Saudi Arabia, for making the full corpus of Muhammad Ibn Abd al-Wahhab's works available to me and to the Center for Muslim-Christian Understanding and the Department of History at Georgetown University, the American Historical Association, and the King Abd al-Aziz Foundation for Research and Archives for their financial support.

Finally, I wish to thank those who have been supportive at a more personal level, particularly by entertaining the children in order to give me space for writing and revisions. I am especially indebted to my "second mother," Ruth Slonaker DeLong, who has stepped in to fill the roles of cherished friend and beloved grandmother; my sister Zedeka, who has always been there in moments of crisis as deadlines approached; our friends Anthony, Ursula, Chantal and Veronica Woodson and David, Pamela, Marissa and Nicole Helms, who have spent countless hours entertaining the children while I was writing and out on the lecture circuit following the September 11 tragedy; and my mother-in-law, Françoise LeSage Bas, for her assistance with the children during the summer of 2002.

My own worldview and faith have been profoundly influenced by the most important people in my life—my family. My father, the Rev. James A. DeLong, has always set a strong example of what scholarship is intended to be and has been the example and role model I have striven to emulate in my own work and life. My mother, the late Grace Ann Toothaker DeLong, and grandmother, the late Florence Margaret Rohe Toothaker, dedicated their lives to loving service of God, community, and family. Their examples of love, encouragement, and insistence that we be hard-working, faithful, and productive citizens responsible for giving something back to our societies have had a profound influence on my life and work.

Finally, and most importantly, I thank my husband Christophe for his encouragement, support, and humor in seeing this project through to the end. His boundless energy, positive attitude, and assistance, both with child care and the never-ending housework and repairs, have made the experience bearable for all of us. Our children, Aurora and Gabriel, have tolerated their mother's preoccupation with Muhammad Ibn Abd al-Wahhab and Osama bin Laden with patience beyond their years. I am grateful for their constant reminders of the importance of seizing the opportunities each day has to offer and of their practical reminders of the importance of peace-keeping, mutual understanding, and the power of dialogue and discussion in resolving disputes. Raising them full time while completing this book has been a challenge, but I am grateful for their animated company and unconditional love.

Contents

Wahhabi Islam

Introduction

Post–9/11, Wahhabism has been identified by governments, political analysts, and the media as the major "Islamic threat" facing Western civilization and the inspiration for Osama bin Laden and his al-Qaida network. It has become infamous for its negative influence on Islam, mosques, and madrasas globally. It is described as extremist, radical, puritanical, contemptuous of modernity, misogynist, and militant in nature. It has been characterized as Islamo-fascism following in the traditions of communism and nazism.[1] It is accused of inspiring militant religious extremism in movements ranging from the Taliban of Afghanistan to the so-called Wahhabis of Central Asia and Osama bin Laden's al-Qaida network.[2] It is targeted as the most intolerant of all interpretations of Islam, seeking to impose itself alone as the expression of "true" Islam.[3] Wahhabi teachings are often referred to as "fanatical discourse" and Wahhabism itself has been called "the most retrograde expression of Islam" and "one of the most xenophobous radical Islamic movements that can be."[4]

Yet Wahhabism is also the conservative creed of the ruling family of Saudi Arabia and has been defended by visionary twentieth-century reformers like Muhammad Rashid Rida of Egypt and the Palestinian American scholar Ismail Raji al-Faruqi as a model for reforming and rejuvenating Islam in the modern era—an interpretation considerably at odds with its supposedly violent and intolerant tendencies. Also at odds with such negative portrayals are the more positive images of Wahhabis distributing copies of the Quran and *hadith* (accounts of the sayings and deeds of the Prophet), funding hospitals, orphanages, and other charitable institutions; and constructing mosques worldwide. Wahhabis have also provided relief following natural disasters globally and in the aftermath of the wars in Bosnia and Kosovo. However controversial the missionary work (daw'ah) accompanying these efforts has been, a strong case can be made for recognition of Wahhabi involvement in charitable works and its provision of educational and worship institutions for Muslims throughout the world.[5] This image does not fit with the more monolithic presentation of Wahhabism as a militant, violent, extremist movement.

For all of the press and academic coverage of Wahhabism, few attempts have been made to define and delineate what makes a Wahhabi a Wahhabi other than broad concerns about tendencies toward violence, extremism, terrorism, and indoctrination of the masses in the conservative Wahhabi creed. There has been little discussion of the Wahhabi interpretation of Islamic law or scripture outside of general assertions of "literalism," "innovation," "heresy," and obsession with ritual matters, such as the precise length and style of a man's beard or the exact fashion in which one is to pray.[6] Having been accused of a paradoxical combination of narrow-mindedness and innovation, Wahhabism is then typically dismissed as being unrepresentative of "Islam" and unworthy of detailed attention to its doctrines. Particularly striking is the lack of attention given to the written works of Wahhabism's founder and ideologue, Muhammad Ibn Abd al-Wahhab, despite the fact that it is assumed that the militance, violence, and extremism displayed by certain Wahhabis today have their origins in Ibn Abd al-Wahhab's own teachings.

Post–9/11, many in the West have struggled to understand the connection between Wahhabi beliefs and the horrendous acts of terrorism that caused the deaths of over three thousand civilians. Fear and uncertainty about the previously little known Wahhabis have led to serious questions. Does Wahhabism represent an ongoing threat to the United States and American interests? Is Wahhabism monolithic? Is it necessarily opposed to Western civilization and values? Can the United States safely have a friendly and cooperative relationship with the Wahhabi monarchy of Saudi Arabia or are Americans being deluded into consorting with the enemy due to the need for oil and a failure to understand the "true" nature of Wahhabism?[7]

In response to the demands for answers, many have asserted that the militant extremism of Osama bin Laden has its origins in the religious teachings of Muhammad Ibn Abd al-Wahhab, who is believed to have legitimated jihad against non-Wahhabis and encouraged the forcible spread of the Wahhabi creed. According to this interpretation, Ibn Abd al-Wahhab is the godfather of modern terrorism and Islamic militance.[8] Like his contemporaries, he is accused of being opposed to modernity, an extreme literalist in his interpretation of Muslim scriptures, a misogynist, and an admirer and imitator of past militant radicals, particularly the medieval scholar Ibn Taymiyya. Like Osama bin Laden, he is believed to have had little formal religious training, and his written works are generally dismissed as mere compilations of Quranic verses and *hadith* without any accompanying commentary or interpretation.[9] Finally, both Ibn Abd al-Wahhab and the Wahhabis are often accused of being outside of the Sunni tradition due to their position as "heretical innovators" and extremists.[10] Although this comparison makes for a simple and clean analysis, it is not faithful to the historical record.

The real Muhammad Ibn Abd al-Wahhab, as revealed in his written works, was a well-trained and widely traveled scholar and jurist, as well as a prolific writer. His extant written works fill fourteen large volumes, including a collection of *hadith*; a biography of the Prophet Muhammad; a collection of *fatawa* (juridical opinions); a series of exegetical commentaries on the Quran; several volumes of Islamic jurisprudence (*fiqh*), numerous theological treatises; and other varied works, including detailed discussions of jihad and the status of women. The scope of his scholarship stands in marked contrast to the few legal rulings (*fatawa*) issued by Osama bin Laden. More importantly, his insistence on adherence to Quranic values, like the maximum preservation of human life even in the midst of jihad as holy war, tolerance for other religions, and support for a balance of rights between men and women, results in a very different worldview from that of contemporary militant extremists. The absence of the xenophobia, militantism, misogyny, extremism, and literalism typically associated with Wahhabism raises serious questions about whether such themes are "inherent" to Wahhabism and whether extremists like Osama bin Laden are truly "representative" of Wahhabism and Wahhabi beliefs.

Wahhabi Islam: From Revival and Reform to Global Jihad presents for the first time in a Western language the themes of Ibn Abd al-Wahhab's writings that are of greatest concern post–9/11: Wahhabi theology and worldview, Islamic law, women and gender, and jihad. Rather than reinforcing the standard image of Ibn Abd al-Wahhab as "an unsophisticated, narrow-minded wanderer" and a "disconnected, footloose son of the remote oases" who became "the archetype for all the famous and infamous Islamic extremists of modern times,"[11] it reveals a more moderate, sophisticated, and nuanced interpretation of Islam that emphasizes limitations on violence, killing, and destruction and calls for dialogue and debate as the appropriate means of prosetylization and statecraft. This new understanding is then compared to the writings of other scholars and activists, both past and present, on the controversial topic of jihad in order to assess Ibn Abd al-Wahhab's influence, or lack thereof, on contemporary Islamic militants, most notably Osama bin Laden, and to explore the roots of the militant extremism inherent in their visions of global jihad.

I

Muhammad Ibn Abd al-Wahhab and the Origins of Wahhabism: The Eighteenth-Century Context

Wahhabism was founded in the eighteenth century in the province of Najd, a broad desert expanse located in central Arabia. Najd has often been described as a desert wasteland, standing in marked contrast to the more cosmopolitan Hijaz region, which houses the Muslim holy cities of Mecca and Medina. While the Hijaz has been at the forefront of international commerce and educational exchanges, Najd has traditionally been considered a more isolated region, off the beaten track of the caravan routes. As such, Najd has not been a prime location for tourism or foreign conquest. This does not mean that it was completely isolated from the outside world. In fact, pilgrims, students, and merchants regularly traveled from Najd to other regions of Arabia and the Middle East to participate in the broad exchange of ideas, culture, and goods. These exchanges were simply on a smaller scale than was the case for the more cosmopolitan regions that served as a point of arrival rather than departure.

The main advantage that Najd enjoyed over other regions, such as the Hijaz, was that it held little interest for foreign conquerors. Consequently, Najd's history has been marked more by local tribal warfare and chieftains struggling for power than by its position as part of a broader state or empire.[1] Even when other portions of Arabia were claimed by the Ottoman Empire, Najd retained its independence.

The fact that Najd has always been independent eliminates the notion of Wahhabism as a response to European colonialism or Ottoman state consolidation. Najd had no claim to commercial or religious importance and thus held no interest for imperial conquest. If

Wahhabism was not a response to external pressures or aggressions, why did it arise at this particular time in this location? How could a movement begun in such an isolated region grow to become a global phenomenon?

Setting the Stage: The Eighteenth-Century Context

Wahhabism was neither a historical aberration nor an isolated phenomenon. It did not arise in a vacuum. In fact, Wahhabism reflects some of the most important trends in eighteenth-century Islamic thought, underscoring the interactions and exchanges that took place between Muslims in cosmopolitan regions like the Hijaz. The fact that Wahhabism so clearly reflects major trends of thought apparent in other contemporary reform movements suggests that it was neither "innovative" nor "heretical." Rather, it can more appropriately be viewed as part of mainstream eighteenth-century Islamic thought, although somewhat tailored to its specific context.

The eighteenth century is often described as the century of renewal and reform in Islam, a time when revivalist movements of various types arose in a variety of locations.[2] Although each movement had its own specific characteristics, reflecting the environments and contexts in which they arose, eighteenth-century revival and reform movements share some common themes and emphases. Unlike the movements of the nineteenth and twentieth centuries, which arose in response to external aggressions, like European imperialism, or the desire for political independence, the movements of the eighteenth century arose largely in response to internal conditions. The most important of these was the perceived deterioration in Muslim beliefs and practices.

For eighteenth-century reformers, one of the major signs of the deterioration of Islam was the adoption of rituals and beliefs from other religions, like praying to saints and believing that saints could grant blessings or perform miracles. In some cases, people had adopted superstitious practices, like spitting in a particular way or wearing charms to ward off evil spirits. Reformers were puzzled and perturbed by these practices, particularly when they were accompanied by a failure to respect Muslim rituals and prayers. They wondered whether the people engaged in these activities knew why they were doing so or what such actions symbolized. Some questioned whether a person engaged in such activities could still be considered a Muslim since their actions reflected a belief that people and things other than God possessed the power to grant requests or provide protection.

This was a serious matter because the major distinctive doctrine of Islam is belief in absolute monotheism (tawhid). In Islam, God alone is considered to be worthy of worship and prayer. This belief is reflected in the defining act of the Muslim, the declaration of faith that proclaims, "I believe that there is no god but The God and that Muhammad is the Messenger of God." Consequently, failure to act in accordance with this proclamation of faith opened the door to questions about the person's status as a Muslim. It was for this reason that the revival and reform movements of the eighteenth century adamantly insisted that a "return" to monotheism was the necessary first step in reforming Islam. This meant getting rid of foreign and superstitious beliefs and practices. Wahhabism shared this common concern and goal, becoming famous for its strict adherence to *tawhid*.

However, this was only a first step. Eighteenth-century reformers believed that adherence to *tawhid* had implications beyond private religious beliefs. They believed that adherence to *tawhid* should also be reflected in public life by placing God at the center of the political order. Theoretically, this meant recognizing God as the creator and sustainer of all life and as the ultimate sovereign and lawgiver. Practically, it meant reimplementing Islamic law (Sharia) as the law of the land. Eighteenth-century reformers believed that this restoration of God to the center of Muslim public life was the key to recovering the power and prestige that Muslims had enjoyed in the past during the rules of the great empires and caliphates.

In general, reformers did not seek to implement their goals by overthrowing the current regimes or insisting that their reforms be applied from the top down by force or government decree. Instead, they believed that reform should be a process, beginning at the grassroots level and moving gradually upward through society as peoples' private ethical and moral beliefs, grounded in their religion, influenced decision making and public conduct. In this way, adherence to *tawhid* was intended to launch the second goal of the reformers, the sociomoral reconstruction of society.

In addition to adherence to *tawhid*, eighteenth-century reformers called for a return to the fundamentals of faith—the Muslim scriptures of the Quran (the word of God as revealed to the Prophet Muhammad) and the *hadith* (records of the sayings and deeds of Muhammad)—as the sources of guidance that would lead to the sociomoral reconstruction of society. This emphasis on the return to fundamentals made the reformists the original Muslim fundamentalists in the same way that nineteenth-century Christian movements dedicated to a "return" to the Bible were the original Christian fundamentalists. There was nothing inherently militant or violent about this return, nor did it necessarily imply a literal interpretation of the scriptures. It was simply an attempt to move away from centuries of historical interpretations and accretions in favor of direct study and interpretation of the scriptures.

The dual emphasis of the eighteenth-century reformers on the Quran and *hadith* was neither unusual nor revolutionary. Muslims believe that the Quran and *hadith* are complementary. The Quran, as God's Word, is a statement of God's will for all of humanity. Although it contains some legal prescriptions, it is not a lawbook. Rather, the Quran provides moral and ethical guidance and values that human beings are supposed to apply in their personal and public lives, individually and communally. The *hadith* provide practical advice on how this is to be done.

Muslims do not worship Muhammad or believe that he is God. Throughout history, they have emphasized that Muhammad was strictly a human being, although they believe that he was the most perfect of human beings. It is precisely because he was a real human being living in the real world in which love and war, family and marital relations, business and commercial transactions, and local and international relations exist that his example is so important for Muslims to study.

Muslims believe that Muhammad's life reflects the perfect living out of the teachings and values of the Quran. Consequently, whenever a question arises about how one should respond to a given situation, they turn to the *hadith* to see how Muhammad reacted. Although some Muslims have taken Muhammad's example very literally, for example, wearing their beards exactly like he did, most do not believe that such strict, literal adherence is necessary or even desirable. Rather, many point to his attitudes and values, such as respect for women, caring for the poor and orphans, and support for social justice, as the correct examples to follow.

The reformers shared the belief that Muhammad's example was very important for Muslims to follow. Consequently, the third major characteristic of the reform movements was a renewed emphasis on the study of the *hadith* but in a new way. Eighteenth-century studies of *hadith* differed from studies of the past because they focused on the content of the *hadith* rather than their chains of transmission. This represented a major break from the past tradition of *hadith* study and authentication.

The *hadith* were initially a series of oral testimonies transmitted by Muhammad's Companions and wives. Because they were oral, *hadith* were originally verified by determining whether the chain of transmitters (*isnad*) was credible. That is, could the original source truly have had knowledge of the issue in question because he or she had direct contact with either Muhammad or one of his Companions? Was the testimony passed down through a credible series of witnesses who were known to have had enough contact with each other to have made accurate transmission possible? Was the chain of transmitters unbroken in time? And were there multiple reports of the same incident, which would bolster the claim to authenticity? In the past, if the chain of transmitters was found to be credible then the *hadith* was declared authoritative and was incorporated into the later written compilations.[3]

Although the reformers believed that authentication of the chain of transmitters was an important first step in determining the potential authenticity of a *hadith*, they believed that verification of the chain was insufficient by itself. They recognized the potential for fabrication not only of the chains of transmitters but also of the content. Consequently, they believed that the content of the *hadith* should also be examined to determine whether its message was consistent with the message of the Quran. They reasoned that the Quran and *hadith* should be in agreement with respect to their content and the values they embodied because they were supposed to serve as complementary sources of scripture. Thus, if a *hadith* had a strong chain of transmitters but contradicted the teachings of the Quran, the reformers believed that it should be declared inauthentic. The Wahhabis were important with respect to this new methodology because the written works of their founder and ideologue, Muhammad Ibn Abd al-Wahhab, are an excellent and compelling example of its use. The Wahhabis also became well known for their travels throughout the Muslim world in search of *hadith* collections.[4]

This new content-driven methodology of *hadith* criticism tied in directly to the reformists' goal of the regeneration of Muslim society through the return to scripture because it offered a new way to interpret and understand it. These reformers did not seek to re-create literally the early Muslim community, as some later movements tried to do.[5] Rather, the goal was to rediscover the meaning of the *hadith* in their original context in order to determine the eternal value or ethical guideline contained within it.[6] This value or guideline was then compared to Quranic teachings about the same, setting the stage not only for a more profound understanding of Islam but also for a more meaningful application of Islamic values in both the private and public spheres. Thus, this new methodology of studying the Quran and *hadith* was not just an intellectual exercise. It had very practical implications for daily life, for both individuals and the broader Muslim community.

The desire of eighteenth-century reformers to embrace and study scripture directly was not simply a matter of religious purity or theological quibbling. These reformers were concerned not only by their belief that Muslims were not paying sufficient attention to Islamic values and ethical considerations but also by the fact that their fellow Muslims did not distinguish between the scriptures and their interpretations. In their experience, many Muslims of their time considered the scriptures and their interpretations to be equally authoritative.

In the more than one thousand years that had passed since the death of Muhammad, religious and legal scholars had written innumerable commentaries, analyses, and exegetical studies of the scriptures. Particularly important among these works were those that detailed and elaborated upon Islamic law. Similar to the role of the law in Judaism, Islamic law plays an important role in Muslim life. The Quran declares that the correct living out of faith (orthopraxy) is a necessary corollary to correctness of belief (orthodoxy). In other words, while it is important to have correct religious beliefs, it is even more important to live a life that reflects those beliefs. The Quran teaches that at the end of time human beings will be judged not on the sole basis of what they believe but on how they lived their lives. However, the Quran is not a lawbook along the lines of Old Testament books like Leviticus and Deuteronomy, which outline long series of exacting legal prescriptions. Rather, the Quran provides moral and ethical values and guidelines, which Muslim legal experts have elaborated and detailed for practical application. While this scholarship was one of the most important contributions and efforts of early Muslim scholars, this process was understood to have been largely completed under the Abbasid Empire (750–1258 C.E.). Although there were always some independent jurists who continued to interpret the law on their own, a practice called *ijtihad*, the guidelines and teachings of the early legal specialists were broadly accepted and utilized intact until the eighteenth century, a practice known as *taqlid*.[7]

Eighteenth-century reformers were concerned by *taqlid* because they perceived that these interpretations had come to be considered as authoritative as the scriptures. Over time, students and scholars had begun to place a heavier emphasis on study and knowledge of the commentaries and interpretations of past scholars than on direct study of the scriptures.

The reformers believed that this practice was inappropriate. They pointed to the fact that interpretations and commentaries often reflected the context in which they were written, both geographical and political, rather than the context in which the scriptures were revealed and originally understood. They questioned whether one interpretation of a legal or religious matter could truly be authoritative for every time and place, as had been claimed by past scholars. Concluding that this could not be the case, they called on each generation and context to be responsible for revisiting the scriptures directly for fresh interpretation. The promotion and exercise of *ijtihad* therefore became another defining characteristic of eighteenth-century reform movements.

The reformers understood their movements to be a process that would necessarily occur gradually. They were evolutionary, not revolutionary, in approach. In general, the movements did not seek to topple governments, engage in coups to replace one political system with another, or organize their followers into cells to carry out terrorist activities or guerrilla warfare against existing governments. They did align themselves with political leaders, but their purpose in doing so was not overtly political.[8] What mattered to the reformers was that the political system in place reflected and supported Islam in both private and public life. They were more concerned with matters of religious practice and adherence to Islamic law than with political systems or geographic boundaries.

The reformers sought to implement a two-tiered approach to the sociomoral reconstruction of society. At the grassroots level, they sought to continually add to the number of their followers, believing that this was the level at which real change needed to occur. Once individuals began to reform their religious beliefs and practices, it was expected that these private beliefs would have a broad impact on public behavior. At the same time, the reformers were practical enough to anticipate popular resistance to the proposed reforms because they represented a change not only in beliefs but also in behaviors at both the private and public levels. Consequently, the reformers sought protection and assistance from local political leaders. According to this arrangement, the political leaders acted as protectors who ensured that the religious teachings of the reformers were respected and implemented. In return, the reformers supported the political rule of their protectors and provided religious legitimation for it.[9]

There were times when military activity occurred under this arrangement, particularly when issues of self-defense arose. However, jihad as holy war was not the primary purpose of the eighteenth-century reform movements. The reformers were not engaged in battles for independence, the end to colonial rule, or global jihad. Engagement in jihad as holy war was not one of the movements' defining characteristics. If anything, their downplaying of jihad as holy war distinguished them from the independence movements of the nineteenth and twentieth centuries, which specifically called for jihad as holy war in order to shake off colonial overlords or respond to other aggressions.

One final hallmark of eighteenth-century reform movements was the fact that they were inspired and led by scholars (ulama) rather than lay activists, as is so often the case in the contemporary era. This does not mean that there was a broad consensus among all ulama that reforms were necessary. In fact, some of the strongest opposition to the reform movements came from the ulama, typically those who held a position within the official religious establishment. These establishment ulama often owed their positions to nepotism and the sale of offices rather than to their scholarly achievements. As a result, they were often more interested in maintaining their own power bases than in the "correct" practice and interpretation of Islam. The reformers, on the other hand, tended to either occupy the lower echelons of the religious establishment or stand outside it altogether, often enjoying mass popularity rather than government favor. Consequently, a subtheme of the reform movements was opposition to reform-minded scholars by establishment ulama, who supported a continuation of the status quo in order to maintain their own positions of power.

The life and teachings of Muhammad Ibn Abd al-Wahhab, the founder and ideologue of Wahhabism, reflect these eighteenth-century themes and power struggles as they were played out first in his home province of Najd and later throughout the Arabian Peninsula. Like his contemporaries, he called for the sociomoral reconstruction of his society through greater adherence to monotheism (tawhid) and renewed attention to the Quran and hadith. He rejected imitation of the past (taqlid) in favor of fresh and direct interpretation (ijtihad) of the scriptures and Islamic law by contextualizing them and studying their content. He was a religious scholar. He established a protective relationship with a local political leader, who agreed to implement his religious teachings. Jihad was neither the primary goal nor the purpose of the movement he inspired. And he was opposed by local religious scholars and leaders who perceived threats to their own power bases from his teachings.

Where he differed from his contemporaries was in the context of Najd and in some of the more specific details of his teachings. Ibn Abd al-Wahhab's biography provides context for understanding who he was as a person, how he implemented these major reformist themes in Najd, and what their impact was upon this environment.

Muhammad Ibn Abd al-Wahhab: Biographical Sources

Most of what is known about Ibn Abd al-Wahhab comes from four types of sources: (1) contemporary chronicles written by his supporters, the most important of whom were Husayn Ibn Ghannam and Uthman Ibn Bishr; (2) polemical works written by his opponents, the most important of whom was Ahmad bin Zayni Dahlan; (3) accounts written by Western travelers to Arabia; and (4) Ibn Abd al-Wahhab's own written works. Of all of these accounts, the chronicles contain the most biographical information and are considered to be the most accurate in terms of biographical information because of the proximity of the writers to their subjects.

Husayn Ibn Ghannam (hereafter referred to as Ibn Ghannam) was the first chronicler of the Wahhabi movement. He was a contemporary and acquaintance of Ibn Abd al-Wahhab. Ibn Ghannam was an Arabic language teacher by profession, a characteristic that comes across clearly in the complex linguistic style of his chronicle. A native of al-Ahsa', Ibn Ghannam is believed to have moved to Najd in order to be close to Ibn Abd al-Wahhab. In addition to providing a year-by-year outline of the activities of the Wahhabis and a biography of Ibn Abd al-Wahhab, Ibn Ghannam's chronicle, *Tarikh Najd* (*The History of Najd*), also contains excerpts of Ibn Abd al-Wahhab's writings and letters. Ibn Ghannam died in 1811 c.e. and was considered "an old man." His birth date is unknown.

Uthman Ibn Abd Allah Ibn Bishr al-Hanbali al-Nasiri al-Tamimi (hereafter referred to as Ibn Bishr) was the second major chronicler of the Wahhabi movement. He was born in the town of Shaqra' in Najd. Ibn Bishr was not a contemporary of Ibn Abd al-Wahhab and did not know him personally. However, he did have direct and personal contact with some of Ibn Abd al-Wahhab's closest adherents, whom he interviewed while writing his chronicle. Ibn Bishr was a student of some of the most important scholars of early nineteenth-century Najd, including Ibn Ghannam, a fact that becomes clear when the chronologies are compared. However, Ibn Bishr's chronicle is not simply a rewriting or recasting of Ibn Ghannam's work. The presentation style of Ibn Bishr's chronicle is less literary and more straightforward and direct in discussion. Although he included much of the information contained in Ibn

Ghannam's work, Ibn Bishr also undertook extensive, systematic interviews with people who had firsthand knowledge and experience of the early days of the Wahhabi movement and had personally known Ibn Abd al-Wahhab. As a result, Ibn Bishr's chronicle is more detailed in many places than Ibn Ghannam's.

Both of these early chronicles provide a wealth of information about Ibn Abd al-Wahhab and the early Wahhabi movement by contemporary observers of and participants in the same. However, it is important to recall that the chroniclers were not official biographers of Ibn Abd al-Wahhab. Stylistically, the chronicles are not written in the hagiographical (manaqib) style typically associated with biographies of Sufi saints. The chroniclers did not seek to establish Ibn Abd al-Wahhab as some sort of holy person or saint or to demonstrate his possession of the capacity to perform miracles (barakah). The inclusion of biographical information about Ibn Abd al-Wahhab had as its purpose the contextualization of the ideologue who inspired the Wahhabi movement. It was the development of the movement, and more particularly the chronology of the Saudi dynasty, that was the main focus of the chroniclers.

Consequently, a few words of caution with respect to the chronicles are in order. First, it is important to note that both chroniclers tended to be supportive of the Wahhabi movement. As a result, they tended to portray the most positive aspects of the movement. At the same time, they emphasized the persecution and oppression often suffered by the Wahhabis. The subtle comparison of Ibn Abd al-Wahhab and the early Wahhabis to the lifetime of Islam's prophet, Muhammad, served in the minds of the chroniclers to demonstrate continuity in the Muslim experience and the attention given by the Wahhabis to the example of Muhammad. It should not be misconstrued as a literal attempt to re-create exactly the life and times of Muhammad, as has been asserted by Wahhabi opponents.[10]

It should also be noted that the more controversial activities of the early Wahhabis are typically portrayed in a somewhat apologetic manner. While it is important to understand the logic and processes that accompanied controversial actions (discussions that will be included in the biography), these discussions should not detract from the fact that the outcomes of certain infamous events were tragic.

Finally, as previously noted, Ibn Bishr was not a contemporary of Ibn Abd al-Wahhab. His methodology of interviewing Wahhabis who had known Ibn Abd al-Wahhab and participated in the early events of the movement provides important information about how the Wahhabis viewed themselves and their past. However, because they were recounting memories, it is possible that their recollections of past events were influenced by subsequent events. Thus, while the chronicles provide eyewitness accounts of the life and times of Ibn Abd al-Wahhab, they must be understood and interpreted within their own biases. Whenever possible, information gleaned from the chronicles has been supplemented either by other historical materials or by Ibn Abd al-Wahhab's own writings.

The second type of primary source material, that of accounts written by Wahhabi opponents, has not been used extensively in the reconstruction of Ibn Abd al-Wahhab's biography for several reasons. First, because opponents of the movement were quite vehement in their opposition, their writings tend to be extremely polemical in style rather than factual or straightforward. At times, this makes it very difficult to discern the difference between facts and rumors.[11] Second, many of these polemical accounts address later developments in the Wahhabi movement rather than the early period and the lifetime of its founder. Because the movement's orientation and even its teachings changed significantly over time, accounts dealing with later time periods cannot be used to portray the early period accurately. The most important examples of the second type of primary source materials are Ibn Dahlan's works, *al-Durar al-Saniyah fi al-Radd ala al-Wahhabiyah* and *Khilasat al-kalam fi bayan ahra al-balad al-haram*, which were written long after Ibn Abd al-Wahhab's death sometime between 1792 and 1797. Ibn Dahlan was born in 1816–17, which means that his knowledge of the movement at the height of Ibn Abd al-Wahhab's leadership would have been garnered more than fifty years after the fact. (Ibn Abd al-Wahhab retired from public life around 1773, although he continued to serve as a consultant and adviser until his death.) Third, because of their polemical nature, these accounts tend to be more useful in reconstructing impressions of the movement than in recounting events or teachings. Thus, polemical works have been largely discarded in the reconstruction of the biography of Ibn Abd al-Wahhab and the early teachings of the Wahhabi movement.

The third type of source material, Western travel accounts, have not been used to reconstruct the biography of Ibn Abd al-Wahhab for similar reasons. Although the travel accounts provide interesting (and often controversial) impressions of Wahhabis and have been used by earlier scholars, none is contemporary with Ibn Abd al-Wahhab's lifetime. Furthermore, none of these writers met Ibn Abd al-Wahhab or read any of his writings. In fact, many never encountered any Wahhabis at all. The accounts generally record information and impressions passed on to them by people who had supposedly encountered Wahhabis. Because of their questionable accuracy, the use of Western travel accounts here has been restricted to discussions of eighteenth-and nineteenth-century impressions of the Wahhabis. They are not used to reconstruct the biography of Ibn Abd al-Wahhab or his immediate context.

Ibn Abd al-Wahhab did not write an autobiography. His written works were dedicated to religious matters, particularly theology and Islamic law. Consequently, what personal information and references to events in his life are contained in his written works are scanty and are used more to illustrate legal issues and theological points than to provide personal information about himself. Nevertheless, there are instances in his written works in which he refers to historical events from his life, particularly his various encounters with local religious *ulama*. They also offer insight into his personality and approach to interpersonal relations. The content of his writings will be discussed more fully in the chapters addressing important themes in his works. Before analyzing his teachings, though, it is important to get a sense of who Ibn Abd al-Wahhab was as a person.

Muhammad Ibn Abd al-Wahhab: A Biography

No physical descriptions of Ibn Abd al-Wahhab have survived the test of time. We do not know if he was short or tall, was thin or heavyset, or had any striking physical characteristics.[12] We do know a few things about his temperament and personality.

Ibn Abd al-Wahhab was a man of intense religious conviction. He believed in the importance of living one's religious beliefs in both private and public life. He valued education and was eager to engage in discussions and debates with others. He was a precise man, who said exactly what he intended and not a word more. He was a master of logic and an able and prolific writer. He was a man who sought to teach and guide individuals from every walk of life, reflecting his belief in the equality of all Muslims, regardless of their ethnic or socioeconomic background. He was devoted to the concept of social justice, dedicating significant portions of his writings to the protection of women and the poor and respect for human life and property. He believed that women had rights in balance with the rights of men in both private and public life, leading him to insist that these rights be restored and protected. He had little patience for corruption, bribery, and hypocrisy, which he continuously and vehemently denounced. He was neither a pacifist nor a warmonger. He believed that there were times when violence was justified, as in the case of self-defense. However, he was neither an active supporter nor a promoter of violence because he believed that it stood in the way of the ultimate goal of Muslims—the winning of converts. He believed that life was something to be not only respected but celebrated. He also had a dry sense of humor, which was particularly evident in his various encounters with the *ulama*, who always looked foolish at the end of his stories and legal discussions.

Ibn Abd al-Wahhab was born in 1702–3 in the town of al-Uyaynah in the Arabian province of Najd. He was descended from a prestigious family of Hanbali jurists and theologians.[13] His grandfather, Sulayman ibn Ali ibn Musharraf, was a judge (*qadi*) and was recognized as the greatest scholar and authority on Hanbali jurisprudence in Najd during his lifetime. His uncle, Ibrahim ibn Sulayman, was both a judge and an issuer of legal opinions (*mufti*), or *fatawa*, in the towns and settlements surrounding al-Uyaynah, where he often was called in to settle disputes.[14] His father, Abd al-Wahhab ibn Sulayman, was the *qadi* of al-Uyaynah and served as his first teacher of both religion and jurisprudence (*fiqh*).[15] Ibn Abd al-Wahhab was clearly well placed in a strong family tradition of legal scholarship and its practical application. Thus, it is not surprising that his writings include detailed discussions of Islamic law.

Ibn Abd al-Wahhab is reported to have memorized the Quran before he was ten years old, an accomplishment that marks his completion of the most basic education that any Muslim undergoes.[16] He took his religious responsibilities seriously and made the Hajj pilgrimage to Mecca as a young teenager. This pilgrimage was followed by a two-month stay in Medina prior to returning home to resume his studies with his father.[17]

In addition to memorizing the Quran, Ibn Abd al-Wahhab also studied the *hadith*, Quranic exegesis (*tafsir*) literature, *fiqh*, and the writings of various *ulama* about the fundamental principles of Islam.[18] Of all of the literature he studied, the *hadith* and *tafsir* were the most influential in developing his worldview. References to the Quran and *hadith* are abundant in all of his written works.

The Quran and *hadith* were particularly influential in shaping Ibn Abd al-Wahhab's understanding of the doctrine of monotheism (*tawhid*), both in terms of how it is to be upheld and what constitutes violation of it.[19] The upholding of *tawhid* was to become the hallmark not only of Ibn Abd al-Wahhab's teachings but also of the Wahhabi movement he inspired. Wahhabis across time and space have been both famous and infamous for their dedication to this principle and their denunciation of any and all activities that either violate it directly or could lead someone to violate it indirectly. Failure to adhere to and uphold *tawhid* has been blamed for the collapse of the social order, evil, tyranny, corruption, oppression, injustice, and degeneration.[20] Like other eighteenth-century reformers, Ibn Abd al-Wahhab taught that the remedy for such sociopolitical ills was simple: the revival and reform of Islam as evidenced by stricter adherence to *tawhid*. Only this could lead to the reestablishment of a just, stable, and powerful society.

His adamant belief that *tawhid* should be at the center of Muslim life led Ibn Abd al-Wahhab to dedicate his life to preaching and teaching the necessity of worshiping the one and only God and the elaboration of how this was to be done in practice. He particularly targeted the foreign and superstitious practices adopted by many Muslims as practices to be eradicated, beginning in his hometown. It was in al-Uyaynah that Ibn Abd al-Wahhab began to preach publicly his message of *tawhid*. Although he has been cast by some writers as a rabid itinerant who preached hellfire and brimstone wherever he went, Ibn Abd al-Wahhab's own writings and the historical record reveal a more subtle and nuanced approach, at least in the early stages of his encounters. Rather than arriving in a town, denouncing every practice with which he disagreed, and threatening the inhabitants with hell and damnation if they didn't change their ways immediately, Ibn Abd al-Wahhab initially sought to engage the inhabitants in dialogue and debate about their various activities and religious practices. He did this because he believed that verbal persuasion was a more effective means of getting the inhabitants to recognize the errors apparent in some of their religious practices. Thus, the tenor of his proselytizing was one of debate and discussion rather than overt violence and destruction. On the occasions when he engaged in more visible symbols of adherence to *tawhid*, this was done only after he had gained a significant following in a given location and generally tended to be a test of the dedication of his followers to *tawhid*. The results of his preaching campaign were often mixed.

For example, when Ibn Abd al-Wahhab began preaching about *tawhid* in his hometown of al-Uyaynah, he started by engaging the townspeople in a series of discussions about what *tawhid* is and how people violate this principle, often unintentionally. In the course of the dialogue, he provided them with specific examples of how some of their religious practices were either wrong or innovative (*bid'a*). It is important to note that his method was clearly one of persuasion rather than accusation because the townspeople did not respond by throwing rocks at him or chasing him out of town. They must have found some truth in what he taught because they allowed him to stay and to continue to teach and preach. It is important to recall that Ibn Abd al-Wahhab did not have a powerful political protector at this point. Consequently, the fact that the townspeople allowed him to continue his discussions indicates that there was at least a tacit level of approval of his teachings.

However, the townspeople did not immediately or completely abandon their prior practices or activities. Listening to a single sermon or teaching session did not result in an immediate and complete life change due to a radical conversion. In Ibn Abd al-Wahhab's approach, the process of adhering to *tawhid* was understood to be exactly that—a process or change that would occur gradually over time as people examined their hearts, thoughts, and activities; gained further knowledge about their religion; and made conscious decisions to change their behavior in accordance with their renewed and reformed beliefs.

Had Ibn Abd al-Wahhab's preaching and teaching been strictly a private religious matter, this state of thoughtful discussion, debate, and gradual change might have continued. However, he did not limit religion and religious beliefs to the private sphere. He believed and taught that religion necessarily has a public dimension because what one believes and the values to which one adheres are not and should not be limited to private life. Because human beings, both men and women, are also public figures who interact with their broader communities, their beliefs and value systems, such as honesty, concern for social justice, and opposition to corruption, necessarily carry over into public behaviors. Consequently, renewal and reform of personal beliefs were intended to carry over into public behaviors and attitudes, ultimately presenting a challenge to the power of the local political and religious leaders. It was at this point, when he began to challenge the leadership of the community, that Ibn Abd al-Wahhab ran into serious trouble.

Local leaders perceived in Ibn Abd al-Wahhab's teachings a challenge not only to their political but also to their moral authority. They discerned that Ibn Abd al-Wahhab's reforms would not remain at the private, individual level but would ultimately have an impact on the public sphere and consequently their own bases of power. When the implications of Ibn Abd al-Wahhab's teachings about *tawhid* became clear and began to have a negative influence on local authorities, the local leaders responded by refusing to recognize any truth in what he taught. They ultimately pushed him to leave al-Uyaynah on a pilgrimage to Mecca.[21] This pattern of acceptance until the local leadership felt threatened enough to encourage, if not force, Ibn Abd al-Wahhab to leave occurred repeatedly in the early years of his teaching and preaching career.

Opponents of the Wahhabi movement point to the fact that Ibn Abd al-Wahhab was pushed into leaving as evidence of the "extremist" and "heretical" nature of his teachings. However, the fact that his teachings were accepted until the local authorities began to feel that their bases of power were threatened makes it clear that the issues were really about power struggles and not so much about heretical religious teachings. Other non-Wahhabi historical records confirm that actual examination of Wahhabi texts revealed consistency with the Quran and *hadith* so that those who bothered to read them did not find any evidence of heresy in Ibn Abd al-Wahhab's writings.[22]

Ultimately, Ibn Abd al-Wahhab gave in to the ruling powers of al-Uyaynah and left. He made the pilgrimage to Mecca and then proceeded to Medina,[23] where he pursued additional studies with two of the most prominent *hadith* scholars of the time, the Najdi Shaykh Abd Allah ibn Ibrahim ibn Sayf and the Indian Shaykh Muhammad Hayat al-Sindi. Mecca and Medina played a special role as major centers of eighteenth-century *hadith* scholarship and important international crossroads for Islamic scholars from throughout the world. Muslim scholars came to the Hijaz for a variety of reasons. Some simply chose to live and teach in the holiest cities in Islam, a venture that was facilitated by the development and expansion of shipping between the Hijaz and other Muslim lands. Others sought to escape foreign encroachment. This was particularly true in the case of Indian *hadith* scholars like Muhammad Hayat al-Sindi, who left behind the deteriorating Mughal Empire and its accompanying Muslim weakness to proclaim the need to recover the glorious past through a return to the fundamental sources of Islam.[24] Thus it was that Ibn Abd al-Wahhab came into contact with some of the major themes of eighteenth-century reform in Medina, in large part thanks to his teachers. He no doubt also engaged in discussion and debate with his fellow students from other parts of the Muslim world. Ibn Abd al-Wahhab's studies and encounters in Medina had a profound impact on both his intellectual formation and his worldview.

Although it is always difficult to determine the exact degree of influence that any teacher has over any student, it is clear that Ibn Abd al-Wahhab was inspired by the key themes taught by al-Sindi and Ibn Sayf: the importance of the *hadith* as a source of scripture, attention to the content of the *hadith* rather than just the chains of transmission, opposition to the imitation of past scholarship (*taqlid*), support for individual interpretation (*ijtihad*), and the urgent need for sociomoral reform.[25] Both of these important scholars were also admirers of the medieval scholar Ibn Taymiyya. Although it is often asserted that Ibn Abd al-Wahhab was an avid admirer and strict follower of Ibn Taymiyya, his writings do not support this assertion.[26] What is important is that Ibn Sayf and al-Sindi included at least some of Ibn Taymiyya's works in their teaching and that Ibn Taymiyya's works therefore would have been one, though certainly not the only, component of Ibn Abd al-Wahhab's studies in Medina.

Perhaps in response to the charges of some contemporaries that Ibn Abd al-Wahhab founded a "fifth," and therefore heretical, school of Islamic law and that he deviated significantly from the teachings of more mainstream Sunni Islam, the chronicles include two anecdotes about his interactions with his famous teachers. These stories demonstrate Ibn Abd al-Wahhab's continuity with their teachings and their encouragement of his preaching and teaching. In the first, Ibn Sayf spends a day with Ibn Abd al-Wahhab and offers him some advice about a "weapon" that will prepare him for his future encounters. When Ibn Abd al-Wahhab expresses interest in seeing this "weapon," Ibn Sayf takes him to a house filled with books, which he commands him to study, making the subtle point that true change can only be brought about through knowledge and discussion, not violence.[27]

The second story occurs later chronologically and describes a scene in which Muhammad Hayat al-Sindi and Ibn Abd al-Wahhab were standing near the Prophet's tomb, watching a variety of people pass by to seek help and intercession from it. al-Sindi asks Ibn Abd al-Wahhab for his opinion about this practice. Ibn Abd al-Wahhab responds that, "These people should wash their hands of what they are doing since what they are doing is worthless/false." Ibn Abd al-Wahhab then proceeds to "correct" this behavior and make it right, apparently without any interference or opposition from al-Sindi.[28]

Whether or not these incidents actually occurred is open to debate. However, it is clear that the chroniclers included these anecdotes to validate and justify Ibn Abd al-Wahhab's mission and demonstrate his continuity with mainstream eighteenth-century thought. The anecdotes are mentioned here because they reflect the worldview that Ibn Abd al-Wahhab came to adopt. He believed in the importance of education, study, and debate as the most convincing means of winning converts, and he was not afraid to carry out the practical application of his theological beliefs, such as preventing people from requesting intercession from tombs. Regardless of whether these anecdotes are true, it is clear that Ibn Abd al-Wahhab left his studies in Medina inspired to engage in a more activist preaching career.

From Medina, Ibn Abd al-Wahhab set out for Basra (located in modern Iraq), where he pursued additional studies in *hadith* and *fiqh* with an important scholar and madrasa (Islamic school) teacher, Muhammad al-Majmu'i. Like Ibn Sayf and al-Sindi, al-Majmu'i also reportedly endorsed Ibn Abd al-Wahhab's public proclamations forbidding associationism (*shirk*) and *bid'a* and confirmed and approved his message of *tawhid*.[29] Al-Majmu'i further reportedly allowed his own children to study with him. It was only when the leaders of Basra decided that Ibn Abd al-Wahhab's teachings represented a threat to their own power and authority that they decided to drive him out in the heat of the day.[30] Al-Majmu'i, though not included in the forcible exile, was injured in the process.[31]

It is believed that Ibn Abd al-Wahhab came into contact with Shiis during this stay in Basra, which would explain his familiarity with their theological beliefs and juridical and religious practices. Although it is often asserted that Ibn Abd al-Wahhab was adamantly opposed to Shiism, he specifically targeted only one particular extremist sect, the Rafidah, in only one treatise.[32] Outside of this treatise, Ibn Abd al-Wahhab never specifically mentioned the Shiis by name, although he denounced some of the practices that he believed violated *tawhid*.[33]

On leaving Basra, Ibn Abd al-Wahhab traveled to al-Zubayr, from which location he intended to continue north to Syria.[34] However, while he was in al-Zubayr he lost his financial support and had to abandon his travel plans.[35] He returned to Arabia and traveled to al-Ahsa, where he stayed with Shaykh Abd Allah ibn Abd al-Latif.[36]

Ibn Abd al-Wahhab's sojourn in al-Ahsa was brief. For undisclosed reasons, he soon left al-Ahsa and headed for Huraymila, where his father lived.[37] On his arrival in Huraymila, he resumed his studies with his father and began preaching against the innovation and associationism practiced there in both words and deeds.[38] It was during this stay in Huraymila that he wrote his most famous treatise, *Kitab al-Tawhid* (*The Book of Monotheism*), copies of which circulated quickly and widely throughout Najd.[39] Although his ideology and the movement he inspired have been dismissed by some, who claim that he had little influence, originality, or lasting impact, the historical record shows that Ibn Abd al-Wahhab's influence spread over a wide area within a short period of time, suggesting that the message he preached found broad enough support not only to last but also to consolidate a movement.[40]

This is not to say that everyone responded positively to his message. Indeed, Ibn Abd al-Wahhab's pattern of preaching prohibitions ultimately caused a rift between him and his father, as well as with the inhabitants of Huraymila.

Ibn Abd al-Wahhab consequently ceased preaching until his father's death in 1740.[41]

After his father's death, Ibn Abd al-Wahhab resumed his preaching and teaching activities. Although some historical records indicate that he at this time declared jihad as holy war against those who did not adhere to the doctrine of *tawhid*, not all accounts agree with this assertion.[42] It is unlikely that jihad as holy war would have been declared at this time because this not only would have been inconsistent with Ibn Abd al-Wahhab's teachings but also physically impractical, if not impossible. Ibn Abd al-Wahhab did not have a political protector at this time. Consequently, he would have lacked the military power to engage in a jihad as holy war. It is more likely that he simply continued his preaching and teaching activities, gradually winning converts.

At least some of the people of Huraymila responded positively to his preaching and offered him their financial support. Huraymila was an interesting test case for the political potential of Ibn Abd al-Wahhab's teachings because the population was divided in its reaction to them. On the one hand, two of the tribes of Huraymila became united due to their support for Ibn Abd al-Wahhab and his teachings, demonstrating the capacity of his message to serve as a unifying force.[43] On the other hand, Huraymila also demonstrated the threat of his message to local political and religious leaders and the power of his message to divide the community. The opposing forces of Huraymila were apparently so threatened by Ibn Abd al-Wahhab's message and so adamant about continuing their "deviant" behavior that they banded together in an assassination plot against him.

The main issue at stake with respect to deviant behavior was Ibn Abd al-Wahhab's denunciation of sexual immorality and his insistence that the people of the region adhere to proper Islamic standards of sexual behavior, that is, reserving sexual relations for marriage. In response, a splinter group, consisting mostly of slaves, attacked him under the cover of night with the intent of killing him. The attempt was foiled when Ibn Abd al-Wahhab realized what was happening and called for assistance.[44]

After the assassination attempt, Ibn Abd al-Wahhab left Huraymila and again returned to his hometown of al-Uyaynah, which had been rebuilt and was now ruled by Uthman ibn Hamid ibn Muammar. Ibn Muammar, as befit a leader of his time, received Ibn Abd al-Wahhab hospitably and honored him by granting him the hand of his aunt, al-Jawhara bint Abd Allah ibn Muammar, in marriage.[45] It was only after this marriage that Ibn Abd al-Wahhab began to teach Ibn Muammar about the principle of *tawhid*.[46] Ibn Abd al-Wahhab and Ibn Muammar then struck a deal. In exchange for Ibn Muammar's support for his religious teachings, Ibn Abd al-Wahhab agreed to support the ruler's political ambitions to expand his rule over Najd and possibly beyond.[47] Ibn Muammar agreed, and Ibn Abd al-Wahhab embarked on a broad public preaching campaign.

The alliance formed between Ibn Muammar and Ibn Abd al-Wahhab was important for several reasons. First, it foreshadowed the later alliance between Muhammad Ibn Saud and Ibn Abd al-Wahhab that led to the foundation of the first Saudi state, which remains intact today as the third Saudi state. This was a tactic adopted by many other eighteenth-century reformers throughout the Muslim world. The formation of a religio-political alliance was not unique to the Wahhabis.

Second, this alliance made clear the religious basis for the political movement that grew out of Ibn Abd al-Wahhab's religious teachings and ultimately became known as Wahhabism. What was important about this religious vision as it was translated into the political sphere was that the leader was to proclaim and adhere to the principle of *tawhid*. That is, all earthly power had necessarily to grow out of recognition of the unique and all-powerful role of God. This approach emphasized the importance of intent in carrying out one's actions, for it makes it clear that one must have the proper intent—recognition and enforcement of *tawhid*—as the basis for one's actions, even, and especially, those concerned with politics, in order to obtain the desired results. Without proper intent, a political leader would only be working for self-aggrandizement, a goal that was clearly at odds with *tawhid*.

The third issue of importance with respect to this time period is the fact that three acts that have come to symbolize the Wahhabi movement occurred during it. These acts were the cutting down of a sacred tree, the destruction of a tomb monument, and the stoning of an adulteress. All of these activities reflected the practical application of Ibn Abd al-Wahhab's overarching message of *tawhid*. They have also come to be considered the hallmark of the Wahhabi movement and prominent examples of the kind of extremism generated by Ibn Abd al-Wahhab's teachings. They not only made Ibn Abd al-Wahhab famous in his own time and place but made both him and the Wahhabi movement infamous across the centuries and throughout the world. Consequently, it is worth examining the circumstances under which these activities occurred in order to determine what can be learned from them with respect to Ibn Abd al-Wahhab's worldview.

All three of the infamous events are recorded by the chronicles in a fair amount of detail.[48] The first, the cutting of the sacred tree, took place following the initial call to *tawhid* issued after the alliance was established between Ibn Muammar and Ibn Abd al-Wahhab. There were in al-Uyaynah at that time a number of trees on which the local populace was in the habit of hanging things in order to request the trees' blessing or intercession on their behalf. Ibn Abd al-Wahhab believed that this practice constituted a direct and serious violation of *tawhid* because it visibly proclaimed the belief that something other than God had the power to grant blessings and intercede for people. He therefore decided that a strong, visible response was in order. Following the example of the Prophet Muhammad, he sent a variety of people out to cut down the trees that served as objects of worship. He saved the most glorified of all of the trees for himself.

While his point was to provide a positive visual aid for the implications of true adherence to *tawhid*, the spectacle of Ibn Abd al-Wahhab personally chopping down this object of popular veneration and worship proved to be a shock to the inhabitants of al-Uyaynah and others who heard about it. Regardless of how much this action was supported by his followers, his willingness to engage in such a destructive act signaled to nonadherents the extremism and intolerance latently inherent in his teachings. This incident made it clear that Ibn Abd al-Wahhab's dedication to *tawhid* was absolute and that worship or veneration of objects, as well as other animist and superstitious practices, would not be tolerated in areas where he and his followers lived. Veneration or worship of anyone or anything other than God clearly had no place in Islam as far as the Wahhabis were concerned.

Similarly, the second incident, that of the destruction of the monument over the tomb of Zayd ibn al-Khattab (one of Muhammad's Companions and the brother of the second Sunni caliph, Umar ibn al-Khattab) was intended to demonstrate visually what it means to adhere to *tawhid*.[49] As in other cases, Ibn Abd al-Wahhab had already carried out a preaching and teaching mission in the area where the tomb was located and had won a significant number of followers. The destruction of the monument over the tomb, which was popularly venerated because of its connection to the early Muslim community, was a deliberate act. It was neither an accident nor a random incident. Ibn Abd al-Wahhab specifically chose this tomb because of its popularity and because it honored a human being rather than God.

As with the tree-chopping incident, the destruction of the tomb represented direct adherence to the example of the prophet Muhammad. The *hadith* record Muhammad's command to destroy tombs and shrines because they can and have led to the veneration and worship of the people buried or commemorated there, an act that clearly violates the principle of *tawhid*.[50] It was because of the possibility that people might be led to worship human beings rather than God that Ibn Abd al-Wahhab was so adamant about tomb destruction. It was not because of a literal approach to the interpretation of scripture.

Ibn Abd al-Wahhab was a pragmatic man as well as a determined preacher. He recognized the importance of this particular tomb and the devotion of the people of the area to it. He knew that there would likely be strong opposition and resistance to its destruction by the local populace, regardless of what they proclaimed to believe. The tomb was an important emotional connection to the early Muslim past. It was probably also an important source of revenue because it served as a pilgrimage site. The local population was not likely to sit by and passively allow its destruction. Consequently, Ibn Abd al-Wahhab asked Ibn Muammar and approximately six hundred of his men to accompany him to the site.

As anticipated, the local inhabitants resisted Ibn Abd al-Wahhab's declared intent to destroy the monument. However, when they saw Ibn Muammar and his men and learned of their resolve to engage in war anyone who stood in opposition, they refrained from interfering with its destruction. As with the tree-chopping incident, the spectacle of Ibn Abd al-Wahhab tearing the monument down with his own hands made a strong impression on both observers and those who heard about the incident later. Equally impressive was the political protection Ibn Abd al-Wahhab now enjoyed. People no longer felt as free to oppose the practical application of his teachings because they had personally witnessed or heard about the military strength that now backed him.

The destruction of the tomb was important for three reasons. First, it again confirmed for non-Wahhabis the extremist nature of the Wahhabi movement, despite the fact that Ibn Abd al-Wahhab had neither done nor encouraged anything that was not part of the Prophet Muhammad's own example. Opponents of the movement looked at the end result—the destruction of an object of popular veneration—and assumed that militancy and destruction of property were inherent to Ibn Abd al-Wahhab's teachings. Thus, the reputation of the Wahhabis for violence and destruction began, although this was not the driving force behind the action.

Second, the destruction of the tomb set a pattern for tomb destruction by the Wahhabis over both space and time. They became notorious for their destruction of tombs that served as objects of popular veneration. This pattern has led to conflict between Wahhabis and Shiis and Sufis up through the contemporary era.

Third, the destruction of the tomb signified that the Wahhabi movement was not simply opposed to non-Muslims. Because this tomb belonged to a hero from the early Muslim community, the message behind the destruction was clear: not even Muslims should serve as popular objects of veneration. Because such objects carried the potential to lead otherwise faithful Muslims from the straight path of *tawhid*, they could not be permitted to remain. Thus, certain battle lines were drawn between Muslims as intolerance for popular practices inconsistent with *tawhid* was declared.

The destruction of the monument produced a variety of reactions. While some of Ibn Abd al-Wahhab's followers found it inspiring and set out to repeat it as evidence of their faith, others were concerned that he had gone too far in carrying his teachings to their logical conclusion. Ibn Abd al-Wahhab himself did not find the destruction of the monument to be particularly troubling because the issue was one of property that was not vital to human survival. As will be shown in his discussion of jihad, he had a very different perspective where life, whether human or animal, and survival were concerned. Destruction of property was permissible in the case of the monument only because of the religious purpose it had come to fulfill. Ibn Abd al-Wahhab did not call for his followers to engage in broad or rampant destruction of property.

The third critical incident, the stoning of the adulteress, was the most troubling for Ibn Abd al-Wahhab because a human life was at stake. Although opponents have pointed to this incident as evidence of the violence and misogyny supposedly inherent to Wahhabism, as well as the supposedly literal interpretation the outcome reveals, Ibn Abd al-Wahhab did not interpret the incident this way. When viewed in its fuller context, it reveals a more complicated, multilayered issue. It is important to note that Ibn Abd al-Wahhab himself was uncomfortable with the outcome of this tragic case.[51]

The historical literature typically mentions only the end result of this incident—the fact that the woman was stoned—and provides neither contextualization nor a discussion of the process that led to the stoning. The impression generally given, therefore, is that a woman was brought before Ibn Abd al-Wahhab and accused of adultery. Ibn Abd al-Wahhab responded by instantaneously stoning her, in accordance with his literalistic interpretation of Islamic law. According to opponents, this incident proved once and for all that Ibn Abd al-Wahhab was a militant extremist who hated women and believed that any indication of sexual immorality on their part deserved the death penalty, regardless of the surrounding circumstances.

This presentation is misleading not only because it does not include any of the details of what actually happened but also because it fails to accurately portray Ibn Abd al-Wahhab's attitude toward women.[52] It is therefore necessary to examine this incident in some detail to understand what it actually conveys about Ibn Abd al-Wahhab's attitude toward women and his interpretation of Islamic law.

The story opens with the woman in question coming to Ibn Abd al-Wahhab of her own accord and confessing to him that she has committed *zina'*. *Zina'* is an act of sexual intercourse that occurs outside of marriage, whether as fornication or adultery. Because the Quran teaches that the only legal avenue for sexual intercourse is within the marriage relationship and further condemns fornicators and adulterers, the sin in question here was a serious one. *Zina'* is one of the four sins included among the crimes punishable by death (*hudud*).[53] The assignment of the death penalty for the commission of *zina'* comes from the *hadith*.[54] It is not specified by the Quran.

It is noteworthy that the woman came to Ibn Abd al-Wahhab of her own free will. No one forced her to appear before him and confess her sins. She was not dragged into a tribunal by her male family members nor was she accused of sexual immorality by her neighbors. Ibn Abd al-Wahhab himself was surprised by the woman's confession because there did not appear to be any reason for it other than to test his sincerity and resolve as a preacher. Interestingly, he did not respond by condemning the woman to stoning on the spot, even though Islamic law gave him the right to do so because she had confessed her sin personally. Neither did he call in her male family members and insist that they do a better job of controlling the woman's sexual activities.

Instead, he spoke directly to the woman and held her personally responsible for her behavior. He admonished her to be chaste, giving her the benefit of the doubt—perhaps she had not known what constituted correct behavior—and the opportunity to repent and change her behavior.

The final outcome of this case was due to the woman's deliberate choice to continue in her immoral sexual behavior. There is no indication that either her honor or that of her family was impugned by her interactions with Ibn Abd al-Wahhab.[55] The case also serves as evidence of Ibn Abd al-Wahhab's concern for justice for women. Throughout the case, he tended to reject condemnation in favor of conversation and education, even where women were concerned. The woman's ultimate punishment was due to her failure to cease her immoral behavior.

The woman responded to her encounter with Ibn Abd al-Wahhab by committing *zina'* again—repeatedly—making it clear that she had no intention of changing her behavior. Puzzled by the woman's odd behavior—she knew what the consequences of her actions were because he had personally made her aware of them—Ibn Abd al-Wahhab launched an inquiry into her state of mind. Was it possible that the woman was insane and therefore not responsible for her actions? After all, what sane person would deliberately and knowingly commit a sin or crime that carried the death penalty?

The inquiry found the woman to be of rational, sound mind. However, Ibn Abd al-Wahhab was still reluctant to stone her. Perhaps there was another reason for her behavior. Was she being raped or otherwise forced to engage in sexual intercourse against her will? Ibn Abd al-Wahhab arranged another meeting with the woman to inquire about her circumstances. The woman informed him that she was not being coerced and that she intended to continue to engage in *zina'*. She left the meeting and continued to engage openly in *zina'*, confessing her sin each time she did so.

It was only at this point—after several discussions, two inquiries into the woman's circumstances, and three opportunities to change her ways—that Ibn Abd al-Wahhab gave in to pressure from the local *ulama* and reluctantly agreed to the implementation of the death penalty in accordance with the example of the Prophet Muhammad. This was not a trivial case of a woman exposing her ankles in public or not appearing properly veiled. The woman was convicted because of her repeated confessions to the act, not because of other peoples' accusations or due to circumstantial evidence such as pregnancy. She had been given ample opportunity for instruction and repentance yet had repeatedly rejected them. Because of the strong stance of the *hadith* on this issue and because the woman had consistently and repeatedly confessed to the crime of *zina'*, Ibn Abd al-Wahhab was left with no choice but to implement the prescribed punishment, however much he personally disliked it.[56]

The case of the adulteress was as much a test of Ibn Abd al-Wahhab's resolve to adhere faithfully to scripture and Islamic law as it was about illicit sexual activity. The chronicles cite the story as positive evidence of Ibn Abd al-Wahhab's faithfulness in adhering to the requirements of the law. However, this should not detract from the tragedy of the loss of human life that concluded the case.

Although Ibn Abd al-Wahhab ended this case without appearing to be a hypocrite, the same cannot be said for the local *ulama*. The same *ulama* who had pressured Ibn Abd al-Wahhab for the stoning sentence then hypocritically used this incident to convince local political leaders that Ibn Abd al-Wahhab was encouraging the local population to revolt against established authority.[57] They further intensified their campaign of defamation and opposition, insisting that Ibn Abd al-Wahhab's teachings were inherently militant and posed a threat to regional stability.

The theme of opposition by local religious scholars and political leaders who feared a threat to their own power bases recurs throughout Ibn Abd al-Wahhab's biography. Many of his writings and some of the most significant events during his lifetime, particularly his forced departure from a variety of locations, were related to his encounters with the *ulama*. How was a group of religious scholars able to wield such power?

The *ulama* possessed such power because of their symbiotic relationship with the communities they served. The *ulama* are neither an ordained clergy nor an officially appointed body of certified or licensed scholars, since neither exists in Islam. They are simply men who have pursued a religious education and are supposed to be knowledgeable about the Quran, *hadith*, and Islamic law and their interpretation. Although they hold official government positions in some countries, this is not always the case and has not always been the norm historically. It would be more accurate to refer to the *ulama* as a social class than as an official body or institution.

The authority of the *ulama* rests in the recognized scope of their scholarship, their ability to attract adherents to their teachings, and the number of students who study with them. Thus, an authoritative *'alim* owes his authority to his popularity, while an *'alim* who lacks popular acclaim likewise lacks authority. Clearly, therefore, the *ulama* of Ibn Abd al-Wahhab's day had a vested interest in preventing the community from changing its allegiance from adherence to its own teachings to adherence to his. Given this vested and personal interest in seeing Ibn Abd al-Wahhab disgraced, defamed, and rejected, it is not surprising that the most lasting negative impressions, rumors, and polemics we have about the Wahhabis and their teachings come from the *ulama*.

The major fear that the *ulama* had with respect to Ibn Abd al-Wahhab's teachings was that they would become not only less powerful but also potentially irrelevant. Ibn Abd al-Wahhab's radical rejection of the imitation of past juridical rulings (*taqlid*) threatened to reduce their control over religious matters, interpretations of the sacred texts and Islamic law, and ultimately the local population's worldview. Ibn Abd al-Wahhab's insistence that every Muslim, both male and female, personally read and study the Quran and *hadith* served not only to undercut the authority of the *ulama* but in many cases to bypass them altogether. Why did he take such a stance?

Ibn Abd al-Wahhab's problem with the *ulama* was not the fact that they existed. In fact, he did not seek to do away with them altogether, since he recognized the value of the *ulama* as repositories of specialized religious knowledge. What he did seek to do was to reserve the title *'alim* for a person who was able to back his religious opinions and interpretations with citations from the Quran and *hadith* rather than simply relying on interpretations.[58] Ibn Abd al-Wahhab's major concern with the *ulama* of his time was that their knowledge consisted of legal manuals and exegetical literature alone and did not include direct study and knowledge of the Quran and *hadith*.

Ibn Abd al-Wahhab sought to counter this tendency by limiting the role of the *ulama* and requiring every Muslim to study the Quran and *hadith* personally and directly. He required this of his followers in order to ensure that all believers would not only have a common base of knowledge, but also a basis for evaluating whether a person claiming to be an *'alim* merited the title. His own personal experience led him to fear that a Muslim without this knowledge base would not be capable of discerning whether the teaching or opinion of another Muslim was correct. The danger in not knowing was that a well-intentioned and sincere Muslim could be led astray, as had already happened numerous times in his own context. It was this concern that led to his adamant teaching that the Muslim must rely on the Word of God, not blind adherence to a fallible and potentially ignorant human being, for guidance.

Ibn Abd al-Wahhab's concern about the *ulama*'s lack of familiarity with the Quran and *hadith* was accompanied by a belief that they also lacked knowledge and understanding of the interpretative texts they taught and cited.[59] He further lambasted the *ulama* for their literal rather than contextual interpretation of the Quran and *hadith*. (Ironically, Ibn Abd al-Wahhab repeatedly had to defend himself from the same charge, launched by the *ulama*!) The danger in a literal approach is that passages such as Quran 2:190–91 which state "Kill the idolaters wherever you find them!" when taken out of context appear to be blanket calls to kill idol worshipers. However, when understood within the specific historical context in which they were revealed—in response to military aggression carried out by idolaters against the early Muslims—they are much more confined in their implications. In this case, the purpose was to grant the early Muslim community the right to defend itself when attacked, even if this meant a preemptive strike in order to prevent further deaths.

Ibn Abd al-Wahhab was also concerned by the fact that many *ulama* gave precedence to customs, traditions, and their own interpretations and beliefs over Islamic law. He charged that when the *ulama* decided to support a particular legal opinion or custom they turned their own opinions into infallible divine directives. Ibn Abd al-Wahhab found this practice, in particular, to be outrageous because it placed the opinions of human beings on a par with divine revelation—a claim that not even Muhammad's Companions could make.[60] He denounced this practice as a departure from *tawhid* and reminded his followers that Muslims are called to worship and serve God not the *ulama*.[61]

Not only was Ibn Abd al-Wahhab upset that the *ulama* would dare to make such an outrageous claim of infallibility, but he was also infuriated that they often promoted outmoded and poor understandings of religious and legal issues.[62] For him, this was made clearest in their tendency to rely on the teachings and interpretations of past scholars (*taqlid*) rather than direct study of the Quran and *hadith* for fresh interpretations (*ijtihad*).[63] All of these factors led Ibn Abd al-Wahhab to the conclusion that the religion promulgated and supported by the *ulama* could not properly be called Islam.[64]

The faults of the *ulama* were not strictly theological. Their teachings and authority also had a very real impact on everyday life. Ibn Abd al-Wahhab's writings mention many times the rampant corruption and nepotism among the *ulama*, the wealthy, and political leaders. For example, he denounced the practice of paying a judge (*qadi*) or issuer of fatawa (*mufti*) to render a particular decision or opinion or to cheat a woman out of her inheritance because such a judgment clearly violated Islamic law. Because they had collaborated with local leaders and the wealthy to cheat women and the poor, in particular, out of their God-given rights, Ibn Abd al-Wahhab declared that the *ulama* had abandoned their moral and religious authority. The need for sociomoral reform was clear. The fact that these practices were apparently so widespread simply added further fuel to his contention that individuals had to read and study scripture for themselves rather than relying on the dubious opinions of religious leaders. The potential threat this stance represented to both the *ulama* and local leaders resulted in their vehement opposition to his teachings.

Not content to let matters rest with the *ulama* alone, Ibn Abd al-Wahhab also criticized their political supporters because it was their political and economic support that allowed the *ulama* such an influential role in the first place. He reserved his harshest criticism in this regard for those who glorified and supported the *ulama*, accusing them of derogating and corrupting Islam.[65]

Not surprisingly, the *ulama* responded very negatively to Ibn Abd al-Wahhab's criticisms. They launched a serious campaign to discredit him, including false portrayals of his doctrines and teachings, in order to protect their own positions of power. This negative campaign of defamation survived the tests of time and found its way into the historical record. Ibn Abd al-Wahhab's own writings and teachings did not. Thus, the defamation campaign of the *ulama* marked the beginning of distortions of Wahhabi teachings and impressions of the same.

Charges leveled against the Wahhabis included accusations of heretical and innovative teachings and their supposed constitution of a new school (*madhhab*) of Islamic law.[66] Ibn Abd al-Wahhab himself was accused of bribery,[67] corruption, killing nonadherents and destruction of their property, falsely devouring the property of the people by claiming that they were indebted to him, and even of outright apostasy.[68] Denunciations of Ibn Abd al-Wahhab and his movement are among the most vehement in Islamic writings, reflecting the danger he represented to the established powers and social positions of his surroundings.

One of the most prominent and repeated charges made against him was the claim that he promoted violence against those who did not adhere to his teachings. This claim, more than any other, has been handed down over time, creating an image of Wahhabism that is bloodthirsty and violent. It is therefore very striking to note that Ibn Abd al-Wahhab himself was aware of these charges and vehemently denied them. He addressed the topic in a legal opinion (*fatwa*) he issued in response to a question about the appropriate response to a Muslim who has been charged with sinful behavior but refuses to repent. It is clear from the question that the person asking it expected Ibn Abd al-Wahhab to give a quick response indicating that such a person was to be considered outside of the Muslim community and therefore subject to jihad as holy war. Ironically, the questioner cited the authority of the *ulama* in support of this expected answer. The *ulama* had declared that any person not supporting his or her leader or accepting his particular interpretation of Islam was both sinful and immoral, rendering such a person an unbeliever (*kafir*) and subject to jihad as holy war. In support of their claims, the *ulama* cited the examples of Muhammad and the Companions.[69]

Ibn Abd al-Wahhab's response to the question was clearly not what the questioner expected. Rather than concurring with the extremist attitude of the *ulama*, Ibn Abd al-Wahhab denounced their interpretation as overly rigid and literalistic because they had taken the example of Muhammad and his Companions completely out of its historical context, making the response to a specific historical situation into a broad value to be applied indiscriminately. Clearly disgusted by the narrowness of vision of these interpreters, Ibn Abd al-Wahhab commented that incidents such as the one cited here must be placed within their historical context in order to understand both the circumstances in which they occurred and the intended broad meaning of the event. One cannot simply look at the end result.

In this particular case, Ibn Abd al-Wahhab declared that the *ulama* were seeking to justify violence and fighting people who did not adhere to their teachings, thereby expanding their own claims to power. Such a distortion of religion had nothing to do with the pursuit of truth or understanding as far as he was concerned. Indeed, Ibn Abd al-Wahhab declared that the *ulama* would have to answer to God for *their* disbelief and for having led others astray.

Having thus shed light on the true agenda of the *ulama*, Ibn Abd al-Wahhab turned to the question at hand: how does one respond appropriately to a Muslim accused of sinful behavior who refuses to repent? He cited Quran

5:41 in his answer. This verse states that temptations and trials are intentionally sent by God as tests. Therefore, no human being has control over what situations he or she might encounter. What God requires is that the Muslim should struggle against unbelievers (*kuffar*) and hypocrites (*munafiq*). However, Ibn Abd al-Wahhab did not declare that such a "struggle" had necessarily to be carried out via jihad as holy war. Rather, he taught that this struggle should begin with education and the call to Islam, relegating fighting and military engagements to a method of last resort and then only in cases in which Muslims actually apostasize.[70]

The battle for power between Ibn Abd al-Wahhab and the established religious and political orders soon became apparent. Not only was he opposed and vilified by the *ulama*, but the local political powers also began to oppose his teachings. The most important incident in this regard occurred while Ibn Abd al-Wahhab was under Ibn Muammar's protection.

When the powerful leader of al-Ahsa and the Bani Khalid tribe, Sulayman ibn Muhammad, heard about his support for Ibn Abd al-Wahhab, he sent a letter to Ibn Muammar, commanding him to either kill Ibn Abd al-Wahhab or force him to leave the area. Sulayman threatened to cut off all of Ibn Muammar's land taxes (*kharaj*) if he disobeyed. This was not an idle threat. Not only did Ibn Muammar's landholdings cover a broad area, but this land produced significant quantities of food and clothing and housed twelve hundred donkeys. All of these items were taxable and provided Ibn Muammar with considerable revenue. Such a great financial loss would have been more than Ibn Muammar's subjects could sustain for the sake of religious teachings—and Ibn Muammar knew it.[71] Consequently, Ibn Muammar wrote his own letter to Ibn Abd al-Wahhab, explaining the situation and asking for his cooperation. Ibn Abd al-Wahhab responded with another letter, reminding Ibn Muammar of his faith and his obligation to uphold *tawhid* at all costs. He thus encouraged Ibn Muammar to consider the ultimatum from Sulayman as a test of his faith.

However, Ibn Muammar was unwilling to take this risk. Although he spared Ibn Abd al-Wahhab's life, he decided to shun him, hoping that this would satisfy Sulayman.[72] Unfortunately for Ibn Muammar, Sulayman was not satisfied. He and his men continued to harass both Ibn Abd al-Wahhab and Ibn Muammar. Finally, Ibn Muammar wrote Ibn Abd al-Wahhab a second letter in which he regretfully informed him of Sulayman's command to kill him and of his own powerlessness in the face of Sulayman because of the inferiority of his forces. Ibn Muammar asked Ibn Abd al-Wahhab to leave voluntarily since he did not want to see him hurt or injured. Although he still respected Ibn Abd al-Wahhab's religious teachings, Ibn Muammar recognized that he also had practical responsibilities to his people and could not reasonably ask them to leave their land.

To facilitate his journey and guarantee his continued protection, Ibn Muammar offered Ibn Abd al-Wahhab an escort for his journey to wherever he sought to go. Ibn Abd al-Wahhab responded by requesting two horsemen to accompany him to al-Dir'iyah, which Ibn Muammar provided. Although some have claimed that these horsemen were instructed to kill Ibn Abd al-Wahhab along the way, the horsemen themselves denied this claim. Ibn Muammar maintained that his decision to withdraw protection and support was politically motivated and in no way reflected negatively on Ibn Abd al-Wahhab's teachings—a claim that is consistent with his later attempts to regain Ibn Abd al-Wahhab's favor.[73]

Upon his arrival in al-Dir'iyah, Ibn Abd al-Wahhab stayed briefly with Abd Allah ibn Abd al-Rahman ibn Suwaylim and his cousin, Hamid ibn Suwaylim. However, he soon set his sights on the local leader, Muhammad Ibn Saud.[74] As with his stay in al-Uyaynah, Ibn Abd al-Wahhab did not immediately engage in public preaching activities in al-Dir'iyah, nor did he immediately preach his message of *tawhid* to Muhammad Ibn Saud. Rather, he conducted his preaching activities in clandestine visits with small groups of people. It was only after gaining some important adherents that a delegation of two blind men and a prominent woman renowned for her "intelligence, knowledge, and religion" was sent to Muhammad Ibn Saud's wife and brother with the express purpose of introducing Ibn Abd al-Wahhab's message to them, particularly his hallmark theme of *tawhid*.[75]

Muhammad Ibn Saud's wife was the first to accept Ibn Abd al-Wahhab's proclamation of God's special role for Muhammad Ibn Saud and to proclaim her belief in it to her husband. Subsequently, two of his brothers, Thunayan and Mashari, also declared their belief and encouraged Muhammad Ibn Saud to support and promote *tawhid*.[76] After these three declarations, Muhammad Ibn Saud ordered that Ibn Abd al-Wahhab be placed under his protection and brought to him under the escort of his own men. When his brothers persuaded him that his personal intervention would be most effective, Muhammad Ibn Saud himself set out to Ibn Suwaylim's house to meet Ibn Abd al-Wahhab in person.

Ibn Abd al-Wahhab greeted Muhammad Ibn Saud with the message of *tawhid*, promising him that if he dedicated himself to the promotion of *tawhid* and the eradication of associationism (*shirk*), ignorance (*jahil*), and divisions among the people, God would grant him and his descendants rule over the lands of Najd and its regions, as well as the people within them.[77] It is clear from his remarks that Ibn Abd al-Wahhab's interest remained in religious issues but that he was also a pragmatic man who realized that no political leader would be willing to take such great risks for the sake of religion unless some kind of earthly reward accompanied it.

Thus, in 1744 the famous alliance that led to the foundation of the first Saudi state was formed between Ibn Abd al-Wahhab and Muhammad Ibn Saud, sealed by a mutual oath swearing (*bayah*) of loyalty.[78] According to this arrangement, Ibn Abd al-Wahhab was responsible for religious matters and

Muhammad Ibn Saud was in charge of political and military issues. Ibn Abd al-Wahhab promised not to interfere with Muhammad Ibn Saud's state consolidation, and Muhammad Ibn Saud promised to uphold Ibn Abd al-Wahhab's religious teachings.

The fault lines of this alliance soon became clear. There is a marked difference between noninterference in military activities and active support and religious legitimation for them. If Ibn Saud had expected Ibn Abd al-Wahhab to legitimate all of his military undertakings for the sake of state consolidation and accumulation of power in the name of jihad as holy war, he must have been severely disappointed. Muhammad Ibn Saud's first conquest, the people of al-Dir'iyah and their possessions, met with neither approval nor condemnation from Ibn Abd al-Wahhab. Rather than actively supporting or promoting this conquest, Ibn Abd al-Wahhab merely "acceded" to it, hoping that Ibn Saud would get his fill of conquest and then focus on more important matters—those pertaining to religious reform. In fact, as evidence of the lack of religious support this military conquest enjoyed, Ibn Abd al-Wahhab left Ibn Saud's company altogether during this campaign, devoting himself instead to spiritual matters and prayer.[79] This was hardly what one would expect had Ibn Abd al-Wahhab believed that jihad as holy war was intended to be used as a tool for conquest.

The tension between the two was also apparent in Ibn Abd al-Wahhab's careful delineation of the parameters to be followed by each in their roles as political leader (*amir*, Muhammad Ibn Saud) and religious leader (*imam*, Ibn Abd al-Wahhab). According to this vision, the *amir* was responsible for political, military, and economic matters and the *imam* for religious issues.[80] Only the *imam* could declare jihad as holy war and this only when the motivating factor was faith alone. Jihad was not intended to serve as a means of acquiring power, wealth, or glory.[81] This did not preclude the *amir* from engaging in military activities that he believed were necessary or expedient. What it did do was to limit the religious legitimation of those military activities. Because only the *imam* could declare a jihad as holy war, the *amir* could not automatically claim that any and all military activities were being carried out in the name of jihad. Thus, Ibn Abd al-Wahhab was able to restrict the declaration of jihad to cases that he believed fit the religious criteria.

Although observers and historians have assumed that any and all military activities undertaken by the Saudis after the 1744 alliance were jihad activities, Ibn Abd al-Wahhab's teachings and writings do not support this contention. His behavior—his tendency to withdraw from Ibn Saud's company during such engagements and his ultimate withdrawal from his position as *imam* in 1773—further makes it clear that he did not actively support all Saudi military actions.[82] In fact, Ibn Abd al-Wahhab's writings and activities after the alliance demonstrate his continued efforts to win converts through discussion, debate, and persuasion rather than force.

For example, during the two years following the alliance, Ibn Abd al-Wahhab engaged in a letter-writing campaign in which he contacted local leaders, scholars, and rulers throughout Arabia, explaining his interpretation of *tawhid* and inviting them to join his movement.[83] Many, though not all, of the recipients responded positively to these missives, although they did not always do so out of religious conviction. These notables were well aware that Ibn Abd al-Wahhab was "in a House of Strength" due to his alliance with Muhammad Ibn Saud and that their own continued power bases necessitated accommodation with these two parties.[84]

Those who did not respond positively to Ibn Abd al-Wahhab's invitation were not immediately or necessarily declared to be unbelievers (*kafirs*), who were therefore subject to jihad as holy war. Rather than engaging in immediate warfare, Ibn Abd al-Wahhab persisted in his attempts to engage those who resisted in dialogue and debate in order to try to work out a formal relationship. The conquests of Riyadh and Washm are particularly instructive in this regard.

The conquest of Riyadh occurred neither quickly nor forcibly. It took the Saudis twenty-seven years to consolidate their hold over this important city, suggesting that a considerable amount of time was allowed for the inhabitants to grow in their understanding of and adherence to *tawhid*.

The conquest began with Ibn Abd al-Wahhab extending an invitation to its ruler, Dham ibn Dawwas, to adhere to his religious teachings. Although Dham ibn Dawwas initially refused this offer, he made peace with the Wahhabis and entered into a truce. This is significant because it shows that a truce with non-Wahhabis was permissible. Initial rejection of Wahhabi teachings did not result in an immediate or permanent state of warfare.

Over time, Dham ibn Dawwas accepted Ibn Abd al-Wahhab's teachings and even invited some Wahhabi *ulama* to live and teach in Riyadh. However, Dham ibn Dawwas broke this truce several times. It was only at this point that protracted military activities began, culminating with the final conquest of Riyadh in 1773.[85]

The conquest of Riyadh did not serve as an opportunity for vengeance or violence against the inhabitants. Although the Wahhabis legally had the right to put to death any person who had actively fought to oppose them, they did not do so. People were not forced to convert, nor were all of their properties or financial assets confiscated. Instead, Ibn Abd al-Wahhab declared that this was an opportunity to offer the inhabitants protection and to implement order and justice.[86] Some of the major accomplishments of the Wahhabis in Riyadh were the establishment of security along the roads, the institution of contracts and other written documentation of legal and commercial transactions, and the development of an organized, written system of communication between Riyadh and outlying towns.[87] The example of Riyadh therefore makes clear that not only were the inhabitants not slaughtered following the conquest, but they actually made important gains in terms of security and communications, lending further evidence to the contention that death and destruction were not the main goals of the early Wahhabis.

Similarly, the conquest of Washm took seven years to accomplish.[88] As with Riyadh, Ibn Abd al-Wahhab first engaged in a letter-writing campaign with the inhabitants of Washm. Although some of the leaders rejected and resisted his teachings, this did not result in an immediate military response. In fact, no overt military action was taken against the region at this time. Instead, Ibn Abd al-Wahhab persisted with his invitations to religious discussions, supporting the notion of a gradual conversion process through education and dialogue rather than a "convert or die" mentality.

That religious issues and debates were really at the heart of the desired conquest of Washm is reflected in the fact that a written war between a number of religious scholars occurred there. Washm was inundated with written religious tracts by a variety of scholars, many from the Hijaz, refuting Ibn Abd al-Wahhab's teachings. Thus, the "battleground" was clearly religious, not just a matter of military might.[89] Indeed, the historical record indicates that the military style adopted in the conquest of Washm was relatively light in touch, with a siege occurring on only a single occasion. Economic pressure was the preferred method in this case.

Those who responded positively to Ibn Abd al-Wahhab's invitations sometimes made a migration (*hijrah*) to al-Dir'iyah to study with Ibn Abd al-Wahhab and his followers. The *hijra* was not a requirement in the way that the seventh-century Kharijites, for example, had required a *hijra* as a way of literally following the example of the Prophet Muhammad. Rather, the *hijra* here simply provided an opportunity for people to come to study directly with Ibn Abd al-Wahhab or one of his followers. In many cases, Ibn Abd al-Wahhab chose instead to send teachers to the other locations so that no *hijra* occurred at all. *Hijra* was not a religious requirement according to Ibn Abd al-Wahhab's teachings.[90]

Ironically, one of the parties who elected to make a *hijra* was Ibn Muammar, Ibn Abd al-Wahhab's previous protector. Claiming that he deeply regretted exiling Ibn Abd al-Wahhab, Ibn Muammar and a contingent of his men arrived in al-Dir'iyah offering Ibn Abd al-Wahhab their renewed protection and pleading with him to return to al-Uyaynah. As proof of their sincerity and ability to provide protection, Ibn Muammar and his men engaged in raids designed to expand Wahhabi influence. However, Ibn Abd al-Wahhab, ever the pragmatist, recognized that Ibn Muammar was more likely motivated by the power and wealth now enjoyed by Muhammad Ibn Saud than by religious zeal. He therefore declined the offer.[91]

Ibn Muammar ultimately left al-Dir'iyah and returned to al-Uyaynah. He was later accused of engaging in subversive activities and of plotting against the newly founded Saudi state. He was assassinated in the mosque of al-Uyaynah in 1749 by a local group of Wahhabi sympathizers, an act that reportedly infuriated Ibn Abd al-Wahhab.[92]

There were other indications of discord within the movement, most notably among those who had elected to make the *hijra* to al-Dir'iyah. Ibn Abd al-Wahhab remained faithful to his vision of reforming Islamic beliefs and practices through education. He did not set up a jihad-oriented community bent on military conquest or a terrorist training camp providing specialized classes in the use of weapons, bomb construction, or the planning of suicide missions. Those who made the *hijra* were immersed in a life of religious study, with particular emphasis placed on *hadith* instruction.

That some of the emigrants were disappointed at what they found in al-Dir'iyah soon became clear. Religious instruction was not what they had expected. Many had seen the growing strength and spreading power base of Muhammad Ibn Saud and no doubt expected that the real purpose of the *hijra* would be military training and preparation for war. It is important to recall that Arabia was a tribal society in which raiding and the taking of booty were prominent political and economic features. Consequently, many of the emigrants found the more peaceful emphasis on education to be particularly "trying" and gave in to the "temptation" to pursue other activities.[93] Ibn Abd al-Wahhab's goal of reforming Islam was overshadowed and ultimately overwhelmed by Muhammad Ibn Saud's quest for state consolidation.

Not surprisingly, it was at this time that organized military opposition to the Wahhabi movement began, supported by the *ulama*. Opponents of the Wahhabi movement claimed religious justification for their military actions by accusing the Wahhabis of ignorance, sorcery, and lies—religious criteria that legitimated fighting according to the Quran.[94] That the charges were untrue was irrelevant—they provided the justification for military action, leading to a strike against the Wahhabis. It was only at this point—when the Wahhabi community was threatened—that Ibn Abd al-Wahhab finally authorized a jihad as holy war to defend the Wahhabis.

However, even this defensive jihad remained limited in scope, as fighting was permitted only against those who had either attacked or insulted his followers directly.[95] This first jihad served to establish the reputation of the Wahhabis as capable of defending themselves. Although the Wahhabis took booty at the conclusion of the conflict, as was their legal right, no rampant violence or destruction occurred, nor were any forcible converts made.[96] Ibn Abd al-Wahhab also took this opportunity to remind his followers that the taking of booty was not meant to enrich the winners. Rather, booty obtained in jihad as holy war was to be used to fulfill the legitimate needs of the people. To prove his point, Ibn Abd al-Wahhab kept nothing for himself.[97]

Ibn Abd al-Wahhab's refusal to emphasize material acquisitions served to deepen the fault lines in his alliance with Ibn Saud. Ibn Saud, as a tribal leader, clearly had no interest in a more ascetic existence because his subjects expected to lead comfortable lives in return for their political loyalty. It was therefore also at this point that Ibn Abd al-Wahhab and Muhammad Ibn Saud had a falling-out of sorts.

Ibn Abd al-Wahhab was appalled by what he witnessed in lands controlled by the Al Saud family. The inhabitants were not following basic Islamic rituals and had adopted a luxurious lifestyle. Incensed by what he perceived to be their "extreme" levels of ignorance (jahiliyyah), he demanded that they abandon their materialism and take their religious duties more seriously. He reprimanded them for neglecting their prayers and other Muslim obligations, particularly the required tithe of 2.5% of a Muslim's wealth (zakat), preached to them about greater and lesser shirk, and reminded them of their pledge to uphold tawhid.[98] Because this territory was held by the Al Saud, who had pledged to uphold and implement tawhid, Ibn Abd al-Wahhab held them responsible for the dedication of their subjects to material pursuits.

Despite this, the Al Saud continued their military exploits to extend their power and expand their wealth. When Muhammad Ibn Saud died in 1767 and was succeeded by his son, Abd al-Aziz, the emphasis on materialism increased. Ultimately, rather than becoming famous as a center for religious learning, al-Dir'iyah became known for its wealth and strength. Whereas the era of Ibn Abd al-Wahhab's prominence was marked by poverty, trial, and temptation, that of Abd al-Aziz was characterized by wealth, power, and luxury, as evidenced by the possession of money, property, arms and weapons decorated with gold and silver, horses, dromedaries, clothing, and luxuries.[99]

This accession to wealth and power was not interpreted as God's favor due to faithful adherence to Islam. In fact, just the opposite was the case, as wealth and power came only when religious reforms and restraints were set aside. Ibn Bishr notes that by the time Abd al-Aziz acceded to leadership the people "had tired of holding back their hearts."[100] They were not interested in pure religious reform. They wanted earthly power and rewards—reflections of the tribal society in which they lived. Thus, the shift from a more religiously oriented era of educational endeavors to emphasis on political and military power is clear.[101]

Finally, Ibn Abd al-Wahhab resigned his position as imam and withdrew from active political and financial life in 1773, following the conquest of Riyadh. He turned over command of the deserts to Abd al-Aziz and entrusted him with command over both his followers and the treasury, the Bayt al-Mal.[102] Abd al-Aziz proceeded to expand his vision beyond the confines of Najd into the rest of Arabia, Iraq, and Syria.[103] His actions made it clear that the Al Saud family had as its ultimate goal the expansion of its territories and power, with or without religious legitimation. In fact, Saudi-Wahhabi power reached its height between 1792 and 1814, long after Ibn Abd al-Wahhab withdrew from public life.

Ibn Abd al-Wahhab remained a consultant to Abd al-Aziz but largely with-drew his legitimation of Saudi military activities. Instead, he devoted himself to learning, teaching, and worship until his death in 1791 or 1792.[104] He left behind four sons who were eminent religious scholars, as well as many students dedicated to his teachings.[105]

Conclusion

Ibn Abd al-Wahhab's influence continued after his death, both in terms of the spread of his religious teachings and in the reinterpretations of the same through the contemporary era. His biography makes certain suggestions about his dedication to return to the fundamental sources of Islam, the Quran, and *hadith*; his hallmark theme of the theological principle of *tawhid* and his op-position to *shirk*; his support for *ijtihad* (the reinterpretation of Islamic law) and rejection of the imitation of the past (*taqlid*); his concern for the rights of women; and his limitation of the use of jihad and discouragement of violence in favor of education and debate. In chapter 2, these themes are explored in more detail in order to provide a fuller explanation of his worldview.

2

The Theology and Worldview of Muhammad Ibn Abd al-Wahhab

Muhammad Ibn Abd al-Wahhab was both a theologian and a legal scholar. The worldview that he espoused reflected both of these traits. In Islam, correct belief (orthodoxy), although important, is not sufficient on its own to achieve salvation in the Afterlife. Muslims believe that God will judge them on the basis of how they lived their lives, not just on the basis of what they believed. Thus, correct practice (orthopraxy) is also a main determinant in whether one will go to Heaven or Hell.

Although many Muslim scholars have therefore chosen to emphasize Islamic law over theology as the most important subject for study,[1] Ibn Abd al-Wahhab gave both equal treatment. He believed that correct belief was a necessary first step in guiding the Muslim in correct behavior. Without correct belief, one would not know how to behave. Consequently, his works provide detailed coverage and analysis of both theology and law.

Ibn Abd al-Wahhab's detailed attention to theology reflected the emphasis he placed on intent rather than ritual perfection. He encouraged Muslims to consider their motivations before undertaking activities—the content of intent—rather than focusing on the form that those activities took. In this way, he demonstrated how the worldview of the Muslim—with God at the center not only of the universe but also of the individual Muslim's heart and mind—is intended to have an impact on every action a human being undertakes and that every action is intended to be a reflection of the faith in the Muslim's heart and mind. It also meant that his worldview was one of an activist, rather than passive, faith, so that faith, as the motivating factor behind every action, was necessarily intended to be lived out in both the private and public realms. In this way, Ibn Abd al-Wahhab demonstrated how even seemingly minor practices or activities can ultimately be expressions of unbelief or violations of God's sovereignty because of the intent behind them and the worldview that they reflect.

Theological Sources

As an eighteenth-century reformer, Ibn Abd al-Wahhab based all of his teachings on the Quran and *hadith*, which he considered to be the only infallible and authoritative sources of scripture. Although he sometimes made use of legal and exegetical commentaries, they were used to support the Quran and *hadith* rather than serving as independently authoritative texts. Similarly, other source materials, such as the examples of the early Muslim community (*ummah*) and the four Rightly Guided Caliphs (632–661 c.e.), were also considered to be enlightening, rather than authoritative. Because the Quran and *hadith* were used most prominently in the elaboration of Ibn Abd al-Wahhab's values, worldview, and understanding of history, the discussion of his theology necessarily begins with an analysis of how he interpreted and used these scriptural sources.

The Quran

As the certain, final and authoritative revelation of the Word of God to the Prophet Muhammad, the Quran is revered by Muslims worldwide as the infallible and eternal means by which God's Will can be known and carried out. Study of the Quran has always been considered the most important component of the Muslim's religious education.

Historically, Quranic instruction has consisted of memorization of its contents and proper recitation under the instruction of a scholar. Such studies are typically completed in young childhood with a recitation of the full text by the child representing the culmination of study. Memorization by its nature requires familiarity simply with the words, order, and proper method of recitation of the text. It does not require contextualization, understanding, or explanation.

Although Ibn Abd al-Wahhab believed that knowledge of the Quran should be required for all Muslims, both male and female, he questioned the usefulness and effectiveness of memorization without understanding. He distinguished between the preservation of knowledge achieved through memorization versus the practical application of knowledge, which becomes possible only with comprehension of the text. While he did not discount the importance of being able to cite scripture, he believed that it was more important to understand it. Without comprehension, he feared that Muslims would interpret the Quran literally, marginalizing the discernment of broad Quranic values in favor of a narrower, more legalistic approach. He also believed that memorization alone overlooked the true purpose for which the Quran was revealed: the putting into action of God's declared will for humanity.[2] He therefore emphasized historical contextualization and understanding of the Quran, rather than strict memorization, as the best way to discern eternal Quranic values and apply them in both private and public life.

Because he emphasized comprehension of the Quran over its memorization, Ibn Abd al-Wahhab's writings reflect a tendency to analyze and discuss the Quran thematically rather than chronologically.[3] Unlike most classical scholars, he never wrote a full exegetical study of the Quran in verse order (*tafsir*).[4] Consistent with his emphasis on contextual rather than literal interpretation, he was always careful to provide historical contextualization for the Quranic verses he used as proof texts for theological or legal points. His discussions typically followed one of two formats. Either he opened with a Quranic verse, which he then explained by referring to other Quranic teachings on the same topic and relevant *hadith*, or he provided the discussion of the point first and provided the scriptural proof texts at the end.[5] Regardless of whether the Quranic text came at the beginning or the end of the discussion, he consistently used scripture to interpret scripture rather than relying on human interpretations alone.

As on many other occasions, Ibn Abd al-Wahhab's new methodology for Quranic instruction met with resistance from a variety of local religious leaders. One group opposing this new methodology was the local *ulama*, who wished to adhere to the old method of memorization. Because the memorization method had been used for centuries, they saw no reason to change or innovate it. In response, Ibn Abd al-Wahhab pointed out that the old methodology of memorization was itself an innovation. It had not been used during the lifetime of Muhammad or the era of the Rightly Guided Caliphs.[6] He believed that this was because the early Muslim community understood the importance of historical contextualization in the interpretation of scripture. Their direct and personal familiarity with events and the context in which particular revelations were received enabled them to contextually interpret the Quran automatically as a matter of common sense. This was the methodology that Ibn Abd al-Wahhab believed was authentic and ought to be used.

A second group concerned by this new methodology of Quran interpretation was the *ashraf*. The *ashraf* were a social class who received prestige and special favor due to their claim to direct descent from the Prophet Muhammad. Not only did they expect to be specially revered by Muslims as Muhammad's descendants, but many of them also claimed special hidden and secret knowledge of the Quran based on that kin relationship.

Although he believed that the *ashraf* were entitled to respectful treatment, Ibn Abd al-Wahhab did not believe that they enjoyed any closer connection to

God than any other human being. Because Islam declares the absolute equality of all human beings before God, regardless of their race, gender, or bloodlines, and because the Quran proclaims Muhammad to be the "seal," or last, of the prophets, Ibn Abd al-Wahhab rejected the notion of any person possessing secret or hidden knowledge of the Quran. In fact, he believed that the claim to secret or hidden knowledge of the Quran was inimical to the Quran's very purpose—calling all human beings equally to belief in the one true God.[7]

Ibn Abd al-Wahhab noted that the *ashraf*'s claims were based strictly on blood descent, not on special behaviors or more faithful adherence to the Quran's teachings. In fact, he classified the *ashraf* as a social class consisting of "unbelievers" because they failed to carry out good works among Muslims, preferring instead to have Muslims treat them with special favor because of their kin relationship with Muhammad.[8] He therefore dismissed the claims of the *ashraf* to any secret or hidden knowledge and thereby to leadership over the *ummah*, declaring that the descendants of Muhammad did not possess any special authority to interpret the Quran.[9]

Although this dismissal specifically targeted the *ashraf*, it also represented a challenge to some of the beliefs proclaimed by Sufis and Shiis. Some Sufis have claimed that hidden or secret knowledge of the Quran is mystical in nature and therefore is accessible only through the achievement of a higher state of spiritual awareness. The liturgies and devotional practices of some Sufi orders are designed to help the believer achieve this special level of awareness in the expectation that they will thereby gain access to this special knowledge.

Shiis believe that the hidden message of the Quran is known only to the *imams*, the male descendants of Muhammad who served as the leaders of the Shii community up until the last *imam* went into "hiding" or "occultation" himself. Because Shiis believe that the *imams* possessed this special knowledge, which enabled them to interpret the Quran infallibly, they consider the legal and theological writings of the *imams* to be additional sources of scripture. Consequently, both Shiis and Sufis also had reason to be concerned by this denial of hidden or secret knowledge of the Quran.

Ibn Abd al-Wahhab's rejection of special human insight into the interpretation of scripture is consistent with his broad worldview, in which every individual believer is capable of and responsible for encountering God directly, without the help of human intercessors. Rather than relying on human interpreters of the scriptures, whether for theological or legal issues, he taught that individuals needed to read the scriptures for themselves in order that they might know directly what God had said. His further emphasis on the need to contextualize Quranic passages and understand their content, rather than focusing strictly on the Quran's memorized form and word order, reflects his approach to scripture in general. He applied the same methodology to the study and interpretation of Islam's other source of scripture, the *hadith*.

Hadith

The *hadith* are a body of literature recording the sayings and deeds of the Prophet Muhammad. Muslims recognize Muhammad as the most perfect of all human beings and believe that his life reflects the perfect living out of the Quran. Muhammad's special status for Muslims is not due to any assertion of divinity but rather to his role as God's Messenger—a role the Quran assigns only to Moses, Jesus, and Muhammad as the recipients of God's three revelations to humanity—the Torah, the Gospel, and the Quran. Because of their special status, these three Messengers are deemed worthy of special respect by Muslims, although such respect should not lead to worship. In fact, Ibn Abd al-Wahhab himself, while declaring that love of Muhammad along with love of God is a "sacred duty" for all Muslims, nevertheless was careful to distinguish between loving Muhammad *and* God and loving Muhammad *as* God. Muhammad was to be respected and ranked higher than any other human being, so that no other human being was to be associated with Muhammad.[10] However, association of Muhammad with God was strictly forbidden.[11]

Muhammad's special status even among the Messengers was for several reasons according to Ibn Abd al-Wahhab. First, Muhammad was distinguished from the other prophets by the fact that he broke their previous pattern of simply weeping and wailing for peace. Previous prophets were also often set apart from society due to their idiosyncratic habits.[12] Muhammad, on the other hand, was not content to bemoan the travails of this world without doing anything about it. Instead, he actively and successfully engaged the affairs of both the Afterlife and life here on earth as everyday people live it out, setting an example that all Muslims can follow.[13]

A second characteristic that Ibn Abd al-Wahhab believed distinguished Muhammad from the other prophets is the fact that he was the only prophet who never committed the sin of disobedience against God. Although many religious analysts and biographers of the prophets tended to assert their special status as being due to their obedience to God's will, Ibn Abd al-Wahhab, on the basis of scriptural analysis, determined that all of the other prophets had disobeyed God in either a major or a minor matter. Therefore, part of Muhammad's distinctive perfection lay in his perfect and complete obedience to God.[14]

A third and final matter that set Muhammad apart from the other prophets was his context. The prophets of the Old Testament and Gospel were sent to people who had clearly fallen away from worship of the One True God. Ibn Abd al-Wahhab noted that Muhammad, on the other hand, was sent to people who were already devoting themselves to His service, making the pilgrimage, giving alms, and practicing *dhikr* (remembering God). Despite these correct actions, they had erred by making idols and calling on created beings to serve as mediums or intercessors between themselves and God.[15] Thus, although

Muhammad's message was consistent with that of prior prophets in insisting on a return to the worship of the One True God and the elimination of mediums and intercessors, his context was different.

Having established the distinctive role of Muhammad in Islam, Ibn Abd al-Wahhab was able to effectively and convincingly argue for the necessity of *hadith* study. What was most important in this process was not a literal understanding of the exact words of the *hadith* but discernment of the legal or theological principle embodied in the *hadith*, which could then be extrapolated and used to interpret other materials or situations.[16]

As an eighteenth-century reformer, and consistent with his approach to the Quran, Ibn Abd al-Wahhab embraced the new methodology of *hadith* study, which emphasized analysis of the content of a *hadith*, rather than acceptance of a credible chain of transmitters, as the appropriate means of determining its validity. He believed that every individual *hadith* needed to be reevaluated for authenticity through use of this new methodology rather than simply accepting the opinion of past scholars about its veracity. He noted that there were cases in which *hadith* reflected Arab and tribal, rather than Muslim, traditions and customs. For him, this rendered such *hadith* suspect, despite their authoritative chains of transmission and the collectors who included them.[17]

From a practical standpoint, this meant that Ibn Abd al-Wahhab investigated a wide variety of potential source materials, including, but not limited to, the six canonical Sunni *hadith* collections.[18] In his quest for authentic *hadith*, he did not declare any limitation on potential source materials on the basis of the collector or the chains of transmission. The only limitations he accepted were those of content.[19]

Ibn Abd al-Wahhab's insistence on careful examination of the content of the *hadith* was due to his concern that distortions and additional material might have been added to the *hadith* over time.[20] Although he never accused any specific individual of committing such an act, he found the writings of the *hadith* commentators to be particularly suspect because it was often difficult to distinguish between the material that was actually transmitted and the opinions of the commentators regarding it.[21] He shared similar concerns with respect to certain Shii groups.[22]

Ibn Abd al-Wahhab felt so strongly about reexamination of the *hadith* on the basis of their content that he outlined his methodology for their authentication. He began by recalling that the Quran proclaims itself to be the completion and perfection of human knowledge as provided by God (Q 5:3) and that Muhammad's life example expresses the perfect living out of that knowledge. Therefore, he declared that no additional scripture outside of the example of Muhammad is necessary: "What is perfect/complete is not in need of augmentation."[23]

Because God has definitively proclaimed His Will in the Quran, the Quran is the most authoritative source of scripture. Believing that scripture should be consistent with scripture, it logically follows that the Quran and *hadith* should be complementary and that neither should ever abrogate the other. As sources of the same revelation, no contradiction, whether in interpretation or meaning, is possible.[24] Ibn Abd al-Wahhab therefore declared the methodology of content analysis to be the only acceptable method of *hadith* criticism or the resolution of any question arising among Muslims.[25]

Ibn Abd al-Wahhab was careful to ground his *hadith* methodology in the teachings of the Quran and *hadith* themselves. He reminded his followers of the Quranic command: "And if you are at variance with each other over a thing, refer it to God and His Messenger" (Q 4:59). He also noted that Muhammad himself had required adherence to his own example and had further recommended following the example of the Rightly Guided Caliphs because they were the most familiar with and dedicated to following his example.[26] This assertion of the scriptural foundation for his methodology of *hadith* authentication both placed Ibn Abd al-Wahhab within the broad Islamic tradition and exonerated him from charges of innovation. He then outlined the specifics of how to carry out *hadith* authentication.

Ibn Abd al-Wahhab taught that the believer should evaluate the content of a *hadith* on the basis of careful comparison with the teachings of the Quran, using reason to determine their compatibility.[27] If a *hadith* contradicts the Quran, both the *hadith* and the principle or value contained within it are inauthentic.[28] Only the Quran can never be dismissed as inauthentic. How, then, should one deal with a case of two contradictory *hadith*?

Many *hadith* collections include several versions of a given incident, typically as recounted by a number of observers. Different people often have different recollections and perceptions of a shared experience, although the broad outlines of the experience tend to be similar. Multiple *hadith* recounting a single event share this general tendency. Many times, the differences are limited to minute details. However, such variance can at times create a contradiction in how different people interpreted, remembered, or recounted a particular event. Ibn Abd al-Wahhab therefore reminded his followers that the same methodology is always to be used when examining a *hadith*: return to God and Muhammad first, not the words of the Companions or the supposedly superior story of two or more narratives or sayings.[29] A correct *hadith* will not contradict the two primary sources.

In support of this approach, he cited as an example the case of two apparently contradictory *hadith* about the permissibility of the Muslim using a talisman. One *hadith*, recounted by Muhammad, permitted the use of talismans in the cases of jealousy and the sting of deadly animals. The second *hadith*, recounted by the companions of Muhammad's Companion Ibn Masud, prohibited the use of talismans altogether, even if they were simply Quranic verses. Ibn Abd al-Wahhab ruled that these two *hadith* were not contradictory because the one recounted by Ibn Masud's companion was not a true *hadith*. A true *hadith* has to come from Muhammad. Therefore, he dismissed the second *hadith* as inauthentic, thereby resolving the apparent contradiction.[30]

If a genuine case of two truly contradictory *hadith* claiming direct transmission from Muhammad does exist, it means one of two things: either the *hadith* supporting it is erroneous or the interpretation contained within it is erroneous.[31] For Ibn Abd al-Wahhab, there was no such thing as two contradictory but authentic *hadith*: "This is not appropriate for you to say. The words of God and the words of His Messenger are exempted from contradiction. All of it is true, and they verify each other."[32] Thus, if there are two accounts that contradict each other, only one can be true. In order to determine which one is correct, the believer must return to the words of God and Muhammad. If the believer is not able to do this independently, Ibn Abd al-Wahhab recommended seeking the opinion of a reliable and trustworthy scholar, who is to be chosen on the basis of knowledge of the Quran and *hadith*, correct interpretation of clear passages, and faithful adherence to the teachings of the Quran and *hadith* in both public and private life.[33]

Ibn Abd al-Wahhab further insisted on the contextualization of both the Quran and *hadith* in order to be certain of their intent. In order to demonstrate the importance of contextualization, he cited several *hadith* pointing to the origins of idol worship. According to the *hadith*, idol worship began when some of Noah's descendants made statues of righteous people who had died and gave those statues the names of the deceased. Although their intent was to honor and respect the dead, over time people forgot the origins of the practices and began to worship the statues.[34] For Ibn Abd al-Wahhab, the value inherent in these *hadith* was the importance of knowing the context in which a particular activity was undertaken. Only knowledge of the context could enable the reader to understand the original intent behind the action. In this case, the original intent of those who made the statues was harmless. However, the loss of historical contextualization resulted in idol worship and associationism—the worst of all sins in Islam. Because of the danger of leading others astray, Ibn Abd al-Wahhab condemned the practice of making or revering statues of living beings. This case also reaffirmed his belief that Muslims must engage in study and learning as constant and continuous processes so that knowledge might be preserved.[35]

Although Ibn Abd al-Wahhab believed that content analysis was the most important element of *hadith* authentication, he did not discard the traditional method of verifying the chains of transmission (*isnad*) altogether. In fact, some of his *hadith* citations include a note indicating the relative strength or weakness of the chain of transmission.[36] Strength or weakness of the chain was due to the proximity of the transmitter to Muhammad. The gender of the transmitter was never an issue in determining the validity of a *hadith*. Ibn Abd al-Wahhab presented *hadith* transmitted by women as evidence equally as compelling as *hadith* transmitted by men as long as the content was consistent with the teachings of the Quran and Muhammad's known example (Sunna).[37] He used the case of a *hadith* transmitted by Muhammad's daughter Fatima to prove his point about content being more important than the chain of transmission.

Fatima had recounted a *hadith* claiming that a repudiated woman has no right to her residence or to maintenance unless she is pregnant. Even though Fatima was the daughter of Muhammad himself, Ibn Abd al-Wahhab did not consider her presence in the chain of transmitters to make a *hadith* infallible. He rejected this particular *hadith* because it contradicted clear passages in the Quran and Sunna. He further noted that there is legal consensus (*ijma'*) on the requirement that the divorced woman be provided with housing and maintenance, so no one, not even Fatima, can override the clear instructions of the Quran and Sunna.[38]

Having definitively outlined his methodology for *hadith* authentication, Ibn Abd al-Wahhab turned to the question of interpretation. He opened his discussion by noting that any given *hadith* may contain more than a single value or legal or theological principle. Consequently, more than one interpretation of a single *hadith* is possible depending on the issue being examined.[39] He then reemphasized the importance of contextualizing Quranic verses, *hadith*, and legal rulings in matters of interpretation. He used this opportunity to criticize again those who literally interpret the Quran and *hadith* as failing to comprehend the intended meaning of the text. Looking solely at what was decided rather than trying to understand the process of reasoning that led to the decision results in a total lack of comprehension of the incident in question. He further noted that anyone, even fanatics or those who are erroneous in their beliefs, can quote the Quran or *hadith* without necessarily understanding them.[40]

The importance of contextualizing *hadith* is made clear in a case in which Ibn Abd al-Wahhab was challenged about a *hadith* that most past scholars had interpreted literally. This *hadith* allowed for delays in payment of the charitable tax (*zakat*), which is one of the five requirements of all Muslims.[41] Ibn Abd al-Wahhab responded to the questioner by noting that the issue was not whether the *hadith* was authentic but rather that the full context of the incident described had been typically overlooked by the interpreters. The interpreters who charged that the *hadith* was inauthentic pointed to the clear example of Muhammad strictly denying the request to delay payment of the *zakat* under normal circumstances. However, Ibn Abd al-Wahhab pointed out that these interpreters had overlooked the legal principle of public welfare (*maslahah*), which allows for a delay in the payment if there are drastic extenuating circumstances, such as a year of drought, which just happened to be the context of this particular *hadith*.[42] He bolstered his argument by citing the similar declaration by the second caliph, Umar, as supportive evidence for this ruling. Thus, contextualization is clearly critical in correct *hadith* interpretation.

Once context and authenticity have been established, the next step is determination of the lesson to be learned in a given *hadith*. Ibn Abd al-Wahhab discussed a *hadith* addressing associationism (*shirk*) in order to demonstrate the multiple meanings potentially contained within a single *hadith*. This *hadith* referred to Muhammad's military campaign against Hunayn, which occurred shortly after his Companions had converted to Islam. Although they were now Muslims, the Companions had not fully grasped the implications of absolute monotheism (*tawhid*). Because they had previously been in the habit of hanging their arms and armor on a sacred tree for good luck, they asked Muhammad to establish another sacred tree for them. Muhammad responded that such ignorance was not worthy of Muslims, who were to trust in God alone and not make other gods for themselves.[43]

Ibn Abd al-Wahhab found several lessons in this *hadith*. The first lesson was contained in the conclusion: the Companions' request was not granted because it was inappropriate. Although this was the most obvious lesson of this *hadith*, Ibn Abd al-Wahhab did not believe that it was the only one. He believed that looking at the broader context and details of the incident would reveal additional lessons.

He began by examining the exact nature of the request made by the Companions and the fact that they did not receive what they had asked for. Thus, the question turns from "What happened?" to "Why did it happen this way and what are we to understand and learn from it?" Ibn Abd al-Wahhab looked for the intent behind the action undertaken by the Companions. He found that their intent was closeness to God. On the basis of past experience, they believed that their requested action would be pleasing to God. Ibn Abd al-Wahhab then pointed out that if the Companions of Muhammad himself did not recognize and understand the implications of what they wanted to do it is logical to assume that others, who do not have the benefit of direct knowledge of Muhammad and the Quran, would be likely not to know it either. Consequently, in the face of ignorance and given the purity of their intent, their actions were credible and deserving of mercy and forgiveness. Indeed, he recognized that the Companions remained Muslims despite the gravity of the sin they had committed.[44] This is hardly the response of a violent literalist. By refusing to engage in a facile condemnation of literal actions, Ibn Abd al-Wahhab dug deeper into the processes involved in deciding on an action and carrying it out. Thus, purity of intent can override the clumsiness of a sin that is committed in ignorance.

In addition, Ibn Abd al-Wahhab recognized that there are different degrees or levels of *shirk*, so that commission of an act of *shirk* in and of itself does not necessarily result in the immediate excommunication of the perpetrator. Indeed, he noted that rather than condemning his Companions Muhammad immediately instructed them regarding the error of their request. He helped them to see beyond their own past experiences and customary practices to the implications of their new faith and the need to rethink their words and actions in light of what they now believed. Ibn Abd al-Wahhab thus noted that conversion to Islam is not an instantaneous process that magically changes a person's outlook and way of living but observed that, practically speaking, some vestiges of former practices and beliefs remain in the recent convert. Therefore, anyone converting to Islam must constantly seek knowledge.[45] This again emphasizes the difference among external, literal, and ritual adherence to religious requirements and internal knowledge and understanding of the implications of faith.

Quran and Hadith Interpretation in Practice

Having established the primary role of scripture and how it is to be used according to Ibn Abd al-Wahhab's methodology, an illustration of how he carried out his analysis is instructive. This is a particularly important endeavor in light of the fact that his opponents over the years have contradictorily accused him of either simply repeating what past scholars, most notably Ibn Taymiyya, have written or of starting his own school of Islamic law (*madhhab*). A quantitative analysis of Ibn Abd al-Wahhab's most important theological treatise, *Kitab al-Tawhid* (*The Book of Monotheism*), offers some important insights.

Kitab al-Tawhid is arguably Ibn Abd al-Wahhab's most famous written work. As an exegetical discussion of the Muslim doctrine of *tawhid* it includes a description of what *tawhid* is and a discussion of how it is to be kept and what kinds of activities and statements constitute violations of it. There are a total of 66 chapters of varying length, organized by theme, and a total of 341 citations within those chapters. Of those 341 citations, 82 (24%) are from the Quran, 195 (57%) are *hadith*, and only 64 (19%) are citations from interpreters, including Ibn Abd al-Wahhab himself. Quranic verses are present in 44 chapters (67%), while *hadith* are present in 61 (92%). Interpretations are present in only 23 chapters (35%). The prominence of *hadith* is also noteworthy in that there are 15 cases (23%) in which a *hadith* is cited without any correlating Quranic verse or interpretation. In comparison, there are no chapters based strictly on the Quran or interpretations of other scholars and there are only 5 chapters (8%) in which the Quran and interpretations are cited without *hadith*. All of the chapters contain references to either the Quran or the *hadith*. The majority of the chapters—39 (almost 60%)—contain citations from both. All three sources are cited in only 11 cases (17%). These statistics clearly bear witness to Ibn Abd al-Wahhab's participation in the broader eighteenth-century revival of *hadith* studies.

Ibn Abd al-Wahhab's typical pattern of writing was recitation of a Quranic verse followed by relevant *hadith*, with only an occasional bit of commentary. Commentary exists only in cases in which a Quranic verse was deemed unclear and required some additional interpretation. In such cases, Ibn Abd al-Wahhab turned to interpreters, Companions of Muhammad when possible and later commentators only when he felt it was necessary.[46]

In terms of *hadith* sources, Ibn Abd al-Wahhab included a total of 210 *hadith* transmitted by 84 different people. The most commonly quoted people are Ibn Abbas (23), Abu Hurayrah (21), Ibn Masud (17), Ibn Umar (8), Qatadah (6), Aisha (5), and Anas (5). Thus, for Ibn Abd al-Wahhab, Ibn Abbas, Abu Hurayrah, and Ibn Masud were generally considered to be the most important *hadith* transmitters.[47] It is interesting that one of the most traditionally important *hadith* transmitters, Ali ibn Abi Talib, is largely absent from this treatise. Ibn Abd al-Wahhab used *hadith* from Ali only twice,[48] suggesting that, although he did not totally discount the observations or interpretations of Ali, he clearly did not consider him to be as authoritative as the three other major transmitters.

An alternative way of looking at *hadith* citations is by category. Out of a total of 210 citations, fully 153 (73%) come from Companions of the Prophet, relatives of the Prophet, or sons or companions of Companions of the Prophet. Only 19 (9%) are identified by their collectors, and 37 come from other sources.

Kitab al-Tawhid reflects a broad base of scholarship, encompassing a total of 34 sources cited in 170 different places. Of the 34 cited and identified sources, 13 were *hadith* collectors, 8 were Companions of the Prophet or companions or relatives of Companions, 2 were Hanbali jurists, 1 was a Zahiri jurist,[49] 1 was a poetry critic and anthologist, 1 wrote exegetical works, and 1 was a genealogist. *Hadith* collectors were responsible for 140 of the total citations (82.4%). The sources most frequently quoted are *Sahih Muslim* (39), *Sahih al-Bukhari* (26, which may be raised to 43 if those referenced simply as "Sahih" are included for al-Bukhari), Ahmad ibn Hanbal (19), *Sahih al-Sijistani* (15), Abu Isa al-Tirmidhi (9), and al-Nasai (6). This is not particularly surprising in that al-Bukhari, Muslim, al-Sijistani, al-Tirmidhi, and al-Nasai are five of what are widely considered by Sunni Muslims to be the six canonical *hadith* sources.[50] The other major canoncial *hadith* source, Ibn Majah al-Qazwini, is quoted twice. The *hadith* collections of Ahmad ibn Hanbal and Malik ibn Anas, also often considered authoritative by Sunnis, are each quoted once.

The total of 34 works cited indicates that Ibn Abd al-Wahhab was well versed in both *hadith* scholarship and legal and exegetical literature. It also indicates that he did not necessarily consider any one source to be singularly authoritative and was open to looking at alternative sources to address specific questions. Of these sources, it is possible to identify some early classical works, such as those by Ibn Jarir al-Tabari (3), as well as medieval sources, such as those by Ibn Taymiyya (3) and Ibn al-Qayyim al-Jawziyah (3). Although Ibn Abd al-Wahhab has historically been labeled a blind follower and even a copier of Ibn Taymiyya's work, this record demonstrates a much broader education and a reluctance to adhere to or imitate any single source. The list of works cited is further instructive in providing evidence of what works Ibn Abd al-Wahhab was authorized to teach and interpret, although this is not necessarily a comprehensive list.

Perhaps most significant is the compilation of interpreters cited in this work. The most frequently quoted interpreters are Companions (6), Ibn Abbas (6), Ibn Abd al-Wahhab himself (6), Ibn Masud (4), Mujahid (4), Qatadah (4), Ahmad ibn Hanbal (3), and Ibn Taymiya (3). Numerically, out of 31 total authors, 13 have been identified as either Companions or companions of Companions, 8 are *hadith* collectors, 4 are Hanbali jurists, 1 is a Zahiri jurist, and 1 is the author of *tafsir*. Of 63 total instances of interpretation, 34 (54%), are attributed to either Companions or companions of Companions, 8 (12.7%) to *hadith* collectors, and 14 (22.2%) to Hanbali jurists.[51] It is clear that the weight of statistics does not favor prior assertions of total reliance on any single individual.[52]

Ibn Abd al-Wahhab's meticulous citation of exact sources was unusual for his time. There was a general tendency among scholars of this time period to cite other scholars without directly crediting them. That Ibn Abd al-Wahhab would not have adhered to this approach is not surprising. It is important to recall that he was constantly defending himself from the contradictory charges of innovation and imitation of Ibn Taymiyya. His extensive citations from a wide variety of sources make it clear that Ibn Taymiyya was, at most, a negligible source of inspiration. By citing such a wide variety of opinions, Ibn Abd al-Wahhab placed himself strongly within a scholarly genre of literature known as *ikhtilaf.*

Ikhtilaf literature consists almost entirely of citations of other scholars and interpreters, which are arranged in a manner that both gives shape and lends authority to the author's own interpretation. Because jurists are supposed to discover rather than create the Law of God, no individual jurist was considered to be authoritative. Placing oneself within a tradition of interpretation was one way of garnering authority for a particular interpretation.[53]

Although Ibn Abd al-Wahhab followed the broad form of *ikhtilaf,* he injected one new element into his writings: the inclusion of his own personal voice. In cases in which he was offering his own interpretation, he clearly said so, usually in the form of "Wa-ana uqul an . . . ," or "And I myself say that . . ." Classical *ikhtilaf* literature did not include such pointed and clear statements of personal interpretation. One other major difference in Ibn Abd al-Wahhab's writings was his purpose in engaging in *ikhtilaf.* Whereas other jurists had as their purpose the development and continuance of reverence for tradition and a subtle demonstration of their own overarching authority in the interpretation of Islamic law because of that reverence, Ibn Abd al-Wahhab rejected such imitation (*taqlid*) outright, favoring instead the exercise of independent reasoning (*ijtihad*).[54]

Ijtihad was not carried out in a vacuum. *Ijtihad,* as it was practiced by Ibn Abd al-Wahhab, was based on the historical precedents of Muhammad, his

Companions, and the early Muslim community. Although he did not consider these two additional sources to be as authoritative as the Quran and *hadith*, Ibn Abd al-Wahhab clearly considered them to be informative and worth consideration. His use of these examples offers additional insight into his method of scriptural interpretation.

The Early Muslim Community (Ummah) and the Four Rightly Guided Caliphs

Like many other theologians, Islamic activists, and jurists, Ibn Abd al-Wahhab frequently used examples from the time of Muhammad to illustrate his points. This was not done in an attempt to re-create the early Islamic community, as some scholars have posited,[55] but to demonstrate the ongoing relevance of their example to the present.[56] Ibn Abd al-Wahhab used examples from this time period in order to demonstrate that the Muslim community of his day was grappling with the same issues as did believers of other times and places. This is not to say that he considered these examples to be infallible or eternally binding on all Muslims. Rather, he taught that these examples must be subjected to broad scrutiny and comparison with the Quran and *hadith*. Unlike the Quran and *hadith*, the examples of the Rightly Guided Caliphs and the early *ummah* were open to critique and criticism.

Ibn Abd al-Wahhab's use of the early *ummah* and the time of the caliphs reveals a critical historical approach to their interpretation. While he acknowledged that the Companions were certainly much closer in time and space to Muhammad and the early Muslim community, he did not believe that this necessarily rendered their interpretations and behaviors perfect. He rejected the assertion of other Sunni scholars that the examples and rulings of the Rightly Guided Caliphs ought to be considered as having same stature as the example and rulings of Muhammad himself. He pointed out that the Rightly Guided Caliphs were not always consistent among themselves in their legal rulings, particularly where an unclear text was concerned, nor were they necessarily consistent with the teachings and practices of Muhammad.[57] In fact, in some cases the Rightly Guided Caliphs themselves introduced innovations that deviated from the Quran and Sunnah.[58]

Variances of opinion were not a matter to be taken lightly for Ibn Abd al-Wahhab. He sharply disagreed with *ulama* who claimed that such variances of opinion should be interpreted as a mercy to the people, noting instead that they actually constituted a source of chaos (*fitnah*) because these divergences obfuscated rather than clarified the issues and judgments.[59] Ibn Abd al-Wahhab made it clear that Muhammad's life and teachings were always binding and authoritative over any other human interpretations, including those of the Rightly Guided Caliphs. The opinion of any other person was simply that—an opinion.[60] Any time one must choose between the human and the divine, the divine must always win.[61] The believer must always turn to the Quran and *hadith* alone, not the words of the Companions, in order to determine the authenticity and binding nature of any given narrative.[62] Ibn Abd al-Wahhab forbade believers from taking the Companions, *ulama*, or anyone else claiming to have knowledge as lords and masters. Respecting them and seeking their opinions was fine, but equating those opinions with the Word of God was not.[63]

There was only one case in which Ibn Abd al-Wahhab declared the example of the Companions to be authoritative: the matter of charitable endowments (*waqf*, pl. *awqaf*). This was because the institution of *awqaf* had no Quranic or prophetic basis. The institution arose during the rule of the Rightly Guided Caliphs. This did not mean that people could do anything that they pleased. Just because the institution had not existed did not mean that it was exempt from the same laws and values that guided the Muslim in every other instance of public life. Ibn Abd al-Wahhab permitted anything with respect to *awqaf* that did not contradict the commands of God and Muhammad and the example of the Companions and their followers.[64]

To illustrate his point that the example of the Companions and the Rightly Guided Caliphs was to be used as potentially supportive, rather than authoritative, evidence in other cases, but always in conjunction with the Quran and *hadith*, Ibn Abd al-Wahhab presented two cases. In the first, the permissibility of delaying payment of the *zakat* tax, he cited Muhammad's general prohibition of such a delay, although he allowed it in cases in which public welfare was at stake. The example of Umar's caliphate is cited as "supportive evidence."[65] That is, when combined with a Quranic precept or clear example from Muhammad's actions, the ruling of a Rightly Guided Caliph becomes authoritative as supportive evidence.

The second case is used to illustrate the opposite—what happens when the example of the Rightly Guided Caliph contradicts that of Muhammad. Here Ibn Abd al-Wahhab particularly took to task the tenure of the first caliph, Abu Bakr al-Siddiq, as an example of fiscal mismanagement. He noted that Abu Bakr had established the practice of the caliph serving as a paid guardian over the people. Abu Bakr justified this practice with a series of Quranic verses that Ibn Abd al-Wahhab described as "vague."[66] He classified Abu Bakr's ruling as "the most astonishing part of his ignorance" precisely because it was based on vague Quranic verses that were not clearly applicable to this situation.[67] He also denounced Abu Bakr's corrupt use of *zakat* taxes for his own private and personal use—an example that the other caliphs subsequently followed by "feathering their nests" from the public treasury, the Bayt al-Mal.[68] In addition to emphasizing the legal error made by the Rightly Guided Caliphs, Ibn Abd al-Wahhab also used this example to demonstrate how such judicial errors come to be entrenched and passed down as normative and binding over time. Although Abu Bakr had perverted the original purpose of *zakat*, his example was followed because he was the first caliph and a close Companion of Muhammad. Yet Abu Bakr's example was clearly not one that should have been emulated.[69]

Ibn Abd al-Wahhab's willingness to examine the early Muslim community, particularly the Rightly Guided Caliphs, from a historical perspective resulted in a "de-deification" of these early Muslims, returning them to the status of fallible human beings. By doing this, he liberated Muslims from strict adherence to or imitation of their example and attempts to re-create literally the early Muslim community. In other words, taqlid of even the early Muslim community and the example of the Rightly Guided Caliphs were rejected in favor of a direct return to scripture as the only perfect and authoritative expression of God's Will for humanity. In this way, adherence to tawhid was made complete.

Having examined the source materials he used for his formulations of theology, it is time to turn to an analysis of Ibn Abd al-Wahhab's theological teachings, beginning with his hallmark themes of tawhid and shirk.

Tawhid: The Theology of Absolute Monotheism

"There is no god but The God." This Quranic phrase and declaration of faith explains in all simplicity and complexity the doctrine of tawhid. Tawhid is typically defined as the "unity of God." However, a more understandable and comprehensive definition would be "the unity and utter uniqueness of God," or "absolute monotheism," so that nothing and no one may be associated with or compared to God in any way.

Although monotheism's origins lie with Ibrahim/Abraham, the common ancestor of Muslims, Jews, and Christians alike, Ibn Abd al-Wahhab taught that absolute monotheism is the distinctive feature of Islam alone. Islam does not recognize different "persons" of God or Jesus as the Son of God. Islam also does not have an ordained clergy, papacy, or binding interpretations of scripture written by rabbis or priests. In Islam, there is only One God who is always and only referred to as God. Descriptions of God refer to His attributes which are His alone. God is never referred to as more than a single being.

For these reasons, Ibn Abd al-Wahhab believed that only Islam adhered to the doctrine of absolute monotheism, setting it apart from every other religion, including Judaism and Christianity.[70] In fact, he declared belief in monotheism to be the first and foremost duty of the Muslim, preceding every other duty, including prayer.[71] Belief in and adherence to monotheism not only makes a Muslim a Muslim but also places the Muslim's property, blood, and fate under God's protection.[72]

It is difficult to express in a single word or phrase all that tawhid encompasses because it is a complex concept that impacts every aspect of faith and human life. For this reason, Ibn Abd al-Wahhab devoted an entire treatise, *Kitab al-Tawhid*, to the definition and exploration of this central theological doctrine. Although some have interpreted this important work as a manifesto for action and a justification for fighting those who hold different beliefs, this is not the spirit in which the work was written. When read in the broader context of Ibn Abd al-Wahhab's full corpus of written works, it is clear that *Kitab al-Tawhid* was intended to explain the central doctrine of *tawhid* and its implications for the daily lives of Muslims. Its purpose was to edify and build up the Muslim community, not to justify jihad as holy war.

The treatise begins with a definition of *tawhid*: "That there is one single God whom we are to glorify/praise in worship. This is the religion of the Prophets whom God sent to worship Him."[73] Thus, *tawhid* necessitates recognizing God alone as Creator, Sustainer, and Director/Administrator of all that is. Recognition of God's bounty and mercy should lead to both joy and fear on the part of the believer because God is also the source of all judgment, reward, and punishment.[74]

When asked to explain how God's uniqueness is overarching and all-encompassing with respect to humanity, Ibn Abd al-Wahhab responded by describing three types of *tawhid*, or unique features of God: the *tawhid* of lordship, the *tawhid* of divinity, and the *tawhid* of characteristics.[75] *Tawhid of lordship* refers to God's possession of absolute power over Heaven and earth, life and death.[76]

The second type of *tawhid*, that of divinity, requires devotion to service and worship of God alone by all of creation. Thus, anyone who serves or worships anyone or anything else, even the Righteous Ancestors (*Salihin*) or angels, has departed from Islam. Muslims are to recognize God alone as the ruler of the universe and without equal.[77]

The third type of *tawhid*, that of God's characteristics, is established by the *tawhids* of lordship and divinity. That is, God's characteristics are defined by God's role as Lord and Divine Being. Consequently, assigning God's characteristics to human beings, even if they are kings or masters of slaves, constitutes a violation of God's uniqueness. Only God truly possesses anything, and only God can truly educate human beings.[78]

Ibn Abd al-Wahhab taught that God's uniqueness is evident in the fact that He created all that is for the purpose of serving Him. Only God can create, and only God is uncreated. To God alone belongs all power in Heaven and on earth, so that no human being, not even Muhammad, has the power on his or her own initiative to bless or curse but must refer the matter to God's control.[79] Therefore, God alone deserves to be worshiped, served, and obeyed.[80]

By clearly and decisively limiting worship, service, and obedience to God alone, Ibn Abd al-Wahhab precluded the possibility of idolatry as a Muslim practice. Idolatry and the creation of images, whether statues or paintings, are strictly forbidden in the *hadith*. The theological basis for this prohibition is recognition that only God can give life. Because the creation of images suggests the giving of life, Muhammad forbade it.[81]

Ibn Abd al-Wahhab also prohibited his followers from making statues or images of living beings and insisted that they remove from sight those that already existed. He was concerned that the presence of such images might tempt someone to worship or sacrifice to them. His concern for others reflects his belief that the individual Muslim is responsible not only for his or her own faith but also for the effects of his or her behavior on another.

Ibn Abd al-Wahhab's stance on this issue emphasized the communal nature of Islam. Rather than being a private matter of individual belief, Islam is necessarily a public religion in which believers are supposed to uphold and help each other in the correct practice of the faith. Ibn Abd al-Wahhab therefore held Muslims responsible not only for their own intent but also for the interpretation of their actions by others, lest they lead another into temptation or sin.[82]

Ibn Abd al-Wahhab taught that God's uniqueness should be the first and foremost remembrance and declaration of the Muslim in every situation. This declaration is also intended to serve as a guideline for interactions between Muslims. Anyone making a request in God's name, whether for protection or for material things, is to be recognized as a Muslim and answered positively. God will reward the Muslim who responds positively to such a request.[83]

Ibn Abd al-Wahhab repeatedly emphasized the importance of placing God first in everything. He declared that the greatest responsibility of every human being is to work in obedience to God and that this should be evident in both the person's actions and the intent behind them. Ibn Abd al-Wahhab believed that adherence to monotheism is so central that God will pardon any other sins committed by a true monotheist because the primary duty and responsibility of the Muslim has been fulfilled.[84] Similarly, ritual perfection and the performance of good deeds either for their own sake or for self-aggrandizement are violations of monotheism because their purpose is the glorification of the individual engaging in them rather than the desire or intent to serve God. In fact, such pursuits demonstrate a lack of faith in God's ability and power because they place the individual, rather than God, at their center.[85]

Ibn Abd al-Wahhab taught that the Muslim should always adhere to *tawhid*, even when it is not the majority opinion. In his opinion, one of the worst violations of monotheism is possessing knowledge of *tawhid* and its implications but deliberately choosing to ignore or reject them. He declared that the Muslim who knowingly violates *tawhid* commits an even greater sin than one who does so out of ignorance. One should not participate in or appear to accept a violation of *tawhid* even as a demonstration of love or respect for a non-Muslim since this constitutes an act of disbelief.[86]

This explanation makes it clear that correct belief is intended to lead to correct behavior. Ibn Abd al-Wahhab used this discussion to highlight the importance of remaining faithful in both beliefs and behaviors, even in the midst of hardship. In a *fatwa* addressing the case of an individual who once had followed monotheism but had chosen to return to a life of associationism, Ibn Abd al-Wahhab expounded on the importance of maintaining consistency between faith and action. He denounced as an unbeliever (*kafir*) anyone who believes in monotheism but fails to obey and act out its consequences. In his opinion, adherence to monotheism should override all other concerns, including national interests. Thus, he denied the designation of Muslim to anyone who participates in killing, hostilities, and/or aggression against monotheism and its adherents, regardless of the level of participation. Whether the person is personally supportive, actively involved in the military campaign, or just providing financing, his or her responsibility and unbelief is the same, even if it is impossible for this person to leave the country due to hardship or oppression.[87]

Ibn Abd al-Wahhab's declarations here suggest that one must be prepared for the possibility of suffering for one's beliefs, even to the point of losing one's home, family, tribe, or property, although he never declared that anyone should deliberately seek such consequences. At no point in any of his writings does he promote the concept of martyrdom or encourage the Muslim to seek it.

Ibn Abd al-Wahhab's denial of the designation of Muslim to anyone who gives a human relationship a higher priority than his or her relationship with God points to the serious implications of belief in *tawhid*. Because adherence to and belief in absolute monotheism is the very essence of what it means to be a Muslim, someone who does not adhere to or believe in *tawhid* is necessarily categorized as a non-Muslim and is excluded from the Muslim community (*ummah*).[88] It is important to note that exclusion from the *ummah* did not mean that such a person was necessarily and immediately subject to *jihad* as holy war. Rather, it opened the door to proselytization and pointed to the need to educate such a person. *Jihad* as holy war became a possibility in certain clearly defined circumstances, but it was neither a requirement nor a foregone conclusion.

How, then, is one expected to demonstrate adherence to *tawhid*? Clearly, the proclamation of the Muslim declaration of faith (*shahadah*) alone is insufficient. In Ibn Abd al-Wahhab's worldview, adherence to monotheism is not just a matter of declaring that "There is no god but The God." This proclamation must be accompanied by an understanding of the full meaning of those words.[89] People's actions must demonstrate their conviction of the truth of what they are saying.[90]

Ibn Abd al-Wahhab therefore required that the declaration of faith be accompanied by the active denial of all other objects of worship besides God in order to be certain and valid. If the denial is doubtful on the basis of the person's actions or if the person fails to make the denial, his or her status and right to protection as a Muslim become open to question.[91]

Ibn Abd al-Wahhab's requirement of consistency between words and actions reflects the social reality that there were always people who paid lip service to monotheism in order to protect their property or their own personal safety.[92] What he wished to highlight was the importance of the intent behind the proclamation. He noted that cleverness in playing with words and philosophical arguments does not constitute faith and will not be accepted as actual belief. In fact, he categorized those who articulate the words but remain unconvinced in their hearts as unbelievers (kuffar).[93] Similarly, those who have some of the other visible trappings of being Muslims, such as making the pilgrimage, paying zakat, remembering God, or worshiping God, without adhering to monotheism cannot be considered true Muslims. Instead, he labeled them associationists or those who commit shirk (mushrikun).[94]

Being a mushrik is a charge with serious consequences. Ibn Abd al-Wahhab wrote of the mushrikun: "And unless these mushrikun witness that God is the sole Creator, they do not believe in Him, and they will not be blessed by Him, and they will not live or die except through Him, and a leader cannot lead except by Him and that all that is exalted from among these and their associates and the seven heavens and among them and their associates, all of these are servants to Him and under His charge and power."[95] It is clear here that the denial of monotheism is tantamount to unbelief, resulting in the loss of God's favor.[96] Everything that one has and does, from life to power and leadership, emanates from God. Considering the importance of the politico-religious alliance into which Ibn Abd al-Wahhab entered with Muhammad Ibn Saud, it is of interest here that he mentions that "a leader cannot lead except by Him," implying that a faithless leader is one who cannot command the loyalty or obedience of true Muslims, who recognize that all power emanates from God alone. He noted that this failure to believe in monotheism ultimately makes the mushrikun liable to being fought by true Muslims, according to the example of Muhammad.[97] However, it is important to note again that such military engagement is neither required nor a foregone conclusion. It is also important to note that Ibn Abd al-Wahhab does not use the term jihad to describe such military action. He uses the term qital, which is a more generic term for fighting. Thus, although the label of mushrikun opens the door to the possibility of military engagement, it does not result in an immediate or required declaration of jihad.

Typical of his age, Ibn Abd al-Wahhab was neither a supporter of nor a participant in ecumenical dialogue. Although they do not constitute a large or even important part of his works, criticisms of pagans, idolaters, Jews, and Christians exist in his written works. His purpose in including these criticisms is not to call for the annihilation or destruction of such religious groups or to call for interreligious hatred, as certain of his critics have charged.[98] Rather, criticism of specific beliefs and practices is used to illustrate theological and behavioral errors, particularly with respect to violations of monotheism. Ibn Abd al-Wahhab pointed to specific examples of what he considered to be associationism inherent in the religious beliefs of particular groups, such as the Christian belief in Jesus as God's son. He also denied claims of superiority and special status on the basis of birth, as in the case of the Jews as God's "chosen people." For Ibn Abd al-Wahhab, the critical issue in true faith was correct behavior and motivation in what one does, not false pride in circumstances that are a matter of birth or reliance on the past.[99]

It is also of interest that, despite his at times vehement denunciations of other religious groups for their supposedly heretical beliefs, Ibn Abd al-Wahhab never called for their destruction or death. While he assumed that these people would be punished in the Afterlife for their incorrect beliefs and false pride, he never suggested that they should be killed on the basis of their faith—or lack thereof. He believed that such punishment was the prerogative of God in the hereafter, not of human beings here on earth.

Ibn Abd al-Wahhab's tendency to criticize specific behaviors, rather than groups of people,[100] is also reflected in his outline of a series of activities that violate the principle of monotheism, including submitting requests to a king, prophet, holy person (wali), tree, tomb, or demon (jinn).[101] This list covers the full gamut of different types of polytheism, other religions, or variations on religion. Worship of a ruler, such as was done in time of Pharaoh, was forbidden. Forbidding the worship of trees and jinn served as a denunciation of pre-Islamic pagan religious and animist practices. The reference to prophet worship was probably a condemnation of the practices of Jews and Christians. Walis and tombs was a double reference, covering the practices of both Shiism and popular Sufism. However, in none of these cases did he target or even name a specific group of people. Rather, he focused on condemning a specific practice. Although his writings here served as a proof text as to what is "wrong" with these other religious practices, he did not condemn the people or the entire religion out of hand. Rather, he left room for improvement and a return to a purer form of religion.

The implications of belief in God's utter uniqueness, or absolute monotheism, are clear. Having defined adherence to tawhid in thought, word, and deed, Ibn Abd al-Wahhab then shifted to an elaboration of the concept of shirk as the violation of tawhid.

Shirk: Violations of Absolute Monotheism

Shirk, the association of anyone or anything with God and/or God's attributes, is the other major theological theme in the writings of Muhammad Ibn Abd al-Wahhab. *Shirk* is always and clearly defined as a violation of and departure from *tawhid*, making it the polar opposite of *tawhid*. *Shirk* is given great attention in Ibn Abd al-Wahhab's written works because, according to the Quran, it is the one unforgivable sin.[102] Anyone who commits *shirk* will be condemned to Hell in the Afterlife.

The *hadith* confirm that *shirk* was the thing that Muhammad feared most for his followers after his death. He warned of the danger when he declared that only those who have never associated anything with God will enter Paradise.[103] Thus, the critical issue in salvation for Muslims is adherence to absolute monotheism. Muslims are not to consider even Muhammad or Jesus to be on a par with God.[104] Furthermore, not even love for God or piety, however great, can excuse *shirk*.[105]

Ibn Abd al-Wahhab taught that obedience and service to God can only be accomplished by absolutely and categorically rejecting and disbelieving in *shirk*, particularly idolatry (*taghut*).[106] Because of its serious nature, Ibn Abd al-Wahhab carefully outlined behaviors that constitute *shirk*. Among the most serious are worshiping, sacrificing to, slaughtering to, praying to, invoking, calling on, seeking refuge in, seeking intercession by, or attributing authority to anyone or anything other than God.[107] He also denounced as *shirk* the practice of considering the writings or teachings of religious scholars, whether priests, rabbis, *ulama*, or jurists, to be as authoritative as God's revelation.[108] He considered such reverence for human interpretations to be blasphemous.[109]

In seeking to define *shirk*, Ibn Abd al-Wahhab posited the same question he had asked when defining *tawhid*: how does intent determine the essence and nature of a particular action? In some cases, he asserted that the answer was quite straightforward. For example, slaughtering an animal as an offering to a *jinn* is prohibited because it entails doing something that is clearly forbidden and detested by the Quran. Such a sacrifice violates the principle of absolute monotheism because it is performed for the benefit and glory of the nondivine and compares the nondivine to the Divine. The comparison alone is an act of associationism because it suggests that God is somehow not entirely unique and incomparable. Thus, Ibn Abd al-Wahhab noted that there was nothing ambiguous about this case.[110]

Associationism is not always a clear-cut matter, though, which is why Ibn Abd al-Wahhab found it necessary to expound on the numerous varieties and types of acts that constitute it. Similar to his approach to *tawhid*, Ibn Abd al-Wahhab understood *shirk* to be an act of intent and meaning. If *tawhid* can best be defined as "belief in God's absolute sovereignty over all of creation and knowledge," then *shirk* is evident in behaviors such as imitation of past juridical rulings and traditions (*taqlid*) and the placement of human knowledge and science over the revelations of the Quran and *hadith* because these behaviors assign power and sovereignty, which are God's alone, to someone or something other than God. For Ibn Abd al-Wahhab, this was the greatest of all sins.[111]

Shirk can be expressed in a person's actions. Ibn Abd al-Wahhab cited the example of the use of bewitchment to make people fall in love with each other as an action that demonstrates confidence in the power of someone or something other than God to provide a specific outcome.[112] Failure to fulfill a vow, unless it involves disobedience to God, also detracts from the image of God because a vow is intended to serve as a tribute to God.[113]

Associationism can also be expressed in what one says. Clearly, prayer to or worship of anyone or anything other than God is associationism. However, even expressing confidence in the ability of someone or something other than God to keep one safe or provide refuge can also constitute associationism. For example, Ibn Abd al-Wahhab related a *hadith* in which Muhammad instructed his followers to proclaim their desire to seek shelter in the perfect words of God from all created evil whenever entering a house. Ibn Abd al-Wahhab interpreted this *hadith* to demonstrate two important things. First, sincerity in making the proclamation is required. The pronouncement is supposed to be a declaration of faith, not a means of seeking self-aggrandizement. Ibn Abd al-Wahhab denounced those who seek material gain by uttering such a declaration since this violates the purpose of making the statement. The second purpose is to distinguish between God and His Word, which are uncreated, and other beings—whether animate or inanimate—which are created. The point is that one should never seek shelter in anything that is created. Only God and His Word can provide protection.[114]

Having thus defined the term and described the types of behavior that constitute it, Ibn Abd al-Wahhab turned to the distinction between different degrees of *shirk*.

Greater and Lesser Shirk

Generally speaking, Ibn Abd al-Wahhab recognized two types of *shirk*: greater and lesser. The greatest *shirk* of all is calling on any being other than God, whether for benefit or harm, even if it is for the most righteous and altruistic purposes.[115] Calling on anyone or anything other than God for help, assistance, refuge, or any other thing is strictly, totally, and permanently forbidden because "this calling signifies worship of the one called upon."[116] Other examples of greater *shirk* include invoking holy men and requesting their assistance, rather than God's, or making vows or offerings at the tombs of holy men.[117]

The theme of the pre-Islamic customs of worshiping idols, sacred rocks, trees, and other gods, whether by direct worship, prayer, and requests for intercession or belief in the power of the same, permeates Ibn Abd al-Wahhab's writings on *tawhid* and *shirk*. He denounced these actions as violations of monotheism because they accord godlike status to created beings and objects. He taught that the only appropriate response to such behavior was to fight such people until they adhere to monotheism.[118]

It is important to emphasize again that Ibn Abd al-Wahhab used the term *qital* to refer to such fighting rather than *jihad*. Thus, the commission of associationism does not automatically result in the declaration of *jihad* as holy war against associationists. Furthermore, the purpose of the permitted fighting is neither killing nor the annihilation of the people in question because this would interfere with the goal of the fighting—changing their behavior. It is also important to note that permission to fight was given only in cases in which the people in question were actively engaged in worship of created beings and objects. While it is important to be aware of these clarifications, it is also important not to overlook the implications of the declaration of the permissibility of fighting in such cases.

Ibn Abd al-Wahhab's definition of *shirk* makes clear why he sometimes referred to Jews and Christians as those who commit associationism. He believed that Christian petitions to Mary or the saints for intercession and worship of Jesus as the Son of God are clear and blatant examples of associationism because Muslims do not consider Jesus, Mary, or the saints to be God. Furthermore, in Islam prayer is an act of worship. Because worship is supposed to apply to God alone, it is also intended for God alone.

This definition of *shirk* also had important implications within Islam. Ibn Abd al-Wahhab specifically denounced those who venerate Ali and/or the Companions of Muhammad to the point of worship as being similarly guilty of ignorance and not understanding the Quran. For Ibn Abd al-Wahhab, veneration of even these special individuals constituted idol worship, if not downright apostasy.[119]

Lesser, or "hidden," *shirk* is defined as "any action purportedly undertaken in order to serve or worship God that actually has the intent of calling attention to oneself." These actions constitute associationism because they place a human being (the self) in the place that rightfully belongs to God.[120] Thus, hypocrisy, such as improving one's manner of praying when observed by others, is an example of lesser or hidden *shirk*.[121] Similarly, the pursuit of worldly goods and luxuries for their own sake is an instance of associationism because it has as its goal glorification of the individual rather than glorification of God.[122]

Ibn Abd al-Wahhab reminded his followers that God knows the true intent behind all actions and that He is more interested in the intent than in the action itself. Because God will reject even good deeds if they are not done purely for His sake, the Muslim is expected to focus all attention and energy on striving in God's cause.[123]

Ibn Abd al-Wahhab was frequently asked to classify various acts according to whether they constituted greater or lesser *shirk*. Those asking the questions tended to take a legalistic approach to the question of *shirk*, indicating that they expected different levels of punishment for different degrees of *shirk*. Ibn Abd al-Wahhab demonstrated very little patience for this type of inquiry, noting simply that an act of lesser *shirk*, such as fearing created beings or hoping or wishing for things through them, inevitably becomes more intense over time, ultimately leading to greater *shirk*.[124] He offered as an example the question of whether it is permissible to build shrines over tombs and to pray at them or if such constructions should be torn down. Ibn Abd al-Wahhab required the tearing down of such structures because he believed that their very existence constituted an act of associationism. However, he equivocated on the question of whether these acts constitute greater or lesser *shirk*. For him, the issue was not the classification of the kind of associationism involved. Rather, the issue was that associationism was present. The degree of the associationism was not important.[125]

Having refused to classify the actions, Ibn Abd al-Wahhab took up instead a discussion of intent and, just as importantly, the potential impact of one person performing an act on another, who sees it and may interpret it differently. The building of domes and shrines over tombs provided an excellent example of this issue.

Ibn Abd al-Wahhab traced the practice of building domes and shrines over tombs to Jews and Christians who sought thereby to show their respect for their prophets. Over time, these locations became sites of worship. While Ibn Abd al-Wahhab recognized that theoretically the entire earth is available for worship of God, he also observed the practical reality that worship at these shrines tended over time to lead people to associate those who were buried there with God. He cited as evidence the popular tendency to petition the person whose tomb houses the shrine for intercession with God.

He was also concerned by the fact that the domes and shrines tended to become adorned over time, particularly with drawings or sculptures depicting likenesses of the people buried there. He feared that this also might lead some people to believe in the efficacy of praying to the likeness itself for blessings or intercession with God. Thus, he made clear the potential for innocent actions to lead, however unintentionally, to idolatry.[126]

Ibn Abd al-Wahhab was careful throughout this discussion to distinguish between two types of intent: the original intent of the people building the domes and shrines simply as memorials or places for quiet prayer or meditation and the long-term intent of the masses, who turned such locations into places for unorthodox practices. He not only held believers responsible for their own intent in undertaking activities but also charged them with thinking about the potential effects on and interpretations of their actions by others. It was because of their potential to lead people astray that domes and shrines over tombs were to be destroyed, not necessarily because the original builders intended to commit *shirk*.[127]

On Shrines, Mosques, and Tombs

Ibn Abd al-Wahhab's concerns about shrines, mosques, and tombs were not merely theoretical. They were based on practical experience, both within his own historical context and in the time of Muhammad and the early Companions. The historical record of eighteenth-century Najd reflects the types of worship and requests made at tombs about which he wrote.

For example, in Wadi Musim, there was a tomb that reputedly belonged to Zayd ibn Umar (the son of the second caliph). This tomb had become a site of popular veneration and requests for material benefits. Similar tombs existed in the town of al-Dir'iyah and were frequented for the same purposes. There was also reportedly a cave in a rocky mountain in al-Dir'iyah that was believed to have been miraculously opened by God in response to the desperate search for shelter by a woman who had been sexually molested by the local tyrant. Because this cave was believed to have had miraculous origins, it had become an object of veneration and a locus for making requests for the intercession of this woman with God because God had clearly answered her prayers for sanctuary.[128]

Ibn Abd al-Wahhab addressed these local customs by referring to early Muslim history—namely, the deaths of Muhammad and some of his Companions—because it was during this period that the question of shrine and dome buildings over tombs came to a head for the early Muslim community. According to the historical record, Muhammad was buried in his house, underneath the apartments of his favorite wife, Aisha. This house was later converted into a mosque. After a time, the tribe that controlled the mosque sought to expand it. This was opposed by some, who claimed that it should not be done because this was also the location of Muhammad's tomb. The tribe in control responded that it had no intention of expanding the chamber where Muhammad was buried but simply wanted to expand the mosque.

In reviewing the record, Ibn Abd al-Wahhab agreed with the decision to expand the mosque because it was confined to the mosque. There was to be no embellishment or expansion of Muhammad's tomb.[129] However, he remained concerned about the precedent that the construction of such a mosque set for future generations. He noted that Muhammad himself had feared that people would come to his grave to worship him. Consequently, he instructed his followers not to place his grave above ground so that it could not be taken for a mosque.

On this basis, Ibn Abd al-Wahhab concluded that mosques generally should not be constructed over anyone's grave lest they somehow be confused as a place of worship for human beings. He then stated his opinion regarding the use of graves as places of worship: "The Prophet, therefore, prohibited it after his life. Then he cursed/condemned—and this is in succession—anyone who does it, even if it is not joined to a mosque. . . . Therefore, the Companions were not supposed to build a mosque around the Prophet's grave."[130]

Muhammad had expressly forbidden people to build graves within their homes or make graves places of celebration, even in the case of his own. Consequently, Ibn Abd al-Wahhab noted that although visiting Muhammad's grave was a worthy act it must not be done in a spirit or intent that compromises monotheism. Finally, prayer should never be conducted in a cemetery.[131]

Ibn Abd al-Wahhab expanded his discussion into a broader analysis of Muhammad's general opposition to shrines and mausoleums. The *hadith* record Muhammad's declaration that all images should be wiped out and all high graves leveled to the ground so that no one could use these images or graves as objects or sites of worship or claim that any human being has the power to grant them souls and life.[132] Ibn Abd al-Wahhab's own commands to destroy elaborate tombs therefore stemmed from Muhammad's similar actions. Because Muhammad himself commanded it, Ibn Abd al-Wahhab considered such actions to be incumbent on all Muslims and instructed his followers accordingly, commanding them to wipe out or break every image.[133]

However, when specifically asked for a legal ruling about the permissibility, indeed the religious requirement, of tomb destruction, his answer was initially deliberately vague. Rather than responding with a clear yes or no, he issued a statement indicating that he understood the reasoning behind such a practice based on various examples in early Islamic history. He made it clear in his *fatwa* that he knew the circumstances behind the question.

At that time, the *ulama* of Najd had begun issuing *fatawa* subjecting anyone who participated in tomb veneration to the death penalty. They claimed that the perpetrators were simply pretending not to know that such practices were forbidden. They further permitted shedding the blood and confiscating the property of such persons because vengeance against such sinners was supposed to bring them closer to God.[134]

Considering the typical image of Ibn Abd al-Wahhab, it is particularly striking that he responded by condemning the *ulama* for their extremism. He noted that rather than attacking people who venerate tombs true Muslims should be asking whether or not these people have renounced their deeds and asked for forgiveness for their error. In fact, the true Muslim should ask whether the people in question were even aware that their actions constituted apostasy, as required by the consensus of all of the Islamic law schools. Had they actually continued with the practices or were the accusations merely a rehash of their past activities, however distant?[135]

These were not academic questions. The issues that Ibn Abd al-Wahhab raised are consistent with all of his other writings and teachings: it is neither reasonable nor just to go around accusing people of apostasy on the basis of literal interpretations of the Quran and *hadith* when there is no hard evidence that the people in question have been properly instructed in matters of faith. Ibn Abd al-Wahhab consistently insisted that rather than condemning people the Muslim was responsible for assuring that anyone committing an act that that Muslim considers to be in error be properly instructed in the faith and given the opportunity to repent and change his or her ways prior to taking any kind of punitive action. Indeed, he appeared to be sympathetic toward those who followed the teachings and examples of the *ulama* without having any personal understanding of the issues involved. Rather than condemning their followers, he held the *ulama* responsible for leading the people astray and even compared them to the rebellious and deviant Kharijites![136] He thus made it clear that whether or not a person has committed associationism is a matter of intent and knowledge. Without deliberate intent and proper knowledge, one cannot be held liable for one's actions.

On the Visitation of Tombs and Idolatry

Muhammad Ibn Abd al-Wahhab considered the issues of tomb visits and requests for the intercession of holy people with God to be so important that he devoted one-sixth of *Kitab al-Tawhid* to their discussion. Out of a total of sixty-six chapters in *Kitab al-Tawhid*, four discuss the prohibition against worship and prayer at or veneration of grave sites and seven discuss the prohibition against requesting intercession with God. Ibn Abd al-Wahhab's discussion was not just a blanket condemnation of such practices but also served as an opportunity to remind his followers that Muslims must consider both their own intent and the potential response and reaction of other people to any actions they undertake prior to engaging in them.[137] Recalling the example of the righteous descendants of Noah whose statues were later worshiped by people who had forgotten their origins, he reminded his followers that even the most righteous people can unintentionally mislead others into unbelief (*kufr*) if their actions are not clearly and properly understood by those who follow them.[138] As additional proof, he noted that worship of the pre-Islamic goddess al-Lat developed out of the practice of people spending long visits at the grave site of a righteous person bearing this name.[139]

Ibn Abd al-Wahhab's concerns about grave visitation included both genders. He recounted a *hadith* forbidding both men and women from visiting graves and setting up mosques and lights over them. He then specified that women as well as men were forbidden from carrying out such practices.

That Ibn Abd al-Wahhab would have repeated this prohibition on the basis of Muhammad's own teaching is not surprising. Historically, women have always been active participants in, for example, popular Sufi rituals involving the presentation of prayers and petitions at the tombs of saints, as well as the care and upkeep of tombs and shrines. Ibn Abd al-Wahhab's inclusive language in this case parallels the Quranic use of the same and serves to emphasize the prohibition of these practices for both genders. The emphasis is made in order to provide clarity, not to single out female adherents or wives or daughters of adherents as being especially open to criticism.[140]

The only instance in which Ibn Abd al-Wahhab singled women out for criticism with respect to the visitation of tombs and the recitation of prayers at them was his prohibition of women working as professional bewailers at funerals and during mourning periods. Because a bewailer expresses disagreement with the will of God (and God holds the power of life and death in Islam), bewailing contests God's *tawhid*.[141] Muhammad himself had admonished such women to repent before Judgment Day or suffer.

On Requests for Intercession with God

Similar to his discussion about tombs, mosques, and shrines, Ibn Abd al-Wahhab also addressed the question of requesting intercession with God, whether from a person or an object, as a practical rather than theoretical issue. History records the popular Najdi practices of venerating certain trees and rocks as capable of bringing good luck, marriage, or pregnancy. In particular, a male palm tree in Bilad al-Fiddah was believed to be capable of granting requests for marriage and thus became a popular site for spinsters to visit.[142] Ibn Abd al-Wahhab himself had chopped down a tree that was popularly venerated for its supposed intercessory and magical powers.

Requesting intercession by anyone with God was one of the most important issues Ibn Abd al-Wahhab addressed in his discussions of *shirk*. He began by citing a series of Quranic verses that clearly and permanently forbid requests for intercession with God.[143] There were two reasons for this prohibition. First, in Islam prayer is an act of worship. Therefore, prayers should be made only to God. Second, only God possesses the power to grant requests. Therefore, making requests to anyone or anything else is pointless.

For Ibn Abd al-Wahhab, there were two main theological problems with requesting intercession. First, it expresses confidence that the person or object to whom the request is made is capable of granting it. Second, it expresses a lack of confidence in God as merciful, compassionate, and benevolent toward believers because it creates the false impression that God either does not care about earthly matters or is incapable of granting such requests. Ibn Abd al-Wahhab taught that intercession is possible only if God permits it. Since no one can control God, only God can know and determine who will be permitted to intercede with Him. The piety or righteousness of the person being prayed to therefore has no effect on the outcome. Even prayers for intercession by the Righteous Ancestors (*Salihin*) and Muhammad himself were not permissible.[144] Ibn Abd al-Wahhab did not allow his followers to even mention another person's name when invoking God.[145]

Ibn Abd al-Wahhab highlighted the gravity of associationism by observing that God sent Muhammad to people who were already doing most of the things God required of them but who continued to place created beings and mediums between themselves and God.[146] Thus, he understood God's purpose in sending Muhammad to "renew them in the religion," which meant teaching them "not to associate anything" with God and "not to give Him associates in authority."[147]

Is there anyone, then, who is permitted to intercede with God on behalf of human beings? According to the *hadith*, Muhammad declared that he would be allowed to fulfill this role but only after performing other duties that proclaimed God's absolute power and sovereignty. Muhammad stated that he would first be brought before God on Judgment Day. However, rather than immediately presenting petitions on behalf of various believers, Muhammad would prostrate himself before God and praise Him. It would only be after his worship of the One True God that he would be allowed to present petitions on anyone's behalf. When Muhammad was questioned about the people on whose behalf he would present his petitions, he responded that it would be those who affirm in all truth and honesty that there is no god but God.[148]

Ibn Abd al-Wahhab's analysis of these *hadith* made it clear that the only "guaranteed" intercessor with God is Muhammad himself. Nothing is said about anyone else interceding with God. Ibn Abd al-Wahhab believed that intercession should be considered a gift from God that reflects His ultimate power.[149] He cautioned Muslims against being overly confident in Muhammad's ability to intercede with God on their behalf, noting that Muhammad himself stated that his capacity to intercede would be restricted by the believer's own faith. Failure by the Muslim to uphold monotheism would prevent Muhammad from interceding on his or her behalf.[150] In fact, Ibn Abd al-Wahhab pointed out that placing greater confidence in Muhammad's ability as an intercessor than on God's mercy and compassion already violates monotheism. He therefore advised his followers to focus on adhering to monotheism rather than counting on intercession for salvation.[151]

To emphasize his point of personal responsibility for salvation, he turned to the example of Muhammad's uncle, Abu Talib. Abu Talib raised Muhammad after the deaths of his parents and grandfather and protected him throughout his preaching career, but he never converted to Islam. As Abu Talib lay dying, Muhammad begged him to proclaim that "There is no god but The God" so that Muhammad would be allowed to intercede with God on his behalf. Abu Talib consistently refused and then died. Muhammad then declared that he would pray for forgiveness for Abu Talib as long as he was not prohibited from doing so. Not long afterward, God revealed to Muhammad the verse Q 9:113, which forbids prayer for forgiveness for unbelievers. God later admonished Muhammad that even he could not guide those whom he loves to faith, but only God can guide whom He wills (Q 28:56).

Ibn Abd al-Wahhab's citation of this case reflects both the historical and contemporary debates about whether Muhammad would be able to gain salvation for those who did not profess Islam as their faith, including Muhammad's ancestors who died before the revelation of the Quran.[152] This idea comes from the importance placed on kin relationships in pre-Islamic tribal Arabia. Some early Muslims assumed that the faith of one family member, when strong enough, ought to be sufficient to save other unbelieving family members on the basis of their kin relationship. However, Ibn Abd al-Wahhab believed that this *hadith* made it clear that not even Muhammad could save people who did not uphold monotheism on their own.[153] He taught that the main point of this *hadith* was the declaration of the personal responsibility of every individual believer for his or her own faith and salvation.[154] Neither blood relationships nor the accomplishment of numerous good deeds, however commendable, can cancel out the missing factor of faith in matters of salvation.

The issue of intercession was a matter of such concern for Ibn Abd al-Wahhab that, in addition to the extensive discussions contained in *Kitab al-Tawhid*, he wrote a treatise entitled "Kitab Kashf al-Shubhat," which served as a "how-to" manual for dealing with people who insist on human intermediaries with God. Throughout the manual, he called for debate and dialogue rather than violence and warfare as the appropriate method for dealing with such people. His discussion addresses the question of intercession from both outside of and within Islam.

He began by noting that historically popular recognition of certain people, like Jesus, as being particularly righteous and close to God led to the popular belief in their capacity to serve as intercessors with God. He believed that this special recognition had led some (namely, Christians) to worship these people as God.[155] In the specific case of Jesus, Ibn Abd al-Wahhab instructed his followers to begin their discussions and debates by outlining verses from the Quran that recognize Jesus as God's Messenger but deny his status as the Son of God. The purpose of this was to remind people that God has stated that He will curse anyone who follows idols, no matter how righteous they might be, because idols "do not possess power/authority over anything but their direction comes from God for their intercession."[156] By deemphasizing the role of the intercessor, Ibn Abd al-Wahhab was able to refocus attention on the individual believer's personal and direct access to God.[157]

In a later discussion, Ibn Abd al-Wahhab addressed the issue of *awliya'* (the plural form of *wali*, or "friend" of God, a term typically used by Sufis for their saints) as supposed intermediaries. He instructed his followers to remind those with whom they were debating about the Quranic admonition that claiming the *awliya'* as intercessors constitutes idolatry.[158] Because adherence to absolute monotheism is supposed to be the distinguishing characteristic of Muslims, violations of monotheism rendered such persons non-Muslims, even if they claimed to be Muslims. However, rather than fighting or killing such people, Ibn Abd al-Wahhab encouraged his followers to continue to encourage debate and discussion with them.

Ibn Abd al-Wahhab believed that the clear logic of his arguments would lead people to recognize their errors and return to the straight path of Islam. He instructed his followers to proceed in their debates as follows:

> Say to him: "You have determined that God has made incumbent upon you sincere devotion to the worship of God and this is truth to you?" And he says: "Yes." Then say to him: "It is clear to me that this is incumbent upon you and this is sincere devotion to the worship of God in His unity and this is truth to you." And he had not known worship, and there are no other types of it clear to him in your saying God Most High said: "Call on your Lord in humility and in secret" (Q 7:55). And you will know Him in this way. And say to him: "Do you know that this is definitely worship of God?" And he says: "Yes." And the Call is the marrow of worship. Then say to him: "Therefore, I tell you that this is worship and God calls you day and night out of fear and greed. Then He calls you in this necessity by the prophets and others like them. How can you associate in worship of God other than Him and not be distant from Him?" And he says: "Yes." Then say to him: "And therefore you work with the saying of God Most High (parting from your Lord and others) and you worship God Most High and you slaughter to Him. Is this worship?" And it is certain that he says: "Yes." Then say to him: "Yet you slaughter to a created being: a prophet or a *jinn* or other than them. Do you associate in this worship other than God?" And he will have no choice but to decide and he will say: "Yes."[159]

It is clear from this discussion that conversion is not intended to occur in a "convert or die" moment. Rather, conversion is understood to be a process achieved through logical, structured discussions of what actions constitute worship and associationism. The purpose is to help people recognize their violations of monotheism of their own accord in the hope that they will be moved to voluntarily adjust their practices in keeping with the profession of monotheism.

On the Use of Amulets, Charms, and Talismans

Similar to requesting intercession by holy people, the use of amulets or talismans either to ward off problems or to cure them constitutes associationism. Ibn Abd al-Wahhab disallowed the use of chains, talismans, amulets, and clothing purported to carry special powers because he believed that belief or trust in the capacity of these objects to cure disease or old age or protect one from evil spirits demonstrates a lack of faith in God to resolve such problems. He stated unequivocally that "ignorance in this matter is no excuse" and that ultimately such examples of what might legally be classified as lesser *shirk* are actually graver in nature than major sins because they violate monotheism. Such acts of associationism are sufficiently grave to merit not only the rejection and condemnation of any person guilty of committing them but also the removal of the talisman from anyone or anything wearing it. The condemnation of the wearing of talismans and amulets applied to both people and animals.[160]

The only instance in which Ibn Abd al-Wahhab hesitated was a case in which the talisman consisted of Quranic verses. Noting that there was no legal consensus (*ijma'*) about the permissibility of Quran verses used as talismans, Ibn Abd al-Wahhab turned to the *hadith*. He found that Muhammad had expressly permitted the use of incantations only for warding off jealousy and in the case of the sting of deadly animals. Ibn Abd al-Wahhab therefore limited the use of Quranic verses as talismans to these two cases in order to uphold the requirements of monotheism.[161]

On Sorcery and Seeking to Know the Future

Sorcery and seeking to know the future were also listed as instances of associationism in Ibn Abd al-Wahhab's written works. Ibn Abd al-Wahhab considered sorcery to be such a grave sin that he classified it as unbelief (*kufr*) and condemned to immediate death any person engaged in it.[162] His extreme stance on sorcery was due to the Quran's condemnation of the same and the fact that Muhammad listed sorcery among the seven grave sins in Islam. Muhammad had further warned that there are three types of people who will not enter Paradise—habitual drinkers of alcoholic beverages, those who deny their blood relations, and those who believe in sorcery.[163]

Because of the serious nature of the charge of sorcery, Ibn Abd al-Wahhab identified the behaviors that constituted it. He included in his list six types of divination: allowing a bird to fly away, drawing lines on the earth, and listening to the voice of Satan; astrology or attempting to draw knowledge from the stars; making a knot and blowing on it; wearing an amulet or talisman so as to be subject to its control; extreme literary eloquence; and lying and spreading false rumors with the goal of spreading evil and ill will.[164] On their own, such activities may not appear to be particularly grave or harmful. It is the intent behind them that renders them so dangerous and blasphemous. All of the activities discussed above entail attempts to gain knowledge about the unknown, control destiny, or attract people into believing and participating in falsehood. All of these intents have behind them the desire to be as knowledgeable as God Himself or to exert control over the activities and understanding of other human beings, all for selfish gain. It is this spirit of intent that challenges God's uniqueness, rendering them unacceptable. Thus it was that Ibn Abd al-Wahhab declared that those who knew better but either engaged in sorcery or associated with those who did were to be found further at fault than those who engaged in sorcery without knowledge of its violation of monotheism.[165]

Because of the similarity of the intent involved, Ibn Abd al-Wahhab also condemned seeking the assistance of a soothsayer to learn about the future or the mind of God. He noted that soothsayers neither receive nor transmit messages directly from God. Only God's Messengers receive such revelations. Since Muhammad was the last of the Messengers, anyone claiming to have received a message from God is clearly a liar, even if the content of the message is true. Furthermore, Ibn Abd al-Wahhab noted that soothsayers are not infallible. He therefore taught that people should ignore these fallible human sources and turn instead to infallible sources—the Quran and Sunna of Muhammad.[166]

Along the same lines, Ibn Abd al-Wahhab condemned diviners and fortune-tellers, as well as those who seek their services, as guilty of blasphemy and denying God's revelation to Muhammad. He defined fortune-telling as seeking to know facts that are hidden, such as the location of stolen items or stray animals, the closely guarded secrets of another person, or the meaning of omens. He condemned those who seek such services because they place their faith in superstitions and human beings rather than God.[167] He believed that reliance on good luck or fortune also constitutes derision and mockery of God by supposing that someone or something other than God is capable of knowing the unknown.[168]

Attempting to read omens is often a matter of seeking to know the future through natural phenomena such as natural disasters like epidemics or contagious diseases, reading the future in nature, belief in a sort of worm-beast reputed to roam around the grave of a nonavenged victim until blood vengeance has been satisfied, tampering with the lunar calendar so as to permit hunting and war, linking storms to astrological configurations, and belief in punishing monsters. All of these phenomena had been explicitly condemned by Muhammad.[169] Only optimism or the expectation that an event will be followed by a better one is permitted because this reflects faith in God's ability to overcome and control any situation and turn it into a better one. Because only God can know the future, the only appropriate response to natural calamities, disasters, and phenomena is to turn to God through prayer.[170]

Ibn Abd al-Wahhab also targeted pre-Islamic practices and behaviors that reflected faith or confidence in someone or something other than God. He singled out pride in the noble achievements of one's relatives, attacks against weak genealogies, seeking rain by means of the stars, and bewailing the deceased as particularly demonstrative of this attitude. He noted that pride in the achievement of one's relatives and ridicule of another's weak genealogies reflects pride in the achievements of human beings rather than in God's achievements and Will. Seeking rain through stars demonstrates unbelief, as though stars could actually control or interfere with life on earth. Bewailing the deceased could be interpreted to mean dissatisfaction with God's Will. All of these are instances of violations of God's unique power.[171]

For Ibn Abd al-Wahhab, the problems associated with such practices were clear and not open to debate. What is interesting in his discussion is that, despite his clear condemnation of such practices in accordance with Muhammad's teachings in the *hadith*, his manner of dealing with people who commit such sins is relatively mild. For example, he made it very clear that there is a significant difference between the person who carries out the sorcery (and is immediately subject to the death penalty) and the person who seeks the services of the sorcerer. Although one might expect a consistently violent and intolerant response toward those who seek the services of sorcerers or at least their damnation to Hell and eternal punishment for their associationism, Ibn Abd al-Wahhab simply reiterated that such people need to be educated. Rather than attacking them, he taught that the appropriate response to such "ignorant" people was to question them indirectly by asking them if they know what God has said regarding such practices.[172] Thus it is that questioning is to lead to discussion and proper instruction so that the offenders can be helped to understand the error of their ways and can change them accordingly.

It is also important to note that, despite his condemnation of astrology and seeking to know the future through the positions and movements of the stars and planets, Ibn Abd al-Wahhab was careful to state clearly to his audience that astronomy—the study of the position of stars and movements of the moon for the purpose of guiding travelers and the pursuit of knowledge—was permitted. Thus, he believed that faith should not preclude attempts to know and understand physical knowledge. In fact, he taught that the Muslim should seek to understand what he or she can of the universe God has created because the entire universe serves as witness to God's uniqueness.[173] He thus distinguished between knowledge of the natural universe and knowledge of future events.

On Breaking Magic Spells and Expressing Faith in God's Will

Tied to the questions of divination, omens, and the use of magic is the question of the breaking of magic spells, which some people believed caused illness. The practice of casting and breaking magic spells (*nushrah*) existed in the time of Muhammad and may have been an issue in the era of Ibn Abd al-Wahhab.[174] According to Ibn Abd al-Wahhab, there are two ways to break magic spells. The first, which is prohibited, is for the person under the spell and the person who is attempting to break it to approach Satan and offer him satisfaction in exchange for breaking the spell. The second, which is permitted, is the invocation of genuine spiritual powers (*ruqyah*) through the recitation of Quranic verses, medicine, and prayers.

It is clear from the discussion that illness is not considered to be strictly physical in nature. Ibn Abd al-Wahhab also recognized a spiritual dimension to physical health. Consequently, he prescribed a combination of medical treatment and Quranic recitation and prayer when dealing with illness as a reflection of belief in God's ultimate power and Will over all situations. In other words, faith was not to be placed in pharmaceutical products alone.[175] Ibn Abd al-Wahhab was also careful to distinguish between actual medicine and magic and incantations used as medical treatments. While actual medicine was allowed—and even required—magic and incantations were not.[176] For Ibn Abd al-Wahhab, the use of magic or incantations violated the command to have complete trust in God alone (tawakkul).[177]

Ibn Abd al-Wahhab believed that this complete trust in God should permeate every statement and action of the believer. He cautioned believers to formulate their responses to adversity as expressions of their submission to God's Will, observing that God sometimes uses adversity as an opportunity to test faith and provide a positive outcome. Thus, he taught that whatever one experiences one should thank and praise God and request His assistance in dealing with the circumstances and their aftermath.[178] He equated a negative response to life events as shirk because it expresses doubt on the part of the believer in God's wisdom and ability to will and decree events, success, and victory.[179]

At stake in the question of absolute faith and trust in God is the matter of God's qadar, or Will. Muhammad himself stated that belief in God's Will was an absolute requirement of faith, along with belief in God, His angels, books, prophets, and the Day of Judgment.[180] God's Will can result in either good or bad things. What is important is not so much what happens as how one reacts to it. Belief in God's Will is what turns faith from a matter of belief into a matter of conviction. It is the attitude that permits the believer to respond appropriately to every situation on the basis of absolute and unshakeable faith in God's control over the universe and all events that occur within it. Without belief in God's Will, true faith cannot exist. Even good works cannot achieve salvation for a person lacking such faith.[181]

Because only God is capable of providing favors, Ibn Abd al-Wahhab taught that even the attribution of an event or outcome to someone or something other than God, like the weather or a person, constitutes associationism. He pointed to the examples of what appear to be harmless statements about the weather—like the wind or rain being responsible for good crops—or people—like someone leaving an inheritance—being responsible for a positive event. He noted the danger of such trends of speaking and thinking because such declarations deny God's role in providing such blessings. Thus, even what might appear to be the most innocent wording can be a reflection of continued associationism in the heart and mind.[182]

Furthermore, one should not combine thanks or credit to God for an action with a declaration of the role played by someone or something else in that event. Credit should go strictly to God in a first statement. Any acknowledgment of the role of someone or something else belongs in a separate statement, even if that person is Muhammad.[183] Ibn Abd al-Wahhab therefore counseled his followers to avoid phrases like "If only such and such had happened" and "If only so and so had done such and such."[184] It was also for this reason that he forbade swearing by anyone other than God or naming a child or taking a name that implies the service of anyone other than God.[185] Even joking or jesting about God, the Quran, or Muhammad was forbidden as an act of unbelief.[186]

Major Sins

Although Islam does not have the Christian concept of Original Sin or divide sins into venial and mortal sins along the lines of Roman Catholicism, Islam recognizes both the concept of sin and human vulnerability to sinful behavior. In Islam, no individual is held responsible for the commission of a sin by a past generation.[187] Instead, Islam proclaims the responsibility of every individual for his or her own behavior.

Islam recognizes two categories of sin: those committed against God and those committed against human beings. Sins that are committed against God are the most serious and will be punished in the Afterlife. Sins against human beings are to be punished in this world. Within these two categories, certain sins have been categorized as "major" and "grave."

The *hadith* record Muhammad's delineation of both major and grave sins. He defined the four major sins as: slaughtering in any other name than God's, cursing one's parents, sheltering the perpetrator of a crime carrying a divine sanction so as to enable the perpetrator to escape punishment, and unjustly altering the boundaries of personal land properties in order to achieve illegitimate advantage.[188] Grave sins were defined as: *shirk*, sorcery, murder, consumption of interest, robbery of the orphan, desertion on the day of battle, and false accusations against chaste women.[189]

Ibn Abd al-Wahhab took up the topic of big sins in his *Book of Big Sins* (*Kitab al-Kaba'ir*). In this treatise, he compiled a list of various types of major sins on the basis of the Quran and *hadith*, arranged according to themes.[190] The purpose of the treatise was an elaboration of various daily life experiences that violate monotheism.

He opened with the identification of the greatest of all sins—those that God has promised to punish via banishment to Hell, cursing/damnation, anger or other types of punishment. The three "biggest of the big sins" are *shirk*, disobedience to one's parents, and false testimony. The other big sin discussed is "the big sin of the heart," which is defined as a lack of goodness or righteousness in the heart that spoils the entire body.[191]

The remainder of the treatise is dedicated to matters of individual and communal behavior and speech. As with his other writings, Ibn Abd al-Wahhab was particularly concerned in each case with the intent behind the listed actions and interpersonal communications and their ultimate meaning with respect to God. Sinful behaviors range from major issues such as hypocrisy to seemingly minor issues such as the failure to keep the achievement of puberty a secret.[192] In each case, it is the relationship between the activity and God's *tawhid* that renders the behavior or statement sinful.

The significance of this elaboration of major sins of words and deeds is that it serves as a catechism of explanation of what it means to believe in and adhere to monotheism and faith in Islam. It is a detailing of the implications of faith in daily life that demonstrates the application of beliefs in every aspect of life and interaction with other human beings. Furthermore, it holds the Muslim ever mindful of his or her responsibility to build up the Muslim *ummah* rather than engaging in destructive behavior toward it, whether collectively or individually. It is in this spirit that Muslims are commanded to be kind to their slaves and livestock, pay fair and just wages, grant shelter to any Muslim seeking it, oppose tyranny and injustice, and always be mindful of the brotherhood and truth of Islam.[193]

Ibn Abd al-Wahhab also included a discussion of major sins that governments should avoid, including being dishonest toward or defrauding subjects; hiding or veiling things from citizens; showing favoritism in governing; engaging in tyranny, oppression, or injustice; and permitting dishonest sales, contracts, purchases, measures, or weights.[194] He commanded governments to be responsible, to demonstrate compassion toward their subjects, and to improve the enforcement of justice.[195] This discussion makes clear his vision of the need for government to reflect Islam's messages of justice, compassion, and equal treatment for all.

Faith (*Iman*)

In all of his discussions about the requirements of faith and the need to avoid sinful behaviors, Ibn Abd al-Wahhab asserted faith (*iman*) as the guiding force that drives every thought and action of the Muslim in both private and public life. Because faith is the measure by which every Muslim will be judged in the Afterlife, Ibn Abd al-Wahhab believed that faith that remained a matter of private, personal belief was unworthy of the title. It was only by acting and living out the consequences of faith that the Muslim could rightfully be called a Muslim.[196]

Ibn Abd al-Wahhab defined *iman* as a belief and attitude that grow out of absolute trust and confidence (*tawakkul*) in God. *Tawakkul* is both a religious duty and a condition of faith. It allows the believer to rely completely on God at all times, particularly in the case of disaster.[197] Thus, despair is labeled a grave sin because it indicates the belief that one is beyond God's reach and expresses doubts about God's mercy, compassion, power, and control over the universe. Ibn Abd al-Wahhab taught his followers that they should always express confidence in God's goodness and mercy and expect that things will turn out well.[198]

Ibn Abd al-Wahhab believed that faith should lead to both individual piety and the pursuit of good works. He noted that it is faith that distinguishes between believers, rather than wealth or nobility, and that God's favor is upon the most pious.[199] Consequently, he taught that faith, rather than works, was the critical factor in matters of salvation. In support, he cited a saying of Muhammad: "Not a single one among you will enter Paradise by his work."[200] Ibn Abd al-Wahhab himself repeatedly asserted that good actions, even when combined with ritual perfection, are insufficient for salvation. What ultimately matters is faith, conviction of the heart, and the intent behind actions.[201] Because salvation should be the ultimate goal of the Muslim, he suggested that the true believer should not be distracted by the benefits and luxuries of this world but should strive instead for constant awareness of the Afterlife. He noted that those who receive their rewards in this life have nothing waiting for them in the Afterlife.[202]

This does not mean that Ibn Abd al-Wahhab discounted works altogether. Consistent with the broad Islamic vision of the necessity of correct practice, Ibn Abd al-Wahhab taught that works were a necessary corollary to faith. Works were insufficient by themselves because the totality of a human being's actions must be considered by God. If salvation were strictly based on a person's actions, Ibn Abd al-Wahhab believed that no one would enter Paradise because all people are capable of both good and evil. It is only because God forgives people for their evil deeds that the attainment of Paradise becomes possible.[203] Thus, the main actor in this equation is God, rather than human beings, making clear humans' dependence on God's goodness and mercy rather than their own capabilities for salvation. Because faith provides knowledge of God's mercy and goodness, only the combination of faith and works together can lead to salvation.[204]

Because of the public dimension that he expected faith to contain, Ibn Abd al-Wahhab specified five activities that were to be carried out by every believer as a demonstration of faith: (1) a return to the Quran and the examples of Muhammad and the early Muslim community for knowledge rather than relying on someone else's explanation (*tafsir*) of the same; (2) basing judgment and wisdom on the direct contents of the Quran rather than interpretations of it; (3) avoidance of bribery and corruption; (4) shunning of superstitious practices; and (5) not disclaiming something that is recorded in the Quran simply because someone else claims that it is not necessary to follow it.[205]

Just as the demonstration of faith is complex and multifaceted, so the absence of faith is more than a difference of opinion about legal or theological issues, particularly where difficult or unclear scriptural passages or issues are concerned. Ibn Abd al-Wahhab recognized the reality of the potential plurality of interpretations on certain matters. He was not interested in condemning people through legalistic and literal interpretations of religion or in assigning labels. In fact, he wondered how anyone could label as an unbeliever someone who is generally pious and avoids forbidden things yet disagrees about a single word.[206]

Faith as a Matter of the Heart

Ibn Abd al-Wahhab understood the heart to be the center from which every-thing else flows to the extremities, decreasing in intensity as one moves out-ward.[207] It is within the heart that the believer carefully examines matters of faith and determines whether or not a particular action is permissible or ought to be opposed. Only the heart is capable of distinguishing between good and evil, between what will bring harm or injury and what is advantageous and meritorious. It is the heart that discerns both hidden and clear *shirk* and en-courages the believer to repent.[208]

Because of the centrality of its role for both mind and body, Ibn Abd al-Wahhab taught that the heart is to be the central location of faith for the gen-uine Muslim. He declared that faith as an attitude and conviction comes from the heart, allowing true faith to permeate the entire body and essence of the believer and to make the Quran the instinct and passion of the believer. The heart must be kept strong in faith so as to prevent the body as a whole from becoming weak and susceptible to hypocrisy and the "snatching away" of faith.[209]

Faith as a matter of the heart is based on a *hadith* that states, "Islam is on the exterior, and faith is in the heart."[210] When asked to explain the difference between Islam and faith, Ibn Abd al-Wahhab replied that speaking of Islam is what leads to faith in the heart. Because faith is a true reflection of what lies in the heart and mind of the believer, Ibn Abd al-Wahhab accorded faith a higher ranking than Islam as ritual perfection. Although he did not consider Islam as outward ritual perfectionism to be necessary, he warned that departure from true Islam is possible only through unbelief (*kufr*), which is never ac-ceptable. In other words, faith and true Islam are necessary corollaries of each other. Faith makes true Islam definite and final, while ritual Islam does not make anything necessary.[211]

Ibn Abd al-Wahhab's emphasis on faith as conviction of the heart, rather than ritual perfection or the pursuit of self-importance, is consistent with his concern with the intent, rather than the form, of actions. He believed that intent should be guided by conviction of the heart.[212] Without conviction of the heart, prostration in prayer, almsgiving, and seeking the face of God and Paradise are meaningless because they reflect love of this world, leadership, kingship, authority, property, and money rather than love of God.[213] In other words, faith directed by the heart is what determines sincerity. Ibn Abd al-Wahhab taught that a person possessing faith from the heart will be able to oppose hypocrisy and any writings or cultural accretions that contradict Islamic precepts.[214]

Ibn Abd al-Wahhab noted that God has declared that He will reassure the heart of the person who believes in Him (Q 64:11). Thus, when questioned about whether one should consider afflictions and suffering in this world to be signs of God's punishment and displeasure, Ibn Abd al-Wahhab responded that suffering in this lifetime is actually a sign of God's love and concern for believers because it gives them the opportunity to demonstrate and grow in their faith, as well as to be rewarded. Therefore, one should approach suffering and affliction with a spirit of contentment and patience, looking toward the longer term goals of salvation and reward. Resentment is strictly prohibited.[215]

Faith versus Unbelief (Kufr)

Kufr is the polar opposite of faith.[216] Ibn Abd al-Wahhab taught that unbelief is never acceptable because people have been told in their own language by a series of prophets what the Word of God is and have deliberately chosen to disobey it. In his opinion, ignorance on the part of a person who verbally professes faith cannot and will not be excused.[217] This denial of forgiveness underscores again the importance of the believer engaging in direct and personal study of scripture so as not to fall into such ignorance. Observing the constant threat of deception and false teachings, Ibn Abd al-Wahhab taught that people must have personal knowledge of their religion in order to be able to defend themselves against "these devils." It is only through knowledge of God's Word and Law that one can be victorious over associationists and unbelievers.[218]

While the distinction between faith and unbelief is clear in Ibn Abd al-Wahhab's works, the consequences of unbelief are not. This is surprising because the standard historical works dealing with the Wahhabi movement posit that the Wahhabis had a very narrow and clear definition of what constituted unbelief: any failure to follow the teachings of the Wahhabis. According to these standard portrayals, such unbelief constituted apostasy, which rendered the offender liable to the death penalty and confiscation of his or her property.[219] It is therefore of great interest that Ibn Abd al-Wahhab's discussions of this topic not only did not support this practice but actually condemned it.

Rather than labeling all unbelievers as apostates, Ibn Abd al-Wahhab presumed all persons to be innocent of unbelief or apostasy unless and until they have been properly instructed in the faith. It is only *after* the declared acceptance of such instruction and adherence to it that behavior contradicting it can be considered to be unbelief or apostasy.[220] The chronological order was of critical importance to Ibn Abd al-Wahhab. He noted that belief cannot exist without faith and that faith cannot exist without proper instruction in the Quran and Sunna. Consequently, charges of apostasy or unbelief against those who have not been properly instructed are necessarily false, particularly where unclear passages of the Quran are in question because one cannot be certain of their meaning.[221] He further distinguished between associationists (mushrikun) and unbelievers (kuffar), with the label of kuffar being more serious, as it was reserved for those who were clearly and deliberately either idolaters or infidels.[222]

However much he denounced certain practices or beliefs, Ibn Abd al-Wahhab never called for wholesale killing of people, not even apostates. Rather, he proclaimed the need to call people to Islam and to educate them. He even insisted that the attitude of unbelievers toward his followers be taken into consideration. For example, he declared that it is perfectly acceptable, and even beneficial, to carry out business with anyone who is friendly to Muslims, regardless of whether they are Muslims themselves. Even in the case of jihad, if Muslims find themselves in need they may enter the territory of non-Muslim tribes that are friendly to them, though only with the express permission of the imam. The simple takeover of property because it belongs to non-Muslims is not permitted.

Ibn Abd al-Wahhab opposed the other major law schools (madhahib), most notably the Malikis, in these teachings because he found the conduct of business to be to the benefit of both the Muslims and the social order.[223] Thus, the interest of public welfare (maslahah) for the Muslim community was served. His position underscored the importance he placed on dialogue and education rather than calls for rampant violence and destruction.

In fact, declarations and accusations of or rulings against apostasy are quite rare in Ibn Abd al-Wahhab's works. His focus on the importance of education, knowledge, intent, and comprehension of God's expectations of humanity led him to restrict accusations of apostasy to a very few extreme cases: belief in Musaylimah,[224] denial of resurrection at the end of time, denial of the teachings of the Quran, and other unspecified types of apostasy. He further cautioned that evidence of apostasy must be very clear, so that the permissibility of seizing property and killing apostates will be neither rampant nor easily practiced.[225]

Ibn Abd al-Wahhab discussed the question of apostasy in two cases: the case of Muslims fighting other Muslims and the case of the Shiis. Consistent with the teachings of the Quran and Muhammad, he declared Muslims fighting other Muslims to be an act of apostasy for which the perpetrators should ask for forgiveness and submit to God.[226] He denied the right of the ulama to defend such activities or claim that they are somehow legal and permissible and noted the impossibility of the Muslim escaping the consequences of such actions because God knows and sees all.[227]

The prohibition of Muslims fighting other Muslims necessarily raises the question of how Ibn Abd al-Wahhab viewed people who claimed to be Muslims but did not share his interpretation of Islam. Although historically the Wahhabis have been accused of labeling anyone who does not adhere to their teachings as a non-Muslim, as had been the practice among the extremist seventh-century Kharijites, Ibn Abd al-Wahhab's writings do not reflect such a rigid division of the world into Wahhabis and non-Wahhabis. Because history has similarly charged the Wahhabis with opposition to both Sufism and Shiism, because Ibn Abd al-Wahhab himself wrote about apostasy with respect to the Shiis, and because contemporary Saudi-Shii relations, both with Iran and the Shii population of the Saudi Eastern Province, remain strained, it is worth examining what Ibn Abd al-Wahhab actually wrote about Sufis and Shiis.

Sufis and Shiis

The historical record has typically depicted the Wahhabis as being vehemently opposed to and engaged in destructive and violent acts against both Sufism and Shiism.[228] There are a variety of reasons for this, including Ibn Abd al-Wahhab's opposition to the practices of building shrines and domes over tombs, the destruction of Shii shrines in Karbala and Najaf,[229] his rejection of human beings, however pious, serving as intermediaries with God, and the fact that Ibn Abd al-Wahhab was a Hanbali jurist. This last point, more than any other, is responsible for the assertion that Ibn Abd al-Wahhab sought the complete eradication of Sufism.

Historically, both Muslim and Western scholars asserted that Hanbalism in general, which was depicted as extremist, rigid, exclusivist, fanatical, and intolerant, was opposed to Sufism, which was portrayed as being inclusivist, flexible and tolerant. Scholars pointed to the tendency of Sufis to incorporate local, non-Muslim customs and religious practices as evidence of the open-mindedness of Sufism and its ability to adapt to new geographic situations. This depiction was then contrasted negatively with Hanbalism's insistence on religious purity. This portrayal of Hanbalism and Sufism as polar opposites and the assumption that the Hanbalis rejected Sufism as being outside of Islamic orthodoxy resulted in the demonization of Hanbalism.[230] However, the historical record paints a much more nuanced picture than this black and white portrayal suggests.

The examination of Hanbali texts and scholars reveals not only the lack of proclamations of the need to completely eradicate Sufism as a mystical tradition but also the reality that some of the greatest Hanbali scholars, including Ibn Taymiyya and his most important student, Ibn al-Qayyim al-Jawziyyah, were Sufis. Both of these Hanbali scholars were members of the widespread Qadiriyya order, and both included some of the works of the great Sufi masters in the sources they examined and deemed worthy of study.[231] In addition, the founder of the first and largest Sufi order, Abd al-Qadir al-Jili, was himself a Hanbali jurist.[232] Furthermore, from their origins Hanbalism and Sufism shared a common emphasis on meditation on the Quran, study of the *hadith*, and belief that the intent behind an action is more important than the form of the action.[233] The emphasis on the *hadith*, in particular, was spearheaded by the Hanbalis so that the Sufi adoption of this emphasis in the eleventh century reflects an ongoing dynamic relationship between Hanbalism and Sufism.[234] Thus, rather than serving as polar opposites, Hanbalism and Sufism actually agreed on many important points of both methodology and interpretation.

The combined evidence shatters the image of Hanbalism as being necessarily opposed to Sufism per se. However, these commonalities do not mean that Hanbalism should be equated with Sufism. Substantial differences still remained, particularly as Sufism developed historically.

The opposition of the Hanbali school to certain Sufi practices developed as Sufism's geographical spread led to the adoption of un-Islamic practices into the devotional practices of certain orders. Thus, what the Hanbalis found to be problematic were certain practices engaged in by certain Sufis rather than Sufism as a mystical tradition as a whole. The Hanbalis recognized a distinction between the Sufism that was based on scripture and Islamic law and the Sufism that adopted un-Islamic practices.[235] Ibn Taymiyya fit the Hanbali tradition of acceptance of the more scripturally based Sufi movements. Consequently, neither he nor the Hanbalis were "the sworn enemies they have been made out to be by previous studies based on their detractors."[236]

It is within this context that Ibn Abd al-Wahhab's approach to Sufism must be understood and examined. Based on his writings, it is apparent that Ibn Abd al-Wahhab was neither the literalist nor the extremist that past scholars have asserted him to be. Instead, he clearly fits the Hanbali tradition of approving practices grounded in and consistent with the Quran and *hadith*, while disapproving and calling for the eradication of practices that do not meet this criteria. It is important to note that Sufis are barely present in Ibn Abd al-Wahhab's written works. In fact, he did not use the term *Sufi* at all. Rather than targeting "Sufism" as a phenomenon or group of individuals, Ibn Abd al-Wahhab denounced particular practices and explained why they were sinful.[237]

The case of the Shiis is somewhat different. Historically, the Hanbalis were in fact opposed to Shiism.[238] Ibn Abd al-Wahhab himself found certain beliefs and practices of Shiis to violate the key doctrine of monotheism. Although he generally denounced its beliefs and practices, rather than Shiism per se, he did write one theological treatise—the only one of its kind—denouncing the extremist Rafidah sect of Shiis. In their case, he believed that their practices violated monotheism to the point where he declared that they had rejected Islam altogether.

In his treatise "Risalah fi al-radd ala al-Rafidah" (Treatise/Letter on the Denial/Rejection Pertaining to the Rafidah), Ibn Abd al-Wahhab addressed thirty-two topics, ranging from political and religious issues such as the caliphate and Rafidah accusations of apostasy against the Companions to legal personal status issues such as marriage and divorce and comparing the Rafidah to other religious groups such as the Christians, Jews, and Magis. He attacked their stances on points of both theology and law, making no distinction between them as to which offense is more grave. Nine of the topics (one-fourth) address the question of women and gender.

With respect to theological issues, Ibn Abd al-Wahhab approached the beliefs of the Rafidah point by point on the basis of what Shii scholars and jurists had written and taught rather than on the basis of hearsay or propaganda. In doing so, he spoke as a scholar who had read and studied at least some Shii scholarly works, giving him a broad and systematic perspective of the Shii worldview and theology.

Prior to addressing specific points of theological doctrine or jurisprudence, Ibn Abd al-Wahhab established his methodology for criticism of the Rafidah. The basis for his criticism of the movement was his perception that it had diverged from Muhammad's example, making the distinction between Sunnis and Shiis one of the authority of scripture. All of the theological and legal issues addressed in this treatise stem from this issue. It was this apparent deviation from accepting the final authority of Muhammad's example that led to charges of Rafidah departure from monotheism. Based on his readings, Ibn Abd al-Wahhab found that the Rafidah assigned greater authority to their current leaders in understanding and interpreting the Quran and Islamic law than they did to Muhammad.[239]

For example, one of the main issues of contention between Sunnis and Shiis is the question of authority: after the death of Muhammad, who was granted authority and the right of leadership? Sunnis believe that the most faithful and qualified Muslim should serve as the leader. Shiis believe that leadership belongs only to the descendants of Muhammad on the basis of kinship. The problem for Sunnis with the Shii approach is that it denies the legitimacy of the first three caliphs after Muhammad—Abu Bakr, Umar, and Uthman—and asserts that they were inauthentic and sinful usurpers of power that rightly belonged to Muhammad's cousin and son-in-law, Ali ibn Abi Talib.

Ibn Abd al-Wahhab denounced the Shii approach because it accused the early Muslim community of wrongdoing and denied the validity of their legal consensus (ijma') over the question of succession. The denial of the validity of consensus was a major problem because it contradicted a *hadith* in which Muhammad stated, "My community will never agree in error." This dual violation led Ibn Abd al-Wahhab to declare the Shii approach to succession to be a false teaching.[240]

Ibn Abd al-Wahhab also took issue with the Shii practice of according infallible status to those descendants of Muhammad who were declared *imams* because he believed that this constituted associationism with God. Ibn Abd al-

Wahhab did not grant anyone, not even Muhammad's descendants, quasi-divine status. However, neither did he believe that they should be reviled. Instead, he upheld their specialness and asserted the responsibility of Muslims to treat them justly.[241]

Ibn Abd al-Wahhab found the logic behind the assertion of the infallible status of the *imams* to be internally flawed. According to the logic, succession to Muhammad was to be passed through the oldest son of the *imam*. However, Ibn Abd al-Wahhab noted that both Hasan, the oldest son of Ali and Fatima, and his descendants were excluded from the succession of the *imams*. For Ibn Abd al-Wahhab, the denial to Hasan of the special status and powers supposedly accorded to the second son, Husayn, and his descendants on the basis of their lineage was illogical.[242]

The exclusion of Hasan was not just illogical. It also created a major theological problem with respect to the coming of the Mahdi. According to the *hadith*, the Mahdi is a messianic figure who is expected to come at the end of time to institute an Islamic society of peace and justice and a reign of a thousand years. This Mahdi is supposed to be a descendant of Hasan, not Husayn. Ibn Abd al-Wahhab observed that if Hasan's descendants were wiped off the face of the earth it would be very difficult for this to occur by natural means. Thus, he concluded that the Shiis had tampered with God's Will by excluding Hasan and his descendants—a sin of major proportions.[243]

It is interesting that Ibn Abd al-Wahhab did not follow the example of some Sunni scholars in practically demonizing Ali and his descendants because of their special veneration by Shiis. On the contrary, his treatment of Ali and his descendants is respectful and supportive of their specialness, although he did not accord them infallibility or the exclusive right to leadership. He thus made clear the distinction between honoring human beings and worshiping them.[244]

In addition to the problems of denying consensus and the associationism involved in considering Muhammad's descendants to be infallible and more authoritative than the Quran and Muhammad's example, Ibn Abd al-Wahhab was deeply concerned by the existence of conflicting *hadith* cited to support both the Sunni and Shii positions on the succession question. According to the most prominent Shii *hadith* supporting the imamate over the caliphate, Muhammad debated with God the wisdom of appointing a caliph after his death out of fear that the person would be deified. Despite numerous requests to the contrary, God stood by His original decision to allow the imamate.

Ibn Abd al-Wahhab rejected this *hadith* as a fabrication on the basis of its weak chain of transmitters (*isnad*), its "false" and "deceptive" intent, and the fact that he found nothing in it contentwise that he believed was authentic.[246] The major problem with this *hadith* for Ibn Abd al-Wahhab was its content because it made sacrosanct something that was clearly forbidden in the Quran and the rest of the *hadith*: the aggrandizement of a single family above all others when all Muslims are supposed to be equal in the eyes of God.[247] In order to disprove the validity of the Shii *hadith*, Ibn Abd al-Wahhab pointed to its deficiencies in both form and content.

First, he noted that the Shii *hadith* stood in opposition to other *hadith*, with much stronger chains of transmission, that supported Abu Bakr's appointment. To solidify his case, he not only cited the sources of the stronger *hadith* but also the numerous compilers and specific collections from which the *hadith* were taken. This careful documentation suggests that this treatise was not merely an academic exercise in which he needed to demonstrate his scholarly credentials but also that it was intended to unequivocally prove the points contained within it to a Shii audience.[248]

Second, he addressed the content of the Shii *hadith*, outlining the theological violations that clearly marked it in his mind as a fabrication. First, this false *hadith* asserted that Muhammad had debated God's wisdom, an act of disobedience that Ibn Abd al-Wahhab classified as an act of unbelief because it challenged God's will. Noting that Muhammad is the example of perfection itself and that Muhammad alone among the prophets was never disobedient to God, Ibn Abd al-Wahhab rejected the notion that Muhammad would have engaged in such an act.[249] He then noted that this *hadith* proclaims Muhammad's preference for his own family—an attitude he completely rejected in the other *hadith* and a clear violation of the repeated Quranic concept of the equality of all Muslims except in matters of piety. Third, he pointed to this *hadith*'s proclamation of Muhammad's lack of trust in God to prevent his community from falling into error. This last point in particular had to be an error in Ibn Abd al-Wahhab's opinion because it contradicted another well-known *hadith* stating that God will never allow the Muslim community to fall into error. Since once cannot accuse God of lying, Ibn Abd al-Wahhab declared that belief in this false *hadith* or following anyone who claims that it is true is an act of unbelief.[250]

Having thus debunked this *hadith*, he turned to others that proclaimed the favored position of Ali ibn Abi Talib. These other *hadith* were recounted by three major Shii theologians: Ibn al-Mathar al-Hilli, al-Tumasi, and al-Sharih, all of whom refer to Ali as "the most preferred of the Companions." al-Tumasi argued that Ali's special stature and privileges were reflected in his ability to perform miracles. He therefore considered Ali as equal to Muhammad. al-Sharih equated Ali with the prophets—equal in mind and knowledge to Adam, equal in strength and vigor to Noah, equal in patience and discernment to Ibrahim, equal in reverence to Moses, and equal in service to Jesus. Ibn Abd al-Wahhab rejected these *hadith* on the basis of their content because it clearly contradicted the Quran.[251]

Fabrication of *hadith* is a serious charge. Because the *hadith* are the major source material for the Sunna, fabrication involves tampering with scripture and the creation of false revelation. Ibn Abd al-Wahhab also accused the Shiis of making life easier by rejecting the restrictions and limitations made by the Quran in their *hadith* fabrications.[252] He further pointed to the hypocrisy inherent in the Shii fabrication of *hadith* while accusing Muhammad's Companions of apostasy for having tampered with the Quran.[253] He found this accusation of apostasy to be particularly troublesome in light of the fact that both the Quran and *hadith* refer to the Companions as faithful and righteous believers and supporters of Muhammad and his message. This denial of the clear teachings of the scriptures led Ibn Abd al-Wahhab to accuse the Rafidah of heresy, apostasy, corruption, and a vicious sin.[254]

These quarrels about the theological matter of the succession to Muhammad and the nature of the authority of his Companions led Ibn Abd al-Wahhab to address one final matter of contention between Shiis and Sunnis: the treatment of Aisha bint Abi Bakr, Muhammad's favorite wife and the daughter of the first caliph. Aisha was known after Muhammad's death for her opposition to Ali's ascent to the caliphate. Because she opposed Ali so strongly, not only in words but also in leading a military contingent against his forces in the Battle of the Camel, Aisha came to be vilified by Shiis across the centuries.[255] Shiis, beginning with Ali, accused Aisha of adultery and whoredom during her marriage to Muhammad, despite the fact that seventeen Quranic verses and numerous *hadith* defended her innocence.[256] Ibn Abd al-Wahhab devoted a lengthy chapter to the defense of Aisha's innocence in the Affair of the Necklace as another means of demonstrating the erroneous beliefs of the Rafidah.

Briefly, the Affair of the Necklace occurred during a trip when Aisha was accidentally left behind by the caravan when she went to search for a missing necklace. When her absence was noted, some of the members of the caravan posited that she had remained behind in order to engage in an illicit love affair. Although Aisha was found alone wrapped in her cloak and proclaimed her innocence, there were those, including Muhammad, initially, who did not believe her story about the missing necklace. Ultimately, God revealed several Quranic verses affirming her innocence.

Ibn Abd al-Wahhab's defense of "Aisha the Innocent" is one of the longest and most detailed discussions in all of his written works. The length and detail of this discussion not only indicate the importance he attributed to the defense of Muhammad's favorite wife but also underscore his theme of support and respect for women in general. This defense consisted of the citation of extensive Quranic verses and *hadith* affirming Aisha's innocence as declared by none other than God Himself, thus proving beyond a shadow of a doubt her innocence of the charges leveled against her.

The very fact that God revealed such a lengthy passage (24:11–21) indicated, for Ibn Abd al-Wahhab, the seriousness of the charges against Aisha. In this passage, God commanded Aisha's accusers to bring witnesses and evidence of her lack of chastity if it in fact existed. When the accusers failed to do so, God declared them liars. Ibn Abd al-Wahhab interpreted God's response to mean that the matter of a woman's chastity is very serious and no one should ever accuse a woman of a lack of chastity lightly or without proof. Such slander and lies will be seriously punished by God.[257]

Ibn Abd al-Wahhab then noted that no less than nine major *hadith* collectors and a large number of Companions tied these verses to the defense of Aisha's innocence.[258] He thus made it very clear that Aisha's innocence and the Quranic verses revealed in her favor were not matters of an obscure verse or a single or weak *hadith* but rather that there were several clear Quranic verses and numerous *hadith* of various chains confirming her innocence. In the face of such overwhelming evidence, Ibn Abd al-Wahhab rejected Shii claims that Aisha was a whore.[259]

One other issue raised by the Affair of the Necklace is the question of whether the greatest prophet of all could possibly have had an adulterous wife. The commentators and *hadith* collectors responded in the negative. Even the wives of great prophets like Noah and Lot, although they were sinful, never committed adultery.[260] How much more so, then, would it be impossible for the wife of the "seal" of the prophets to commit adultery?[261]

Ibn Abd al-Wahhab explained Shii vilification of Aisha by the fact that one of her major accusers, Abd Allah al-Athim, was a strong supporter of the right of Muhammad's descendants to special status among Muslims. Ibn Abd al-Wahhab accused this man's followers not only of fabricating lies and slander against Aisha, but also of damaging Muhammad himself and even God because the continuation of these false accusations despite the revelations received in defense of Aisha's innocence ultimately constituted unbelief in the Word of God and in His Messenger. Ibn Abd al-Wahhab had harsh words for those who persisted in such unbelief:

> Anyone who lies about God has committed *kufr* (unbelief) and anyone who falsely accuses her [of fornication] with allegations that she was not his wife or left behind her purity for prostitution, therefore we say: If it has been proven definitively that she was innocent by these verses then persisting in her defamation is what proceeds from evil. As for the occurrence of her defamation, how is it possible for God Most High to lie in His revelation about her innocence unless one is speaking calumny in it? Some of the investigators said plainly: 'As for her defamation now, it is *kufr* (unbelief) and *irtidad* (apostasy). Do not believe in it steadfastly because it is a lie addressed by seventeen verses from the Book of God.[262]

Ibn Abd al-Wahhab's use of strong theological language—*kufr* (unbelief) and *irtidad* (apostasy)—with respect to this issue indicates the serious nature of discounting or setting aside scriptural passages, even when the subject is a woman. The fact that he denounced the false accusation of a chaste woman in such great detail and with such powerful scriptural support underscores the importance he placed on the assertion of women's God-given rights and his denial of the right of any political or human power to alter those rights. The defense of Aisha is one of the extremely rare cases in which Ibn Abd al-Wahhab not only permitted but actually called for violence, as he justified fighting and even killing those who defame Aisha because of the defamation of God and Muhammad that occurs in the process.[263]

Ibn Abd al-Wahhab's defense of Aisha's innocence led him to address infringements on women's rights committed by the Rafidah sect generally, which he believed served as further evidence of its failure to adhere to Islam. Among the types of "illegal" and "debased" treatments of women committed by the Rafidah were the Shii practice of temporary marriage (*mut'ah*), which legalizes sexual intercourse without granting the woman the right to inherit or receive maintenance for her waiting period; the pronouncement of the triple divorce by repudiation (*talaq*) at a single session rather than at spaced intervals; permitting the marriage of a woman without the presence of her marriage guardian or witnesses; the authorization of sexual relations with slave girls, licentious sexual practices, and the giving of women in polygamous marriages to serve as cowives along with their maternal and paternal aunts.[264] In all of these cases, Ibn Abd al-Wahhab cited the writings of a prominent Shii jurist, typically al-Hilli, and Shii *hadith* permitting such practices, so that what he recounted was not a matter of hearsay or misunderstanding, but consisted of citations from authoritative Shii texts.[265]

One final point of contention between Ibn Abd al-Wahhab and the Rafidah was the Rafidah's claim to have the exclusive truth of Islam. This charge is, in and of itself, significant because the Wahhabis are typically accused of making the same claim and declaring jihad upon anyone who differs from their beliefs. Not surprisingly, Ibn Abd al-Wahhab denied this claim, noting that exclusive truth belongs to the Quran and Sunna alone. All else is human interpretation and prone to error.[267] He observed that the Shiis in general and the Rafidah in particular had themselves diverged from Muhammad's practices, as well as those of the Companions, making them guilty of departure from Islam.

However, rather than calling for violence and warfare against them, Ibn Abd al-Wahhab ordered his followers to clarify their own legal teachings to point out where such offenders were incorrect. He instructed that this procedure of education and debate should be carried out with the support of truthful *ulama*, *hadith* transmitters, and righteous members of their own community.[268] At no point did he ever suggest that violence of any sort should be used against the Rafidah or Shiis. Rather, he employed logic, rhetoric, examination of the primary texts, and debate among leaders and scholars as the tools with which to "combat" the Rafidah and the Shiis.

Conclusion

The important role of theology in the definition and elaboration of Ibn Abd al-Wahhab's worldview is clear. Correct belief is intended to be the guiding force that motivates correct thoughts, words, and actions. Rather than focusing on ritualistic correctness and literal interpretation of the Quran and *hadith*, Ibn Abd al-Wahhab emphasized the necessity of appropriate intent behind every action and statement undertaken and made by the Muslim. He believed that the content of a person's words and actions, rather than their form, determines their correctness because content reflects the person's intent.

The most important and defining belief for Muslims is adherence to the principle of *tawhid*, as required by God's uniqueness, so as to avoid *shirk*, whether intentional or unintentional. Ibn Abd al-Wahhab devoted extensive time and space to the elaboration of these two theological principles, not as an abstract exercise in intellectualism but in order to respond to the realities of cultural and popular practices in his time and place. Throughout his discussion, he was careful not to target specific groups of people, such as Sufis, but instead chose to target specific practices. In doing so, he did not isolate or cut off any group of people from salvation or membership in the Muslim community. Rather, he pointed out the errors inherent in certain practices because of the incorrect beliefs that they reflected on the part of the person carrying them out or because of the risk that they entailed for people observing them. This approach enabled him to emphasize the more positive, community-building capacity of Islam to draw believers ever closer into fellowship with and support for the Muslim community (*ummah*) rather than focusing on a more negative, exclusionary approach in which violence and military action would have played a more prominent role. Thus it was that even the Rafidah in its extensive violations of the principle of *tawhid* did not necessarily become subject to jihad as holy war or even violence. Rather, its adherents were to be engaged in dialogue and debate in order to demonstrate, on the basis of logic and absolute belief in the Quran and Sunna as authoritative scriptural sources, where their practices were in error in the hope of helping them return to the straight path of Islam. It is this worldview that permeates all of Ibn Abd al-Wahhab's writings and is elaborated thematically.

Having established the primary importance of theology as the foundation of correct belief required for all Muslims, the next issue for analysis is the question of how faith is to be lived out. The next chapter analyzes Ibn Abd al-Wahhab's legal thought.

3

Islamic Law: Separation of the Divine from the Human

Similar to the Jewish emphasis on adherence to the law, as outlined in the Torah, adherence to Islamic law has served as one of the distinguishing characteristics of the Muslim faith historically. Muslims across the centuries have believed in the importance of living out the implications of their proclaimed faith as outlined in the Quran and *hadith* and have devoted significant scholarly space and attention to the elaboration of Islamic law.[1] Islam's emphasis on orthopraxy (correct behavior) is reflected in the legal literature of Muhammad Ibn Abd al-Wahhab.

As a Muslim scholar and jurist, Ibn Abd al-Wahhab devoted a significant portion of his writings to the interpretation of Islamic law in both private and public life, in both religious and temporal matters, for both men and women. His legal writings, which include several volumes of jurisprudence (*fiqh*), as well as a collection of legal opinions (*fatawa*) provide insight into several aspects of Islamic thought: the methodology and interpretation of jurisprudence, including source materials and legal devices used; the characterization of what it means to be affiliated with the Hanbali school (*madhhab*) of Islamic law; and the reflection of some of the most important trends in eighteenth-century Islamic thought, notably the revival of *hadith* studies and criticism and the radical rejection of the imitation of past scholarship (*taqlid*) in favor of independent reasoning (*ijtihad*).[2] Given Ibn Abd al-Wahhab's significance as the leader of a major revival and reform movement that continues to have an impact on contemporary Islamic thought and legal reforms, his reflection of these intellectual trends, as well as the content of his writings, are important not only in terms of increasing our understanding of eighteenth-century trends of legal thought but also in better understanding his influence on contemporary Islamic revival and reform.[3]

This chapter provides both a contextualization of Ibn Abd al-Wahhab's legal thought and a broad analysis of his legal literature, highlighting his understanding and use of the four sources of Islamic law: the Quran, Sunna, analogy (*qiyas*), and consensus (*ijma*). The chapter then moves to a discussion of legal principles: the role of public interest (*maslahah*) in the interpretation of Islamic law, the concept of abrogation (*naskh*), the rejection of *taqlid* in favor of *ijtihad*, the role of those who exercise independent reasoning (*mujtahid*), and the appropriate consideration of the schools of Islamic law (*madhahib*), *fiqh*, and the role of those who offer legal opinions (*mufti*) or *fatawa*. Finally, interpretational issues, including literalism, ritualism, and the role of intent, are addressed. In all of these cases, his attention to the theological principle of absolute monotheism (*tawhid*) is apparent.

Ibn Abd al-Wahhab as a Legal Theoretician and Practitioner

Ibn Abd al-Wahhab was born into a family with a long history of theoretical legal scholarship and practical experience in its application. His theoretical knowledge of *fiqh*, affiliation with the Hanbali school of Islamic law, and careful study of the Quran and *hadith* can all be traced to his formative years studying with his father and in Medina. He was therefore well-placed to follow in the family tradition of legal scholarship and practice as both a judge (*qadi*) and a *mufti*.[4] Although the chronicles do not specify either of these roles by name or indicate whether he received payment for his work, they, as well as Ibn Abd al-Wahhab's own writings, make clear both that he issued legal opinions and that these opinions were followed in at least some cases.

As with his theological writings, Ibn Abd al-Wahhab's legal literature reveals careful consultation with a variety of sources—the Quran, *hadith*, the opinions of close Companions of Muhammad, and the writings of the founders of the Hanbali, Hanafi, Shafii, Maliki, Zahiri, and even Jafari schools of Islamic law.[5] His purpose in including such a broad discussion was to demonstrate familiarity with a variety of opinions and a wide body of literature, as well as to favor the original opinions of those who either had direct contact with the early Muslim community or those who formulated the principles of *fiqh*. However, he did not consider any of these sources, outside of the Quran and *hadith*, to be authoritative.

The fact that he consulted a large number of sources was in keeping with the classical genre of Arabic literature known as *ikhtilaf*, in which the author cites a variety of opinions about a given question but does not indicate any as being correct.[6] Ibn Abd al-Wahhab varied from this trend by including his own personal opinion as to which interpretation was correct, typically using the phrase "and as for us." Occasionally, he took personal credit for finding the "correct" answer. That he did so was important not only because he felt confident enough in his answers to take credit for them but also because this was a subtle way of expressing his opposition to *taqlid*, even when these opinions were a matter of legal consensus, in favor of *ijtihad*. By expressing his differing position, Ibn Abd al-Wahhab risked opposition by local power holders.[7]

Because of the risks involved and because he sought to irrefutably prove his points, Ibn Abd al-Wahhab always included in his discussions not only a variety of opinions but also the the legal reasoning and supportive evidence behind them. This approach demonstrated that his legal opinions were not made in a vacuum. It also made clear that he did not expect the reader to find them believable just because he said so. It was because his legal opinions were carefully grounded in the Quran and *hadith* that Ibn Abd al-Wahhab proclaimed his interpretations to be correct. In his opinion, only a source-driven approach to Islamic law could be faithful to God's Will.

The Sources of Islamic Law

Sunni jurists generally assert four binding sources of Islamic law: the Quran, the Sunna of Muhammad (as recorded in the *hadith*), *ijma'*, and *qiyas*. The status of the Quran and Sunna are due to their nature as the Word of God and the living out of the meaning of that word. The belief in *ijma'* as a source of law is based on a *hadith* of Muhammad that declares, "My community will never agree in error." Historically, *ijma'* is believed to have occurred in the early centuries of Islam on specific issues addressed by numerous jurists and about which they reached the same conclusion. Thus, *ijma'* has been considered a binding source of Islamic law. The use of *qiyas* was generally approved as a legal principle because Muhammad did not issue specific rulings about every potential topic. *Qiyas* was understood to be a means of applying known Islamic law to new situations. Historically, *qiyas* entailed the extrapolation of a legal principle or value from a specific situation and its transfer to a similar case.[8]

As an affiliate of the Hanbali school of Islamic law, Ibn Abd al-Wahhab generally followed the Hanbali methodology of jurisprudence. Hanbalis traditionally considered the Quran and Sunna to be the first and primary sources of law, followed by the consensus legal opinions of Muhammad's Companions, as long as they did not contradict these primary sources. Sayings of individual Companions could also be used, provided that they conformed to the teachings of the Quran and Sunna. The Hanbalis in general were uncomfortable with the use of analogy and tended to use it only in cases of absolute necessity.[9]

The Quran and Sunna

As was seen in his theological treatise, "Kitab al-Tawhid," Ibn Abd al-Wahhab relied most heavily on the Quran and *hadith* in his interpretation of Islamic law. Interpretations were used only occasionally, reflecting his belief that only the Quran and Sunna were binding sources of Islamic law (Sharia). As sources of divine law, they were of much greater importance than works of *fiqh*, which were mere human interpretations of divine law. Ibn Abd al-Wahhab asserted that refusal to consider the Quran and Sunna as the primary sources of Sharia was a grave sin.[10]

Ibn Abd al-Wahhab restricted his use of interpretations to cases in which Quranic verses were unclear. In such cases, he cited Companions where possible, turning to later commentators only when he felt it was necessary or the interpretation of a Companion was unavailable. By doing this, he added the interpretations of the Companions as a source of Islamic law, although he did not consider them to be independently authoritative or infallible because there were many cases in which some Companions contradicted others.[11] He therefore remained cautious in his employment of the interpretations of the Companions, using them only when they when they did not contradict the Quran and Sunna.

Qiyas

Ibn Abd al-Wahhab's use of *qiyas* was extremely rare. Like other Hanbali jurists, he believed that *qiyas* was best understood as an interpretative legal tool to be used only in cases of extreme necessity rather than as a source of Islamic law. Generally speaking, the Hanbalis favored a methodology that considered everything that was not explicitly forbidden to be permissible. This is not because the Hanbalis tended to be literal in their interpretation of Islamic law but rather because they differentiated between legal issues that were clearly stated, such as the prohibition of female infanticide, and legal issues that were unclear. Because the Hanbalis were well known for forbidding only what was strictly forbidden by clear passages, it could be argued that the Hanbali rejection of *qiyas* as a binding source of law actually allowed the Hanbalis greater flexibility in the application of the law than was the case with other law schools.

For example, on the question of dower (*mahr*), the Hanbali approach allowed for a much broader definition than other schools. Although the founder of the Hanafi school, Abu Hanifah, forbade giving a slave woman her freedom as her dower, Ibn Abd al-Wahhab permitted such a dower because the man was giving up some notion of his "property" by freeing a slave.[12] Abu Hanifah had forbidden the practice because it is not specifically permitted in the Quran. Ibn Abd al-Wahhab, on the other hand, permitted it because it is not specifically forbidden by the Quran. This permission reflects greater flexibility on the part of the Hanbalis, rather than a literal approach to Quranic interpretation.

Ijma'

Ijma' is the legal principle of consensus whereby the agreement of the scholars of a certain age on a particular topic is considered to be binding. Similar to his use of *qiyas*, Ibn Abd al-Wahhab did not make extensive use of the principle of *ijma'*, reserving it for obvious and prominent cases such as the interpretation of clear Quranic passages.[13]

Ibn Abd al-Wahhab's legal writings include a methodological discussion of *ijma'* based on two broad requirements for validity. First, as with any other source, *ijma'* must be consistent with the teachings and values of the Quran and *hadith*.[14] Second, *ijma'* is to be used as a tool for interpretation of the Quran and *hadith* rather than as an independently authoritative legal source. Ibn Abd al-Wahhab taught that proper use of *ijma'* can only be made in conjunction with its corroboration of the Quran and *hadith*. The following case is instructive because of its demonstration of the authority assigned to each source and the insight it offers into Ibn Abd al-Wahhab's legal reasoning. The case questions whether a woman is entitled to a *mahr* upon marriage.

According to the Quran, a woman is entitled to a *mahr* upon marriage as a gift. The Quran states that this is a required religious duty for men. Thus, for Ibn Abd al-Wahhab the question of whether or not the *mahr* is due to a woman was unequivocally answered by two Quranic verses (4:24 and 4:4). The *hadith* record Muhammad's responses to questions about the amount of the *mahr*, asserting that it is in fact required, so that only the amount is open to debate. The question then becomes whether the *hadith* should be interpreted literally or contextually. A literal interpretation would mean that the actual amount prescribed by Muhammad should always be the amount of the dower (one gold piece in the *hadith* cited) and that no variations should be permitted, regardless of changes in context. A contextual interpretation would attempt at the very least to determine the actual value of the specified dower in that time and place and to recalculate it accordingly. *Ijma'* comes into play, therefore, not in declaring that the *mahr* is required but in determining the amount of the *mahr*.

The law schools varied in opinion about the question of the amount of the *mahr*. Malik ibn Anas and Abu Hanifah taught that there was a set minimum amount for the *mahr*. Al-Shafii and Ishaq taught that there were no predetermined minimums or maximums. Ibn Abd al-Wahhab, in keeping with his typical rejection of *taqlid*, returned to the Quran and *hadith* to seek evidence in the matter.

He noted that Q 4:24 states, "They [the women] seek from you your prop-

erty," indicating that women have a claim to the property of their husbands.
From the *hadith*, he made two observations: one, that Muhammad, when questioned about the requirement of *mahr*, responded, "If it is sealed, it is in iron,"
meaning that the agreement made about *mahr* was binding once made,
whether orally or in writing; and, two, that the second caliph, Umar, said, "Do
not fetter/shackle the dowers of the women."[15] Ibn Abd al-Wahhab understood
these sayings to mean that there are no set minimums or maximums for the
dower but that they are a matter for negotiation in the marriage contract. Once
the contract is agreed on, the amount of the *mahr* is set and cannot be
changed.[16] Although in agreement with the *ijma'* of certain legal specialists,
Ibn Abd al-Wahhab's preference was to return to the Quran and *hadith* directly,
with *ijma'* serving merely as a tool for interpretation of the details.

In his legal literature, Ibn Abd al-Wahhab was careful to distinguish between two types of *ijma'*: the *ijma'* of Muhammad's Companions and the *ijma'*
of legal specialists after his time, particularly where the founders of the various
law schools were concerned. He reserved a special authority for the *ijma'* of
the Companions because, having lived during the lifetime of Muhammad, they
had direct contact with him and were able to seek his counsel about legal
matters. There are many instances of Quranic verses that were revealed to
Muhammad in response to such questioning. Ibn Abd al-Wahhab therefore
believed that the Companions were able to assert a certain authority in matters
of law and interpretation of the Quran that later generations could not. It was
for this reason that he asserted the binding nature of the *ijma'* of the Companions, such as in support for the Sunni institution of the caliphate, which
was established by their consensus.[17]

The other type of *ijma'*, that of the legal scholars, was rarely invoked by
Ibn Abd al-Wahhab, largely because he found that it rarely existed. He noted
that the reality was that the law schools often agreed on the broad principles
of a case but varied in their opinions about the details. For example, on the
question of who is eligible to enter into a protected treaty relationship as protected people (*ahl al-dhimmah*), he cited *ijma'* several times as confirming that
Jews and Christians are entitled to do so but noted variances concerning the
Magi.[18] He was therefore reluctant to recognize *ijma'* of the law schools because
of the rarity of its occurrence. He specified that true *ijma'* had to be the consensus of all of the legal scholars rather than specific to a particular law school
or group of scholars. Where true *ijma'* actually existed, he declared it to be
binding on the Muslim community.

Ibn Abd al-Wahhab's reference to *ijma'* typically occurred in cases in which
he was responding to charges by the scholars (*ulama*) that he was introducing
some sort of innovation or heresy. He silenced their arguments by appealing
to the works of prior scholars in support of his own approach. For example,
he appealed to *ijma'* in his rejection of the claim that the Quran contains hidden
or concealed knowledge that can only be known by the descendants of Mu-

hammad (*ashraf*)—a claim that had been rejected historically on the basis of *ijma'*.[19]

Ibn Abd al-Wahhab most frequently used *ijma'* in cases in which he sought to demonstrate his consistency with prior scholarship on sensitive issues. For example, in response to the question of whether bribery and corruption were ever permissible, he responded in the negative. Having defined bribery and corruption as the unlawful and deceitful taking of property until receiving a bribe, he noted that they were forbidden (*haram*) according to *ijma'*. Consequently, he denounced anyone who claimed a bribe as his lawful right as diverging from *ijma'*.[20]

In his denunciation of bribery and corruption, Ibn Abd al-Wahhab particularly singled out the judicial system, as supported by the *ulama*, as being guilty of a conspiracy to deprive the people of justice. He specifically cited the case of "gifts" given to the judge (*hakim*) in exchange for a particular judgment. He commented that no '*alim* had ever permitted such a practice historically and expressed incredulousness that the *ulama* of his own time and place permitted it. He rebuked the *ulama* of his own time by reminding them that the purpose of court litigation is the pursuit and declaration of justice between two opposing parties. There can be no justice if the judge is bribed to deliver a certain outcome for one party on the basis of money.[21]

The vehemence of Ibn Abd al-Wahhab's condemnation suggests that bribery and corruption were widespread in his time and were probably supported not only by the political leadership but also by the religious establishment. By invoking the principle of *ijma'*, he strengthened his own condemnation by citing supportive evidence from the very scholars the *ulama* claimed to follow, placing them in a position where they condemned themselves. When he was challenged on his position with a demand to know by which Sharia he passed judgment on such practices, he cleverly responded by claiming the Sharia of Muhammad and the *ulama* of his community. Thus he was able to mockingly return their question by wondering: "Praise be to God, which Sharia did *you* rule by in solving this?"[22]

Ibn Abd al-Wahhab cited the use of *ijma'* in a second case of corruption regarding debt and repossession of the property of the debtor as a means of fulfilling his financial obligations. He noted that the repossession of property is allowed according to *ijma'* and stated that he would therefore not issue a *fatwa* about such a case. However, he noted the importance of studying the context in which such cases arise, since abuses of this *ijma'* had been made in the past. He commented that there had been cases historically in which the ruler had declared the needs of the general public (*maslahah*) as a reason for confiscating property, although the reality had been the desire of the ruler to cheat and deceive the people out of their property in order to accumulate greater wealth for himself. This is obviously wrong because the Quran and Sunna clearly affirm justice and forbid deception and treachery. For Ibn Abd al-Wahhab, this case underlined the importance of contextualizing Quranic verses, *hadith*, and the cases to which one applies them.[23]

Ibn Abd al-Wahhab's examination of the *ijma'* of the law schools was designed to demonstrate his familiarity and consistency with the opinions of other jurists. Although he did not consider their true *ijma'* to be as authoritative as the Quran and *hadith*, he did believe that their true consensus should be given careful consideration, though always with awareness of the context of the ruling and its compatibility with the Quran and *hadith*. When asked about whether it was permissible for Muslims to join with Jews and Christians in attacking other Muslims, Ibn Abd al-Wahhab was careful to examine the context prior to issuing an opinion. What he found problematic in this case was not the presence of Jews and Christians or Muslim cooperation with them per se but the fact that Muslims were fighting other Muslims. According to *ijma'*, such an action constitutes apostasy. Ibn Abd al-Wahhab concluded that if all of the law schools unanimously agreed about this particular ruling then surely this *ijma'* must be right.[24]

However, he was also careful to assert that *ijma'* should not be confused with majority opinions or the rule of the majority in legal matters. He warned against *ulama* who claim to represent the great majority and base their own power structures and opinions on the supposed sayings and deeds of past Muslims.[25] He further cautioned against broad use of the term *ijma'*, as any number of supposed scholars might agree on an error based on false evidence or failure to contextualize a given Quranic verse or *hadith* if their purpose was to support political leaders or gain personal wealth. *Ijma'* can therefore be misleading, which is why scholars should always verify a ruling's consistency with the Quran and *hadith*.[26]

Clearly, Ibn Abd al-Wahhab used *ijma'* only as a tool for legal interpretation. He did not believe that it should be used as a legislative tool or to assert the rule of the majority. This understanding was in keeping with the classical interpretation of *ijma'*.[27]

Other Sources

In addition to the four standard sources of Islamic law, Ibn Abd al-Wahhab addressed the question of whether local customs, traditions and literature should have any role to play in the theoretical elaboration and actual practice of Islamic law. His writings make it clear that, while historically many societies with Muslim majorities have attempted to synthesize Islamic law and local custom, this was not an appropriate legal methodology. He differed sharply here with the Maliki law school, which tended to assert the customary practices of Medina as authoritative.[28] Ibn Abd al-Wahhab remained consistent in his methodological assertion of the Quran and *hadith* as authoritative sources. Where the Quran and *hadith* offered clear and specific guidelines, he saw no need to refer to local customs or traditions. Even in cases in which the Quran and *hadith* were not clear, he did not consider local customs to be worth consideration.

His reasoning was based on the fact that these local customs and traditions tended to be pre-Islamic in their origins. For example, when asked about the permissibility of cutting the beards of one's deceased enemies after a battle he responded that this was not an Islamic practice. Its origins lay in pre-Islamic literature (*adab*), which describes it as something that people did during war as a means of humiliating the proud and arrogant. Ibn Abd al-Wahhab found that the intent of the *adab* literature was the glorification of pre-Islamic ancestors and practices rather than God. Over time, this glorification had led to claims of nobility and assertions of rank among the believers—assertions that clearly had no place in the radically egalitarian vision of Islam. Having thus made clear the origins, purpose, and inappropriate ways in which people had made use of the *adab* historically, Ibn Abd al-Wahhab dismissed it as a source of Islamic law.[29]

Ibn Abd al-Wahhab's consideration and usage of the sources of Islamic law provide a framework for analyzing his use of legal principles and theories in their interpretation. We now turn to his use of the legal devices of *maslahah*, *naskh*, *taqlid*, and *ijtihad*, and the roles of the *madhahib* and *fiqh*.

Legal Devices for the Interpretation of Islamic Law

Public Interest (Maslahah)

Maslahah is the legal principle of the consideration of public interest or public welfare in interpreting Islamic law. Although mainly upheld by the Maliki law school, it was also supported by the Hanbalis and Shafiis as a principle of jurisprudence.[30] *Maslahah* as a principle declares that when there is a choice among several possible interpretations of the Quran or Sunna on a particular point of jurisprudence the jurist should proceed according to a descending ladder of priorities: first, necessities (*daruriyyat*), then needs (*hajiyyat*), and finally improvements (*tahsinat*).[31]

Ibn Abd al-Wahhab supported the use of *maslahah* in legal decisions because the stated purpose of the Quran is to be a help and guide to humankind rather than a burden. *Maslahah* is one way of ensuring that Islamic law is used in this way. While it cannot override clear commands or prohibitions for the most part, it can be invoked in extreme cases of urgency, such as starvation or the threat of death, to allow what would not normally be permissible if the goal is the preservation of human life. The reasoning behind this is that the preservation of human life is considered to be a greater good than the keeping of ritual law in such extreme cases.

For example, Ibn Abd al-Wahhab supported the use of the principle of *maslahah* in order to allow for a delay in payment of the almsgiving (*zakat*) tax in cases of dire necessity. This support was based on Muhammad's ruling allowing a delay in payment in cases in which the public welfare was at stake, such as a year of drought.[32] However, Ibn Abd al-Wahhab was careful to note that *maslahah* was necessarily restricted to urgent situations and was to be used in a limited fashion. He rejected a broad usage of the principle as a general procedure for the accumulation of power or self-aggrandizement.[33] For example, he rejected the use of *maslahah* by the first caliph, Abu Bakr, to justify unlawful spending of *zakat* for the purpose of bribery. Ibn Abd al-Wahhab declared that Abu Bakr's claim that such spending was "for the sake of the good of the people" (*maslahat al-nass*) was an "awesome lie."[34]

Maslahah, as a principle, is intended to serve the public good rather than to fulfill individual desires. For example, because marriage is the only legal means by which sexual activity is to take place in Islam Ibn Abd al-Wahhab asserted that it justified the public announcement and punishment of sexual activity outside of marriage. He believed that such public consequences would encourage the preservation of the accepted social order.[35] He also applied the principle of *maslahah* to jihad against unbelievers. When he discussed the treatment to be accorded to captives after jihad, he asserted, on the basis of *maslahah* and *ijtihad*, that the captives (limited to adult males) should be given the choice between death or submission to the Muslims via payment of a poll tax *jizyah*.[36] The presentation of a choice was considered to be a matter of public interest with a dual purpose: first, to prevent greed, whether for blood or for property; and, second, to remind Muslims of their responsibility to be merciful to those who are willing to lay down their arms and submit to them.

This is not to say, however, that *maslahah* could only be applied in public situations. There were some private, individual cases in which Ibn Abd al-Wahhab applied the principle of *maslahah* because of their broader repercussions across time and space. For example, when asked about the permissibility of the guardian of an orphan selling the orphan's immovable property on the basis of *maslahah*, Ibn Abd al-Wahhab noted that the purpose behind such a sale was the benefit of the guardian not the orphan. He believed that *maslahah* could be better served by maintaining the property in the orphan's name.[37] This private situation reflected a broader social trend of abuses of the powerless by the powerful being justified on supposedly religious grounds. By focusing on the nature of the activity rather than the letter of the law, Ibn Abd al-Wahhab opened the door to correction of such abuses.

Ibn Abd al-Wahhab also used the principle of *maslahah* in addressing the question of how to finance public welfare activities. Because *maslahah* was intended to fulfill a public service role, Ibn Abd al-Wahhab argued that it should be financed in a public way. He therefore declared that one-fifth of the booty obtained during jihad activities should be assigned to the service of *maslahah*. His reasoning was based on the fact that this one-fifth was assigned to God and Muhammad by the Quran, thus signifying its intended use for public benefit and service of God rather than individual aggrandizement.[38]

While he was selective in his use of the principle, it is clear that Ibn Abd al-Wahhab considered *maslahah* to be an important guiding principle in the interpretation of Islamic law, particularly when the broader good of the community could be served.

Abrogation (Naskh)

The legal principle of *naskh* considers that a Quran verse revealed at a particular time may have been overridden by a later revelation. The classic case in point is the drinking of grape wine. Initially, this was permitted for Muslims, although the consumption of date wine was forbidden. However, over time the right to drink grape wine came to be restricted and was finally outlawed altogether.

Naskh is a source of controversy among theologians and legal scholars alike because of the implication that there is an error in the revelation itself. Consequently, rather than focusing on the question of why contradictory texts existed historically, jurists chose to focus instead on the matter of how to determine which text abrogated another and why.[39] Some scholars have argued that the process is a gradual one meant to give people the opportunity to adjust over time as they move toward greater restrictions and stricter observations. Others have argued that the ultimate universal principles were revealed in the beginning in Mecca but that these principles were adjusted in Medina so as to make them more palatable to the Muslims of that time and place. The eventual goal, though, was a return to the original, universal principles.[40] Ibn Abd al-Wahhab did not refer to the principle of *naskh* frequently, so it is worth examining the cases in which he did in order to see how he applied it.

Ibn Abd al-Wahhab's assertion of *naskh* was limited largely because he believed that scripture should be used to interpret scripture. Further he did not easily accept the notion of contradictory passages of scripture, in much the same way that he did not accept the concept of the existence of two valid but mutually contradictory *hadith*. In cases in which the Quran appears to possess an ambiguity or contradict itself, he believed that the verses in question should be carefully studied to see if they offer any insights into each other. He cited the case of the question of the legality of sexual relations between men and their slave girls. Many legal scholars, both Sunni and Shii, have argued that this is allowed on the basis of Q 70:29–30, which mentions "those who have preserved their chastity except regarding their spouses or what they possess by their right hands." "What they possess by their right hands" is usually interpreted to mean slave women or women who have been captured in battle.

Ibn Abd al-Wahhab disagreed with this interpretation because it violates the important Quranic principles of limiting sexual relations to marriage and the general prohibition of licentiousness. For him, the phrase "what they possess by their right hands" was simply another way of affirming a state of marriage. He cited an additional Quranic verse, Q 24: 33—"And do not force/compel your young women into prostitution"—in support of his own interpretation because according to his worldview sexual relations outside of marriage could only be the result of the prostitution of women.[41] Thus, he argued, it is not always a matter of one Quranic verse abrogating another; rather, the Muslim must seek the intent and value inherent in the Quran and its treatment of specific topics as a whole in order to interpret it properly and discover the actual legal principle. Likewise, one must take care not to read something into a verse that is not there, particularly when it contradicts other Quranic verses.

The cases in which Ibn Abd al-Wahhab did cite the principle of *naskh* typically occurred with respect to Muhammad's personal declarations about specific issues. For example, when questioned about temporary marriage (*mut'ah*) Ibn Abd al-Wahhab cited several *hadith* sources, including Muslim and al-Bukhari, which contain several *hadith* showing a movement from initial permission to total prohibition over time. In the initial case, *mut'ah* was allowed, but the rights of repudiation (*talaq*), the waiting period and inheritance that normally accompany marriage, were not. Ibn Abd al-Wahhab's interpretation of the ultimate prohibition of *mut'ah* was that it had been outlawed because it opened the door to unlawful sexual intercourse (*zina'*), which was not permitted.[42] Thus, rather than asserting that God had changed His mind over time, Ibn Abd al-Wahhab saw in such revelations an increasing clarification of the implications of the Quran in cases in which believers continued to go astray.

Another case in which he mentioned the possibility of *naskh* was in the event of a change in status of the Muslim community. This issue was addressed in the question of whether jihad is intended to be a collective duty (*fard kifayah*) or an individual duty (*fard 'ayn*). The Quran can be interpreted to support either position. Ibn Abd al-Wahhab outlined the arguments of both sides. Those who claimed it was a *fard 'ayn* based their assertions on Q 9:122, which states, "And the believers should not go out collectively." Those who claimed it was a *fard kifayah* based their assertions on three different verses: Q 9:41, "Go forward lightly and heavily"; Q 9:39, "Unless you go forth He will punish you"; and Q 4:95, "Not equal are those who are idle among the believers."

In order to determine which verses abrogated the others, Ibn Abd al-Wahhab sought to contextualize these revelations. Contextually, he argued that while *jihad* as military duty was undertaken on an individual level in the early years of Islam, in accordance with the Quranic revelation, collective military action became necessary over time due to the aggression the early Muslims were suffering. As opposition grew, individuals standing alone became increasingly unsuccessful in defending themselves against their persecutors. Therefore, they began to act collectively, giving them a better chance to overcome their enemies—an action that was legalized by Quranic revelation. This argument was further bolstered by the testimony by one of Muhammad's most prominent Companions, Ibn Abbas, that Q 9:122 had been abrogated. On the basis of historical developments, therefore, Ibn Abd al-Wahhab asserted that jihad as a collective responsibility had overtaken jihad as an individual duty.[43]

It is important to note that Ibn Abd al-Wahhab's use of *naskh* differs slightly from its classical use. The classical interpretation of *naskh* asserted an absolute change regardless of historical context. Ibn Abd al-Wahhab's interpretation, on the other hand, suggests not so much *naskh* as absolute abrogation as it does *naskh* as allowing for interpretations that are context sensitive.

He also applied the principle of *naskh* to cases in which there are apparent contradictions between the Quran and *hadith*. He emphasized the importance of contextualization in such cases because Quranic verses were sometimes revealed not only in response to specific situations but also to correct prior practices. A case in point is the question of the distribution of booty after jihad. Here, the Quran abrogated the *hadith*. The *hadith* record that after the Battle of Badr Muhammad allowed those who had taken specific items to keep them. However, the result of this was a great deal of quarreling among the Companions. Consequently, God abrogated this practice by revealing Q 8:1, which declared, "Say: The booty/spoils belong to God," thus asserting God's ownership of everything captured during jihad and laying the foundation for the collection of goods after battle and their distribution according to specific guidelines.[44] Without contextualization, it would be very difficult, if not impossible, to determine which of the two practices was correct. The subtler message of this passage is that one should always look to the Quran as the final authoritative source when contradictions appear. The Quran always outweighs the *hadith*.[45] Ibn Abd al-Wahhab therefore believed that *naskh* is God's prerogative, not that of human beings.

Taqlid *versus* Ijtihad

Taqlid refers to the legal practice of imitating or adhering to the juridical rulings of the past. *Ijtihad*, on the other hand, is the practice of the individual engaging in personal interpretation of the Quran and Sunna. There has been a considerable amount of scholarly literature devoted to the question of whether the "gate to *ijtihad*" was closed in the ninth century or later at the end of the eleventh, whether theoretically or in practice. While some scholars have argued that the gate was closed, others believe that *ijtihad* has been consistently practiced historically, though in different ways.

Those who believed that the gate had been closed in practice in the ninth century argued that Islamic law had been largely elaborated and that all essential questions had been thoroughly discussed and definitively answered by the beginning of the tenth century. Therefore, in their opinion the practice of *ijtihad* became unnecessary, explaining the broad continuity of rulings within the law schools.[46]

Other scholars have noted that debates about the "closing of the gate of *ijtihad*" were not apparent in legal literature until the end of the eleventh century,[47] and even then only as a theoretical issue as Muslim jurists pondered the question of whether practitioners of *ijtihad*, known as *mujtahids*, continued to exist.[48] In fact, the phrase, "the closing of the gate of *ijtihad*" was not used until well after the sixteenth century. The issue was raised out of recognition that *mujtahids* of the caliber of the founders of the Islamic law schools no longer existed. In addition, Muhammad's Companions were also long deceased by this point. Historically, as noted by scholars who believed that the gate to *ijtihad* had been closed, those who claimed the title of *mujtahid* tended to follow the patterns and methodologies already established by the law schools with which they were affiliated. Thus, there was a certain continuity in their legal rulings, so that *ijtihad* as a methodology for finding new answers to old questions was no longer practiced.[49] That is, although some claimed to practice *ijtihad*, it was no longer carried out in the same way as had been the case with the early generations of Muslims.

The historical record reveals a general tendency away from the practice of *ijtihad* by the Hanafi and Maliki law schools, as well as the majority of Shafiis.[50] However, *ijtihad* was consistently practiced by the Hanbalis and a number of prominent Shafiis historically because they believed that true consensus (*ijma*), apart from that of Muhammad's Companions, did not exist and because they believed that the constant and continuous existence of *mujtahids* was a theological requirement.[51] They did not believe that God would leave Muslims without juridical scholars capable of reinterpreting the Quran and Sunna in order to keep scripture fresh and relevant for daily life in constantly changing contexts. This stance was adopted by many eighteenth century revivalists and reformists, who shared a broad tendency toward rejuvenation of the practice of *ijtihad*.[52] Ibn Abd al-Wahhab followed this tendency.

As a Hanbali jurist, Ibn Abd al-Wahhab asserted the theological necessity of the constant existence of *mujtahids* in history. He commented repeatedly that knowledge of the truth could not cease to exist on the earth and that a faithful minority would continue to uphold it.[53] He believed that this knowledge of the truth could only be determined through the continual practice of *ijtihad*.[54] Thus, one of the hallmarks of his approach to Islamic law was the radical rejection of *taqlid* in favor of *ijtihad*.

Ibn Abd al-Wahhab's *ijtihad* was grounded in the firm belief of the necessity of returning directly to the Quran and Sunna to research any given topic. His rejection of *taqlid* was due to the fact that he considered it to be a form of *shirk*. He believed that blind adherence to the jurisprudence of a human being constituted associationism with God and the teachings of the Quran. He did not believe in the infallibility of jurists because jurists are human rather than divine beings. Because no human being is perfect or immune to error, it stands to reason that no jurist's interpretation of the divine word can be perfect or immune to error either, even if the jurist in question was a Companion of Muhammad or one of the Four Rightly Guided Caliphs.[55] Believing that no human being except Muhammad was perfect in interpreting Islamic law, Ibn Abd al-Wahhab proposed a case-by-case study of an individual's rulings in which the content of the ruling was to be compared to the teachings of the Quran and *hadith*. In his opinion, this was the only certain way of separating the good judgments from the bad. It also allowed for analysis of the intent and consequences of the ruling rather than adherence to the letter of the law.

Ibn Abd al-Wahhab's opposition to *taqlid* was due in part to its role in the perpetuation of both false *hadith* and erroneous practices, such as false *hadith* asserting the special status of Ali as a prophet and the rampant bribery and corruption of Abu Bakr's reign, both of which obviously contradicted Quranic values.[56] He also pointed to the impact of juridical *taqlid* on the general population because people tended to follow traditions and juridical teachings without necessarily understanding them or questioning their bases.[57]

Ibn Abd al-Wahhab particularly faulted the practice of *taqlid* as serving as a means of preventing, rather than promoting, the pursuit of knowledge. He wrote, "The key of knowledge is questions."[58] For him, it was only by constantly questioning the purpose and intent of the Quran and Sunna that one could discern their true meaning. This explains why he found the emphasis of the religious sciences, including the interpretation of Islamic law (*fiqh*), on memorization to be so problematic. In his opinion, comprehension and knowledge of the truth were more important than memorization of words without meaning. Consequently, he advised his followers to "look down on" the antiquated sciences and abandon them.[59]

Ibn Abd al-Wahhab further guided his followers not to seek counsel or "knowledge" from repetitions of juridical writings because many of the questions posed in the older sources were no longer issues of concern in his day. Furthermore, the logic and solutions were not always clear. Particularly problematic was the intent behind this practice—maintaining coherence and continuity with the past. In his opinion, seeking guidance and information from the "signs of God" in the present was a more important task than worrying about consistency with past practices, particularly when the texts in question incorporated local practices, customs, and traditions into their interpretations and rulings rather than relying solely and completely on the Quran and Sunna.[60]

This is not to say that Ibn Abd al-Wahhab's *ijtihad* was necessarily designed to provide new answers to old questions. However, neither was it an attempt to simply re-create the past. His *ijtihad* was designed to return to the primary sources of Islam in order to determine how the Quran and Muhammad dealt with specific situations. He insisted on contextualization of the Quran verses or *hadith* in question so as to avoid a literal interpretation. In his opinion, contextualization was critical to understanding the full spectrum of issues involved, as well as the legal thinking behind the proposed solution. What he sought was to understand not only how the issue was resolved but also the intent behind the resolution and what it meant to the people of that time. Only then would it be possible, in his opinion, to fully comprehend the legal ruling and its implications for the present.

Ibn Abd al-Wahhab's radical rejection of *taqlid* did not mean that he eschewed familiarity with the legal literature. Rather, his written works demonstrate a vast and detailed knowledge of the legal opinions of a variety of law schools, which he outlined prior to stating his own opinion and presenting his reasoning as to why he was correct and the others were incorrect. Such an approach makes abundantly, though subtly, clear his radical rejection of *taqlid* in practice.

IMITATION OF IBN TAYMIYYA? Despite Ibn Abd al-Wahhab's clear, frequent, and radical rejection of *taqlid*, he is often accused of being a strict and blind follower of the thirteenth-century Hanbali jurist Ibn Taymiyya. Because this supposed imitation has been asserted for so many years by a number of prominent scholars up through the present and because the supposed radicalism of both Ibn Taymiyya and the Wahhabis has come to play such an important role in contemporary terrorist movements, the evidence for such a claim must be carefully examined.

The assertion of Ibn Abd al-Wahhab's heavy reliance on the writings of Ibn Taymiyya was first made in the West by Ignaz Goldziher, one of the pioneers of the Western study of Islamic law, on the basis that certain manuscripts preserved at the University of Leiden were copies of Ibn Taymiyya's works recorded in Ibn Abd al-Wahhab's handwriting.[61] The existence of these manuscripts, while important, should not overshadow the more important evidence of Ibn Abd al-Wahhab's own writings.

As was mentioned in chapter 1, it is known that Ibn Abd al-Wahhab studied Ibn Taymiyya's works as part of his education. Given that Ibn Taymiyya was the most important Hanbali jurist historically, one would expect to find his writings as part of the curriculum for any Hanbali jurist. There is, however, a major difference between being a blind imitator of another person's works and having simply studied them.[62] The existence of references to, copies of, or brief notations about Ibn Taymiyya's writings and teachings should not be misconstrued as blind adherence to them or a failure to write anything original.

In order to evaluate the assertion of heavy reliance on Ibn Taymiyya fairly and accurately, a quantitative analysis of Ibn Abd al-Wahhab's writings is in order. Such an analysis reveals that Ibn Abd al-Wahhab only rarely referred to Ibn Taymiyya. Analysis of *Kitab al-Tawhid*, for example, reveals only 3 references to the works of Ibn Taymiyya out of a total of 170 citations (less than 2%

of all citations). A similar approach can be found in his treatise on marriage, *Kitab al-Nikah*, which includes a total of 376 citations from 90 different sources. Ibn Taymiyya is not mentioned by name *at all* in this treatise, although it is possible that the person identified simply as "The Qadi" was Ibn Taymiyya. However, even The Qadi is cited only 4 times in the entire treatise (less than 1% of all citations), one of which was in opposition to his teachings. The plethora of other sources and scholars cited in both of these important treatises simply does not support the notion of Ibn Abd al-Wahhab's blind adherence to any single source or scholar, particularly not Ibn Taymiyya.

Having definitively rejected *taqlid* to any scholar on the part of Ibn Abd al-Wahhab, we now turn to the question of how he engaged in *ijtihad*, the personal interpretation of scripture.

Ijtihad *and the* Mujtahid

As an eighteenth-century reformer, Ibn Abd al-Wahhab promoted the exercise of *ijtihad* by people whose knowledge, mastery and understanding of the Quran and *hadith* qualified them to act as *mujtahids*. According to his vision, the exercise of *ijtihad* had to be in keeping with the spirit of upholding Quranic values. *Ijtihad* was not to be used as a tool for building personal bases of power or wealth.

Ibn Abd al-Wahhab was particularly concerned by the tendency of the *ulama* of his day to use the interpretation of Islamic law in a spirit of protectionism and self-aggrandizement. In fact, he accused them of using *ijtihad* as a means of supporting their own corrupt and immoral customs, of causing divisiveness within the Muslim community, of leading the people into disobedience, and of justifying unlawful spending and political agendas.[63] He also noted the tendency of the *ulama* to include as source materials for legal rulings the heroic books of legends and myths, as well as the commands of the political leadership, ultimately allowing the desires and writings of human beings to outweigh the Word of God and even to slander Muhammad.[64] He condemned the Shii exercise of *ijtihad* for similar reasons, noting that the Shii imams exercised *ijtihad* on the basis of their supposed secret knowledge of the Quran and according to birthright, rather than on Quran and *hadith* scholarship.[65]

Because of his concerns, Ibn Abd al-Wahhab was careful to specify how the *mujtahid* should set about engaging in *ijtihad*. First, he charged the *mujtahid* with undertaking *ijtihad* with purity of heart rather than a set agenda with a predetermined outcome. He then reminded the *mujtahid* that the goals of *ijtihad* were understanding of the Quran and discernment of truth.[66] In his opinion, true understanding of the Quran required the *mujtahid* to actively grapple with the Word of God in order to determine how it might best be applied to daily life. Thus, *ijtihad* was not intended to be simply an exercise of the mind. Its very purpose was real life application. At the same time, he cautioned against the use of *ijtihad* as a means of overriding clear legal principles or rules. Because of the connection he asserted between *ijtihad* and truth, he repeatedly emphasized that *ijtihad* was never to be used to override or twist what God had clearly revealed and that anyone who attempted to use *ijtihad* in this way would be punished.[67]

A prominent example of such a misuse of *ijtihad* in his time was the question of whether the triple declaration of divorce by repudiation at a single instance (triple *talaq*) was legal.[68] Three *hadith* deny the permissibility of this kind of divorce. Two of these *hadith* are attributed to Muhammad. The third was transmitted on the authority of the first two caliphs, Abu Bakr and Umar, who stated that "The three are one." Because of the weight of the *hadith*, Ibn Abd al-Wahhab declared that there was no need to engage in *ijtihad*. This case was very clear-cut. The only possible purpose in engaging in *ijtihad* would be to reach a different conclusion, an act that would result not only in contradicting the declarations of both Muhammad and the first two caliphs but would also violate the consensus of the early Muslim community. Ibn Abd al-Wahhab therefore denied the right to engage in *ijtihad* on this issue, believing that nothing but deception could possibly result from it. He then used this case to underline yet again the importance of people being educated and informed about what constitutes correct practice and understanding so as not to be caught in the errors of the *ulama*.[69]

Ibn Abd al-Wahhab believed that *ijtihad* should be restricted to cases in which there was disagreement or a controversy that rendered correct and proper interpretation unclear. Thus, the exercise of *ijtihad* became most important when cases were being disputed either by the law schools (*madhahib*) or by various scholars.[70] This raises the important question of the role of the Islamic law schools in Ibn Abd al-Wahhab's legal thought.

Madhahib: The Schools of Islamic Law

Although Ibn Abd al-Wahhab never directly claimed to be a Hanbali jurist, he clearly drew inspiration from the teachings of Ahmad ibn Hanbal and had extensive familiarity with Hanbali jurisprudence and theology through both his family connections and his studies.[71] This does not mean that he blindly adhered to Hanbali jurisprudence in a spirit of *taqlid*.[72] He always reserved the right to exercise *ijtihad* and in fact varied from classical Hanbali jurisprudence on certain points of law. However, in general his methodology and legal interpretations are largely consistent with Hanbalism as both a theological and a law school, particularly with respect to emphasis on the Quran and *hadith*, contextualization of these sources, and attention to intent.[73] He also followed the Hanbali methodology of extreme conservatism in interpretation of the Sharia, taking matters of public interest (*maslahah*) and justice (*'adil*) into consideration and generally avoiding the use of analogy (*qiyas*) in favor of a meth-odology that considered everything not explicitly forbidden to be permissible. These legal methodologies and attitudes led Ibn Abd al-Wahhab to take an activist stance toward the question of justice in this world. He charged his followers to address and resolve complaints of injustice in the here and now rather than ignoring, hiding, or dismissing them as matters to be addressed in the Afterlife.[74]

Some of the negative perceptions of Ibn Abd al-Wahhab both in his own lifetime and across history are due to this connection to the Hanbali law school.[75] At the same time, consistent with the schizophrenic accusations typ-ically launched against him historically, Ibn Abd al-Wahhab was also viewed negatively because of his supposed foundation of a new, and therefore inno-vative and unorthodox, law school. His critics pointed to his failure to identify himself clearly as a Hanbali, combined with his radical rejection of *taqlid* in favor of *ijtihad*, as evidence of his innovation, a charge that was tantamount to an accusation of apostasy because starting a new school of Islamic law was unthinkable at the time.

Ibn Abd al-Wahhab responded by dismissing this accusation as ignorance on the part of such *ulama* of their own legal tradition. He claimed that, rather than introducing new concepts or principles, he was simply returning to the practices of his predecessors.[76] At the same time, he did not assert the supreme authority of any of them. When pressed to choose between rulings by Ibn Hanbal and Ibn Taymiyya, he asserted the superiority of neither, preferring to return directly to the original sources in order to form his own scripturally based opinion.[77]

Ibn Abd al-Wahhab's attitude toward and association with the law schools in general can best be described as one in which he examined both their legal methodologies and their rulings. His openness to the use of legal materials outside of his own law school reflected his rejection of *taqlid* in favor of rec-ognition that only God possesses authority.[78] He therefore consistently em-phasized the necessity of grounding legal rulings in the Quran and *hadith* and cautioned against placing too much emphasis on the teachings or rulings of any law school or sect within Islam because of the variances between each group on both major and minor points of law. This warning reflected his con-cern that the law schools of his time tended to inject personal opinion on the basis of traditions and past experiences into issues already clearly determined by the Quran.[79]

He was similarly concerned by the use of contradictory *hadith* by the var-ious law schools on the basis of convenience rather than systematic compari-son of the content of the *hadith* with the Quran. He noted numerous instances of the law schools declaring the *hadith* cited by other law schools to be inauth-entic without provision of Quranic evidence to support their claims.[80] In his opinion, no *hadith* could ever contradict the Quran, regardless of what any law school claimed. Therefore, he did not consider the opinion of any law school to be binding. Where clarification was needed from an external, nonscriptural source, Ibn Abd al-Wahhab encouraged his followers to turn to the example of Muhammad's Companions rather than the opinions of the law schools.[81]

He offered as an example the question of whether a Muslim has an absolute right to recover property or money stolen from him by unbelievers (kuffar) and later recovered during jihad. The Companions and law schools appear to disagree on the issue. Certain Companions asserted that the Muslim is entitled to recovery only before division of the booty. Other Companions, notably Umar and Ali, negated the claim to recovery when the claim is made after the division. al-Shafii and Ibn al-Mundhir asserted that the Muslim had the inherent right to the property regardless of the timing of the claim. Abu Hanifah claimed that the property was recoverable only if it was included in the division of the booty. Even Ahmad ibn Hanbal noted that there were apparently two contradictory hadith about this matter, one denying the right to recovery if the claim was made after the division and the other granting the Muslim the right to claim only the value of the property if the claim was made after the division.[82] Clearly, there were a variety of opinions about this issue. How was one to definitively answer the question when so many interpretations were possible?

Ibn Abd al-Wahhab taught that the appropriate method was not to follow the teachings of a given law school but to return to Muhammad's example to look for similar cases. He was particularly concerned that the chain of transmission for the hadith asserting the right to recovery only prior to the division was "admittedly weak," making clear the need for a more authoritative hadith.[83] He also noted that the two potentially contradictory hadith cited by Ahmad ibn Hanbal were not as contradictory as they initially appeared. The legal issue in these two hadith was the point in time at which the claim was made, not the entitlement of the Muslim to his property. Both hadith support the entitlement of the Muslim to compensation for the value of lost property in cases in which the claim is made after the division of the booty or if the property is no longer extant.[84]

Returning to the hadith, Ibn Abd al-Wahhab found a case with a strong chain of transmission in which a non-Muslim tribe raided the grazing lands of Muhammad and stole a slave girl and a female camel. The Muslims responded by attacking the tribe and recovering the slave girl. Unfortunately, by this time the tribe was no longer in possession of the camel. However, because the slave girl had cared for the camel and knew it well she was able to identify it later. Thus, Muhammad recovered both his slave girl and his camel. For Ibn Abd al-Wahhab, God's judgment in this case was clear—Muslims are absolutely entitled either to direct recovery of their property or compensation for its value from the booty taken during jihad.[85]

This case is an excellent illustration of contextualizing and deriving a legal precedent directly from the Quran and *hadith* rather than following the teachings of a particular law school. It was precisely because the law schools were unable to reach an agreement about this case, as well as many others, that Ibn Abd al-Wahhab denied their authority. He believed that the methodology and the content of both the source materials and the final ruling had to be examined in order to determine the truth of the conclusion. This raises the question of how he believed that jurisprudence (*fiqh*) in general should be approached.

Fiqh and the Mufti

Fiqh is typically defined as the "interpretation and elaboration of the Sharia." It is a purely human endeavor rather than a divine directive. Historically, the distinction between *fiqh* and Sharia has often been blurred, as many jurists and scholars have considered *fiqh* to be as authoritative, divine, and infallible as Sharia. One of the hallmarks of Islamic revivalism and reform from the eighteenth century through the present has been the attention given to distinguishing between *fiqh* and Sharia in order to allow for reinterpretation on the basis of a direct return to the Quran and *hadith*.[86]

Ibn Abd al-Wahhab's legal writings share this concern about the confusion of *fiqh* with Sharia. He was careful to identify and distinguish between them in his writings because of his recognition of the difference between their natures. He was particularly concerned by the tendency of Muslims of his time to accord too much importance to *fiqh* and not enough to the Quran and *hadith*. He therefore warned them about the dangers of adhering unquestioningly to *fiqh*. First, he noted that God commanded believers to adhere to the Quran rather than *fiqh*. Second, he cited a *hadith* that stated that pursuit of knowledge of *fiqh*, rather than knowledge of the Quran, would lead to misery, wretchedness, agony, worry, poverty, injustice, hostility, and hatred in this world. He believed that the negativity of this imagery reflected the serious nature of looking to human reasoning to achieve salvation rather than recognizing salvation as the prerogative of God. He was also concerned that excessive adherence to *fiqh* might lead to dedication to the law schools and deification of the instructor.[87]

These concerns about assigning too much authority to *fiqh* do not mean that Ibn Abd al-Wahhab categorically rejected the use of it altogether. Rather, these concerns highlight the importance of assigning the correct authority to each source so as to remain faithful to the values and teachings of the Quran and *hadith*. On this basis, he developed his own methodology of *fiqh*.

As with his theology, Ibn Abd al-Wahhab's methodology of *fiqh* is based, first and foremost, on a return to the Quran and *hadith* to search for clear and specific legal examples and proclamations. At the same time, he admitted that most cases are neither simple nor clear but have many parameters and involve numerous considerations. In fact, some cases may appear to have no precedent at all in the Quran and *hadith*. In such cases, he proposed the reference of such questionable problems to clear situations in order to eliminate the obscurity.[88]

In support of this approach, he cited a *hadith* featuring a man who had sworn to make a sacrifice to God in a specific location. Prior to setting out, the man sought Muhammad's permission to carry out his vow. Because the sacrifice was being made in God's name, it did not initially appear that there was a problem with this situation. However, Muhammad made it clear to the man that he must consider the full context of the place where he proposed to make his sacrifice. Were sacrifices made to idols in this location? Did unbelievers celebrate any feasts there? When the man responded negatively, Muhammad gave him permission to carry out his vow but advised that vows that could potentially involve disobedience to God ought not to be carried out.

Ibn Abd al-Wahhab emphasized two points of contextualization and interpretation in this *hadith* that reflect his use of the source materials. First, he noted the importance of considering the implications of one's actions, however innocent and pure in intent they may be, because any action has the potential to be confused with the activities of nonbelievers and thus be seen as somehow justifying and approving non-Islamic practices.[89] There is a suggestion here, although it is not stated directly, that such situations help to explain why the adoption or even adaptation of local, non-Islamic practices by Muslims is problematic. Any appearance of sanctioning such an activity by conducting a similar activity could mistakenly lead someone to believe that non-Islamic practices are accepted by Muslims, thus encouraging the "pollution" of Islamic practices with non-Islamic ones.

The second major point was recognition of Muhammad's explicit permission to seek the opinion of a *mufti* in cases that are not clear. A *mufti* is a scholar who serves as both a legal and religious consultant and adviser by issuing *fatawa* (sing. *fatwa*), or legal opinions, to either judges (*qadis*) or to private individuals on request. The opinion of the *mufti* is not considered to be binding in court but offers a recommendation as to how a particular situation is to be handled. The *mufti*'s authority is based on his popularly recognized knowledge and scholarship rather than an officially held or appointed position.

Similar to his concerns about the law schools, *fiqh*, and the *ulama*, Ibn Abd al-Wahhab was concerned by the level of authority granted to *muftis* in his time. In his experience, too many people had come to rely more heavily on the interpretations and opinions of *muftis* than on the Quran and *hadith*. Ibn Abd al-Wahhab rejected the notion of any human being, however well educated, being more authoritative than these two primary sources. Consequently, he warned believers against adhering too closely to the teachings of any scholar or *mufti* and promoted instead direct and personal reading of the Quran and *hadith* by individual believers. His purpose in doing so was not to do away with *muftis* altogether but to limit the seeking of a *mufti*'s opinion to cases in which difficult or unclear situations were encountered. Only when there was a need did he explicitly permit seeking the opinion of a *mufti*.[90]

Interpretational Issues: Literalism, Ritualism, and Intent

Historically, Ibn Abd al-Wahhab has been portrayed as a literal interpreter of the Quran and *hadith*, holding to the letter, rather than the spirit, of the law. However, his writings reveal a very different methodology and approach. In every discussion about legal issues, Ibn Abd al-Wahhab carefully highlighted the importance of the intent behind the actions taken, that is, their purpose and goal, rather than just the actions themselves or the ritualism involved in them. In his opinion, it was the spirit driving an action that determined its value and outcome, not the action itself.[91]

Consequently, rather than supporting ritual perfectionism he looked to the purpose of the believer in pursuing various activities. For example, when asked to explain Quran 11:15–16, which addresses the question of what will happen to those who desire worldly benefits and do not care about the Afterlife, Ibn Abd al-Wahhab used this as an opportunity to expound on the importance of intent in carrying out good works. He stated that the performance of devout acts, such as almsgiving, assembling, and doing good, while refraining from evil and injustice only with the purpose of preserving or expanding money and possessions or preserving one's family or perpetuating a life of comfort and luxury, was hypocrisy, which would not be rewarded in the Afterlife.[92] It was because these actions shared the common goals of self-glorification and the achievement of rank and status in this life, rather than rewards in the Afterlife or service of God, that they would not be rewarded.

Ibn Abd al-Wahhab repeatedly emphasized that God will reward or punish in the Afterlife on the basis not only of *what* one does, but *why* one does it. He based this opinion on a *hadith* outlining three groups of people who are destined for Hell: those who study knowledge in order to be called a scholar (*'alim*), those who give alms in order to be called generous, and those who struggle and fight in the way of Islam (i.e., participate in jihad) in order to be called brave and heroic. For Ibn Abd al-Wahhab, this *hadith* made it clear that those who seek knowledge for profit or leadership or study the Quran and pray for the sake of position in the mosque and the commendation of the people would come to nothing because their intent was not correct.[93] Thus, intent, rather than ritual perfection or correctness, is the most important factor in determining whether an action is acceptable or not.

Ibn Abd al-Wahhab considered literalism and ritualism to be intimately connected. In his opinion, an overly literal interpretation of the Quran and *hadith* would lead to an inappropriate obsession with ritual perfection over what he considered to be the essence of religion: intent and action. In a *fatwa* addressing this exact question, he cited the example of someone who extends his lip and sticks out his tongue in the ritually prescribed manner as deviating from *tawhid* because he saw no connection between these physical expressions and the ultimate message of God, regardless of how faithful they might have been to the exact ritual example of Muhammad.[94] Later in the same *fatwa* he refused to elaborate specifically and in minute detail on what exactly was permitted and forbidden, what could be sold, and what was to be given in marriage because he felt that this was superfluous. He stated instead that the most important command of religion was the performance of works. He denied the importance of going into extensive detail about how this was to be done because "detailing/elaborating on what was narrated about what is preferable necessitates elaborating what the written text did not permit. It would have been in the writings if its being brought to perfection is God's will."[95] In other words, detailing and elaboration that are not contained directly within the Quran and *hadith* are not pursuits worthy of the believer. Ibn Abd al-Wahhab believed that performing good works was a far more important task for the believer than the achievement of empty ritual perfection. This ruling also reinforced his message that faith as the path to salvation is a matter of what one does in broad terms—worship, charity, moral living, and so on—at both the individual and community levels, not a matter of minute details that are focused only on the relationship between God and the individual. It is a reminder of the communal nature of Islam and a call to action within one's community, not a call to asceticism.

It is of interest that, while he denounced ritual perfection without accompanying intent of the heart, at the same time he denounced actions that are opposed to one's true intent. He cited as an illustration a *hadith* in which Muhammad told a parable about two men who passed by a town that contained an idol. The people of the township required that any passerby make a sacrifice to the idol in order to pass through their territory. The first objected that he had nothing to sacrifice. The people told him that anything, even a few flies, would suffice. So the first man, even though he was a Muslim and knew that what he was doing was wrong, sacrificed the flies—a seemingly harmless action—in order to gain passage. This man achieved his earthly goal of passage through the territory but was consigned to Hell in the Afterlife because he had committed an act that he knew was wrong. The second man refused to sacrifice anything to anyone or anything other than God and was immediately killed. The second man, because he was faithful to the faith in his heart, went to Paradise.[96]

Ibn Abd al-Wahhab used this *hadith* to emphasize the difference between external acts and the work of the heart, noting that the most important consideration was what was in one's heart. The first man, because he had made an issue of not having anything to sacrifice as his main reason for refusing to commit the sacrifice, indicated that what was in his heart was a willingness to make a sacrifice to an entity other than God in order to achieve his immediate goal. The second man allowed the faith of his heart to guide his external actions, despite the physical danger that he knew would ensue. Ibn Abd al-Wahhab pointed to this second man as setting the correct example because what is in the heart should drive one's external acts. Muslims must be sufficiently confident in their faith to act accordingly, even if it means that they will suffer great hardship, even to the point of death, for their faith.[97]

Not only did Ibn Abd al-Wahhab not support a literal interpretation of the Quran and *hadith*, but he also denounced those who did for their ignorance. He was opposed to literal interpretations and the pursuit of literal knowledge because such literalism did not offer any evidence of discernment or understanding of the content of the text or its contextualization. He particularly singled out as an example of such ignorance the Kharijites—an early group of Muslims known for their purist and literal interpretation of the Quran—and literalists who believe that they please God by their strictness and harshness. Ibn Abd al-Wahhab considered such literalism to be tantamount to exaggeration and charged that people who literally interpret the Quran clearly do not comprehend its meaning.[98]

Likewise, he berated his contemporary *ulama* for their rigidity in interpreting the Quran and *hadith* without placing the events into historical context. His concern was that this practice typically reflected the self-serving purposes of local power holders rather than faithful adherence to the principles of Islam.[99]

Finally, he was opposed to literal adherence to the law that resulted in trickery in legal and financial matters, such as transactions designed to avoid the appearance of charging of interest but in reality accomplished exactly that. He declared these practices to have as their purpose the cheating and swindling of God, actions that could never be considered permissible or lawful.[100] The critical factor in determining the legality of actions was, as always, the intent of the person carrying out the transaction.

Ibn Abd al-Wahhab clearly does not fit into a literalist mode with respect to Islamic law because he did not allow literal adherence to the law to supplant adherence to the intent of the law. This is why he believed that it was so important for Muslims to possess individual and personal knowledge of the scriptures. Without education, one cannot know and adhere to the requirements of Islam or distinguish between Islamic and customary practices. He pointed out that various types of legal trickery came about long before his time and had been practiced so widely in the area in which he lived as to have been sanctified by the leadership. Thus, he made it clear that the declaration of the leadership of the permissibility of an action was not sufficient to render it so.[101]

Ibn Abd al-Wahhab was also concerned about the literal use of prior judg-

ments on legal issues because the ruling did not always include the logic of
the legal opinion or the details of the case. The danger of adhering to such a
ruling was that one might fail to understand the actual issues involved. He
believed that this had proven to be a problem particularly in the citation of the
examples of the Rightly Guided Caliphs and Muhammad's Companions because of the variances in their legal opinions. He believed that these variances
were most likely due to differences in circumstances in what outwardly appeared to have been similar cases.[102]

The question of literalism versus intent was particularly relevant to Ibn
Abd al-Wahhab's discussion of inheritance law. If he were truly a literalist, one
would expect to find strict literal adherence to inheritance law as it is outlined
in the Quran and classical *fiqh* literature.[103] However, his discussion of this
topic in particular reveals a reluctance to adhere to a literal interpretation of
Islamic law in favor of careful examination of the intent behind the legal rulings.

Inheritance as a Case Study of Interpretational Issues

In general, Ibn Abd al-Wahhab followed classical interpretations of Islamic
inheritance law as it is laid out in the Quran and *hadith*. This is significant
because adherence to the Quranic precepts appears not to have been the norm
in the Arabian society of his day. For example, when asked to issue a ruling
on whether or not a person is permitted to will both a bequest *and* a third of
his property, Ibn Abd al-Wahhab replied that the bequest should be taken *from*
the third of the property normally allotted for bequests unless it was contested.
This ruling was in keeping with classical interpretations of inheritance law.
Unfortunately, he did not offer a ruling on the situation when the bequest was
contested. However, within the same ruling he noted the hypocrisy apparent
in the application of Islamic inheritance law in his own time, commenting that
the division of the estate only became an issue when the poor were named as
beneficiaries. As long as the wealthy retained their hold on their wealth, no
issues were raised at all.[104]

The instances in which Ibn Abd al-Wahhab diverged from classical interpretations of inheritance law were guided by his concern for the intent of the
Quranic texts. He particularly took into consideration the Quranic values of
justice and equity in the interpretation of inheritance law rather than adhering
to the literal classical interpretation. He believed that classical jurists had overlooked the matter of intent with respect to inheritance issues. The major case
in which he outlined these issues was the division of the estate of the deceased.

In the case of the division of the estate, Ibn Abd al-Wahhab asserted the
primacy of direct descendants rather than ascendants. He noted, for example,
that estate issues were to be handled, resolved, and agreed on by the primary
heirs, who were descendants, rather than secondary heirs. Once this has been

done, none of the secondary heirs who might have inherited under certain conditions have any claim to anything. In practical terms, this meant consideration of sons and grandsons as primary heirs over parents and grandparents. He specifically stated, "Place the son of the son as a son, and do not place the father of the father as a father."[105] According to this interpretation, the grandchild is placed in the position of a primary heir in cases in which the son is no longer living. However, a grandparent is not entitled to take the place of a deceased parent as an heir. Ibn Abd al-Wahhab's ruling emphasized Quranic intent rather than literal interpretation, leading him to contradict classical interpretations of inheritance law.

Under classical law, orphaned grandchildren are excluded as heirs of their grandfather.[106] The portion that would normally have gone to the parent is redistributed in the event of the parent's death. Ibn Abd al-Wahhab believed that this interpretation was unfaithful to the Quranic intent of the inheritance verses, which proclaim appropriate portions for relatives of the deceased. Thus, he declared that keeping the spirit of the law was more important than adherence to the letter of classical practice. Clearly, in the case in which the parent inherited the allotted portion that portion would have gone to the children on the parent's death. Consequently, he asserted the right of the grandchild to inherit in the parent's place as being in keeping with the principles of justice and equity intended by the Quran.[107]

One other point of inheritance law where Ibn Abd al-Wahhab differed from classical interpretations was his assertion, on the basis of several *hadith*, that if the only heirs of an estate are brothers and they differ in their circumstances the estate ought to be split according to their needs rather than according to strictly allotted portions. In defense of this ruling, he noted that, whatever the classical interpretation, Muhammad's Companions did not completely agree as to how inheritances were to be split. He specifically noted that Abu Bakr, Ali, Ibn Masud, and Zayd all had their own divergent opinions on the matter, so that assertions of *ijma'* on this particular issue are patently false.[108]

Waqf

Tied to Ibn Abd al-Wahhab's discussion of inheritance law is the question of *waqf*. *Waqf*, or charitable endowments, are a common establishment in the Islamic world although they have no Quranic basis. The purpose of *waqf* is to provide revenue for charitable purposes, such as aiding the poor and hungry. A *waqf* can consist of a building, fountain, orchard, or any other type of property. It is overseen by an administrator who provides the upkeep necessary for it to continue to be profitable. Although *waqf* is theoretically intended to be purely charitable, the historical reality is that it *waqf* has sometimes, though certainly not always, been used as a means of circumventing inheritance laws because the person establishing the *waqf* has the right to specify who the caretaker will be—often a friend or family member, sometimes in perpetuity or until the family line dies out.

Ibn Abd al-Wahhab upheld the legality of *waqf* and the necessity of respecting and adhering to the terms under which it was established. For example, he was presented with the case of a date palm that had been established as a *waqf* but had, after a certain time, failed to produce the fruit whose sale was intended to provide the income to be given to charity. The caretaker decided to rent half the tree for a period of ten years in order to finance improvement of the other half, whose proceeds would continue to finance charitable works. Unfortunately, the man leasing half the tree died two years into the leasing period. The lessor, not surprisingly, wanted to cancel the lease, but the heirs of the man who had established the lease argued that it should continue.

When Ibn Abd al-Wahhab was asked to rule on the legality of the lease, he declared that it was valid and fixed and that the death of the leaseholder did not terminate the lease. He supported the heirs of the leaseholder because they were claiming the lease as part of their inheritance. Citing Quran 5:1, "O you who believe, complete contracts/commitments," he declared the word of the Muslim to be binding, regardless of changes in circumstances or context.[109]

Ibn Abd al-Wahhab further asserted the perpetuity of a *waqf* until the beneficiaries have died out, referring to *waqf* as a duty. However, he did not support the establishment of *waqf* as a means of circumventing the Islamic law of inheritance. When asked about the legality of a woman without a husband establishing a *waqf* to benefit her son, he replied that this was not legal because it made the son the only heir of the property rather than splitting the estate among appropriate heirs. Likewise, a *waqf* established for the purpose of benefiting an heir was not generally acceptable unless it was the only source of sustenance for that heir.[110] It is clear that Ibn Abd al-Wahhab's declaration of the legality or illegality of the *waqf* was based on the intent behind its establishment rather than on the institution itself.

Conclusion

Muhammad Ibn Abd al-Wahhab was consistent in his interpretation of both theology and Islamic law. He emphasized the importance of the intent behind an action rather than whether it was permissible according to a literal interpretation of the Quran or *hadith*. Further, he never focused strictly on the performance of the action or adherence to ritual in his determination of the legality or illegality of an action, believing instead that the intent behind the action indicates what is in the heart of the actor. He consistently interpreted theology and Islamic law through a direct return to the Quran and *hadith* for individual interpretation (*ijtihad*) rather than simply following the teachings of the past (*taqlid*), thus making clear the difference between human interpretations (*fiqh*) and divine ordinances (Sharia).

The past few chapters have served to contextualize both the historical person of Ibn Abd al-Wahhab and his intellectual and methodological placement in history. His guiding methodologies of theology and Islamic law, which formulate his worldview and approach to and interpretation of scripture, have been analyzed in detail. We now take this theoretical framework and analyze how it was applied to particular themes in his writings.

The next two chapters address three important themes in Ibn Abd al-Wahhab's theological and legal writings—the role of education and missionary work (*da'wah*), jihad as an armed struggle for the defense of Islam, and the status of women and women's rights in Islam. The practical application of his theoretical concepts and methods demonstrates the implications of his theological beliefs, as well as the use of key legal interpretational tools such as the prominence assigned to the Quran and *hadith*, the use of *ijma'* and *maslahah*, and emphasis on the importance of knowledge and intent, rather than literalism, in distinguishing truth from falsehood. These themes also reflect his adherence to broad Quranic values, particularly the concern for social justice, the protection of women's rights and property, and the correct and acceptable means of spreading and defending the faith. We now turn to the topic of women and gender.

4

Women and Wahhabis: In Defense of Women's Rights

Wahhabism in the contemporary era is largely portrayed as misogynist, denying women their human rights, insisting on strict gender segregation, forbidding women access to public space, and subjugating them by considering them inferior to men. Women under Wahhabi regimes are assumed to have second-class citizenship, if not slave status. Critics of Wahhabism point to extreme examples like the Taliban and Saudi Arabia's requirement that women wear the full *burqa'* or *abaya* covering them from head to toe, leaving barely enough room to breathe; the ban on women driving or being recognized as heads of households; and the Taliban's forbidding women to go to school, work, or seek medical care as evidence of Wahhabism's oppression, suppression, and repression of women in accordance with an extremely conservative interpretation of Islamic law.[1] All of these stereotypes and images are assumed to be based on the conservative Wahhabi interpretation of Islam despite the fact that no systematic analysis of Muhammad Ibn Abd al-Wahhab's writings about women and gender has ever been undertaken. In addition, no distinctions have been made between tribal customs, local traditions, and Islamic law in these portrayals.

While these contemporary views and concerns have come to define Wahhabism for Western human and women's rights activists and Muslim feminists alike, the assertion that these attitudes are characteristic of Wahhabism risks inaccuracy because the term *Wahhabism* is rarely defined. Many of the regimes and movements labeled as Wahhabi in the contemporary era do not necessarily share the same theological and legal orientations.[2] The reality is that *Wah-*

habism has become such a blanket term for any Islamic movement that has an apparent tendency toward misogyny, militantism, extremism, or strict and literal interpretation of the Quran and *hadith* that the designation of a regime or movement as Wahhabi or Wahhabi-like tells us little about its actual nature.[3] Furthermore, these contemporary interpretations of Wahhabism do not necessarily reflect the writings or teachings of Ibn Abd al-Wahhab.

In fact, Ibn Abd al-Wahhab's life and writings reflect a concern for women and women's rights reminiscent of Muhammad. Like Muhammad, he sought to ensure that women's rights, as granted by the Quran, were implemented and that women were aware of them. Like other jurists and Muslim legal thinkers of his time, he was engaged in the discussion of the appropriate place of women in Muslim society.[4] His interactions with women indicate that he recognized them as human beings capable of serving as positive, active agents in both the private and public realms and who therefore deserved access to both education and public space. Rather than demonstrating misogyny or the relegation of women to seclusion, these interactions and encounters reflect the consistent application of the principles of social justice, the equality of all believers, and the need to preserve public welfare and order that permeate all of his other theological and legal writings.

These interactions also stand in marked contrast to conventional wisdom about customs and traditions in Arabia both during this time period and in the contemporary era, as well as traditional interpretations of Islamic law. Consistent with his legal and theological methodologies, Ibn Abd al-Wahhab sought to rediscover the earliest sources of Islamic revelation with respect to gender issues in order to reinterpret them (*ijtihad*) through contextualization, both historically and in terms of the broad values taught by the Quran and *hadith*. He used this methodology to construct an Islamic vision of gender.

Gender Themes in Ibn Abd al-Wahhab's Writings

The defining theme of Ibn Abd al-Wahhab's writings with respect to gender is that of balance. Rather than reflecting an attitude of misogyny or male superiority, his writings argue, in painstaking detail, for the balance of rights and responsibilities between men and women in both human interactions and their relationships with God. The overall image of women in his works is based on an appreciation of human life and the human condition in which women are viewed as divinely created people who not only have a part to play in the process of salvation in the Afterlife but are also expected to play an active role in this life in the establishment of an Islamic order on earth in both the private and public realms. Ibn Abd al-Wahhab's writings therefore contend that women have a place in society and that they possess rights and responsibilities that that society is obligated to respect and protect.

Ibn Abd al-Wahhab's theme of gender balance is remarkable for two reasons: first, because of the content of what he actually said; and, second, because of who he was. If, as has been claimed, the apparent oppression of women by contemporary Wahhabi regimes is due to their adherence to the Wahhabi interpretation of Islam, then one should expect to find indications of such misogyny in Ibn Abd al-Wahhab's writings. The fact that his writings do not contain such an attitude raises the question as to whether contemporary misogyny is truly due to Wahhabism or if it has more to do with patriarchy and local customs.

This is not to assert that Ibn Abd al-Wahhab's writings on gender are unique. Had they been unique, then the charges of heretical innovation would be applicable. Instead, analysis reveals that they were both fairly mainstream for his time and place and were in keeping with the broad Hanbali tradition of protecting women.[5] As will be seen, on matters such as dower (*mahr*), marriage contracts, and divorce his writings reflected fairly standard interpretations and teachings, presenting an evenhanded treatment of gender that is neither literalist nor misogynist. In the few instances in which his teachings do represent a departure from more standard treatments about topics like concubinage, the right of the father and grandfather to compel a minor daughter/granddaughter in marriage, the stipulation of conditions in the marriage contract, the wedding feast, and inheritance law, he tended to place greater power in the hands of the woman than was typically the case for other jurists. Thus, rather than seeking to deprive women of power Ibn Abd al-Wahhab was actively engaged in the empowerment of women through support of awareness and enforcement of their rights.

This approach, while certainly not what one would expect given standard stereotypes of Wahhabis, was consistent with Ibn Abd al-Wahhab's methodology for directly and personally interpreting and applying the Quran and *hadith*. It is important to recall that one of the most shocking messages of the Prophet Muhammad was his raising of women's status through his proclamation of social justice for women; his granting to women the right to be parties to, rather than objects of, their marriage contracts; his requirement that the *mahr* be property payable to the bride rather than her father or guardian; his outlawing of female infanticide; and the special protection offered to widows and orphans.[6] Because of the heavy emphasis he placed on the Quran and *hadith*, it is not surprising that Ibn Abd al-Wahhab would have underscored both these legal teachings and their underlying values. The fact that he dedicated an entire treatise to women's issues—"Kitab al-Nikah" (The Book of Marriage)—further serves to demonstrate his concern for the discussion of gender issues and his insistence on enforcing the God-given rights of women as outlined in the Quran and *hadith*, even when these were not in accord with local customs or traditions.

It was perhaps because he anticipated opposition to his teachings, as had been the case with his theological teachings with respect to *tawhid*, that Ibn Abd al-Wahhab was careful to present highly detailed evidence for his construction of gender, including not only extensive Quran and *hadith* proof texts but also a highly inclusive discussion of classical legal rulings on various topics from all of the major law schools. By grounding his teachings in scripture and continuity with past jurisprudence, he subtly sought to refute charges of heretical innovation while grounding himself strongly in the historical scholarly tradition.

"Kitab al-Nikah" includes a total of 376 *hadith* citations and interpretations from 90 different sources. In keeping with the classical *ikhtilaf* genre of legal writing, he included opinions with which he both agreed (248 or 66%) and disagreed (128 or 34%). No individual is ever cited as being singularly authoritative. In fact, Ibn Abd al-Wahhab disagreed more often than not with the people he cited most frequently, al-Shafii and Malik.[7] Not even Ahmad ibn Hanbal was considered absolutely authoritative, although Ibn Abd al-Wahhab generally agreed with him.[8] Similarly, important Companions of Muhammad were also cited but never as absolutely authoritative.[9]

It is significant that Ibn Abd al-Wahhab did not extensively cite one of the most misogynistic of all *hadith* transmitters, Abu Hurayrah.[10] Abu Hurayrah is cited only twice (about 0.5%), both times in disagreement with his opinion, indicating that, despite his status as a Companion, Ibn Abd al-Wahhab did not consider his opinion to be at all authoritative or even important, particularly with respect to women and gender. In contrast, the person with whom Abu Hurayrah tended to disagree most, Muhammad's favorite wife, Aisha, is cited by Ibn Abd al-Wahhab seven times (almost 2% or four times more frequently than Abu Hurayrah), all in agreement. This preference for Aisha over Abu Hurayrah is significant not only because Ibn Abd al-Wahhab showed preference for *hadith* transmitted by a woman, even when they contradicted those of a man, but also because Aisha's *hadith* tend to grant women more agency and voice than Abu Hurayrah's.[11] Thus, the very fact that Ibn Abd al-Wahhab showed a preference for Aisha's *hadith* reflects his emphasis on broad Quranic values rather than literal adherence to specific proclamations taken out of context.

Ibn Abd al-Wahhab addressed two spheres with respect to women's rights and responsibilities: the sphere of spirituality, or the relationship between human beings and God (*ibadat*); and the sphere of interpersonal human interaction (*muamalat*). In matters of faith, he asserted the equal responsibilities of both men and women. He taught that any mature man or woman, whether slave or free, who possessed understanding was permitted to recite the Quran.[12] Significantly, he did not exclude women who were menstruating. Rather than declaring a menstruating woman impure to the point of exclusion from communal religious activities, he noted instead that the *hadith* required only that a woman be veiled while she was praying.[13] The fact of menstruation had no impact on God's hearing or receiving the prayer.

Similarly, he expected both men and women to observe the five pillars of Islam—declaration of faith, prayer five times daily, pilgrimage to Mecca, payment of the charity tax (*zakat*), and fasting during the month of Ramadan. To emphasize the point that every individual, whether male or female, is responsible for his or her own faith and salvation, he cited a *hadith* in which Muhammad proclaimed that no one would be able to rely on kinship for his or her salvation. Not even his own daughter, Fatima, would be able to claim her salvation on the basis of her relationship with Muhammad.[14] Thus, he made it clear that men and women were equal in terms of their responsibilities toward God.

In the realm of human, specifically male-female, interactions, the most important topics are matters of personal status, specifically, marriage, divorce, and procreation. "Kitab al-Nikah" was written to address these topics, reflecting the importance of marriage and parental relationships in Islam, both of which are accompanied by a spectrum of rights and responsibilities delineated according to gender. Despite the fact that certain responsibilities and rights vary according to gender, Ibn Abd al-Wahhab did not use these differences to assert that women are inferior to men or to place men in a superior position. Rather, he insisted on a balance in rights and responsibilities between men and women "requiring like her to like him."[15]

Within this framework, he demonstrated sensitivity to two types of rights with respect to gender: absolute rights and negotiable rights. Absolute rights are those to which every woman is entitled, regardless of socioeconomic status, geographical location, or age. Examples of absolute rights include the right to receive a *mahr* upon marriage, the right to stipulate conditions in the marriage contract, the right to maintenance during marriage and the divorce process, the right to initiate a divorce, and the right to education. Negotiable rights tend to address details of the absolute rights. Examples of negotiable rights include the amount of the *mahr* and the amount of maintenance during marriage and divorce, all of which are contingent on the socioeconomic status of the husband. This distinction between absolute and negotiable rights is very striking in Ibn Abd al-Wahhab's writings because he focused on absolute rather than negotiable rights to the immense frustration of his petitioners. For example, he made clear in his discussion of *mahr* that he believed that the most important right of the woman was the absolute right to receive the *mahr*. He refused to issue a ruling about the negotiable right of the specific amount of the *mahr* because the amount fluctuated according to socioeconomic status, making an absolute ruling impossible. Thus, although he was sensitive to the reality of socioeconomic differences between women, he did not make a legal issue of them.

This chapter now turns to a detailed analysis of the contents of "Kitab al-Nikah" in order to explore Ibn Abd al-Wahhab's construction of gender through the topics of marriage, divorce, and widowhood.

The Purpose of Marriage

Marriage is the intended norm of life for both men and women in Islam, the legal means by which procreation is to occur and carnal desire is to be fulfilled. It is expected that every Muslim man and woman will marry and have children. As a life-affirming religion, Islam both acknowledges the reality and existence of human desire and provides a legal mechanism for its satisfaction, namely, marriage.

Ibn Abd al-Wahhab wrote of marriage, "It is required (*yajib*) if one fears for oneself hardship/affliction in a general saying of the *fuqaha'*. If one does not fear and has a carnal appetite, it is commendable (*istihabb*). And it is preferable (*afdal*) for his rightful property (*haqqihi*) to give it up/withdraw from it as a supererogatory act of worship (*li-nawafil al-'ibadah*)."[16] The terminology of this statement indicates that this is the binding declaration of legal doctrine that serves as the point of departure for Ibn Abd al-Wahhab's elaboration on the topics of marriage and sexual relations.[17]

The requirement of marriage in the case of "fear of hardship/affliction" refers to a fear that one would not be able to control one's sexual desires. Such a person would be at risk of committing a sin by engaging in a forbidden sexual relationship due to his or her inability to control sexual desire. By requiring marriage as the solution, Ibn Abd al-Wahhab made it clear that marriage is the only appropriate and legal means of satisfying this desire.

This notion is further supported in the second scenario in which a person does not fear a lack of self-control but nevertheless experiences sexual desire. The word *commendable* (*istihabb*) is still a strong legal term, though not an absolute requirement. Ibn Abd al-Wahhab's reasoning behind not making this an absolute requirement was that a person experiencing but capable of controlling sexual desire would not have been at risk of engaging in a forbidden sexual relationship. Nevertheless, he recommended marriage out of recognition of the existence of sexual desire and the need for a legal outlet for it.

The third scenario, that of "his rightful property," refers to the potential sexual relationship between a master and his female slaves. The wording of this third scenario suggests that Ibn Abd al-Wahhab recognized the reality of the existence of such relationships but did not approve of them because they did not constitute marriage. By making "withdrawal" from such relationships a superogatory act of worship (i.e., a laudable extra expression of faith rather than a requirement), he sought to discourage this practice and encourage Muslims to seek sexual satisfaction through marriage alone.

Ibn Abd al-Wahhab's discussion makes clear Islam's recognition of both the reality of sexual desire and the need to fulfill it. His support for marriage was followed by a rejection of the state of celibacy because the "chastity" that Muslims are required to uphold is not the same as celibacy.[18] Ibn Abd al-Wahhab believed that God's command to "Be noble and chaste" (Q 3:39) should be interpreted in accordance with the admonition of Muhammad to "Marry the woman, and anyone who withdraws from my Sunna [example] is not from me."[19] That is, he defined *chastity* as the reservation of sexual relations to the marital relationship, not as the need to abstain from sexual activity altogether.

Having made his declaration of binding legal doctrine, Ibn Abd al-Wahhab then turned to the elaboration of how this doctrine was to be carried out in practical terms.

On Sexual Relations

Ibn Abd al-Wahhab's statement on marriage makes it clear that marriage is the only legal means for the satisfaction of sexual desire. To underscore this point, he carefully outlined various types of illicit sexual relations—fornication, adultery, and rape—and elaborated on the topic of sexual relations with slaves and servants in order to strengthen his argument that sexual relations should be restricted to the marriage relationship. He also provided guidelines for how sexual relations should occur within marriage. He did this not to compile a laundry list of sinful activities or permitted actions according to a literal inter-pretation of the Quran and *hadith* or of Islamic law, but rather to demonstrate how the broader Quranic value of concern, protection, and respect for women was to be carried out in this most intimate relationship between a man and a woman. His overriding concern was to protect women in the sphere in which they were the most vulnerable—sexual relations.

Fornication (*zina'*), whether by a man or by a woman, is strictly forbidden in Islam, constituting one of the punishments carrying the penalty of death by stoning (*hudud*).[20] Defined as sexual relations outside of marriage, fornica-tion can take place either between unmarried people or as adultery.[21] Ibn Abd al-Wahhab emphasized the forbidden nature of such sexual relationships by addressing the case of a man who fornicates with a Muslim woman. He taught that any man, whether Muslim or non-Muslim, who fornicates with a Muslim woman is to be put to death.[22] This is a very strong statement, making it clear that sexual relations with a Muslim woman outside of marriage are never acceptable, regardless of whether she is free or a slave. However, it also raises some other issues, namely, the responsibility of the man in sexual relationships and the implications of such teachings for the master-slave relationship.

Ibn Abd al-Wahhab's prescription of the death penalty for the male partic-ipant in a sexual liaison with a Muslim woman makes it clear that men are to be held responsible both for their sexual activities and for controlling their sexual desires. This stance is in keeping with his statement of legal doctrine about marriage. The fact that he did not prescribe the same punishment for the woman in this situation is striking and raises the question why. Shouldn't the woman also be held responsible for her participation in this forbidden act?

Ibn Abd al-Wahhab did not look strictly at the sexual act that occurred in this scenario but considered the question of whether the woman was a willing participant. Rather than simply assuming that the woman in question had to have been a willing participant or was somehow responsible for inciting the man's sexual desire, so that he could no longer control it, Ibn Abd al-Wahhab first declared that men should be held responsible for controlling their own sexual desires and then recognized that women generally are vulnerable in the face of male desire. Consequently, while he condemned the man for his participation in this act, he used this case as an opportunity to explore the topic of female vulnerability in the face of male sexual desire.

Concern for female vulnerability is most apparent in Ibn Abd al-Wahhab's discussions of sexual relations with female slaves. Although some law schools asserted that sexual intercourse with female slaves was permissible, Ibn Abd al-Wahhab strongly disagreed, as is suggested by his preference that a man withdraw from such sexual relations.[23]

Many jurists and scholars have argued that the Quran permits sexual relations with female slaves. The standard verse in support of this is Q 70:29–30: "And those who have preserved their chastity except regarding their spouses or what they possess by their right hands." The phrase "what they possess by their right hands" is typically understood to mean slave women. Ibn Abd al-Wahhab did not agree with this interpretation because he believed that it allowed men to engage in licentiousness and lowered and debased such women to the status of prostitutes, a status that is clearly forbidden by both the Quran and the *hadith*.[24] In support of his own position, he cited Muhammad's own teachings, noting:

> And He [Muhammad] denied/repulsed this forbidden thing in the
> saying of the Most High: "And those who have preserved their chas-
> tity except regarding their spouses or what they possess by their
> right hands," Q 70:29–30. And it is well known that this was trunca-
> ted and that having sex with her [a female slave] is not by marriage
> and not by possession of the right hand. And the Most High said,
> "And do not force/compel your young women into prostitution."
> (Q 24:33)[25]

By citing the authority of the Quran in forbidding the practice by comparing it to prostitution, Ibn Abd al-Wahhab demonstrated great concern for the vulnerability of women in a patriarchal society in which men make the rules and hold power over women, including the right to possess their sexuality. Rather than focusing on male rights or privileges, Ibn Abd al-Wahhab argued forcefully for male responsibility for self-control where women are concerned and that women should be treated honorably and respectfully. He recognized the right to sexual relations in marriage alone. It is marriage, he argued, that is intended by the phrase "what they possess by their right hands," not slavery. Consequently, although he recognized that other jurists had permitted this practice historically, Ibn Abd al-Wahhab, in keeping with his broad theme of marriage being the only legal state in which sexual relations can occur, declared sexual relations with slave women to be forbidden because they occurred outside of marriage.[26]

He further forbade the purchase of a female slave or servant with the expectation of gaining sexual favors from her, noting that this reflects not only a spirit of greed on the part of the man but also a violation of the protection with which he is supposed to provide her. Through the citation of several *hadith*, he made authoritatively clear the protective relationship that is supposed to exist between master and servant/slave, whether male or female, so that what is highlighted are not the master's rights over the servant/slave but the master's responsibilities: protection from harm and provision of sustenance. He specifically stated in the case of the purchase of a slave girl/woman that a man should not make such a purchase with greed in his heart because "She was placed under your protection from her calamity."[27] He then compared this purchase to the purchase of a camel, the clear implication being that the purpose of such a purchase is to obtain labor, not satisfaction of greed or carnal desire.[28] Thus, he held the Muslim man responsible for controlling his sexual impulses and fulfilling his duties toward others.

Consistent with his teaching that it is preferable for a man to withdraw from sexual relations with his female slave, Ibn Abd al-Wahhab recognized the permissibility of and even encouraged the emancipation and marriage of any slave/servant woman who is the mother of her master's child. Muhammad himself had established this practice by manumitting his female slave Safiyah as her dower prior to marrying her. Thus, Ibn Abd al-Wahhab declared that, "There is no objection to manumitting the mother and marrying her."[29] By emancipating and marrying the woman, the man renders sexual relations legal and sets the stage for recognition of the child.

On the basis of the same *hadith*, Ibn Abd al-Wahhab recommended manumission in the case of a proposed marriage between a female slave and her master.[30] Here again, he showed genuine concern for the status of the woman, recognizing that a slave married to her master is on an unequal footing with him. Through her emancipation and subsequent marriage, the slave woman is raised in status to a free married woman and receives the financial and legal obligations of the husband toward her. Ibn Abd al-Wahhab's stance here is preferential to women, ensuring that they will receive what is due to them legally and financially by reserving sexual intercourse for the marriage relationship.

In addition to asserting that men not only do not have the right to sexually possess whatever woman they "own" or are married to, Ibn Abd al-Wahhab also taught that men do not have the right to any kind of sexual relations they desire. He declared that certain ways of having sexual intercourse are unacceptable. He particularly objected to the practice of taking a woman in the buttocks (anal sex), which he classified as no less than an act of *kufr*.[31] Justification for the permissibility of this practice is typically based upon Q 2:223, which states, "Your women are tillable soil to you, and you take your tillable soil as you wish." While some men have interpreted this to mean that they can do as they wish in matters of sex, Ibn Abd al-Wahhab disagreed. He noted that the consideration of women as "tillable soil" refers to their reproductive capacities, so that the only permissible forms of sex are those that could potentially result in procreation. Anal sex is thus precluded.

Ibn Abd al-Wahhab's description of the act, the title of the discussion, and its position in a treatise addressing similar topics make it clear that he considered anal sex to be degrading to the woman and an act of pure licentiousness, reflecting a lack of male self-control.[32] Consequently, the intent behind the discussion was not only the limitation of sexual relations to ways in which procreation can occur but also the protection of women's sensibility and the insistence on treating women honorably and respectfully, even in bed.

Ibn Abd al-Wahhab's support for a woman's right to dignified treatment is followed through in his prohibition of rape, regardless of the woman's status as free or slave.[33] He noted that rape can result in pregnancy, in which case the family of the woman in question would be entitled to retaliate. Furthermore, the man would be responsible for raising the offspring—something that could become quite expensive, even "overwhelming," in the long run.[34] It is interesting that he not only forbade the practice but sought to explain to men why raping a woman is a bad idea due to its potential consequences for the man. There is no sense of loss of honor or shame for the woman in his discussion of rape.

Having made clear the status of marriage as the legal means by which sexual relations are to occur, Ibn Abd al-Wahhab turned to other considerations in undertaking marriage.

The Motivation for Marriage

Although marriage is the only legal means for the satisfaction of carnal desire, carnal desire is not the sole determining factor in whether a man should marry because there are cases in which men do not experience carnal desire but seek to be married anyway. When asked whether a man not experiencing carnal desire should marry, Ibn Abd al-Wahhab responded in the affirmative, noting that the real deterrent to marriage is not lack of desire but lack of the financial wherewithal to support a wife.[35]

According to Ibn Abd al-Wahhab, any man who possesses sufficient means to support a wife should marry. A man who does not possess sufficient means cannot marry, even if he has carnal desire.[36] There is no time limit on the state of insolvency—it can last a lifetime—so that financial ability, rather than age or sexual maturity, is the determining criterion for marriage.

The question of the financial ability to support a wife serves to place a limitation on the practice of polygyny according to Ibn Abd al-Wahhab's inter-pretation. While he noted that Q 4:3 tacitly allows a man to marry up to four wives simultaneously, he tempered this permission with recognition of the Quranic teaching that marriage is contingent on the man's ability to support those wives. He noted that God's limitation was not made out of coincidence or necessarily to block such marriages but in order to clarify that the same authorization for marriage applies to every marriage, not just the first.[37] Thus, although tacitly allowed, polygynous marriages are required to follow the same regulations applying to a monogamous marriage. This underlines the impor-tance of the ability to fulfill one's financial obligations in marriage and deem-phasizes the factor of sexual desire. This is not a case of preferential treatment for wealthy versus poor males. Rather, it reflects the Quranic emphasis on economic justice for women by reinforcing the right of every woman to the financial obligations undertaken by her husband upon marriage.[38]

Who Should Marry?

The expected norm in Islam is that every man and woman should marry. Marriage of a Muslim man to a Muslim woman is always preferable.[39] Muslim men also have the option of marrying a woman considered to be among the People of the Book, that is, Jews, Christians, and Zoroastrians.[40] Muslim women are not permitted to marry non-Muslim men.[41] Only prisoners are discouraged from marrying.[42]

Ibn Abd al-Wahhab recognized that the ideal situation of a free Muslim man being able to marry a free Muslim woman does not always exist. Therefore, in cases in which the man fears hardship, affliction, or an inability to control his desire when he is outside of the Muslim community (ummah), it is permissible for him to marry a non-Muslim woman, provided that the legal requirements for Muslim marriage are in place.[43] This is even the case when the man is in the land of the enemy because absence from the Muslim ummah does not excuse the man from the need to adhere to Islamic law and refrain from sexual relations outside of marriage. In Ibn Abd al-Wahhab's opinion, it is better for the Muslim man to recognize his inability to control his sexual desires and pursue a legal means of satisfying them than to prohibit the man from marriage altogether and to leave him no alternative but illegal means of satisfying his desires. He emphasized the fact that the man is responsible for controlling his desires and recognizing when he is reaching a point where he can no longer do so. He did not blame the woman for the man's experience of sexual desire or for the man's inability to control himself.[44]

Although he taught that the man should return to the *ummah* as expediently as possible, this did not necessarily mean the end of the marriage. Rather, it reinforced his belief that Muslims need to live within a Muslim community.[45] Thus, Muslim women should always be removed from the land of the enemy.[46] In the case of marriage of a Muslim man to a non-Muslim woman, Ibn Abd al-Wahhab presumed that the wife would benefit from living within the Muslim community. He also recognized the possibility that she might eventually become a Muslim, making such a return even more urgent.

The Mechanics of Marriage (*Nikah*)

Marriage in Islam is understood to be a contractual relationship and is often compared in legal literature to a business contract. As such, the bride and groom are both considered to be parties to the contract, with each party gaining certain rights by undertaking certain responsibilities. According to Islamic law, the wife is responsible for providing sexual intercourse and children to her husband and for being obedient (*nushuz*) to him.[47] In exchange, the husband is responsible for providing his wife with a dower (*mahr*) and maintenance, including food, clothing, and shelter, as well as sexual intercourse.

The actual marriage takes place in a session where the offer of marriage is made and accepted and the marriage contract is agreed to by the bride and groom. The contracting of marriage is a serious matter, which should not be undertaken with a spirit of levity. Ibn Abd al-Wahhab noted that Muhammad himself stated that there were three matters about which one should never joke: marriage, divorce/repudiation, and return after divorce.[48]

Ibn Abd al-Wahhab clearly subscribed to the Islamic teaching that marriage is the norm for all Muslim men and women, as well as the teaching that sexual intercourse can occur legitimately only within marriage. Consequently, he used the opportunity of his discussion of marriage to note that, although the standard and expected way in which a marriage is to occur is through the negotiation and signing of a marriage contract, there is one alternative method for entering into a state of marriage: sexual relations. On the basis of the *hadith*, he taught that the presence of intimacy between a man and a woman is considered to enter them into a state of marriage, making it clear that sexual relations are never a matter of levity but carry serious financial repercussions for the man.[49]

The Five Required Elements of Marriage

Ibn Abd al-Wahhab noted five conditions imposed by Muhammad for the contracting of a valid marriage: (1) determination of the spouses, (2) consent of the spouses, (3) contracting of the marriage by a male guardian (*wali*), (4) presence of two reliable/just witnesses, and (5) equality of status between the man and the woman.[50] Each condition was the subject of a lengthy description and analysis in Ibn Abd al-Wahhab's writings.

Determination of the Spouses

In determination of the spouses, Ibn Abd al-Wahhab required that the wife be present and specifically named at the contracting of the marriage so that no ambiguities exist, such as the confusion of one daughter or sister with another. He noted the existence of such cases historically, which allowed a guardian to obtain a dower for a mistaken bride due to the guardian's deception of the husband.[51] It is of great interest here that the punishment for such an error falls on the men involved rather than on the woman. In a case of mistaken identity, the woman who was wrongly sent to the marriage bed remains entitled to her *mahr* as compensation for what she lost, namely, her virginity, even if she was not a virgin.[52] Such a woman is to be returned to her guardian, but she is entitled to maintenance during her waiting period (*iddah*), which must be observed due to the sexual activity that has occurred. Furthermore, the sister who was supposed to have been given in marriage is also entitled to the *mahr* because she was the intended bride according to the contract.[53]

If the case is one in which two men married two women and the husbands were sent the wrong wives but consummated the marriage prior to realizing that they were doing so with the wrong woman, each woman is entitled to receive her *mahr* and then must observe the *iddah* prior to being sent to the correct husband.[54] It is clear from this discussion that Ibn Abd al-Wahhab supported the woman's financial rights in marriage even in cases in which there has been some confusion about which woman was actually married. He believed that the woman's financial rights should never be held hostage to errors made by the men involved.

Agreement of the Spouses

The second point, the agreement of the two spouses to the marriage, is generally required.[55] Exceptions are made only for an infirm or diseased youth.[56]

In a statement of legal doctrine, Ibn Abd al-Wahhab declared it "commendable" for the father to ask the permission of the virgin in contracting the marriage.[57] In his opinion, the need for the daughter's consent (*idhn*) was determined by her status as a virgin, not by her age. He underscored this teaching by declaring invalid any marriage contracted by a father or his authorized agent for a minor son or a virgin daughter "by other than their consent." Such a marriage can only be validated by the subsequent consent of the spouses.[58] Consistent with the example of Muhammad, he also included the mother in the marriage negotiations by "recommending" that she be consulted for her permission in the giving of her daughter in marriage.[59]

Ibn Abd al-Wahhab's stance here reflects his concern about the possibility of a woman being forced into a marriage she does not desire because of the broad powers granted to the father or his authorized agent in contracting a marriage for her. Historically, all of the Sunni law schools had allowed the father or grandfather to compel a virgin minor daughter (defined as a girl under the age of nine) into marriage.[60] Only the Shafiis limited this practice by requiring that the girl be given a "choice" upon reaching maturity. Ibn Abd al-Wahhab specifically denied the right of the father or grandfather to compel a virgin minor daughter into marriage.[61] Because he departed so strongly from classical teachings on this topic, he provided a detailed discussion of the consideration of the rights of the daughter given in marriage by her father, beginning with the question of her age at the time of the marriage.

Prior to delivering his own judgment about the permissibility of marrying off a young girl under the age of nine, Ibn Abd al-Wahhab outlined the juridical arguments in favor of child marriages. He noted that the Sunna contains the historical example of Aisha, who married Muhammad at the age of six, although the marriage was not consummated until she was nine, and that this example has been used as the norm for determining the legal majority of a girl as being nine years of age. Furthermore, there is a *hadith* that records Muhammad's permission for the marriage of "those who do not menstruate," to which later jurists (most notably al-Shafi'i and Malik) added the provision that it is preferable that the girl be of an "appropriate/fit condition for marriage" and be capable of expressing either her aversion to the marriage or tacitly approving it by abstaining from comment.

The historical examples from the Sunna made it impossible for Ibn Abd al-Wahhab to outlaw the practice of child marriage outright. However, he clearly found this practice to be potentially abusive for the girl. Thus, he ruled that such a marriage should only take place with the girl's consent, leaving the power in her hands rather than those of her father or his authorized agent.[62] He further stated that a girl who was "not mature" at the age of nine should not be married off but required the marriage guardian to wait until the girl was mature.[63]

In the case of the mature virgin (*al-bikr al-balighah*), Ibn Abd al-Wahhab stated unequivocally that her consent is required in order for the marriage to be contracted.[64] That is, although he allowed the father to contract the marriage, he required the mature virgin woman's consent in order for the marriage to be valid (sahh).[65] In cases in which the woman in question is deflowered but unmarried, that is, no longer a virgin, he also absolutely required the woman's authorization of the marriage.[66] In support of this teaching, he cited the example of al-Khansa', who was married off by her father without having given her permission. Because she detested her marriage, al-Khansa' sought Muhammad's counsel. Muhammad decreed that she was to be separated from her husband because she had not given her authorization to the marriage and she had been a deflowered but unmarried woman. Again it was her status as a deflowered woman that was the defining legal issue of this case, not her age.

The only exception Ibn Abd al-Wahhab made in allowing the marriage of a woman who had reached her majority without her permission was when the woman was recognized as being crazy or insane (majnunah), as evidenced by her visible inclination toward a particular man. He allowed the marriage guardian to contract a marriage between the majnunah woman and the object of her insanity without her verbal consent because her visible attraction or reaction to the man in question provided tacit permission for the marriage.[67]

In looking at the full discussion of the necessity of the woman's consent to any marriage contracted for her, it is clear that Ibn Abd al-Wahhab steered away from the marrying off of any girl under the age of nine and then followed this by not permitting the marriage of any female, whether virgin or nonvirgin, without her permission. In this subtle way, he offered a critique of child marriage, despite the historical example of Aisha, suggesting that the woman always ought to have some say in her marriage, regardless of her age or level of maturity. His protection of the minor female is consistent with his emphasis on adherence to broad Quranic values rather than literal interpretations or ritualism and his broad theme of the protection of women's rights, particularly where matters of marriage and protection from rape are concerned. He did not limit his protection of women to cases in which women were legally recognized as having reached their majority but included minor women. Thus, women's rights were to be applied equally on the basis of gender rather than age or status as a virgin or nonvirgin.

THE WOMAN'S CONSENT. The question of the woman's consent occupies an important place in the literature about marriage because there are variant opinions about what constitutes consent. The definition of consent is important because, unless the way in which it is expressed is clearly defined it is not clear how the woman's consent is to be determined.

Ibn Abd al-Wahhab taught that the woman's consent may be either verbal or silent. Silent consent should be accompanied by an approving gesture of some sort during the actual contracting of the marriage in order for the contract to be valid. In his opinion, a marriage contracted without the woman's consent is never valid (sahh).[68] Similarly, he taught that once given, even if only by hinting, the woman's consent is considered binding and dissolution of the engagement is not permitted.[69]

Ibn Abd al-Wahhab's absolute requirement of the woman's consent was a departure from the teachings of the other Sunni law schools, most notably the Shafiis. His departure was due to a difference in interpretation of a *hadith* about Fatimah bint Qays who had declared about her marriage, "Asamah gave me in marriage." al-Shafii interpreted this *hadith* literally, understanding it to mean that Fatimah herself had played no role in the process of contracting the marriage and that her male marriage guardian, Asamah, had sole responsibility for contracting it. Ibn Abd al-Wahhab disagreed with this interpretation because it was literal and did not take into consideration the context in which the statement was made.

In his opinion, there were two critical legal issues addressed in this *hadith*. First, Fatimah remained engaged to the man and ultimately married him. In his opinion, these two facts indicated her consent. Had she not consented to the marriage, she would not have kept the engagement or married the man. Second, the context of this *hadith* was a discussion about the permissibility of a man publicly declaring an engagement. Therefore, when Fatima stated, "Asamah gave me in marriage," she was not declaring the man's prerogative to give a woman in marriage but was granting approval to the practice of the marriage guardian granting his permission by making it a matter of public knowledge. Thus, Ibn Abd al-Wahhab emphasized the need for historical contextualization of *hadith* in order to discern the values and legal precedents established within them.

In a further elaboration of the definition of *consent*, Ibn Abd al-Wahhab noted that the state of the woman must be determined in order to ascertain whether or not she has consented to the marriage. He required verbal consent in the case of a deflowered but unmarried woman receiving news of a proposed marriage.[70] How the woman came to be deflowered—whether by permitted or forbidden intercourse—was irrelevant to him.[71] In the case of a virgin, he abided by the classical ruling that her permission or authorization is given via her silence upon hearing about the proposed marriage.[72] In the event that there is a dispute about whether the woman's consent has been given, he followed majority opinion in granting the woman the right to reject the marriage, provided that no sexual activity has occurred.[73]

In each of these cases, Ibn Abd al-Wahhab noted as the most important element the girl/woman's consent. In his opinion, it was the *girl/woman* who determined the validity of the marriage by either consenting to it or declining it. Thus, he believed that the woman was always a critical party to the marriage contract, regardless of her age or status as a virgin or deflowered woman.

Because men had greater control over marriage because of their right to repudiate marriages without a reason, Ibn Abd al-Wahhab did not give great attention to the question of male consent in marriage. The exception was in the case of a minor male who is the ward of a guardian other than his father. In this instance, he required the permission of both the guardian and the ward in order for the marriage to be valid. However, he allowed the ward to marry if he felt a need to do so and was unable to request the authorization of his guardian for some reason. The critical element in such a case was whether it was possible for the ward to request the guardian's authorization. If the ward could have requested the guardian's permission and failed to do so, then Ibn Abd al-Wahhab declared the marriage contracted by the ward to be invalid.[74]

As for the status of servants/slaves in marriage, Ibn Abd al-Wahhab noted that a master has the right to marry off a minor male servant/slave without his permission, but he cannot force or coerce a male servant/slave who has reached his majority to marry provided that the servant/slave is in full possession of his mental faculties. Rather than literally interpreting Q 24:32, which commands men to "Marry those among you who are widows/widowers/single," Ibn Abd al-Wahhab qualified this verse by noting that such a command to marry was specific to the condition of the request by the servant/slave, evidence of which is his inclination toward and affection for a particular widow or single woman. Not only did he require the mature male servant/slave's permission to be given in marriage, but he also granted the mature male servant/slave permission to marry himself off.[75]

Permission of the master of the male servant/slave comes into play not because the master owns or controls the sexuality of his servant/slave, whether male or female, but because, in a case in which a mature male servant/slave desires to marry himself off, it is the master's responsibility to ensure that the servant/slave is capable of fulfilling the financial requirements of marriage. That is, the master is responsible for providing him with a fixed sum for maintenance of the wife, the *mahr*, which the husband is required to give his wife; authorization to select his wife without restrictions; and permission to divorce his wife if he wishes. The master is also responsible for the financial obligations associated with any potential divorce.[76] All of the financial obligations that the man undertakes in marriage fall to the master in the case of his servant/slave marrying because the he is understood not to have the financial means to fulfill the obligations that his marriage brings.

However, it is of fundamental importance that this does not mean that the servant/slave lacks the right to marry. Ibn Abd al-Wahhab recognized the right of every human being to marriage and thus sexual fulfillment. It was because of the master's obligation to meet the financial responsibilities of his servant/slave's marriage that he required the master's permission. By the same token, any marriage by a servant/slave contracted without the permission of the master was to be considered void.[77]

Marriage Guardianship

On the third point, that a marriage guardian (*wali*) must contract the marriage for the woman, Ibn Abd al-Wahhab taught that any marriage contracted by someone other than the woman's marriage guardian, even if it is the woman herself, is not valid and the marriage is void.[78] Thus, the woman's consent to the marriage was insufficient on its own to constitute a valid marriage. Her male marriage guardian had to handle the legal transacting of the marriage. Although this teaching was in keeping with the Hanbali tradition, Ibn Abd al-Wahhab nevertheless presented his contextual interpretation of the Quran and *hadith* in support of this statement of legal doctrine. By doing so, he affirmed the authority of scripture rather than of Ahmad ibn Hanbal.

Ibn Abd al-Wahhab began with the citation of Q 2:232, which states, "And do not prevent them from marrying their husbands." Although some law schools, most notably the Hanafis, believed that this verse gave women the right to contract their own marriages, Ibn Abd al-Wahhab did not. Instead, he noted the double negative in the verse, which prohibited the forbidding of marriage. For him, this was not the same as granting women the right to contract their own marriages. Thus, he turned to the *hadith* for clarification.

The requirement of the woman's marriage guardian contracting the marriage for her in the presence of witnesses is supported by *hadith* in a variety of collections.[79] Although the marriage of a woman without her marriage guardian or witnesses had been permitted by the early Muslim community and some jurists, most notably the Shiis, this practice was ultimately forbidden.[80] Muhammad himself had said: "No marriage except by a guardian and honorable witnesses" and "If a woman marries herself off by other than permission of her guardian, then her marriage is void."[81] Ibn Abd al-Wahhab believed that these two *hadith* combined with the Quran verse set a legal precedent requiring that the marriage guardian contract the marriage. He also noted that Umar and Ali, who were both close Companions of Muhammad and two of the first four caliphs, had unequivocally supported this interpretation and had ordered the punishment of the men involved in a case in which the legal requirements were circumvented.[82]

Muhammad charged the male protector with contracting the marriage as a matter of preserving a social order centered on a legally constructed family unit. According to the patriarchal social order, males are in charge of females' honor. Therefore, the protecting male must contract legal permission for another male to assume responsibility for a given female's honor. It was for this reason that Muhammad required that a woman be given in marriage only with the permission of her guardian. He believed that a woman giving herself in marriage was tantamount to harlotry.[83] Muhammad further required tangible evidence of the marriage via a document/evidence, notably the marriage contract, in order for the marriage to be valid because without it there was no proof of the marriage, reducing the woman to the status of a prostitute.[84] Because marriage is intended to be a public act of declaring a legal state for permissible sexual relations and reproduction, the fact of the marriage itself must be a public, legal record rather than a hidden, illicit act.

Ibn Abd al-Wahhab's upholding of the requirement that a marriage be contracted by the male guardian reflected his belief that men were responsible for protecting women and the social order. He therefore held both the male marriage guardian and the husband responsible for ensuring that proper procedure was followed in the legal mechanics of contracting marriage, providing a double insistence upon male responsibility.[85] Thus he taught that a woman who contracts her own marriage in order to prevent her father from marrying her off is to be loathed and the marriage is void. Likewise, any marriage contracted by the slave/servant without the permission of the master, even when it is contracted by a *qadi* (judge), is also to be considered void.[86]

Nevertheless, as a practical man Ibn Abd al-Wahhab recognized that there are exceptional cases in which the marriage guardian's action is not required, such as when he delegates the right to contract the marriage to the woman herself. In such a case, the woman must be trustworthy and reliable in judgment. Once given, the guardian cannot retroactively deny his permission, even if he has forgotten that he granted it. Ibn Abd al-Wahhab believed that forgetfulness should not serve as an excuse for prejudice against or harm to the woman.[87]

Ibn Abd al-Wahhab also granted the marriage guardian the right to appoint a proxy to represent him at the contracting of the marriage. Whether the guardian was absent due to force or other than force was irrelevant.[88] The critical legal point was that the proxy had to be duly and legally appointed.

Proxyship could be granted either without restrictions or with limits and restrictions. A restricted proxy was the person getting married. An unrestricted proxy was the one who was giving in marriage someone who desired it.[89] The fact that either the guardian or the proxy could contract the marriage emphasizes Ibn Abd al-Wahhab's understanding of the male role in the contracting as one of an overseer of an administrative process. The more substantive issue of the woman's consent could not be fulfilled by anyone other than the woman herself.

It is important that Ibn Abd al-Wahhab was always careful to distinguish the difference between the guardian contracting the marriage as an administrative requirement and the woman's consent as an absolute substantive requirement. While the guardian's contracting of the marriage was required, this did not in any way negate the requirement of the woman's consent to the marriage.[90] Thus, although the guardian has the legal prerogative in the actual contracting of the marriage, the woman remains a critical party in the process of approving the marriage in order for it to be valid.

Ideally, the marriage guardian should be the father. In a case in which the father is deceased or otherwise unavailable, Ibn Abd al-Wahhab assigned guardianship first to the woman's brother, then to the paternal grandfather, then to the woman's son. If none of these are available, guardianship passes to the tribe of the brother, unless it is low/base/despicable, in which case the paternal uncle takes over, followed by his son, then other relatives in paternal relationships.[91] In any case, guardianship always rests with a male, paternal relative. Maternal relatives only have a claim to marriage guardianship if there are no paternal relatives. In such a case, guardianship passes to those who are heirs by religious duty or tribal relations or to someone who serves as a protector or benefactor to the paternal relatives.

In a case in which the otherwise appropriate marriage guardian is unavailable due to either absence or nonexistence, the sultan or political leader may serve as the marriage guardian because of the protective role he assumes for people under his rule. However, the political leader may serve in this capacity *only* if he is a just man. It is further provided that the political leader can serve in this capacity only if the woman lives far away from her relatives due to their "fault," not hers.[92] Thus, if a woman has deliberately run away from her family, a marriage contracted for her by the political leader is not valid because she has deliberately created the distance. Similarly, if there is no great distance separating the woman from her appropriate marriage guardian, any marriage contracted by the political leader is invalid.[93] Ibn Abd al-Wahhab did not allow for the circumvention of legal requirements simply because literal adherence to the law could not be achieved. Thus, if a woman's intent is to get around the literal legal requirements in order to obtain a substitute marriage guardian, the marriage is invalid.

Ibn Abd al-Wahhab was also careful to note that the fact of being a political leader was not a sufficient criterion to become a woman's marriage guardian. Recognizing the possibility of a corrupt leader being in power, he specified that, in a case in which the political leader is either unavailable or unsuitable and does not have a son fit to serve in this capacity, any just man may fill in as the marriage guardian. Such a man is required to demonstrate his just nature by protecting the woman's right to equality of status with her husband, as well as to the appropriate *mahr*.[94] Thus, the critical factor in selecting an alternative marriage guardian is the man's adherence to justice, not his political position.

Because of his responsibility to protect the woman for whom he is contracting the marriage, Ibn Abd al-Wahhab charged the marriage guardian with responsibility for verifying six conditions in the potential husband: intelligence/ability to reason, freedom (i.e., whether he is a free man or a servant/slave), religion (he must be a Muslim if the woman is a Muslim), sexual ability, maturity, and integrity/honorable conduct.[95] The purpose of such conditions is to verify that the marriage meets the criteria for validity and that the husband will be an honorable man who will treat his wife justly, as well as to try to match spouses of an equal social status.[96]

Ibn Abd al-Wahhab recognized that the selection of the marriage guardian is not always an obvious choice. Indeed, it is possible that a woman will have more than one marriage guardian, a situation that can raise some difficulties, such as when the woman authorizes each one separately to seek a marriage contract for her. If both guardians are successful in contracting a marriage for her, which marriage is the valid one?

Ibn Abd al-Wahhab responded that several criteria must be examined in such a case. First, the antecedents of the two husbands should be analyzed. If they are known and acceptable, then, according to the *hadith*, whichever husband married her first chronologically is the valid husband, even if the woman has already consummated her marriage with the second man.[97] However, if the marriage has been consummated with the second husband and the wife has returned to the first husband without his being informed of the consummation with the second husband, then Ibn Abd al-Wahhab decreed that both marriages are abolished and the two husbands should exchange rebuttals or thrash it out.[98] The legal reasoning behind this ruling is that the first man, in contracting the marriage, gained the right to sexual intercourse with the wife as a consequence of the marriage. Because that right was in effect stolen by the second husband, the first husband is entitled to compensation for his loss by the offending party. The issue of property rights remains one for the men to resolve. The woman is absolved from all fault in such a case.

The fact that the Hanbalis did not allow the woman to contract her own marriage independently does not mean that they ruled out the possibility of her participation in the contracting of the marriage altogether. According to the Hanbali tradition, the woman has the right to be an active, not just a passive, partner in the contracting of her marriage.[99] Ibn Abd al-Wahhab confirmed this right in his discussion of what the woman and her marriage guardian should do in cases in which more than one man has proposed marriage. Some respect is to be given to the order in which serious proposals are made, particularly if the proposal has already been accepted, regardless of whether the proposing and/or accepting has been done by the woman or her guardian.[100] This wording is very significant because it recognizes the legality of the woman proposing and/or accepting a marriage. The legal concern addressed in this discussion is not about whether a proposal or acceptance of a marriage can permissibly be made by a woman because the discussion clearly recognizes her legal capacity to do so, as well as that of her guardian. Rather, the issue is one of determining which proposal is to be accepted.

Ibn Abd al-Wahhab taught that if the first proposal has somehow been weakened in the interim between the first and second proposals then it is permissible to accept the second proposal and reject the first. However, if the first proposal has not been weakened, then it should be accepted, regardless of who either made or accepted it, the woman or her guardian. To do otherwise would cause harm to the one who made the proposal, whether male or female.[101] Although the discussion is subtle, the message is clear that the woman has the legal right to issue and accept marriage proposals. Such proposals cannot be overturned merely because they were made or accepted by the woman. Rather, they must be considered on the basis of the strength of the proposal and the qualities of the prospective husband.

Witnesses

The fourth condition Ibn Abd al-Wahhab required for a valid marriage is that there be two male witnesses of just and reliable character at the conclusion of the marriage contract.[102] Although this teaching was in keeping with most classical interpretations, Ibn Abd al-Wahhab felt it necessary to outline the scriptural bases for witnesses to the marriage because there had been variances and divergences in both Muhammad's example and the historical practices of the early Muslim community.

The Quran does not specifically require witnesses in the case of marriage, although it does require two reliable male witnesses for any contract of sale. Although marriage is not considered a contract of sale in Islam, it is nevertheless a contractual agreement. Historically, the marriage contract has been considered analagous to the contract of sale with respect to the form, thus carrying over the Quranic requirement for two reliable male witnesses for the contract of sale to the contract of marriage.

Some *hadith* support this legal analogy. Muhammad himself stated: "No marriage except by a guardian and honorable witnesses" and "The lowest of what is to be in marriage is four: one who marries, one who is to be married, and two witnesses."[103] The Companions and caliphs Umar and Ali both required two male witnesses as a condition of marriage, as did Ibn Umar and Ibn Zubayr. However, the *hadith* also record Muhammad as having given Safiyah in marriage without witnesses present. Malik ibn Anas and Ibn al-Mundhir believed that this act negated the *hadith* requiring witnesses. Their opinion was supported by Yazid bin Harun, who held that marriage was exempted from the requirements applicable to the contract of sale.

In reaching his own legal decision, Ibn Abd al-Wahhab looked at the intent and form of the contracts in both sales and marriage. He concluded that both contracts were matters of public concern requiring public records.[104] Indeed, Muhammad is reported to have said, "Make marriage public."[105] Thus, Ibn Abd al-Wahhab required two reliable male witnesses in order for the marriage to be valid. He also permitted the substitution of two female witnesses for one male witness because this is permitted by the Quran with respect to legal testimony. It was therefore possible for two women and one man to fulfill the Quranic obligation of witnessing.[106]

In addition to the contract, Ibn Abd al-Wahhab addressed the intent and purpose of marriage in his discussion of witnesses. He taught that any marriage conducted in secret—that is, with only the man and woman present—is not permitted because there is no public proclamation of the marriage and only the man and woman themselves can testify to the fact of it.[107] Failure to make marriage a public act has implications for the social order—anyone could claim to be married to anyone. Without witnesses, it cannot be proven. Without witnesses, a woman attempting to claim her financial rights—dower, maintenance, inheritance—has no solid evidence that the marriage ever existed. Any children born of such a union could potentially be declared illegitimate, which would result in the denial of inheritance rights and would make maintenance by the purported father a questionable obligation. Finally, the man and the woman open themselves to charges of unlawful sexual intercourse (zina') and its accompanying punishments.

On the basis of scripture and the greater good of maintaining public order, Ibn Abd al-Wahhab declared that if only the man and the woman are present at the marriage the woman is to be returned to her guardian and the husband is to be cursed, symbolizing the illegality of the act and a return of the implicated parties to their previous unmarried status as though no marriage had taken place at all.[108] No mention of the stoning punishment for zina' is made here. The return of the woman to her guardian without punishment while declaring social disgrace for the man reflects Ibn Abd al-Wahhab's vision of the man bearing responsibility for undertaking an illegal action. The woman is considered an innocent party.

Equality of Status

The fifth and final condition for marriage is that the man be of equal status to the woman. The phrase "equal status" was a subject of debate and difference among jurists. Ibn Abd al-Wahhab noted that the Quran and hadith consider status as a Muslim to be the defining characteristic of equal status, rather than social status, skin color, or tribal affiliation.[109] Therefore, outside of requiring that a Muslim women be married only to a Muslim man, Ibn Abd al-Wahhab left the determination of equal status to the marriage guardian and granted the guardian the right to abolish the marriage if he was not satisfied with the man's status.[110]

The right of the marriage guardian to request the invalidation of the marriage if he was not aware of the man's lower status prior to the marriage, regardless of the opinion of the bride, reflects his responsibility to ensure that the woman is married to an appropriate man.[111] Because a marriage to a man of lower social status would lower the woman's status, investigation of the man's status was a serious responsibility. For this reason, Ibn Abd al-Wahhab also entitled the future bride to the right to know her future husband's status and granted her the right to request that the marriage be invalidated if she was not aware of the husband being of a lower status prior to the marriage.[112] However, if she was aware of the man's lower status prior to the marriage and she accepted the marriage anyway, he denied her the right to request that the marriage be invalidated on the basis of status because she was aware of the difference in status and deliberately chose to marry the man despite this.[113]

Neither the guardian nor the woman had the right to request that the marriage be invalidated in a case where the man was of higher status because the marriage raised the woman's status. Ibn Abd al-Wahhab underlined this understanding by teaching that in a case in which the woman in question is a slave and the man to whom she is to be married is a free man it is best for the woman to be emancipated as a public and visible symbol of her heightened status.[114]

Preparations for Marriage

The Right to Stipulate Conditions in Marriage

In addition to the five required elements for marriage, Ibn Abd al-Wahhab, in keeping with the Hanbali tradition, also granted the prospective bride the right to stipulate conditions in the marriage contract, the violation of which would result in the wife's right to request a divorce by *talaq*, in which she would retain all of her financial rights.[115] The right to stipulate conditions gives the woman both power and agency within marriage and can help her to achieve balance with the husband's rights. Ibn Abd al-Wahhab taught that as long as the conditions are lawful they are permissible and should be enforced.[116]

Of all of the law schools, only the Hanbalis granted the woman the unequivocal right to stipulate conditions in her marriage contract. The Shafiis and Malikis expressly forbade the stipulation of conditions, noting that Muhammad had said: "Every condition that is not in the Book of God is void/invalid" and "Except a condition permitting what is forbidden or forbidding what is permitted."[117] Ibn Abd al-Wahhab believed that these *hadith* did not forbid the stipulation of conditions per se but rather made it clear that stipulated conditions cannot permit what is forbidden or forbid what is permitted. Thus, he ruled that any condition stipulating something that was not expressly forbidden was permissible.[118]

It is in the discussion of conditions that the marriage contract is most comparable to a business transaction because it reflects marriage as a negotiated contract between two partners. The woman's right to stipulate conditions and the requirement for her consent to the marriage reflect her role as a party to the contract rather than an object of it.

Conditions may be stipulated either in writing or orally. Oral conditions should be agreed upon by both spouses and are considered as binding as written conditions because both go through a process of negotiation and are agreed upon by both spouses. In fact, Ibn Abd al-Wahhab declared an oral condition to be an oath, so that, if the man misleads the woman by verbally agreeing to a condition and then leaves her or denies it to her, the man forfeits his rights and must fulfill his obligations to the woman.[119] The woman has the right to request that the marriage be annulled if the man refuses to honor the condition unless she voluntarily submits to the violation of the condition after a fixed period of time.[120]

Ibn Abd al-Wahhab defined two possible types of conditions in marriage—valid and invalid. Valid conditions include the legal transaction of marriage, such as handing the bride over to the groom. Although the handing over of the bride is not specified by the Quran and *hadith*, it is clearly a requirement for marriage because a marriage cannot exist if the two spouses have no access to each other.[121] Other valid conditions are those that profit or benefit the *woman*, such as specifying money for her support, stipulating that the man may not remove the woman from her home (i.e., from her hometown) or country, or that the husband will not marry additional wives or take a concubine.[122] It is very significant that Ibn Abd al-Wahhab approved *only* of those conditions that would benefit the woman. He made no mention or consideration of conditions that would benefit the man.[123]

Granting the wife the right to stipulate that her husband not marry additional wives or take a concubine was a source of great power for the woman. It differed from the historical practice of the husband granting his wife the option of requesting a divorce in such a case, a practice known as *tamlik*, because the inclusion of this restriction as a condition of the marriage contract meant that violation of the condition rendered the contract invalid. Thus, rather than constituting a matter of choice, as was the case with *tamlik*, the stipulation of a legal condition in the contract results in the negation of the contract through judicial divorce in the event of its violation. Stipulation of a condition grants the woman greater legal power than stipulation of an option.

This is not to say that Ibn Abd al-Wahhab granted the woman unlimited power in the stipulation of conditions, however, particularly where justice toward other women was concerned. For example, he did not allow a woman to stipulate that the man divorce another woman to whom he is already legally married prior to entering into a new marriage because this would have been unfair to the woman already married.[124] However, he did allow a woman to stipulate that the man will not be allowed to marry additional women after marrying her. By granting such power and control to the woman, Ibn Abd al-Wahhab ensured the protection of both current and future wives.

Ibn Abd al-Wahhab identified three types of invalid conditions: what is void or invalid in marriage, denial of the woman's rights, and the man stipulating conditions that are outside of the eight acceptable imperfections that can invalidate a marriage. In cases in which invalid conditions are included in the marriage contract, the invalid conditions are considered null and void but the marriage contract itself remains valid, provided that the marriage is legal.[125]

There are three types of void conditions in marriage: marriage of the unprotected, marriage of one who is unsuitable, and temporary (*mut'ah*) marriage. Marriage of the unprotected occurs when a female ward is married off by her marriage guardian but does not receive her *mahr*. Ibn Abd al-Wahhab prohibited this because payment of the *mahr* to the bride is an *absolute* requirement of marriage in Islam, regardless of the circumstances of the marriage.[126] Thus, in order for the marriage to be valid the ward must be given a *mahr*.[127] It is preferable that the *mahr* be specified in the marriage contract so as to avoid confusion. However, in a case in which the *mahr* is not specified the wife is to receive the "equivalent" *mahr*, that is, the *mahr* that would be paid to a woman of comparable status, beauty, and disposition.[128] The bottom line for Ibn Abd al-Wahhab was that there is to be no marriage without *mahr*. He allowed no exceptions.[129] By insisting that the *mahr* be paid to the bride, he sought to ensure both that the woman, rather than her father or guardian, received her *mahr* and that the *mahr* was actually paid, as opposed to being a theoretical agreement that would never be fulfilled in practice.

The second type of void condition, marriage of one who is unsuitable, is not defined. Ibn Abd al-Wahhab simply stated that such a practice was forbidden (*haram*).[130]

The third type of void condition, *mut'ah* marriage, was forbidden by Ibn Abd al-Wahhab, even though the practice was generally known among the Companions and was practiced in some parts of the Muslim world. *Mut'ah* marriage was a pre-Islamic institution that survived among Shiis but was outlawed by Sunnis on the basis of numerous *hadith* and the belief that the stipulation of an end to the marriage rendered the marriage itself invalid.[131] Thus, Ibn Abd al-Wahhab considered invalid any conditions specifying either the date of the end of the marriage or that the marriage will end when the wife no longer fulfills the husband's needs.[132]

Ibn Abd al-Wahhab's opposition to *mut'ah* marriage was based on his dual concerns about the legalization of *zina'* according to the man's convenience and the denial of the rights of a valid marriage to the woman because none of the legal implications of a regular marriage—the right of the husband to repudiation (*talaq*) and its accompanying financial obligations toward his wife, the waiting period for the woman, or mutual inheritance rights—apply in the case of *mut'ah*. Consequently, he considered calling such an arrangement a farce. He understood *mut'ah* to be a means of legalizing sexual relations out-

side of marriage, thus encouraging licentiousness and discouraging social responsibility.[133]

The second type of invalid condition would be one that denies the woman
her rights in marriage. Ibn Abd al-Wahhab specifically forbade the man to
stipulate that the woman not receive her *mahr* or maintenance or to assign her
a *mahr* or level of maintenance that was less than what a woman of comparable
status should receive. He likewise forbade the man to prohibit his wife from
spending his money, thus making it clear that a wife is to have access to her
husband's financial resources.[134] However, the reverse is not true. The
woman's *mahr* and maintenance belong to her alone. She cannot be required
to provide for household expenses out of that which belongs to her. The husband is required to make these provisions. All of these prohibitions serve to
protect the woman's financial rights in marriage.[135]

Ibn Abd al-Wahhab forbade conditions prohibiting sexual intercourse between the husband and wife because such a condition violated the purpose of
marriage—the legalization of sexual intercourse and the production of children.[136] He recognized the importance of companionship and family time by
forbidding the man from stipulating that he would be physically separated from
the wife or only in her company at night or during the days but not at night.[137]
Clearly, a man should be available to his wife as much as possible in order to
promote marital harmony. This remains the case even in instances of a plural
marriage, whereby the husband is required to divide his time equally among
his wives. Ibn Abd al-Wahhab did not allow the man to assign all of his days
to one wife and all of his nights to another. He allowed only the woman to
decide to "give up" her days or nights to another. If the woman wished, Ibn
Abd al-Wahhab granted *her* the right to offer the man his days or nights as a
gift. The man had no right to seize them, even if it was to make peace with a
cowife.[138]

The third type of invalid condition is one stipulated by the husband that
falls outside that to which he is legally entitled if this stipulation would increase
his benefits or advantages over the wife. This prohibition underscores Ibn Abd
al-Wahhab's broad theme of gender balance in rights, so that neither spouse
holds exclusive or greater power over the other. In a male-dominated society,
men would clearly have expected to play the more powerful role within the
family. By setting limits on what the husband could stipulate of his wife outside
of the basic responsibilities of marriage, Ibn Abd al-Wahhab sought to curb
what he perceived to be abuses of women in marriage and to protect their
financial interests and rights. By allowing women to stipulate conditions in the
marriage contract to their own benefit without allowing men to do the same,
he placed greater power in the hands of the wife, at least in theory. This hardly
fits the typical misogynistic portrayal of Ibn Abd al-Wahhab and the Wahhabis.

Examples of invalid conditions unfairly increasing the husband's benefits include the husband stipulating that the wife not receive her *mahr* until some-time after the marriage is consummated. Ibn Abd al-Wahhab believed that this was such a serious violation of the woman's rights that he declared the marriage itself, as well as the condition, to be invalid.[139] Along the same lines, he did not allow the man to stipulate that the woman not receive any *mahr* at all or that she forfeit her right to maintenance. He allowed for only one exception to this rule: the case in which the man was impoverished at the time of the marriage and the woman was aware of his financial status and consented to the marriage anyway. In such a case, he held that the woman had no right to demand maintenance because her demand came after the fact of the marriage.[140] Other than this, he held that payment of *mahr* and maintenance to the woman are absolutely required, with no exceptions.

Interestingly, Ibn Abd al-Wahhab did not allow the man to stipulate that the woman be a virgin. If the man made such a stipulation and then found that the woman had been deflowered, Ibn Abd al-Wahhab did not allow the man to withdraw from the marriage by demanding that it be invalidated.[141] He denied the man this option because it does not meet any of the eight short-comings that are accepted as criteria for the invalidation of a marriage.[142] His stance on this issue again serves to protect the rights of the woman. Invalidation of the marriage would not only mean the loss of the *mahr* for the woman, but she would also lose her right to maintenance, inheritance, and the legitimacy of any child born of the union. Because presumably the only way for the husband to determine whether the woman is a virgin is through sexual intercourse, the woman has already given what is required of her in marriage, regardless of her status as a virgin or a deflowered woman. The end result is the same: following the consummation, the woman is necessarily deflowered. Ibn Abd al-Wahhab's refusal to allow the husband to demand that the marriage be invalidated on the basis of the wife's nonvirginity means that the woman's financial rights remain intact. She is still entitled to her *mahr* and maintenance. She also remains the man's heir, and any child born to her as a result of the consummation is legitimate in the eyes of Islamic law. The man, of course, retains the option of divorcing her, but the woman's financial rights again remain intact during her waiting period (*iddah*). Ibn Abd al-Wahhab's position here is consistent with his protection of women's rights in general and his opposition to practices like *mut'ah* marriage, which are designed to give a facade of legitimacy to sexual intercourse without requiring the man to fulfill the financial obligations that are intended to accompany it.

The only stipulations by the man that Ibn Abd al-Wahhab recognized as valid were that the woman be beautiful (specified here as not being ugly in the sense of misshapen), that she not be too close of kin, and that the she not be the daughter of people who are beneath him.[143] It is of interest that the three points addressed here were covered in the prior discussions by Ibn Abd al-Wahhab about what is and is not permissible and required in contracting a marriage. His discussions specify ways in which these three conditions are to be avoided prior to contracting the marriage. Allowing the man to look at the woman, for example, would resolve the question of whether she is beautiful or misshapen. The clear prohibitions against kin of certain relations should guide the man in selecting a potential wife. The requirement of equality between the spouses and the necessity of the woman's marriage guardian contracting the marriage should give the man some indication of her status prior to the marriage. Thus, granting the man the right to make these stipulations was more a matter of assuring that he selected an appropriate bride than a matter of granting him greater power in the marriage.

Ibn Abd al-Wahhab consistently held the men responsible for any problems resulting in the contracting of the marriage because they were responsible for it. In a case in which the woman is blind, mute, or deaf, circumstances that are typically grounds for dissolution of the marriage according to the other law schools, Ibn Abd al-Wahhab allowed dissolution of the marriage *only* if the woman was found to be responsible for not informing the future husband of her state prior to the marriage. If the husband found out only after the fact and through no fault of the wife, Ibn Abd al-Wahhab did not allow the man to demand that the marriage be invalidated. The reason for this is the same as the reason for not allowing dissolution of a marriage to a virgin: "If virginity does not exist in her there is nothing for him, and the virginity he took from her is greater than menstruation (*haydh*) and jumping (*wathbah*) and spinsterhood/aging (*ta'nis*) and the carrying of a heavy burden (*haml al-thaqil*)."[144] That is, the man owes the woman some recompense for having taking her virginity.

The most striking point in all of these discussions of invalid conditions is that Ibn Abd al-Wahhab consistently and continually emphasized that the rights of the woman cannot be denied while severely restricting the stipulations that a man could make in contracting a marriage. He clearly assigned power in the process of making the contract to the *woman*, not the man. Because the man was already receiving the benefits of sexual intercourse, control over the woman's reproductive capacities, and the right to his wife's obedience through marriage, Ibn Abd al-Wahhab's stance was geared toward assurance that the woman be treated neither as a slave nor as an object for sale. By assuring her right to the financial consequences of marriage—*mahr* and maintenance—and by denying the man the right to demand that the marriage be invalidated except on extremely narrow grounds, he sought to guarantee that the woman would not be subject to destitution, despair, or abuse.

Imperfections in Marriage

As previously mentioned, there are some imperfections in either the husband or the wife that can render a marriage invalid.[145] However, imperfection in and of itself does not automatically invalidate a marriage. Thus, a man finding an imperfection in his wife does not have the right to return her to her marriage guardian on the basis of that imperfection alone.

Some imperfections are specific to men, some are specific to women, and some can apply to either spouse. For men, the inability to perform sexually, whether due to impotence or lack of proper equipment, is grounds for invalidation of the marriage. For women, lack of a hymen or a hymen that is so strong that it cannot be broken is grounds for invalidation of the marriage. In the case of either spouse, the presence of mutilation, leprosy, or insanity is grounds for invalidation of the marriage.[146]

The legal reasoning behind these imperfections relates to the important elements of sexual intercourse and reproduction that are critical components of marriage. If one partner is unable to fulfill the requirement of sexual intercourse for whatever reason, this is considered not only unfair to the spouse but an actual violation of the spouse's marital rights. If the purpose of marriage cannot be fulfilled, the marriage is to be declared invalid so that neither party will suffer injustice.[147]

Likewise, the ruling that disease, whether mental or physical, invalidates a marriage is designed to protect the spouse from injury and/or life-threatening illness. The focus in all cases is on protection of the "innocent" spouse rather than punishment of the one who is imperfect. Dissolution of the marriage is not always immediate, however. For example, if man appears to be impotent the dissolution of the marriage is to be postponed for a year in order to give the man time to overcome his physical difficulty. If during that time the man manages to have sex with his wife at least once, the condition of impotence is considered to be no longer existent and the grounds for dissolving the marriage disappear. Furthermore, such an annulment can only be declared by a judge (*hakim*), who is then responsible for demanding that the man pay the woman her *mahr* because both she and her marriage guardian were deceived in this matter.[148]

Again, it is clear that Ibn Abd al-Wahhab sought above all to protect the woman's rights in marriage so that, whether the marriage is declared valid or dissolved, she, as the innocent party, receives what is due her. Because the woman has experienced a "loss" in this marriage, she is entitled to seek restitution from her husband.[149] This again is in keeping with the understanding of justice that entitles one who has suffered a loss due to the actions of another to seek restitution from the wrongdoer. In the case of a dissolved marriage, the woman not only suffers humiliation, but it is assumed that she has attempted to fulfill her duties in the marriage bed. She is therefore entitled to compensation.

On Selecting a Wife

Ibn Abd al-Wahhab taught that selection of a wife should be based on several criteria and should be a carefully considered, and therefore somewhat lengthy, process. The emphasis he placed on the criteria for the selection of a wife indicates that marriage, like divorce, is a serious matter in Islam and is intended to last rather than being undertaken or ended on the spur of the moment. Criteria to be considered in the selection of a wife include verification that the woman is not forbidden to the man and the woman's beauty and character.

Ibn Abd al-Wahhab followed the classical prescriptions about who is permanently forbidden to whom in marriage, so there is little discussion of this topic outside of a brief mention of the prohibition of marriage between two people who directly shared a suckling relationship.[150]

Declarations of engagement provided him with an opportunity to address women who are forbidden in marriage on a temporary basis. For example, he prohibited the declaration of an engagement to a woman who is currently observing her waiting period (*iddah*) from another marriage or who is revocably divorced because a woman observing her *iddah* was still under her husband's jurisdiction and the woman who is revocably divorced could potentially be reclaimed by her husband.[151] He was less rigid with respect to a woman who has been irrevocably divorced by three *talaqs* or whose marriage has been annulled due to suckling or an accusation of *li'an* (unproven adultery). In such cases, he permitted intimation of betrothal to another man because the marriage had been irrevocably ended.[152]

The case of a woman who has been irrevocably divorced by other than the three *talaqs* or who has been divorced by *khul'* are less clear-cut.[153] Although Ibn Abd al-Wahhab believed that it was permissible to become engaged to such a woman because her former husband no longer had any claim to her, he still found it preferable that the man not be openly demonstrative or verbal about his intentions until she has completed her waiting period and is in a valid state for marriage.[154]

In general, public declarations of the intent to marry by other than the parties concerned were not permitted by Ibn Abd al-Wahhab without the express permission of the groom. In matters of engagement, he believed that a public declaration of the betrothal was "desirable," though not "required."[155] This is in keeping with his concern for the preservation of social order, as was previously indicated in his stance on the requirement that marriage be a public act. The announcement of the betrothal served to publicly declare that the woman was no longer available for marriage and pushed the man to declare his honorable intentions toward her.

The other criteria for selecting a wife, the questions of the woman's beauty and character, is particularly striking in Ibn Abd al-Wahhab's writings because they serve to assert the right of the prospective couple to meet and converse *prior* to any declaration of engagement or the actual contracting of the marriage. Ibn Abd al-Wahhab felt that the most effective way for a couple to know if they were compatible and to avoid issues such as mistaken brides, mismatched couples, and forbidden relationships was for the couple to meet face to face. The question of this meeting provided him with the opportunity to engage in a discussion about the broader issues of veiling and seclusion, which were of concern to the society of his time and remain a matter of contention today.

In addition to commenting that it is desirable for a man to choose a wife of the same religion (i.e., a Muslim) because that woman will bear his children, Ibn Abd al-Wahhab also noted that the woman should preferably be a virgin possessed of both a charitable nature and beauty.[156] In support of this position, he cited a *hadith* in which Muhammad was asked, "Which woman is good?" To this he responded, "The one who makes him happy when he looks at her."[157] The repetition of the importance of the woman's appearance in Ibn Abd al-Wahhab's writings is not an insistence on a woman's value resting solely in her beauty. Rather, it opens the door to a discussion about whether it is permissible for a man to look at the woman he wishes to marry. Given the emphasis on absolute gender segregation and full veiling manifested in contemporary Saudi Arabia, this topic is an important one in the consideration of permissible contact between men and women who are not as yet married or related to each other. What contact did Ibn Abd al-Wahhab allow and what was the basis for his determination?

First, he made a statement of legal doctrine: "We do not know any variation in permitting the looking at the woman for anyone desiring to marry her."[158] That is, after carefully examining the texts of the various law schools he found no basis for denying a man the right to look upon the woman he is considering marrying.[159] However, this looking was to be a relatively private matter between the prospective spouses in that the man should not disclose to anyone else what he has seen that is not normally visible or looked at by men not considering the woman as a potential marriage candidate.[160] While this should not be misconstrued as an opportunity for the couple to be completely alone in each other's company or the right of the man to view the woman in the nude prior to marriage, it nevertheless makes it clear that (1) the couple has the right to meet prior to entering into the marriage contract, and (2) the man has the right to look at his potential wife prior to marrying her. That said, Ibn Abd al-Wahhab launched into a discussion about what it is that the man has a right to view because it is clear that he has the right to view more than what would normally be exposed.

First, he outlined what is normally considered proper for *general* viewing—the face, the two hands/palms, and the two feet. He specifically focused on the general permissibility of seeing the woman's face—that is, viewing her face unveiled—by those not of her acquaintance.[161] As proof texts, he cited two *hadith* recording that Muhammad's Companion Abi Sufyan had "inspected" Umm Habibah when she appeared unveiled while the two of them were in the company of his friends. On this basis, he denied face veiling as a requirement for women. Covering of the hair was a different matter.

Although he did not consider a woman's hair to be permissible for general view, he did allow the prospective husband to see the woman's hair on the basis of Quran 24:58 and *hadith* supporting the right of the woman to leave her hair uncovered in the presence of her family.[162] Ibn Abd al-Wahhab concluded that it is not sinful for a man to view the hair of a woman he is considering marrying precisely because he is a potential future family member. He then went a step further by granting the future husband the right to look not only at the "isolation of the face" but also to view the potential wife's full head and legs/thighs, both of which would be permissible to show among family and men who are forbidden to her in marriage.[163] He did not consider this viewing to impugn the woman's honor. What he did was to restrict more extensive viewing to a situation in which there was a valid reason for doing so.

Although one could argue that such an inspection sounds as though it has more in common with the examination of horseflesh than it does with modern concepts of marriage partner selection, the point is that insistence on the couple not meeting at all prior to the signing of the marriage contract or not allowing the man to see any part of the woman at all prior to the wedding night is inconsistent with Ibn Abd al-Wahhab's teachings.[164] His writings reflect, above all, recognition of the practical need to determine compatibility of some sort between the future couple. Having the right to meet and see each other was to him one way to accomplish this goal.

Within his general discussion of meetings between potential marriage partners, Ibn Abd al-Wahhab made some distinctions between virgins and deflowered but unmarried women. In the case of the deflowered but unmarried woman, he permitted a potential husband to see her clothed but unveiled (including exposed extremities), provided that the clothing is not what she would normally wear in the privacy of her own home.[165] This more open view was not permitted in the case of a virgin.

He also distinguished between Muslim versus non-Muslim women, not because he believed that non-Muslim women were less worthy of respect but because their social customs and religious prescriptions were different.[166] Indeed, he declared that the Muslim man should treat a non-Muslim (*dhimmi*) woman with the same honor as he would a Muslim woman when seeking her hand in marriage.[167] In addition, he taught that both men and women should behave and dress respectfully in the presence of non-Muslim women. He charged the Muslim woman to behave modestly in the company of such women, respecting the veiling she would normally observe when out in public rather than the more relaxed norms that exist when Muslim women are in the company of other Muslim women. It is clear from the discussion that the purpose of respecting these norms was to demonstrate both modesty on the part of the Muslim woman and respect toward women of other faith traditions. Thus, even a non-Muslim woman is not to be viewed as a mere object for male desire. To emphasize this point, Ibn Abd al-Wahhab strictly forbade men from looking upon foreign women without a good reason, except for the face and the two hands, making it clear that the lack of a veil does not imply a lack of virtue or the presence of sexual promiscuity on the part of the woman.[168] The clear message is that men are responsible for controlling themselves and their carnal desires, regardless of whether the woman in question is veiled or un-veiled.

Although Ibn Abd al-Wahhab permitted some visibility between potential marriage partners, he was careful to maintain the woman's responsibility to dress modestly so as not to expose herself to unrelated men. However, this prescription was to be relevant only with respect to those men who could potentially experience carnal desire for her. Ibn Abd al-Wahhab was concerned that carnal appetites can be powerful if given free rein, potentially leading the man and woman into contemplation of satisfying them.[169] Having made it clear that marriage is the only legal means by which sexual desire can be fulfilled, he concluded this discussion by commanding women to veil in the presence of such men. The purpose was self-protection, particularly if a woman is beautiful.[170]

Ibn Abd al-Wahhab warned of the potential for chaos (*fitnah*) when the woman is beautiful. However, rather than placing the blame on her he defined *fitnah* as the state of anxiety and confusion that may be present in the heart of the man looking at her. He therefore held the *man* responsible for avoiding situations that could potentially result in his being in a state of *fitnah*. Specifically, he forbade the man from looking at a beautiful woman to whom he is neither related nor married, thus providing a mechanism enabling men to control their sexual desires and impulses. He did not place blame on the woman for inciting the man to lust or for tempting him, as is often the case in both historical and contemporary conservative writings that insist on the full veiling of women.[171] His assertion that the social order was the responsi-bility of both genders provided a gender-balanced vision of society.

This gender-balanced vision is also reflected in his recognition that both men and women experience carnal desire, so both genders are held responsible for avoiding situations that might incite such desire. Thus, just as he forbade men to look at women they were not considering marrying, he forbade women to look at male visitors in their homes who are not there for the express purpose of seeking to marry them.[172] Because visual contact can result in lust on the part of the observing party and because both men and women are considered actors and initiators in the quest to satisfy desire, both parties are to be re-stricted from excessive viewing of the other.[173]

The critical factors in determining whether or not a man should generally remain apart from a woman are whether he has reached the age of discernment and whether he experiences carnal desire.[174] Similarly, an old woman who possesses no lust or desire is not as strictly bound by the rules of modesty as a younger woman because there is no harm in looking at what is normally visible to the majority. A very young girl (a baby or toddler) is also exempt from veiling requirements, and it is perfectly permissible for a man to hold her in his arms or on his lap and be friendly with her whether he is related or not. It is only when the man experiences carnal desire that he is to refrain from the presence of such young girls. Generally speaking, it is only when the girl reaches maturity, that is, that which marks her as appropriate for marriage (menstruation), that a man who could potentially marry her should refrain from her company.[175]

It is of interest that Ibn Abd al-Wahhab consistently placed the responsibility for control of social behavior and preservation of modesty on the one who is actually experiencing the desire, whether male or female. That is, the person who would potentially be experiencing the carnal desire is the one who is responsible for removing himself or herself from the company of the opposite sex. Lack of reproductive capacity is not the determining criterion in matters of keeping company. Rather, the issue is carnal desire and the possibility of illicit sexual activity, regardless of whether it could lead to pregnancy.[176]

At the same time, Ibn Abd al-Wahhab recognized that there were legitimate instances outside of marriage considerations in which unrelated men and women might meet. These included business transactions in which the woman is selling something and situations in which a woman is in need of assistance, sanctuary, or medical care to be provided by a male physician. In the case of medical treatment he asserted that not only is it permissible for the woman to uncover whatever part of her is in need of treatment, so that the doctor can perform his duties, but she is *commanded* to do so, in accordance with the prophetic example.[177] This teaching reflected Ibn Abd al-Wahhab's belief that the preservation of human life is a higher priority than the preservation of female modesty.[178]

On the broader question of appropriate dress for a Muslim woman in general, Ibn Abd al-Wahhab issued a *fatwa* in response to some questions by a petitioner about some minute details of women's dress. Is it necessary to prevent the appearance of carnal appetites that result from the way in which a woman is dressed? When the woman is to dress for her wedding, is the man responsible for clothing her prior to her entering his home or is he only responsible for her clothing once she is there? What is the proper way for a woman's clothing to be closed—should it be buckled once at the top, once in the center, and once at the bottom or should it be more elaborate? When the woman is to dress before leaving a place, is the husband responsible for dressing her? What about when she returns?[179]

Ibn Abd al-Wahhab's response is both entertaining and enlightening. Surely, if he was the extremist misogynist he is often made out to be, his response ought to have been highly detailed, admonishing women to keep themselves covered to the extreme. Instead, his response reflects a certain degree of exasperation with the questioner for going into such minute detail over a matter that is not covered in such a way in the Quran. Indeed, he said that anyone giving a legal opinion on such a matter must necessarily be citing a prior jurist because such matters have long been transmitted. Although he indicated his awareness of the existence of legal rulings on such matters, he did not express his accord with them or reiterate what had already been written. Instead, he stated that clothing and maintaining the wife are the responsibility of the husband and ended the discussion.[180] Thus, it is left to the husband, rather than an external party, to decide how his wife ought to dress.

The discussion contained in this *fatwa* potentially sheds some light on the social realities of the time in which Ibn Abd al-Wahhab lived. It has been posited that *fatawa* should be considered enlightening resources for historical study because they form the bridge between legal theory and lived human experience. *Fatawa*, rather than court records, reflect the changes taking place in doctrinal development as *muftis* were able to draw on their knowledge of legal theory while relying on their own interpretations through *ijtihad* to deliver opinions that were relevant and useful to members of their communities.[181] As opposed to court records, which provide the details of the case along with a judgment but without any explanation of the *qadi*'s thinking, *fatawa* tend to demonstrate the thinking process of the *mufti* by including relevant Quranic verses or *hadith*, the rulings of prior jurists on the topic,[182] and the legal mechanisms used to arrive at a conclusion.

Ibn Abd al-Wahhab's *fatwa* demonstrates not only that he was not a literalist in his interpretation of Islamic law and that he was not overly concerned with the minute details in the elaboration of that law, but also reflects his concern for determining and applying broad Quranic values in legal matters. This *fatwa* also serves as evidence of what types of issues related to gender were of concern to his immediate community: appropriate dress for a woman, the degree of control the husband is to exercise in the marriage, and whether women are responsible for inciting carnal desire in men. Through his responses, Ibn Abd al-Wahhab demonstrated his recognition of the responsibility of both genders to control their own carnal desires tempered by practical advice to women to dress modestly for their own protection. Thus, there is a balance in gender rights and responsibilities, as well as an emphasis on individual responsibility, in Ibn Abd al-Wahhab's construction of gender.

Responsibilities of Marriage

The act of marrying in Islam carries with it certain responsibilities for both parties. The wife is responsible for providing her husband with sexual intercourse, the reproduction of children, and obedience (nushuz).[183] However, the wife is not obligated to cook or bake bread.[184] The husband is required to provide his wife with sexual intercourse, a dower, and maintenance. Ibn Abd al-Wahhab's discussions of marriage included elaborations of these duties, which appear below.

Dower (Mahr)

Payment of the mahr to the bride is an absolute requirement of marriage in Islam, assigned directly and clearly by God in the Quran: "And lawful to you in addition to submitting to you that they [i.e., the women] seek from your property" (4:24) and "And give the women their dowers as a gift" (4:4). For Ibn Abd al-Wahhab, these verses were very clear in setting the mahr as an absolute requirement. Thus, the only question open to debate was the amount of the mahr because this is not specified in the Quran.[185]

Ibn Abd al-Wahhab noted that the amount of the mahr was a matter of considerable debate among both Muhammad's Companions and various jurists. The debate was an interpretational issue because Muhammad himself, in response to a question about the appropriate amount of the mahr, stated that the amount should be one gold piece.[186] The question was whether this prescription should be followed literally—all mahr should be one gold piece regardless of the status of the families in question, their geographical location, or the actual value of one gold piece—or whether the amount should be interpreted contextually by determining how much one gold piece was worth in that time and place and recalculating the mahr accordingly.

Having examined a variety of opinions,[187] Ibn Abd al-Wahhab concluded that no generic minimum or maximum should be set for the mahr. Instead, he believed that it should be a matter of negotiation for the couple and that a specific amount should be agreed on in the marriage contract.[188] Once the amount of the mahr has been agreed on, it cannot be changed.[189] The husband is absolutely required to pay the contracted mahr because this is what he promised the woman in exchange for her marrying him.[190]

From a legal perspective, Ibn Abd al-Wahhab taught that the agreed on mahr is to be considered a debt is owed to the wife.[191] This is the case even if the man dies prior to the consummation of the marriage. In such a case, the mahr is still owed to the woman because it has been promised to her, it was a condition of the marriage contract, and the fact that the marriage did not take place was due to no fault of hers. Had the man lived, his intent was to marry

the woman and consummate the marriage. His death should not be misconstrued as an indication of a change in his intent. Rather, it should be viewed
as an unintended interruption of the process of contracting the marriage. Ibn
Abd al-Wahhab held the man's estate responsible for the *mahr* in such a case
because of the man's intent, rejecting the more literalist approach of law
schools that ruled that the woman was not entitled to compensation for that
which she had not lost, that is, her virginity.[192] He did not allow for the nulli-
fication of the *mahr*, which had been negotiated according to intent, over a
legal technicality. In this way, he sought to protect the rights of women and
deny men, whether husbands or jurists, the right to override authentic *hadith*
in order to excuse themselves from their responsibilities toward women, even
if this was inconvenient or a customary social practice in their context.

It is interesting to note here that, although both *mahr* and sexual relations
can be considered to be the consequences of marriage, Ibn Abd al-Wahhab
was careful to distinguish between the two as legal issues because different
parties were empowered in each case. He noted that there are two types of
power of attorney over the woman: "proxy of the vulva" (*tafridh al-bidhah*) and
"proxy of the *mahr*." Proxy of the vulva indicates who has ultimate control over
the woman's sexuality—either the father who is giving his virgin daughter in
marriage or the woman who is giving herself in marriage via her consent.[193]
Proxy of the *mahr* is different because it does not take into account who is
contracting the marriage. Rather, it addresses what is appropriately due to the
woman as a result of the marriage taking place, thereby protecting her rights.

Ibn Abd al-Wahhab was aware that despite these regulations there remained men who tried to skirt their way around payment of the *mahr*. One
way that men tried to do this was by failing to specify the amount of the *mahr*.
Consistent with his concern for the financial rights of women, Ibn Abd al-
Wahhab stated unequivocally that failure to specify the amount of the *mahr*
does not excuse the man from his responsibility to pay it. In a case in which
the amount of the *mahr* is not specified prior to the contracting of the marriage,
the man is required to pay the "equivalent *mahr*," that is, the amount that
would be paid to a woman of similar status. Even if the husband chooses to
repudiate the woman after signing the marriage contract, he remains obligated
to pay her the *mahr*. Dissolution of the marriage does not cancel his debt to
her. Even in a case in which the marriage guardian was desperate to marry off
his ward and failed to specify the *mahr* as a means of disposing of her, Ibn
Abd al-Wahhab maintained that the woman remained entitled to the equivalent
mahr, even if she was "odious" or "offensive" and regardless of her status as a
virgin or deflowered but unmarried woman.[194] The *mahr* is always owed to the
woman, no matter how odious she might be.[195]

As to what the *mahr* should consist of, Ibn Abd al-Wahhab interpreted Q
4:24—"They seek from your property"—to mean that anything that the man
possesses is permissible for the *mahr*. Thus, the *mahr* is not restricted to cash

or gold. As an example, Ibn Abd al-Wahhab cited the manumission of a slave woman as a potential *mahr* because legally speaking the man was giving up a portion of his property by freeing her.[196]

It is significant that the Quran specifies the payment of the *mahr* to the woman rather than the traditional pre-Islamic dowry, which was paid to the woman's family in exchange for turning her over to the husband. Ibn Abd al-Wahhab was careful to maintain this distinction between *mahr* and dowry in order to protect the woman's rights. Perhaps in recognition of the continued practice of the marriage guardian claiming the woman's entire *mahr* for himself, he allowed for a compromise solution, supported by the *hadith*. He permitted the father of the woman to stipulate a *portion* of the dower for himself in exchange for marrying off his daughter. What is important is that only a portion, not the entire dower, can go to the father and this only when the father is acting as the woman's marriage guardian. Otherwise, the full dower was to go to the woman.[197] Furthermore, the father has this right only if he specifically stipulates it in the marriage contract, which implies that the woman would be aware of this condition and would have approved it prior to agreeing to the marriage. If it is not included as a stipulation in the contract, the father has no claim to the *mahr*. These specifications were clearly designed to prevent abuses that denied the woman the right to her *mahr* on marriage.

In the case of a slave, permission of the master is a prerequisite to marriage. If the slave who is marrying is male, the master is required to provide both the *mahr* and maintenance for the slave to provide to his wife.[198] Ibn Abd al-Wahhab's purpose in making this declaration was to demonstrate that payment of *mahr* and maintenance were not class issues. They are due to every woman, regardless of her status, and are required of every man, regardless of his. In this way, all Muslims are expected to fulfill the same obligations in matters of marriage.

Even in the case of divorce by repudiation, Ibn Abd al-Wahhab asserted that the wife has an absolute right to her *mahr* if the marriage has been consummated. If the marriage has not been consummated, she is entitled to half the *mahr*.[199] This is in accordance with the Quranic prescription (2:236) that the man owes the woman a "consolation gift" in order to appease her for her loss. If the *mahr* was not specified, the woman is entitled to half of the equivalent *mahr*.[200] Here, again, he made it clear that no woman is to be punished financially for the failure of the marriage prior to consummation. Citing the support of six Quranic verses and five *hadith*, he allowed no conditions, stipulations, or exceptions to this regulation.[201]

Ibn Abd al-Wahhab taught that the woman loses her right to *mahr* in only one case: when the marriage is imperfect (*fasid*) and the couple is separated prior to consummation.[202] If the couple has consummated the marriage by the time the imperfection is discovered, the woman is entitled to her *mahr*, either what was designated in the contract or the equivalent, because she retains the right to compensation for that which was lost through sexual intercourse, regardless of the marriage's status.[203]

In an interesting twist to the discussion of *mahr* and marriage, Ibn Abd al-Wahhab took on the problematic question of rape (*ightisab*). Islamic law recognizes rape as a crime of property usurpation in which a person's right to use his or her own body is violated, thus entitling the victim to compensation for the loss in much the same way that a loss of limb entitles the victim to compensation.[204] Ibn Abd al-Wahhab's recognition of rape as a legal crime is significant because it opposes the increasingly common practice in the contemporary era of denying rape as a legal category. In some countries today, rape is considered to be a form of *zina'*, or illicit sexual intercourse, that, while theoretically carrying punishment for both parties, in practice is usually applied only to the woman.[205] Ibn Abd al-Wahhab, on the other hand, recognized the reality of forced intercourse and, typical of his protective stance toward women, insisted that the man compensate the woman for her loss in the form of *mahr*. His legal reasoning is quite instructive.

He began by commenting that *zina'* is a despicable act for which the *man* always bears responsibility. However, the *woman* should not always be held accountable for her participation in *zina'* because it may have been forced. If she was forced, Ibn Abd al-Wahhab taught that the woman is entitled to *mahr* from her rapist as "the blood money of virginity."[206] This choice of words indicates legal recognition that the woman suffers an amputation of sorts through the act of rape and therefore she is entitled to compensation for that part of herself that she has lost, especially if she was a virgin. This legality is apparent in Ibn Abd al-Wahhab's reference to the loss of virginity as a kind of "cutting up" or "amputation" necessitating compensation, setting the legal precedent for the consideration of *mahr* as blood money.[207]

It is significant that Ibn Abd al-Wahhab did not restrict the right to compensation in rape cases to Muslim women. Rather, he taught that *any* woman who is the victim of forced sexual intercourse, whether Muslim or foreign, is entitled to the equivalent *mahr* of one of her status.[208] This declaration made it clear that men never have the right to coerce women into sexual intercourse. If they do, they will not only be punished for having committed *zina'*, but they will also be required to compensate the victim for her loss. In this way, he upheld justice and the protection of the rights of all women.

Having established the absolute right of the woman to her *mahr*, Ibn Abd al-Wahhab turned to the practical issue of when payment of the *mahr* is to take place. This issue was important because there were occasions when the amount of the *mahr* was specified but payment either did not take place or occurred only in part.[209] Because the timing of the payment of the *mahr* was not consistent during the lifetime of Muhammad,[210] Ibn Abd al-Wahhab concluded that there was no absolute requirement that payment of the *mahr* precede consummation, although at least the declaration of the husband's intent to pay it is required.[211]

Calculation of Maintenance (Nafaqah)

In a Muslim marriage, the husband is responsible for providing his wife with maintenance (*nafaqah*), which includes, but is not limited to, food, clothing, and shelter for the duration of the marriage and during the waiting periods following a divorce by *talaq* or the death of the husband. Similar to the *mahr*, Ibn Abd al-Wahhab taught that the fact of maintenance is an absolute requirement of the marriage. Only the amount is open to negotiation.[212]

Maintenance was not the prerogative of the wife alone. Ibn Abd al-Wahhab also required the husband to provide maintenance for his minor children, both male and female. He further required the man to provide maintenance for his father, mother, or grown children if they were poor and he had the means to do so.[213] Need rather than age was the determining criterion in Ibn Abd al-Wahhab's assignment of maintenance payments, underscoring the notion of parenting as a lifelong responsibility rather than one that ends with the boy reaching maturity or the girl being married.[214] He extended the obligation to pay maintenance to include any heir of the man's estate if that heir is poor, although this responsibility was limited to paternal relatives[215] and *mamluk* slaves (slave soldiers).[216] Reasoning that the heir would eventually have a claim on the inherited property, Ibn Abd al-Wahhab granted the heir the right to the property during the lifetime of the man in the event of poverty. By doing so, he upheld the broader Quranic principles of justice and social responsibility rather than strict chronological adherence to Islamic law.

Ibn Abd al-Wahhab taught that maintenance should be calculated according to the financial state of the husband and wife together.[217] He cited as proof texts Q 2:233, in which God commands the husband to provide for and clothe his wife and children, and Muhammad's admonition to husbands to observe what is sufficient for a person of similar status and to provide the same for his own family according to convention. He believed that the reasoning behind these admonitions was to require that the man provide for his family in a manner befitting their social status but not to place hardship upon him by requiring more than what he was capable of paying. Thus, he ruled that if both parties are wealthy the husband should pay his wife the maintenance due to a wealthy woman, such as hiring a domestic servant if the woman had not worked prior to the marriage.[218] If both parties are in the middle, the husband should pay his wife the maintenance due to a woman of middle income. If only one of the two of them is wealthy, he required only the maintenance of a middle income.[219]

In the event that the husband fails to pay the wife maintenance appropriate to her status, Ibn Abd al-Wahhab granted the wife the right to take what she needs from the husband's property without seeking his permission. If the cause for the husband's failure to provide appropriate maintenance is the husband's poverty, he gave the wife two choices: either persevere in the marriage and endure a lower level of maintenance than what is due her or be separated from him.[220] In support of this declaration, he cited Q 2:229, which commands the husband to hold fast to what is conventional and kind and to dismiss his wife out of benevolence. In his opinion, the husband's failure to pay his wife maintenance violates the Quranic injunction to fairness, regardless of the reason behind the failure.[221] Furthermore, because the payment of maintenance is one of the husband's responsibilities in marriage, his failure to do so violates the marriage contract, thus giving the woman the right to seek an end to the marriage.[222] In such a case, the man had the option of either paying the wife the back maintenance owed and continuing in the marriage or divorcing the wife by *talaq*, guaranteeing her the financial rights of this kind of divorce, as well as the back maintenance owed. In either case, the back maintenance remained a debt owed by the husband to the wife.[223]

Ibn Abd al-Wahhab strengthened this teaching by declaring that the husband's failure to pay the maintenance did not cancel the woman's right to it. Because maintenance is the absolute right of the wife, he taught that any unpaid maintenance was to be considered a financial debt owed to the wife that could not be avoided or excused. Furthermore, he did not allow for the husband's other financial debts to be paid out of the wife's maintenance money. Thus he upheld the absolute right of the wife to maintenance, regardless of changes in the husband's financial status.[224]

The Wedding Banquet

The inclusion of this topic in Ibn Abd al-Wahhab's discussion of marriage may seem somewhat out of place because it addresses a social custom, rather than a Quranic injunction, and it is not typically understood to be a requirement of marriage. In fact, legal discussions of the wedding banquet are very rare, even in the Hanbali tradition, despite the emphasis given to the need to publicize a marriage and the general prohibition against secret marriage.[225] The fact that Ibn Abd al-Wahhab included a discussion of the wedding banquet reflects his recognition of the broader social dimensions of marriage and his assertion that marriage, as a contract, is a community affair rather than a strictly private arrangement involving only the bride, the marriage guardian, and the groom.

Ibn Abd al-Wahhab began his discussion by noting that, regardless of what the majority of jurists think about it, the reality is that wedding feasts are present in the Sunna and Muhammad commanded that they take place. Therefore, he asserted that not only are wedding feasts permissible but they are to be publicly announced and should serve as a "joyful/delightful occasion" with plenty of food.[226] The imagery in this passage provides a sharp contrast to the typical portrayal of the Wahhabis as austere and puritan in their approach to life, forbidding music, the wearing of silk, and just about every other popular social custom or occasion. Ibn Abd al-Wahhab's portrayal of the wedding feast conveys a sense of joy and community building, demonstrating that feasting and joyful celebration are not anathema to his interpretation of Islam but rather constitute an important element of living out one's faith.

Ibn Abd al-Wahhab found strong religious purpose in the wedding feast because it served as an opportunity for community building and carrying out the message of social justice proclaimed by the Quran and Sunna. It was a time for asserting the life-affirming message of the Quran, which proclaims marriage as the preferred state for all believers. Therefore, what he denounced in the typical practice of wedding feasts was not their occurrence but the fact that they were typically closed to the broader community and simply served as an opportunity for the wealthy to congratulate themselves and engage with others of similar social status.[227] Because Muhammad himself had taught that "The evil of food is the food of the banquet to which the rich have been invited and the poor excluded, and anyone whom it is not necessary to invite," Ibn Abd al-Wahhab asserted that in order for a wedding feast to be legal all must be invited, regardless of status. The wedding feast should be thought of as an opportunity to share with the less fortunate rather than an occasion for boasting.[228]

He then outlined certain rules of etiquette to be followed by the Muslim attending wedding banquets. First, no invitation should be left unanswered. Second, one should always respond in the affirmative whenever possible, even if one is observing a fast. While there is no requirement that one has to eat while at the feast, attendance is preferable. A person observing a supererogatory fast, that is, one that exceeds the requirements of Islamic law, can either break or uphold it according to personal preference. Breaking the fast is required only when the purpose of the person fasting is to proclaim his or her piety to the rest of the community—an act that negates its religious validity.[229]

Ibn Abd al-Wahhab's reasoning behind accepting the invitation is that attendance demonstrates an act of communal solidarity. Therefore, acceptance is not so much about whether one wishes to eat as it is about participating in communal life. This is why a length of time one must stay at the feast is not stipulated. What matters is putting in an appearance. Once one has appeared at the event, there is no requirement to stay or participate further in the festivities.[230]

The third rule of proper etiquette was that a written response to the wedding feast invitation should be sent. Fourth, guests are to conduct themselves properly and avoid sinful behavior. The topic of sinful behavior is addressed in a question about whether it is appropriate to invite a man with effeminate behavior or who is known to be bisexual. The response is that the invitation remains appropriate, as does the man's acceptance, but that it is incumbent on the man to control himself and avoid sin in fulfilling his communal responsibilities.[231]

This is a particularly interesting discussion because it reflects several points. First, the man with the effeminate behavior or bisexual preferences is not to be ostracized. Whatever his sins, he is still considered to be a member of the community and worthy of receiving an invitation. Second, the man is responsible for controlling his sexual urges and behaving appropriately at the wedding feast. It is not anyone else's job to police him. Third, Muslims are not to live in fear of those whose behavior is considered to be sexually deviant, but they are to continue to reach out to such people and try to include them in communal life. While this does not serve as a license for people to behave in a sinful manner and expect that everyone should accept them, it does emphasize the responsibility of the Muslim community to reach out to all of its members and remind them that they are part of a greater whole.

Although it is not stated as an absolute requirement, it is apparent in Ibn Abd al-Wahhab's discussion that those who are invited are expected to contribute to the celebration in some way. He specifically mentioned that items that are brought in order to provide entertainment, such as tambourines, are not to be returned to the person who brought them.[232] Likewise, guests should not abscond with things that are specific to the feast, such as sugar and almonds.[233] The fact that he specifically approved the use of tambourines at wedding feasts negates the claim that Wahhabis are opposed to all forms of music, including the use of the tambourine. This narrative makes it clear that tambourines and music have an appropriate time and place for use, even among Wahhabis.[234] Wedding feasts are one of those instances.

Ibn Abd al-Wahhab also approved the use of tambourines in making knowledge of the marriage public.[235] In fact, he not only allowed the use of the tambourine for this purpose, but he actually recommended that it be used *by women*. That is, he specifically declared it permissible for women's voices to publicly proclaim the fact of the marriage. In addition, he permitted the recitation of love poetry and the mingling of guests at the wedding feast.[236]

The celebratory, life-affirming nature of the marriage feast is made very clear in Ibn Abd al-Wahhab's discussion. It is supposed to be a time of joyful celebration in which activities that otherwise might not be permissible are allowed. Even women, music, and love poetry have very public roles to play in marriage celebrations. These points cannot be overemphasized, as they portray a very different picture of women's participation in communal life than what is typically imagined with respect to Wahhabi practices.

Another striking point in Ibn Abd al-Wahhab's discussion of the wedding feast has to do with whether decorations are appropriate. Ibn Abd al-Wahhab asserted, on the authority of Muhammad, that it is not only permissible but appropriate to decorate the walls and floors of the area where the feast takes place in order to honor the bride.[237] This teaching is significant because it places a woman in the seat of honor, recognizing her important role in family life. It stands in sharp contrast to the opponents of decorations, most notably Abu Hurayrah, who "despised" the practice precisely because they were prepared for the bride's honor and amusement. Ibn Abd al-Wahhab's support for honoring the bride reflects his favor for communal celebrations of life-affirming events and his recognition of the central role of women in such affairs.

The discussion of decorations continued with a discussion of what kinds are permissible. Ibn Abd al-Wahhab considered representations of living creatures to be one of the most questionable types. He generally discouraged the representation of human beings because he feared that people might be mistakenly led into worshiping them, as had occurred in the past with representations of people by their graves. However, in his discussion of the wedding feast he was careful to assure guests that they need not fear that they are committing sinful acts simply by entering a place where representations are present. He stated that it is not forbidden to enter an apartment where representations or illustrations are present because historical precedents for this exist.[238]

This does not mean that he encouraged the practice of hanging representations. Consistent with the rest of his theological writings, he noted that in general it is preferable not to have representations hanging about. Where they exist, it is preferable to cover them with a curtain or veil so that they are not generally visible.[239] This discussion recalls his theological teaching that representations become problematic only when they are misused. Thus, it is the prevention of their misuse that is incumbent on the Muslim, not necessarily their complete and total prohibition. At the same time, he distinguished between representations and entertainment, teaching that entertainment is not problematic.[240]

A discussion of the wedding feast would not be complete without some mention of food. Ideally, the wedding banquet should take place at the time of the signing of the marriage contract.[241] Although serving a sheep is always nice, it is not required.[242] Guests are supposed to mingle with the family, and it is recognized that some people will eat more than others. Food is to be served freely, with no restrictions as to what food is to be served to whom. All guests are to be treated as equals and should have equal access to the food provided. Table manners are discussed, indicating that guests are to behave with respect. Meat can be cut with a knife. Guests should eat with their right hands from the food placed on the right. Three fingers are to be used when eating, and one should lick one's hand prior to wiping it off. One should never eat while seated, and one should always eat everything that is set before one. Finally, it is despicable to find fault with the food—one should never criticize what is served.[243]

It is clear that Ibn Abd al-Wahhab believed in the joyous and full celebration of marriage, making it a community affair in every sense of the word rather than simply a private matter between two individuals. Having addressed the communal aspect of marriage, he then turned to the more intimate question of the marital relationship between husband and wife.

Relations between Husband and Wife

Ibn Abd al-Wahhab recognized that married life is more than a matter of who is supposed to pay for what and who is entitled to what rights. There is another, more personal, dimension of marriage, which is the actual relationship between husband and wife as they live together from day to day. Ibn Abd al-Wahhab taught that the Quran provides guidance in the personal relationship of marriage, as well as the legal obligations.

First, he noted that the Quran commands men to live in kindness and equity with women (Q 4:19 and 2:228). Men are not entitled to abuse their wives, physically or emotionally, by demonstrating dislike.[244] Ibn Abd al-Wahhab associated this responsibility not to abuse with the man's legal and social obligation to set a positive example. That is, because the man enjoys superior rights in marriage (an absolute right to divorce his wife), his behavior should reflect a superior benevolent treatment of those who are in his charge, namely, his wife or wives, so that his rights do not translate into an abuse of power. Lest there be any doubt as to how this should be done, Ibn Abd al-Wahhab commanded both husband and wife to smile and be cheerful with each other, to not seek to damage or annoy the other, to not make dislike of the other obvious, and to protect each other. He believed that this was the "kindness" in marriage commanded by God.[245]

It is clear from this description that unlimited and unconditional access to sex is not what is meant by "kindness" on the part of the wife. Although he taught that the husband certainly has the right to enjoyment and pleasure from his wife, this was not to be done in such a way as to distract the wife from her religious duties or cause any sort of damage or harm to her.[246] By phrasing it in this way, Ibn Abd al-Wahhab asserted that, although the right to sexual intercourse is an important component of marriage, the wife does not enter into sexual slavery through it. The fact that the wife is not obligated to engage in any sexual activity that harms her in any way or interferes with her religious duties indicates that even sexual intercourse is subject to some sort of negotiation process and that the kindness commanded for marriage generally is particularly important in the marriage bed.

Ibn Abd al-Wahhab provided several guidelines for when and where sexual activity should occur in order to maintain sex as a private matter between the spouses. Although the fact of the marriage is to be a public matter, he believed that what goes on between the husband and the wife privately is not. Thus, he forbade the man from sexually touching or having sex with his wife near other people. Sexual activity in the public realm was inappropriate in his opinion. Furthermore, he stated that the man should not have sex with his wife in such a manner that the "sensation" of either of them is audible. The man should not even talk about what occurs between the two of them in the marriage bed.[247] All of these prescriptions preserve the woman's modesty by keeping sex out of the public realm, while asserting the need for the husband to treat his wife with respect both in public and in private.

Ibn Abd al-Wahhab further underscored the right of the husband and wife to privacy by including in this discussion a reminder that the husband does not have the right to combine two women within a single dwelling or house except by their agreement.[248] Here, again, he placed the power of decision making about sexual and housing matters in the hands of the women, not the men. Because cowives have an absolute right to equal treatment, discussions about arrangements can take place only at the initiative of the wives.[249]

Equal treatment of co-wives includes the absolute right of each wife to sex with her husband. Ibn Abd al-Wahhab, in keeping with classical practice, set the maximum length of time between sexual relations at four days due to the man's legal right to have up to four wives. Logically, a man with four wives would need a four-day cycle in order to fulfill his responsibilities to each wife.

Ibn Abd al-Wahhab placed power in this matter in the hands of the woman by declaring that only the wife can release the husband from his obligation to spend the night with her. The man cannot withhold himself from this duty. The only exception to this rule occurs when the man marries a new wife. If the new wife is a virgin, the man has the right to spend seven consecutive nights with her. If she is not a virgin, he has the right to only three consecutive nights. The wife can forfeit her right to sex with her husband if she refuses to travel with him or spend the night with him or if she travels without him and without his permission. In these cases, it is clear that the wife has chosen to make herself unavailable to her husband. Because she is denying him his rights as a husband, she therefore forfeits her own.[250]

Ibn Abd al-Wahhab's theme of placing power in the hands of the woman with respect to sexual matters is also apparent in his placing limitations on the man's right to demand sex while highlighting the rights of the woman. First, he forbade the husband of a free woman to "cut her off," that is, refrain from sex with her, unless she authorizes him to do so. Second, he required the man to spend one night out of every four with his wife.[251] The husband has the option of being by himself the other three nights, but once every four nights he must share his wife's bed.[252] This prescription makes it clear that the husband is not in total control over the couple's sexual life. Rather, both partners have a right to sex within a set time period.

The wife's right to sex with her husband does not cease to exist due to his absence. If the husband travels for more than six months, the wife has the right to join him permanently, provided that this does not cause any harm to the husband. Ibn Abd al-Wahhab's concern here was that temptation was likely to arise on both sides during such a lengthy separation.²⁵³ In order to avoid a potentially sinful situation, the husband and wife need access to each other. Thus, he placed a maximum limit on the amount of time that the couple could reasonably be expected to spend apart.

Furthermore, sex, like the marriage itself, is to be a matter of negotiation for the couple. The woman should not be pressed for sex more often than she is capable of fulfilling her duties. Likewise, the man should not weaken or exhaust his body by engaging in too much sexual activity, meaning that the wife cannot force the man to spend nights outside of her calculated times with her. Thus, neither party has the right to be excessive in his or her demands of the other in sexual matters.²⁵⁴ Gender balance in rights and responsibilities applies even in this most intimate of relationships as a protection to both spouses.

Because sex is such an important, though not the only, component of marriage, questions often arose about what to do in a case in which one partner refuses to fulfill his or her sexual duties. The wife's refusal to grant her husband sexual relations is typically referred to in legal literature as *nushuz*, meaning that she has not fulfilled her marital duties. A *nushuz* wife, in practice, opens herself up to discipline by the husband. In many countries, this assertion is used to legitimate a culture of domestic violence.²⁵⁵

It appears from Ibn Abd al-Wahhab's discussion that domestic violence was also a problem in his time. He went to some length in his discussion of how the husband is to respond to a *nushuz* wife. He wrote, "If there appears from her indications of *nushuz*, in that she does not respond to him for pleasure/enjoyment or she responds to him with unwillingness or reluctance, he should admonish her. And if she persists he should part company with her. And if she still persists he should strike her *other than violently/intensely/excruciatingly*, that is, *other than forcefully*, according to the saying of the Most High: 'And those women from whom you fear disobedience then admonish them' Q 4:34 the verse."²⁵⁶

Ibn Abd al-Wahhab did not look to a literal interpretation of the Quran in this discussion. Yes, the Quran does give the man the right to strike his wife, but Ibn Abd al-Wahhab placed it in context here by emphasizing the chronology in which events must unfold in order for a blow to be permissible and then allowing this *only* when the wife is refusing sexual relations with her husband. His careful definition of the term *nushuz* meant that it could not be applied outside of sexual matters. Therefore, a wife's disobedience to her husband's

WOMEN AND WAHHABIS 171

commands about something other than sex could not be considered *nushuz* and thus was not subject to the same admonition and punishment.[257]

Ibn Abd al-Wahhab's insistence on a specific chronology of events recognized that there are other methods of dealing with a wife who does not wish to fulfill her marital duties and that these must be undertaken first—verbal admonishment and physical separation. The blow, then, becomes a method of last resort to be used only when the other avenues have failed. Even then, Ibn Abd al-Wahhab went to great lengths to emphasize that the authorization to strike is not a license for committing violence against one's wife, nor does it make domestic violence a religious prescription or right. Rather, the purpose of the blow is to emphasize the admonition, not the man's physical strength or power over his wife.[258]

This recognition of the apparent tendency for men to abuse their Quranic right here led Ibn Abd al-Wahhab to severely limit the ways in which men were permitted to act toward their wives. In keeping with his general recognition of gender balance in terms of rights and responsibilities, he concluded his discussion by recognizing that women are not the only ones who can be *nushuz*. Men can also be considered *nushuz* if they neglect their marital duties. Ibn Abd al-Wahhab thus noted that the Quran also provided for the woman ways in which she could admonish her husband for his commission of *nushuz* so that they can reach some sort of mutual agreement.[259]

Throughout his discussion, Ibn Abd al-Wahhab made it clear that both husbands and wives have the right to sexual fulfillment in marriage. Neither party holds a monopoly on this right, and neither has absolute control over it. Sex, like the marriage contract itself, is a matter of negotiation for the couple within certain legal boundaries.

Ending a Marriage

Islamic law recognizes two means by which a marriage may be brought to an end: divorce and the death of either spouse. The Quran specifies three possible types of divorce: divorce initiated by the husband (*talaq*), divorce initiated by the wife (*khul'*), and divorce due to the husband's unsubstantiated accusation that his wife has committed adultery (*li'an*). Historically, men have wielded the most power in matters of divorce because they are not required to offer a reason for repudiating their wives. The woman's right to divorce by *khul'* has been more limited. Ibn Abd al-Wahhab's discussion of both types of divorce argues that the fact that the Quran grants the right of divorce to both parties reflects the gender balance present throughout the Quran. His discussion of divorce therefore gives more power than was traditionally allotted to the woman to request divorce in order to allow her to exercise her God-given right.

Repudiation or Divorce by the Man (Talaq)

Talaq is the legal mechanism by which a man may divorce his wife. It is simply a declaration by the man that he repudiates his wife. Despite the apparent simplicity of divorce by *talaq*, it is a serious matter in Islam and is not to be practiced lightly. Ibn Abd al-Wahhab noted that permission for the man to divorce his wife was granted according to necessity. Thus, he taught that if divorce occurs other than out of necessity, defined as a case in which the continuation of the marriage would cause harm or damage to either party, it is to be despised.[260]

There are specific regulations surrounding repudiation by *talaq*, which are designed to ensure justice and rationality in carrying it out. First, *talaq* cannot occur during a woman's menstruation or the time period immediately following it when she is in the process of attaining ritual purity. This is regulated because it is recognized that the man could be declaring a *talaq* on the basis of sexual frustration because his wife is not sexually available to him during menstruation and times of ritual uncleanliness. Prohibiting *talaq* during such a time is designed to prevent a frivolous declaration of that would later be regretted, underscoring its seriousness.

Second, once the *talaq* has been declared, the man should not leave his wife until she has completed her waiting period. The waiting period is set at the completion of three menstrual cycles. If the husband wishes to irrevocably divorce his wife, he must declare a *talaq* between each cycle, totaling three. Upon the third *talaq*, the divorce becomes irrevocable and the woman is forbidden to the man. This process is the one commanded by Muhammad and is designed to give the couple a period for reconciliaton prior to pronouncing the irrevocable divorce. This is the only method of divorce by *talaq* that Ibn Abd al-Wahhab recognized as valid.[261]

In order to validly declare a repudiation by *talaq*, the husband must have attained the age of reason. The father of the husband can demand that the son repudiate his wife by *talaq* only if his father is a just man. The husband must be considered mentally competent at the time of the declaration. Thus, for example, a *talaq* pronounced in a state of drunkenness is not valid.[262] Ibn Abd al-Wahhab compared the *talaq* declared in a state of drunkenness to prayers conducted in a state of drunkennness—neither one is valid, and both require repentance on the part of the man. He placed power in the hands of the woman in such a case—if she decides that the man has returned to her, the husband must accept this claim.[263] The critique of the man is subtle: had he not been drunk—a state of being that is forbidden in Islam—the situation would not have occured. By placing the power of witnessing solely in the hands of the other party to the matter, Ibn Abd al-Wahhab demonstrated the potential consequences of the man's failure to adhere to the precepts of his faith.

One of the most controversial divorce practices in the Muslim world is the custom of pronouncing all three *talaqs* at a single session rather than waiting for the legally required three menstrual cycles between pronouncements of divorce. Although many scholars have recognized such a practice as being an innovation (*bida'*), it has nevertheless been legally recognized historically and has been particularly practiced in Saudi Arabia. One of the most significant reforms of the twentieth century in some countries has been the outlawing of the triple *talaq* pronounced at a single session, counting it as only a single *talaq* regardless of how many times it was actually pronounced.[264]

When Ibn Abd al-Wahhab was asked for a legal ruling about this controversial practice, it was framed within the context of three *hadith* questioning the practice. In two of the cases, Muhammad himself denied the permissibility of such a practice; in the third case, the first two caliphs, Abu Bakr and Umar, denied it, stating that, "The three are one."[265] Interestingly, Ibn Abd al-Wahhab did not directly answer the question with a yes or no. Instead, he stated that this is a case in which the exercise of independent reasoning (*ijtihad*) would be inappropriate because all of the narrators came to the same conclusion, constituting consensus (*ijma'*) of the community, which is unchanging over time. He believed that attempting to create a divergence of opinion in such a case would be inappropriate because all three *hadith* make it very clear that this practice is *not* acceptable. For Ibn Abd al-Wahhab, anyone who contradicted Muhammad or opposed what he commanded was clearly in error and ought to be well noticed for it.[266]

Ibn Abd al-Wahhab's vehemence in denouncing the triple *talaq* pronounced at a single session was due to its legal implications. The triple *talaq* was not part of Muhammad's example. Rather, it was the work of a transmitter of *hadith* (*muhaddith*), who claimed, "I played/dallied with the Word of God and have a clearer vision of it than you."[267] To Ibn Abd al-Wahhab, this was clear evidence that the addition of the triple *talaq* was exactly that—an addition to the Sunna that rendered it impermissible. He even went so far as to say that it was not part of the authentic *hadith* and declared sinful and criminal anyone who claimed that it was.[268] This discussion makes clear the absolute authority that Ibn Abd al-Wahhab assigned to the Quran and Sunna and his rejection of any tampering with them.

Ibn Abd al-Wahhab emphasized the illegality of the triple *talaq* at a single session by requiring that a woman who is divorced in this manner be returned to her husband.[269] This was an important position because it departed from classical teachings, including those of Ahmad Ibn Hanbal, which "did not approve" of this practice, but nevertheless recognized it as valid.[270] Ibn Abd al-Wahhab's declaration that the wife should be returned to the husband in this case reflects his belief that only a single *talaq* had occurred. This was not intended as a punishment for the wife because when she was returned to her husband he was required to resume her financial maintenance. In addition, Ibn Abd al-Wahhab punished the husband by denying him the right to sexual intercourse with his wife until she had purified herself after two menstrual cycles. Only then did he permit the husband to either resume sexual relations with his wife or reiterate his pronouncement of *talaq*.[271] This allowed the wife to complete her religiously required waiting period while receiving maintenance and leaving the man in sexual limbo with her. In this way, Ibn Abd al-Wahhab emphasized the husband's responsibility to carry out his religious and legal duties properly while exempting the wife from punishment in instances in which she was not at fault.

The only method of divorce that Ibn Abd al-Wahhab accepted was the man's repudiation of his wife by *talaq* three times during a period of purity for her and this only if the man had refrained from sexual intercourse with her throughout that time period. Only then did the husband and wife become forbidden to each other.[272] He also adhered to the Quranic teaching, supported by numerous *hadith*, that a woman who has been repudiated by her husband three times must have been married to another and then either divorced or widowed after consummation before she can be legally married by the first husband again.[273]

On the question of the appropriate response to a man who makes an oath of divorce (*hilf al-talaq*), Ibn Abd al-Wahhab taught that any man who lied about his wife or made false charges against her should retire from her. This teaching was not based on the right of the man but on concern for the woman because the man clearly intended to harm his wife with such accusations. Ibn Abd al-Wahhab believed that the woman had the right to be divorced from such a man, subtly placing greater power of divorce in the woman's hands. He denied the man any claim to his wife after such an action.[274]

As with other questions of faith and practice, Ibn Abd al-Wahhab placed the most importance on the man's intent when declaring the *talaq*. He declared despicable any man who declares a *talaq* and then leaves the woman hanging in limbo as to whether or not he intends to carry on with it. Interestingly, because he considered the husband to be at fault for failing to make clear his intent in such a case Ibn Abd al-Wahhab freed the wife from her normal obligation to be obedient to him.[275] He believed that no man had the right to make his wife's life miserable or force her to live in a state of uncertainty.

This issue leads to the question of direct versus indirect repudiations by *talaq*. One of the reasons that Ibn Abd al-Wahhab preferred direct to indirect *talaq* is that an indirect *talaq* may be misinterpreted by those hearing it or those hearing it may not be aware that it is an indirect *talaq*. He cited as an example the case of a man who was asked whether or not his wife was with him. The man replied that she was absent. The person asking the question stated that the man's wife was in fact with him, to which the man replied that she was not and that it was his desire that she not be with him. The person hearing this understood it to be an indirect declaration of *talaq* and so the wife was considered to be divorced. However, for Ibn Abd al-Wahhab the case was ambiguous because the intent behind the man's declaration was unclear—did he actually wish to repudiate his wife or was he merely stating a preference as to where and whether his wife should accompany him? Ibn Abd al-Wahhab concluded by castigating the man as a liar and a deceiver for being ambiguous about his intent because as a result his wife had been left in limbo, not knowing whether or not she had been divorced.[276]

This case is significant for two reasons. First, it raises the issue of social order—an indirect *talaq* creates confusion for all who hear it because it is unclear in its intent, raising the possibility of confusion of the social order because no one knows whether the woman is still to be considered married and, if repudiated, how many times she has been indirectly repudiated. Second, it suggests that the woman has the right to know for certain that she has been repudiated, making her a direct party to the divorce, as well as to the original marriage. This is not to say that Ibn Abd al-Wahhab did not recognize the validity of an indirect *talaq*. In a case in which it was perceived that an indirect *talaq* had been declared, he required that the husband be asked directly about his intent. This is the husband's opportunity to declare publicly whether a *talaq* has been declared. If the husband states that he did not intend a *talaq*, then it did not occur.[277]

Ibn Abd al-Wahhab used the matter of intent as his response to every question about the validity of *talaq* rather than declaring blanket assertions about *talaq* pronounced under a variety of circumstances and mental states. The man's intent is known only to himself and God. No one else is capable of knowing the man's intent, apparently not even his own wife.[278] Thus, if the man claims that in his heart he did not intend to repudiate his wife the *talaq* is invalidated. However, Ibn Abd al-Wahhab cautioned the man against abusing this right because God knows what was truly in his heart and soul and God hates those who are deceitful. No man should claim that he has repudiated his wife when he has not. Likewise, no man should claim that he has not repudiated his wife when he has made an indirect *talaq* with intent.[279]

In some respects, Ibn Abd al-Wahhab's ruling can be viewed as frustrating for women because it leaves them subject to the man's whim and mood and allows him space to declare that words she understood to be a declaration of divorce were not intended to be. On the other hand, he did not approve of indirect declarations of divorce since such declarations leave the woman in limbo. By pressuring the man to declare the intent behind his words, he subtly placed the man in a position of having to inform his wife and the general public of the wife's status. Thus, it can be argued that, although the content of his ruling might not have been popular with women, it certainly could be used as a means of clarifying their status—a status that in other times and places would have remained ambiguous due to the lack of declaration of intent. To make his point clear, he required that the man "reveal" or "make known" his *talaq* directly to the woman during a period of purity in which he has not had sex with her. Furthermore, the third *talaq* must be made in the woman's presence.[280]

To further limit the man's right to claim that any pronouncement qualifies as an indirect declaration of *talaq*, Ibn Abd al-Wahhab noted seven ways of indirectly declaring a *talaq*: (1) You are void, (2) You are clear, (3) You are irrevocable, (4) You are cut off, (5) You are concluded, (6) You are a free woman, and (7) You are forbidden.[281] In a case in which the husband informs his wife that she is forbidden, this is considered to be a legally binding oath that the husband must adhere to, even though it is an indirect declaration of *talaq*.[282] Ibn Abd al-Wahhab thus made it clear that even indirect declarations of *talaq* should not be made lightly. Muslims are always expected and required to keep their oaths.

He also ruled that indirect declarations of *talaq* cannot be counted toward the three *talaqs* required to render a divorce irrevocable. Consequently, one might argue that a husband could constantly threaten his wife with divorce, only to retract it upon deciding that divorce was not his intent. However, Ibn Abd al-Wahhab's insistence on pushing the man to declare his intent resulted in either a retraction or a declaration of direct *talaq*, rendering her status clear.

The importance of making a woman's status with respect to her husband clear lies in the question of whether sexual relations between the husband and wife are permissible. If the husband is supposed to be respecting his wife's period of purity between declarations of *talaq*, engagement in sexual intercourse is problematic because it renders the wife's status unclear. If a woman has been irrevocably divorced and is not aware of it, she will not be aware that engaging in sex with her former husband is forbidden because she is not aware of the fact that he is no longer her husband. It was for these reasons that Ibn Abd al-Wahhab taught that secrecy in the matter of repudiation is a sin because the wife cannot know for certain if she is committing a transgression if her status is either unclear or unknown to her.[283] At the same time, he asserted that the man's resumption of sexual relations with his wife is an intentional act and thus constitutes a declaration of the woman's return to her husband.[284]

Ibn Abd al-Wahhab granted the woman some bargaining power when the man seeks to repudiate her. He allowed the woman to give up her right to maintenance and separate housing as a means of encouraging the man to "hold her fast."[285] He also allowed the man to assign to the wife his right of *talaq*. In doing so, the man placed the power of repudiation entirely in the woman's hands, obligating him to abide by her declarations. The woman remained entitled to maintenance during her waiting period, regardless of who pronounced the *talaq*.[286]

Ibn Abd al-Wahhab adhered to the practice of arbitration in the case of a desired divorce as outlined in the Quran. In a case in which the couple is experiencing serious marital problems, a judge should appoint two representatives, known as *wukala'* (pl. of *wakil*), to investigate the problems. One *wakil* is to represent the man. The other is to represent the woman. Thus, both sides are represented equally in the arbitration process. The *wukala'* are then to report back to the judge what they have seen, both together and separately.[287]

In a case in which the wife is divorced, she is to be "returned" to her people, though not necessarily to her marriage guardian. A returned woman is a wife against whom a *talaq* has been declared, even if this was done through indirect methods such as comparing her to his mother or other female relatives (*zihar*) or the husband's oath that he has refrained from sexual relations with her for four months. If the divorce was revocable, the man has the right to demand that his wife be returned to him. Indications that the man has resumed his married status include his having sex with his wife; his traveling with her in a way in which she is secluded or isolated with him, thereby making sexual intercourse a possibility; or the wife adorning herself for her husband so that he understands that she is available to him. However, even in this discussion Ibn Abd al-Wahhab did not place complete power in the hands of the husband. If it is determined that the man engaged in sex with his repudiated wife but that he detests her, the *talaq* stands and he owes her the dower (*mahr*). The woman must complete her waiting period to determine whether she is pregnant.[288]

Ibn Abd al-Wahhab further limited the man's right to demand that his wife be returned to him to a case in which the man desires a restoration of the marriage and is willing to reclaim his wife as his wife, rather than allowing the man to assert his right to sex with the woman without having any intent of redeclaring their marriage. Here, again, he pushed the man into clearly declaring his intent so that both the woman and society could be certain of her status. To further solidify the woman's right to know her status, he allowed the woman to include a stipulation in her marriage contract that any repudiation take a written form.[289]

Ibn Abd al-Wahhab considered the matter of the woman's status to be so important that he required the man to declare his desire for his wife's return, as well as of her dismissal, with a written declaration being preferred. He also allowed a woman to appear before a judge and swear that she has been repudiated by her husband by *talaq* and has completed her waiting period. If the judge finds her to be truthful, he then has the right to give her in marriage to another man.[290] In all of these cases, the woman's status and honor are protected by making her status a matter of public declaration and record rather than simply the private, undeclared decision of the man. By insisting on the clarification of the woman's status, Ibn Abd al-Wahhab placed power in the hands of the woman to pursue another marriage, rather than waiting in limbo ad infinitum or potentially engaging in an illicit action.

One other noteworthy ruling of Ibn Abd al-Wahhab with respect to repudiation by *talaq* is his declaration that the husband who permanently repudiates his wife via an irrevocable *talaq* must house her in his home or its equivalent with the same number of servants to attend her. He also required the husband to continue to pay her maintenance. He did not set a time limit on these requirements, suggesting that there is no predetermined end to the time period during which these pronouncements are applicable.[291]

The Financial Consequences of Divorce by Talaq

Like marriage, divorce by *talaq* carries important financial obligations for the man because he has chosen to end the marriage. Upon repudiating his wife, the man takes on two major financial obligations: the provision of maintenance to his former wife during her waiting period and the payment of any portion of the *mahr* that remained unpaid after the contracting of the marriage.

MAINTENANCE. The man's responsibility to pay his wife maintenance is subject to several considerations, such as whether the marriage has been consummated. In a case in which the woman has been repudiated by *talaq* prior to consummation, no maintenance is due to the woman because the actual state of marriage never occurred. This exemption from maintenance also applies to cases in which the couple has been separated due to the annulment of the marriage or there is something that renders it invalid, such as a suckling relationship, an imperfection in either spouse, a difference of religion, or manumission. However, in a case in which the marriage is invalidated and consummation has occurred, the woman is still required to observe the waiting period, even though no maintenance is due to her. This is also the case for a woman who has been sexually active due to a judicial error. The reasoning behind this is that maintenance is not due because the marriage was not valid, but a waiting period is still required in cases in which sexual activity has occurred because the woman could potentially be pregnant and the lineage of the resulting child would need to be determined.[292]

The most difficult cases with respect to the payment of maintenance are those in which the husband removes himself from the marriage without giving any direct declaration of either repudiation or when he intends to return. Historically, women who were abandoned by their husbands for whatever reason were left without a male protector, often without maintenance, and facing difficulty in extricating themselves from the marriage in order to contract a marriage with a different husband. Although *khul'* divorce is the wife's prerogative, the husband's presence is generally required in order to determine his opinion about it. Likewise, because a divorce by *talaq* is the husband's prerogative, his absence precludes the possibility of his making such a declaration known to his wife, unless he notifies her via a messenger or through the mail. Recognizing the financial hardship that this entails for the woman, Ibn Abd al-Wahhab allowed an abandoned woman who has no access to her husband's property or money in his absence to seek and receive an annulment.[293]

In his discussion on this important topic, what Ibn Abd al-Wahhab did not say is as significant as what he did. First, he did not set a minimum time period for the man's absence before allowing the wife to appeal for an annulment. His failure to do so stood in marked contrast to the Hanafi school, which required an absence of ninety-nine years, ostensibly to be certain that the man would be deceased, and the Maliki, Shafii, and Hanbali schools, which required a four-year absence on the basis of the caliph Umar's practice. Ibn Abd al-Wahhab did not hold to the four-year requirement because he believed that Umar's purpose was to approve the annulment, not the time period. He noted that other cases required only one year's absence reflecting the flexibility of Islamic law in considering the context of the absence, rather than only the fact of the absence. By refusing to set an absolute time requirement, Ibn Abd al-Wahhab opened the door for the woman to demand an annulment much sooner than the other law schools would have allowed.[294]

Second, because he tied permission for the annulment to the woman's inability to acquire from her husband's property the maintenance to which she is entitled, this would seem to suggest that a woman could apply for an annulment within a relatively short time period on the basis of her need for maintenance. The legal reasoning behind the permissibility of the annulment is that the man, by absenting himself, has made sexual intercourse—one of the rights to which both parties are entitled—impossible, as would be the case if the man were impotent (legally a grounds for annulling a marriage). Furthermore, the requirement that the man provide his wife with maintenance is also being violated because the man in such cases has left his wife in a state of poverty that she is otherwise helpless to escape. Ibn Abd al-Wahhab ruled that, because the man has failed to fulfill his main responsibilities to his wife in marriage, a judge therefore has the right to declare that the marriage has ceased to exist, thus freeing the woman from her obligations to her husband. In such a case, the man does not have the right to demand that his wife be returned to him.[295]

One other possible means of ending such a marriage allowed by Ibn Abd al-Wahhab was for the husband's marriage guardian to declare the *talaq* repudiation to the wife. In this case, the wife must then observe the waiting period prior to remarrying.[296] Unlike the adherents of other law schools, Ibn Abd al-Wahhab allowed several legal mechanisms by which a woman could seek an end to a marriage in which the husband absented himself rather than forever remaining subject to his whims. In doing so, he asserted the balance in the rights and responsibilities of both men and women in marriage, so that the man never holds complete control over the status of the marriage and is held responsible for his failure to fulfill his marital duties.

This does not constitute blanket approval for the woman to seek an annulment, however. For instance, Ibn Abd al-Wahhab did not allow the wife of a prisoner to remarry until the prisoner's demise has occurred and been made known. In a case in which the husband is absent and his location is unknown, but his absence has occurred during a time of peace, the man was engaged in trade or commerce of some sort, and the man has maintained contact with his wife, Ibn Abd al-Wahhab did not allow for the wife to be considered abandoned unless or until the man's death becomes known.[297]

Thus, Ibn Abd al-Wahhab's permission for annulment was restricted to cases that truly represented issues of public welfare (maslahah) in which the woman was left in poverty with no other viable alternative rather than being intended to serve as a blanket means for women to easily obtain a divorce or annulment. The purpose of his ruling was to provide social justice for desperate women while upholding the status of marriage and the social order.

THE WAITING PERIOD (IDDAH). The requirement that the woman repudiated by talaq must observe iddah serves two purposes. First, it allows for the determination of the existence of a legitimate pregnancy, and, second, in a case of revocable talaq it provides the couple with time to reconcile and resume their married status.

Ibn Abd al-Wahhab required the waiting period and the cessation of sexual relations in a case in which the husband and wife have been legally separated, whether due to the determination that the marriage was invalid due to a judicial error or because the husband has declared a talaq against his wife. Even if the couple has not had sex but has been alone together, so that sex would have been possible, the woman is required to observe the waiting period—even if the husband did not so much as touch her. If the couple reconciles in a married state, either because the judicial error or problem blocking the marriage has been resolved or because the husband has revoked the talaq, the woman still must complete her waiting period and be finished with her menstrual cycle before sexual relations can resume.[298] Ibn Abd al-Wahhab also required a waiting period when a woman with a child from a previous marriage marries another man and the child from the first marriage dies. He required the man to withdraw from his wife for the period of one menstrual cycle in order to determine whether the woman is pregnant because her pregnancy would provide an additional heir to the estate of the deceased child.[299]

Ibn Abd al-Wahhab noted three different means of determining how long the woman is entitled to maintenance and how long the waiting period is to last in the case of her repudiation by talaq, all based on the status of her menstrual cycle: (1) when she is pregnant, in which case the maintenance is due to her until the end of the pregnancy, whether via a live birth or miscarriage;[300] (2) when the woman is menstruating, in which case maintenance is due to her through the completion of three menstrual cycles; and (3) when a woman is menopausal or otherwise nonmenstruating, in which case the waiting period is calculated according to a number of months. If the woman has an irregular menstrual cycle, he recommended that the waiting period be nine months long—the duration of a pregnancy.[301] He specified that there may be two types of irregular menstrual cycles. In the first, the woman knows that she menstruates once a month, but is uncertain as to when during the month the menstruation will occur. In this case, he set the waiting period at three months so that three menstrual cycles can occur. If, however, irregularity means that the woman does not menstruate regularly once a month, then he recommended that she wait until three menstrual cycles have been completed, up to a length of the nine months specified previously.[302] Significantly, the only distinctions he made among women were on the basis of their menstrual cycles, or lack thereof, rather than the classical distinctions made between slave and free women.[303] His failure to distinguish between these social classes demonstrates his belief that financial support during the waiting period was an absolute right of the woman, regardless of her social status.

Ibn Abd al-Wahhab also addressed the case of a minor female who had never menstruated prior to the waiting period. If she begins menstruating at any time during the waiting period, the calculation of the waiting period must begin anew. If she does not begin menstruating until after the completion of the waiting period, it does not begin anew.[304]

In a case in which the woman is menopausal, he required the woman to observe a waiting period of one year.[305] The unusual length of time in this case is due to the judicial need to be certain that the woman is not pregnant.[306] Ibn Abd al-Wahhab guaranteed the woman's right to maintenance during this lengthy waiting period, provided that she has been divorced. If at any time during the waiting period the woman suspects that she may be pregnant, she remains in the waiting period until the suspicion has ended, whether due to menstruation or the completion of the pregnancy. During this time, the marriage remains valid, although sexual relations are not permitted between the husband and wife. If the suspected pregnancy occurs after the completion of the waiting period or before another marriage, the woman should not be given in marriage until the suspicion of pregnancy has been resolved, whether via a miscarriage or the birth of a baby.

If widowhood has occurred prior to consummation, there is no waiting period. If there was consummation, the waiting period is four months and ten days, regardless of whether the woman is a minor or has reached her majority. This four-month, ten-day waiting period also applies to any woman who is already observing a waiting period due to repudiation by *talaq* and whose husband dies during that time.[307]

It is of interest that Ibn Abd al-Wahhab again placed the woman in the position of power with respect to the calculation of the waiting period because only the woman knows the intricacies of her menstrual cycle. In doing so, he recognized her as an honest and reliable single witness. No one else was permitted to engage in this kind of witnessing about the woman. It was her responsibility alone. Not only did he charge the woman with the responsibility of calculating her waiting period, but he also held her responsible for recognizing why her menstrual cycle has stopped. Possible explanations include the arrival of menopause, pregnancy, illness, and breast-feeding of an infant. If it has ceased for a reason other than these, then he declared that she should not begin her waiting period until she has had a menstrual cycle.[308] While one could argue that this represents an injustice for the woman, because it delays the possibility of her remarrying and consequently denying her sexual fulfillment, it can also be argued that this measure serves to protect the woman financially because the man is required to continue to pay for her maintenance during the determination period and then throughout the waiting period. Ibn Abd al-Wahhab further noted that any time the woman is observing a grieving period, her waiting period is suspended. Once the grieving period is over, the woman should wait for a menstrual cycle and then begin her waiting period. If she has already observed a waiting period of a year, then she is exempted from any further waiting period.[309]

The only time Ibn Abd al-Wahhab exempted the woman from such lengthy waiting periods was when she is left in poverty. In such a case, he granted her the right to seek elimination of the waiting period by a judge (hakim).[310] Here he rejected literal adherence to Islamic law in favor of consideration of public welfare (maslahah). As applied in this case, Ibn Abd al-Wahhab recognized the injustice of making a destitute woman continue to live in poverty by denying her the right to seek another husband. Therefore, he allowed a judicial cancellation of the waiting period in a case of destitution, while leaving the woman the right to a lengthy waiting period whenever it was financially in her favor to do so. This clearly demonstrates his concern for and protection of women.

Divorce Initiated by the Wife (Khul')

Khul' is a divorce initiated by the wife that involves giving her husband some kind of compensation in exchange for her freedom from the marriage. Unlike talaq, khul' does not carry with it a required waiting period because the issues of menstruation and ritual purity are not of concern.[311] Furthermore, unlike talaq, khul' is an immediate and permanent divorce. The husband does not have the right to demand that his wife return after the declaration of a khul' divorce.[312] Although khul' provides the woman with agency in divorce, there are nevertheless some disadvantages for her in it. For example, if the wife is pregnant at the time of the khul' divorce, not only is the husband not obligated to provide the wife with maintenance, but he is not obligated to provide maintenance for the child until he or she is weaned. If the child is an infant at the time of the khul' divorce, the husband has the right to demand that the child be suckled until he or she is two years old.[313]

Khul' is a legal mechanism recognized by all of the law schools and is broadly present in the court records of various countries.[314] However, the historical records make it clear that, although practiced, the manner in which *khul'* has been carried out historically has not necessarily been in accordance with the original intent behind it. It is this question of intent that Ibn Abd al-Wahhab sought to redress in his juridical discussion of the topic, so as to correct the manner in which it was carried out.

Two major difficulties associated with the practice of *khul'* divorce historically have continued into the contemporary era. Both are associated with the man's desire to either continue or end the marriage. On the one hand, men have often sought to push their wives into a *khul'* divorce, rather than one by *talaq*, in order to free themselves from the financial obligations they would have in the case of a divorce by *talaq*. If a man convinced his wife to purchase her freedom via *khul'*, he not only would obtain from her a payment of some type (typically the amount of her *mahr*), but he also would absolve himself of his responsibility to pay maintenance during her waiting period.[315] Alternatively, some men have refused to grant their wives a divorce altogether, whether by *khul'* or *talaq*, in order to keep the marriage intact. In such cases, the men either refused to come to an agreement about the amount the woman is to pay or have set the payment at an astronimcally high cost in comparison with her financial status so that she cannot possibly pay the amount demanded in exchange for her freedom.[316] Ibn Abd al-Wahhab's support of the woman's absolute right to *khul'* divorce reflects his insistence on gender balance in rights, even in matters of divorce. Although his position is not unique among jurists, it is an important stance because of the agency he granted to the woman.

In a declaration of binding legal doctrine, Ibn Abd al-Wahhab granted the woman the right to *khul'* divorce in cases in which she either despised or disliked her husband to the point where she believed that she could not carry out the duty of obeying him as required by God.[317] On the basis of Q 2:229—"It is not permitted to you [masculine pl.] that you [masculine pl.] take from what you gave to them [feminine pl.] anything except that both fear not being able to adhere to God's limits. If you [masculine pl.] fear that the two will not adhere to the limits of God, then there is no sin on either one of the two in what she sacrifices by it." Ibn Abd al-Wahhab understood this verse to mean that the woman has the absolute right to ransom herself from the marriage when she fears that she will not be able to fulfill her duties. He therefore recognized the woman as the agent in *khul'* divorce.

It is important to note that the only legal requirements for obtaining a *khul'* divorce are the woman's cognizance of disliking her husband to the point of not being able to fulfill her marital duties and the woman's granting of compensation to the husband accordingly. There is nothing in this statement that requires the husband's agreement to *khul'* because it is the wife's prerogative, not the husband's. Ibn Abd al-Wahhab's association of *khul'* with obedience to God renders the decision to request a divorce by *khul'* a religious matter rather than strictly a matter between husband and wife. The implication is that no one, not even the woman's husband, therefore has the right to deny a *khul'* divorce because doing so would result in the woman's inability to fulfill her religious duties. By further emphasizing the fact that the Quran absolves both parties from sin and error in a case in which there is fear that the couple will not adhere to the limits set by God, Ibn Abd al-Wahhab removed any religious stigma or stigma against the husband in *khul'*, as well as any arguments about its permissibility. Thus, the only time the man's honor comes into question is when he refuses to agree to a *khul'* divorce.[318]

Ibn Abd al-Wahhab's insistence on the permissibility and legality of *khul'* underscores his emphasis on reciprocal rights and responsibilities in marriage and divorce for both the husband and the wife. Just as the husband has the absolute right of *talaq* and the financial obligations it entails, so he recognized that the wife has the absolute right of *khul'* and the financial obligation it entails, all on the basis of *her* conclusion that the marriage can no longer remain intact.[319] Furthermore, similar to the husband's unfettered right of *talaq*, Ibn Abd al-Wahhab taught that the woman's use of *khul'* should be easy and convenient for her.[320]

The reciprocity of financial obligations in *talaq* and *khul'* divorces was due to recognition that the party seeking the divorce owed compensation to the party being divorced as a legal means of ending the marriage contract. Ibn Abd al-Wahhab's phrasing on the compensation owed to the husband in the case of *khul'* is strikingly similar to the wording typically associated with the compensation due to the wife in the case of a divorce by *talaq*. He required compensation to the husband so that the husband was not to be left poor or in need by the loss of his wife.[321] It is significant that he stated the justification for compensation in this way because it serves to underscore his insistence on reciprocal rights in divorce. Just as the woman is entitled to maintenance during her waiting period (*iddah*) following the pronouncement of repudiation by the husband (*talaq*) so that she will not be left destitute, so the wife is required to compensate her husband when she is the one initiating the divorce so that he is not left destitute.

The amount of compensation for a *khul'* divorce has traditionally been understood to be the amount of the *mahr*. Thus, the ending of the marriage contract results in the wife returning to the husband what he gave her in order to initiate the contract. Ibn Abd al-Wahhab declared as binding legal doctrine that this is the *only* instance in which the man has the right to take back the *mahr*, indicating that the appropriate amount for the *khul'* was the amount of the *mahr*.[322] Any other return of the *mahr* was *tahrim* (forbidden)—the strongest legal term for forbidding something.

Khul' was the only type of divorce that Ibn Abd al-Wahhab approved for a woman to initiate, noting that other types initiated by women should be considered despicable and defaming, although he did not forbid them.[323] When specifying what he meant by this, he tied *khul'* to the financial obligation of the woman, that is, giving the *mahr* back to the husband, so that the legal issue is one of compensation—the legal mechanism by which the divorce occurs—rather than of the inherent right to initiate the divorce.

In a *khul'* divorce, it is typically asserted that the husband is still required to declare his repudiation of his wife, although this remains a divorce by *khul'* rather than *talaq*. This approach is based upon an interpretation of Q 4:4, which states, "If they [feminine pl.] remit to you any part of it [the *sadaq*] of their own will, then take charge of it as delicious and wholesome." Those requiring the agreement of the husband point to the "taking charge of it" as the indication of the husband's agreement, leaving the husband in control of whether the divorce takes place or not.

Ibn Abd al-Wahhab disagreed with this interpretation, citing instead the interpretation of Ibn al-Mundhir that permission is not requisite/imperative (*la yulazim al-jawwaz*) in anything but an oath of permission in a commutative contract (*mu'awidhah*) according to the evidence of God's forbidding (*haramahu*) of interest in the contract and His giving of permission in the gift.[324] He interpreted this saying to mean that requiring the husband's permission in order to grant the divorce by *khul'* constituted nothing less than preventing the woman from marrying by holding her for ransom (*'adaliha li-taftadi*), which he declares invalid (*batil*). Examples of holding his wife for ransom include the husband treating his wife badly, harming her in order to force her to stay with him, and trying to get her to seek a divorce by *khul'* rather than *talaq* so as to escape his financial responsibilities to her.[325] Ibn Abd al-Wahhab responded by placing agency of *khul'* strictly in the wife's hands by declaring in his own personal voice (*qulna*) that the *khul'* occurs as a *talaq* retroactively (*al-khul' talaq waqi' talaqan raji'an*), thus making it clear that a husband who attempts to block a *khul'* divorce will still be divorced in the end, but by a means that requires him to issue compensation, rather than his wife![326]

Ibn Abd al-Wahhab did not view *khul'* as a method that was to be restricted in practice because it was approved by both the Quran and Muhammad. He did not allow the man to place any limitations on a *khul'* divorce by dragging out endless negotiations about the amount of the compensation. By noting the *hadith* in which Muhammad stated that giving the man back the *mahr* that he had paid to the wife upon the marriage results in a divorce by *khul'*, Ibn Abd al-Wahhab set a clear legal precedent for the wife paying to her husband the amount of the *mahr* and the man recognizing this as a legal *khul'* divorce.

He further despised the attempts by men to demand excessive amounts of compensation in exchange for agreeing to a *khul'* divorce. He cited Q 4:19, which states, "And do not take away from them [feminine pl.] in order to steal from some of what you gave to them [feminine pl.] except that they [feminine pl.] give exorbitantly." He interpreted this verse as a prohibition against male greed in seeking an exorbitant amount from the wife in exchange for agreeing to a *khul'* divorce.[327] He further stated that it is "despicable" (*yukarih*) for the husband to demand from his wife more than what he had originally given her, in keeping with the Quranic teaching that, "There is no sin upon either of them in what she sacrifices by it!" (Q 2:229).[328] In other words, he forbade husbands to imprison their wives in marriage by demanding excessive compensation in exchange for the divorce. Because *khul'* is supposed to be the wife's prerogative and is based on her concern that she cannot fulfill God's commands, it is unfair and unreasonable for the man to demand more than what the wife can give in exchange for the divorce.

Ibn Abd al-Wahhab recognized that there were other ways in which men might try to avoid the financial responsibilities associated with a divorce by *talaq* by trying to push their wives into requesting a divorce by *khul'*. He therefore stated very clearly, "*Khul'* divorce by a subterfuge is not valid."[329] As a further precaution against male abuse of *khul'*, he forbade the man from stipulating in the marriage contract that any divorce would have to occur by *khul'*. Such a stipulation would be invalid. The only thing that he allowed the husband to stipulate with respect to a *khul'* divorce was the amount of compensation he would require.[330]

Ibn Abd al-Wahhab's lengthy discussions about various abuses of *khul'* indicate great familiarity with a variety of ways in which men have sought to extricate themselves from marriage without having to pay the amount normally due from them. By addressing them and consistently repeating that the main point of concern in *khul'* is that agency belongs to the woman alone, he sought to redress the injustices dished out to women trapped in unhappy marriages. His consistent interpretation of Islamic law in favor of gender balance in rights and responsibilities stands in marked contrast to the typical image of Wahhabis as being predisposed to misogyny and support for patriarchy.

Divorce by Oath of Allegation of Adultery (Li'an)

In keeping with the Quran, Ibn Abd al-Wahhab also permitted a third type of divorce, that of *li'an*, a situation in which the husband accuses the wife of having committed adultery but without supportive evidence. In such a case, the couple must appear before a judge. The husband must swear four times that his accusation against his wife is true and call God's wrath down on himself if he is lying. The wife, in turn, proclaims her innocence four times and calls down God's wrath on herself if she is lying. The judge then declares the couple irrevocably divorced. Ibn Abd al-Wahhab noted the seriousness of this type of accusation and divorce by prohibiting the husband from his wife *forever* in such a case.[331] Even if the wife were to marry someone else and be divorced or widowed by him, she would remain forbidden to the husband who divorced her by *li'an*.

Widowhood and Its Repercussions

Widows enjoy a special, protected status in Islam. The Quran commands Muslims to care for widows, orphans, and the poor. Widows were among the most susceptible members of pre-Islamic society to fall into destitution. Historically, even after the revelation of Islam widows remained vulnerable members of society because of their loss of a male protector.

While in Europe widows often ironically enjoyed greater freedom after the death of a husband, in Muslim society widows had to be extremely careful to avoid any behavior that could be considered suspicious or immoral. Ibn Abd al-Wahhab cautioned widows to avoid social interactions or displays that could potentially attract undesirable attention. He cautioned them to avoid being overly friendly, well dressed, or adorned or to use kohl to darken their eyes and further recommended that they should stay at home so as to avoid attracting attention to themselves. He went into some detail about what he meant by being well dressed and adorned. He forbade the widow to wear clothing that is dyed to be beautiful, particularly if the colors were red or yellow. He preferred the more neutral and somber colors of black and dark green as colors for widows.[332]

What is the intent of this approach? Does it signify that widows, as a social group, are somehow outside of normal society and should be avoided? Ibn Abd al-Wahhab's intent here was not one of purposeful misogyny. The spirit of these prohibitions was to ensure that the widow would be treated with respect and could live a quiet life rather than engaging in an ostentatious display of her wealth or charms. Under Islamic law, a widow is to observe her waiting period in a quiet and respectful manner. Indeed, Ibn Abd al-Wahhab granted her the right to observe an even longer waiting period if she so desired.[333] The purpose was to allow the woman to determine the length of time during which she desired to mourn the passing of her husband so as not to be rushed into another marriage. That is, while he recognized a minimum time period for mourning, he did not set any maximum. Such an approach suggests that the legal precepts of the Quran are the minimum requirements that Muslims are to obey, leaving the door open for people to do more than what is absolutely required. This is an important legal precedent because it allows for the possibility of expanding the minimum requirements in other areas, such as the length of time during which a man is to pay his wife maintenance following a divorce—a legal argument that has been made in modern India with respect to Islamic law in the matter of divorce.[334]

Ibn Abd al-Wahhab's restrictions on the widow reflect the Quran's pronouncements about the ways in which she may abandon her rights if she behaves ostentatiously. Q 2:240, for example, allows a widow to remain in her matrimonial home until she chooses to leave it. Ibn Abd al-Wahhab upheld this pronouncement, even though some scholars claim that it was abrogated by a later verse. Although he taught that the woman lost her right to the matrimonial home when her behavior was inappropriate (defined as behaving like a whore by engaging in open lewdness, cursing or abusing her family, or defying her father-in-law), Ibn Abd al-Wahhab asserted the right of the widow to continue to live in her matrimonial home, as well as to receive her portion of the inheritance. Lest there be any doubt, he specifically stated that the other heirs to the estate did not have the right to make the widow leave her matrimonial home.[335]

Ibn Abd al-Wahhab was also careful to explain what he meant by "leaving the matrimonial home," because this phrase had been interpreted extremely literally by other jurists. He did not forbid the widow from ever physically leaving the premises of her home because he allowed her, for example, to leave freely during the day to take care of her needs. According to his interpretation, "leaving the matrimonial home" referred to the abandonment of that home as her residence. He particularly emphasized the requirement that the woman be permitted to continue to reside in her matrimonial home after being either widowed or repudiated by *talaq* if she is pregnant.[336]

Custody of Children

Custody of children becomes a concern only in the case of divorce or the death of one of the spouses. Ibn Abd al-Wahhab concurred with the general guidelines of classical Islamic law in determining who had the right of custody over children, but he commented that, "Custody over a child is not immovable/unshakeable,"[337] setting a precedent for the removal of a child from the custody of the usual legally prescribed adult. For example, if the usual legally appropriate adult is godless or sinful or determined to be a *kafir* and the child is a Muslim, that adult forfeits his or her right to custody of the child.[338]

Generally speaking, Ibn Abd al-Wahhab asserted the right of the mother to custody of her child, even if she is frail or infirm.[339] Although the classical law schools allowed the mother custody only until the boy was seven years old and the girl had begun menstruation, at which point the father became their legal guardian and no further provisions were made for the mother, Ibn Abd al-Wahhab understood parenting to be a lifelong commitment, regardless of the child's age or who has custody. Thus, he allowed a boy who had reached seven years of age to select his own guardian. On the basis of Muhammad's practice, he stipulated neither the father nor the mother as the "preferable" guardian. Rather, he underlined the importance of *both* parents being involved in the boy's life. If the father goes missing or has failed to participate in the boy's upbringing, Ibn Abd al-Wahhab did not automatically assign the boy to the paternal relatives. Rather, he granted the boy the right to choose between living with his mother or his paternal relatives.

Only in the case of the mature girl did Ibn Abd al-Wahhab state a preference that she live with her father, presumably because he is her marriage guardian. He did not subscribe to the declaration that every girl reaches maturity at the age of nine. Instead, he noted that this may be possible but is not necessarily the case. The father has the right to custody of the daughter only after she has reached maturity.[340] In cases in which the parents are divorced, the mother does not automatically lose custody of her daughter upon her remarriage. Rather, in such cases custody of the girl passes to a maternal aunt.[341]

Inheritance Law

The Quran raised the status of women in Arabia by granting them the right to inherit. Actual practices have varied over time and space, often resulting in women being denied their rightful inheritances in favor of male relatives. This appears to have been the case in Arabia in the time of Ibn Abd al-Wahhab. When asked to rule on matters of inheritance, he defended the rights of women. For example, when asked about the right of those possessing kinship without being agnates (paternal relatives), he ruled that those who possessed kinship to the deceased had priority over the state treasury.[342] This ruling would apply, for example, to the widow of the deceased.

Ibn Abd al-Wahhab also protected the right of an unborn child to inheritance. When questioned about a woman who had been pregnant for a year and was known to have been righteous prior to the death of the testator, he stated that the case was clear and there was no ambiguity.[343] The woman's pregnancy had been established prior to the death of the testator, rendering the unborn child heir to one-sixth of the property if born alive and none if born dead.[344]

Ibn Abd al-Wahhab also sought to prevent the twisting of inheritance laws so as to circumvent their intent. Such actions were often undertaken historically to dispossess women of their rightful inheritances. It is interesting that he did not base his rulings about inheritance on gender but rather emphasized the intent behind the action undertaken. For example, in a case in which a woman with no husband set up a charitable endowment (waqf) benefiting her son, he ruled that this was not a legal transaction—not due to the gender of the founder but due to the fact that the purpose of the waqf in this case was to circumvent inheritance law so as to provide for a single heir. However, he also noted that, although such twisting of inheritance issues is typically wrong and not authorized, there are cases in which waqf are founded in order to provide sustenance for the person appointed as caretaker. In cases in which there is need or necessity on the part of the caretaker, the waqf may be allowed to stand, regardless of the gender of either the founder or the beneficiary.[345]

Conclusion

It is clear from the above analysis that Ibn Abd al-Wahhab's construction of gender was not one that displayed misogyny or sought to render women as second-class or invisible citizens. On the contrary, he not only recognized women as individuals with rights and responsibilities, but he also recognized their capacity to serve as positive and active agents in both the private and public spheres as individuals, wives, daughters, mothers, and members of the broad Muslim community. He granted them the right to participate in and even initiate both marriage and divorce. He recognized the validity of their testimony in matters of marriage and divorce and sought to redress the abuses of the Quranically intended gender balance in both rights and responsibilities in marriage and divorce. Through both his interactions with women and his writings, he recognized the validity of men interacting with women and men considering women to be trustworthy and appropriate partners, both in family matters and in business transactions.

Throughout his writings, Ibn Abd al-Wahhab emphasized the themes of respect, protection, and justice for women and the requirement that men adhere to their God-given rights and responsibilities. It is noteworthy that he dedicated as much space, time, and evidence to the protection of women, seeking to avoid their debasement through licentious practices and upholding the limitation of sexual relations to marriage so that women could not be exploited. While one might argue that he did nothing more or less than uphold the strict and clear teachings of the Quran, the very fact that he did so suggests that these were areas in which the society of his time and place was in serious violation of such principles. Consequently, the assertion of women's rights and their protection was an important contribution to the construction of gender in eighteenth century Arabia.

Ibn Abd al-Wahhab's teachings are also significant for their positive contributions in challenging traditional and more literally oriented interpretations of Islamic law in favor of consideration of public interest (maslahah). His assertion that every girl/woman, regardless of age or status, has the right of consent in any marriage contracted for her established the girl/woman as a legal entity with basic rights, which the law was intended to protect. His prohibitions of concubinage, sexual relations with slaves, and rape demonstrate his protection of women where they are most vulnerable in interpersonal relations and present a more logical elaboration of what the requirement of sexual intercourse within marriage alone should mean as a lived reality. His granting to women of the right to stipulate conditions in marriage contracts favorable to them, particularly denying the husband the right to marry additional wives or take on concubines, while denying the same right to men, helped to redress the balance of power within marriage. His recognition of the rights of women to be educated, to be considered proper business partners, and to participate in wedding feasts and the publicity of weddings solidified the right of women to access to public space. All of these themes highlight his concern for gender balance and the protection of women's rights. These themes also demonstrate how he sought to empower and reempower women, all on the basis of their God-given rights, as spelled out in the Quran and *hadith*.

By grounding his teachings so strongly not only in scripture but also in classical jurisprudence, Ibn Abd al-Wahhab presented an authentic, indigenous, and effective means of rejuvenating the actual practice of gender-balanced rights while reforming social practices as they existed during his lifetime. As such, they offer significant insight into the social and religious worlds of eighteenth-century Arabia. His teachings also provide a possible springboard for reform in the twenty-first century, as marriage and divorce laws in particular come under increasing scrutiny throughout the Muslim world.

5

Jihad: Call to Islam or Call to Violence?

There is no more controversial or troubling topic with respect to Islam than that of jihad. Public debates over whether use of a term that many have come to associate with terrorism should even be permitted in the public sphere have come to dominate American discussions of Islam in the aftermath of the terrorist attacks of September 11, 2001.[1] These events raised many questions about the relationship between Islam and terrorism. Were the two irrevocably connected or was this a perverse distortion of Islam's teachings?

As information about the perpetrators of these horrific events slowly became available, Americans not only heard a great deal about the exiled Saudi dissident Osama bin Laden and his shadowy Al-Qaida terrorist network, but they also became familiar with the term *Wahhabi* and the fact that fifteen out of the nineteen hijackers involved in these attacks were Saudi. For some, the implications were clear. Wahhabis and Saudis were inherently terrorists.

However, this portrayal makes many assumptions that are based more on reactive emotions than they are on data and factual evidence. In the aftermath of 9/11, soul-searching for answers to the question, What went wrong?[2] has been accompanied by a national need to assign blame and seek justice for the victims. Unfortunately, these quests for definitive answers have tended to project current events backward in time rather than analyzing the past within its own context and trying to understand how events, contexts, and new developments over time have resulted in reinterpretations and even distortions of the past that have led some to proclaim the militant version of Islam preached by Osama bin Laden and his followers.

Sadly, in the process not enough recognition has been given to the fact that the majority of Muslims throughout the world, including in Saudi Arabia, decried and denounced the attacks of 9/11 as being anathema to Islam rather than inherent to it. The actions of a minority of extremists have come to define for many non-Muslims the religion of Islam, creating another barrier to understanding between world religions and fueling fears of an impending clash of civilizations.[3]

This chapter fills an important void in the quest for answers by analyzing the writings of Muhammad Ibn Abd al-Wahhab on the important topic of jihad. If militant extremism is inherent to Wahhabism, then this theme should dominate the writings of its founder and ideologue. The fact that it does not suggests that more careful attention needs to be paid to when and how this term was used by Ibn Abd al-Wahhab and for what purposes.

The chapter begins by asking, "How did Ibn Abd al-Wahhab believe that Islam should be spread?" Although many have claimed that Wahhabis believe that jihad is the appropriate means of proselytization, Ibn Abd al-Wahhab's writings make it clear that he believed that *da'wah*, or missionary work, was the preferred method for gaining true adherents. According to his vision, becoming a Muslim was to be the result of an educational process rather than a one-time declaration of belief made under the threat of death. Only when this approach to the call of Islam is made clear can the topic of jihad be undertaken—What is its purpose; against whom is it to be undertaken, and under what circumstances is it invoked? What is revealed is an approach to jihad that places severe and strict limitations on its declaration, scope, and purpose rather than one that seeks to expand its appropriateness and engagement at all times and against all people. Ibn Abd al-Wahhab's teachings are then compared to the writings of other jurists and activists on this topic, both past and present, placing him within a long tradition of jurisprudence on this topic and demonstrating a marked contrast between his teachings and those of contemporary militants.

On the Importance of Knowledge and Education

One of the most important and prevalent themes in Ibn Abd al-Wahhab's works is the importance of individual knowledge, study, and understanding. He required that all believers, both male and female, engage in study and the acquisition of knowledge because he believed that this was the only means of gaining true understanding of Islam. He commanded that "the majority of the people" were to learn and understand both the fundamentals and the details of religion so as to "abide by" and "prevail in" them.[4] In this way, he made it clear that he did not consider knowledge of Islam to be the hallowed ground of a few select scholars or specialists. Rather, study and knowledge of Islam were to be a mass affair.

The requirement of individual knowledge and study of the Quran and *hadith* is based on the Quranic assertion that every individual will be judged and held responsible for his or her own actions. No one, not even Muhammad's own family members, will be judged according to the deeds of his or her friends or relatives.[5] Ibn Abd al-Wahhab emphasized these themes in his own teachings, both to encourage his followers to become more knowledgeable and acceptable Muslims and to reiterate the initially shattering message of Islam that faith in God is more important than kinship and power structures.

Ibn Abd al-Wahhab broke with past patterns of Quranic and *hadith* study that focused strictly on memorization of the texts in favor of an approach that emphasized understanding them through contextualization and searching for their intent and purpose. He required the individual to scrutinize each text for its intent rather than just its literal meaning.[6] This does not mean that he did not believe in memorizing the Quran at all. It simply means that he emphasized the importance of the material rather than the importance of the memorization. His requirement of constant study of the Quran and *hadith* was designed to prevent the Muslim from forgetting what he or she had learned and to encourage the constant increase of the individual Muslim's faith.[7] He also required Muslims who were already knowledgeable to help dissipate the misunderstandings and doubts of others.[8]

In Ibn Abd al-Wahhab's opinion, one of the major problems of his time was the lack of understanding of the meanings of the texts among the people. His personal experience demonstrated that ignorance not only leads people astray but also causes people to lead others astray; results in thinking that one is performing a correct action without understanding the purpose behind it; and, most importantly, leads people to follow those who claim to have understanding without this actually being the case. He particularly targeted the *ulama* and *mujtahids*, who sought to raise themselves in the eyes of the people because of their claims to knowledge as being guilty of failure to fulfill the responsibility of acquiring and sharing that knowledge.[9]

Ibn Abd al-Wahhab was particularly concerned about ignorance among the religious and political leaders of the community because of their potential for sanctifying customs and traditions potentially contrary to Islamic law. His insistence on the right and responsibility of every individual to engage in direct and personal study of the Quran and *hadith* served to place a check on the power of these leaders by empowering the people to verify that the practices of the leadership are in keeping with the teachings of Islam. He asserted the responsibility of the individual to know right from wrong so as not to be led into condoning or participating in practices contrary to Islamic law. Following the crowd was not an acceptable reason for committing sin in his opinion. He commanded Muslims to discern, be smart, strive for understanding, and study and read in order not to be trapped by such trickery.[10]

Ibn Abd al-Wahhab's definition of *knowledge* was rooted in religious knowledge. Believing that direct knowledge of the Quran and *hadith* should be the foundation for all other knowledge, he rejected leaders whose knowledge of Islam was limited to the writings of a few jurists about financial matters such as sales and inheritance. In his opinion, such people lacked the scriptural foundations for discerning truth from falsehood, increasing the likelihood that they would lead followers astray.[11]

Ibn Abd al-Wahhab's vision of knowledge emphasized individual interpretation and scrutiny of the Quran and *hadith* rather than adherence to the teachings of other human beings. Only with a strong foundation of personal knowledge could an individual begin to sift through issues such as two contradictory *hadith* and come to a correct conclusion on the basis of content. Ibn Abd al-Wahhab taught with respect to such issues that "It is incumbent on the believer in an instance of this that he seek the answer in the words of God and the words of His Messenger . . . and therefore the truth becomes clear to him. And in what he says and in what he does, he must adhere to and defend God and His Messenger by knowledge/being informed."[12] According to this vision, it is the responsibility of the individual leader to seek the truth because it is only by possessing knowledge that one can both adhere to and defend God. There is no suggestion of militancy or violence here, only an emphasis on knowledge of scripture.

Ibn Abd al-Wahhab taught that believers should be forthright about defending God and what they know with certainty. At the same time, they should "keep their tongues in check" about that which only God knows. He reminded his followers that, no matter how much knowledge people are able to achieve, it is still minimal compared to God's knowledge.[13]

Accordingly, Ibn Abd al-Wahhab divided knowledge into two types—direct knowledge of the authoritative sources (the Quran and Sunna) and so-called knowledge based on interpretations of ambiguous or vague passages or the "hidden" meanings of the Quran. The direct and clear passages of the Quran far outweigh and outnumber the ambiguous, vague, or obscure passages. For this reason, he believed that the credibility and selection of leaders and scholars should be based on their solid knowledge of the clear passages rather than on interpretations of the vague passages.[14] He pointed to the Kharijites[15] as a negative example of those who "drew their false conclusions from obscure passages of the Quran."[16] He also cautioned against using unclear Quranic passages to justify opposition to or conflict with other Muslims, as the Kharijites and Mutazilites had done.[17]

Ibn Abd al-Wahhab further cautioned against those who try to twist the meanings of clear passages or make them into obscure passages in order to override clear commands, declaring that God will punish anyone who tries to twist or argue about clear commands, even if this person claims to be a religious scholar (*'alim*) or *mujtahid*.[18] He also expressed frustration with those who reject scholars whose explanations and interpretations of clear passages are sound because of disagreements over their interpretations of the obscure passages.[19]

In the end, Ibn Abd al-Wahhab recommended that the Muslim seeking a reliable leader or religious scholar should look first to see if that person understands the meaning of a clear passage and, second, whether the person carries out what it says. In this way, he drove home his point that the interconnection between faith and action cannot be set aside without rendering faith meaningless.[20]

Islam and Politics

According to Ibn Abd al-Wahhab's worldview, knowledge of Islam is the source of all legitimacy. This is particularly true in the political realm. Rather than the typical worldly values of power, prestige, wealth, and birth, Ibn Abd al-Wahhab declared knowledge to be the critical factor in determining leadership of the Muslim community. In his opinion, the best leader was the one who was the most correct in faith, the easiest to reconcile with the teachings of the Quran and *hadith*, and the most capable in matters of interpretation.[21]

Ibn Abd al-Wahhab taught that the ideal political leader was one who served God, rather than himself, through his position. For him, the relationship between ruler and ruled could best be described in terms of faith: a true believer holds his or her faith dearer than any family relation or friendship because faith means loving God first and foremost. Other human beings are loved for the sake of God. According to this vision, true authority over the community is based on a shared faith in God and a vision of the brotherhood of all believers rather than kinship, friendship, or worldly power.[22] The leader is to serve rather than to be served.

As with all else for Ibn Abd al-Wahhab, the nature of political authority was inextricably tied to the question of intent. He declared that those who seek leadership positions for their own sake, rather than for the sake of God or the community, are not fit to serve. He singled out as unfit leaders those who seek knowledge in order to be called scholars, those who give alms in order to be called generous, those who struggle in the way of Islam in order to be called brave and heroic, those who do good works or go on the pilgrimage in order to gain money and property, and those who marry a woman or fight for the sake of booty.[23] He also declared those supporting or allowing bribery (refusal to turn over lawful property until the owner has paid a bribe or given gifts to the judge [*hakim*] in order to purchase a particular judgment) and corruption to be unfit for leadership because of their proven propensity for misusing and

abusing the power invested in them.[24] In addition, those who engage in financial finagling, such as circumventing the prohibition on interest by forward
buying commodities prior to taking possession of them or selling commodities
at a low price in order to repurchase them later at a higher price, were also
declared unfit to rule.[25] He recalled one of Muhammad's sayings warning believers to beware the servants of money because power and money are not the
goals of a faithful believer.[26]

According to this vision, the people have the right to select their own
leaders on the basis of their adherence to Islamic teachings and values. This
not only implies that the people have the right to pass over unfit candidates
for leadership but also raises the question of what is to be done in the case of
an unfit person already serving in a leadership capacity. It is important to note
that Ibn Abd al-Wahhab did not give outright permission for or call for the
violent overthrow of such a person, as is the tendency among contemporary
extremists. Rather, his writings indicate that the appropriate reaction of the
people in such a case is to pursue the same pattern they would be expected to
pursue in the case of encounters with non-Muslims or Muslims who have
gone astray: issue the call to Islam and engage the person in dialogue, study,
and debate about the practice in order to demonstrate where they are in error
in the expectation that they will change their ways.

Da'wah: The Call to Faith

Although Ibn Abd al-Wahhab's vision of the pursuit of knowledge began with
the acquisition of knowledge by the individual, this was not the end goal. He
also required that the Muslim then seek to spread knowledge to other people,
both unbelievers and Muslims who have gone astray in their practice of the
faith. In other words, the acquisition of education and knowledge was not to
be a passive experience. It necessarily had an active component as well—proselytization.[27]

Ibn Abd al-Wahhab taught that guiding people to Islam is the most important and worthy action a Muslim can carry out and that it should always be
carried out sincerely. He forbade the practice of pretending to call people to
God when one is actually calling them to follow oneself.[28] He did not support
the creation of personality cults or seek to position himself as a dictator.[29] His
vision of the call to Islam (da'wah) was rooted in an educational process designed to win converts to God through discussion and debate rather than violence and killing.

According to this plan, education was intended to be a gradual process
over time, not a one-shot deal, such as those who believe in conversions by the
sword would promote.[30] Ibn Abd al-Wahhab taught that emphasis should be

placed on "teaching by degrees."[31] He therefore encouraged his followers to engage in a process of education by steps.

The first step in the proposed educational process was the declaration and explanation of the central theological doctrine of absolute monotheism (tawhid). It was only when the person responded to tawhid that the next step in the process, the prescription of the five daily prayers, was to occur.[32] If the person accepted the five daily prayers, then he or she was to be instructed in the duty of almsgiving (zakat). If the person obeyed all of these injunctions, then he or she was to be considered a true Muslim and could enjoy the benefits of membership in the Muslim community. The attention of the proselytizer was then be turned to addressing the complaints of those who claimed to be suffering from injustice.[33]

The chronological order of these steps is very important. Acceptance of tawhid as evidence of faith of the heart must come first. It is only after this faith of the heart has been established that concern with ritual obligations begins, suggesting that the questions of faith and intent are of greater importance than ritual perfection. It also shows that, while winning individual converts is an important first step, the main goal of expanding the Muslim community is to create a just society.

In order to ensure proper missionary work, Ibn Abd al-Wahhab wrote the treatise "Kitab Kashf al-Shubhat" as a "how-to" guide for his followers in matters of conversation and debate.[34] Typical in these discussions is comparison with the experiences of Muhammad and the Companions in order to emphasize the continuity of the Muslim experience across time and space and to legitimize his approach by demonstrating the historical precedents for his methods. This treatise is particularly instructive for the emphasis it places on the use of words, arguments, and language, with violence being a means of last resort.

Ibn Abd al-Wahhab's emphasis on God's Word as revealed in the Quran as the source of all power and victory made it clear that argument and language were critical to the cause of monotheism.[35] In referring to his followers as "the army of God" and "the victorious ones, in argument and in language, just as they are victorious by the sword and by the spear," he made clear the importance of discussion and conversion by conviction rather than violence.[36] At the same time, he also noted that one should not just naively charge into a place with only words as support. "The Muwahhid fears following the path and not having with him weapons."[37] His point about weaponry was not to suggest that those undertaking missionary work should do so by the sword, but rather that they had both a right and a responsibility to physically defend themselves, not just with words but with weapons.

Ibn Abd al-Wahhab recognized that neither he nor his followers would be able to convince everyone of the truth of their message. Not even Muhammad had been successful in converting everyone he met to the truth of Islam.[38] Because he recognized the historical reality of rejection of Muhammad's message even during his own lifetime, Ibn Abd al-Wahhab felt that it was also important to observe how Muhammad had handled such rejection.

Ibn Abd al-Wahhab noted that Muhammad had responded by doing four things: (1) he denounced the claims of his opponents to superiority (2) he took up his sword (3) he demanded that people cease their lies about the Muslims and recognize that his teachings did not contradict or diverge from monotheism, and (4) he called on them to repent for such lies. By highlighting the series of four steps, Ibn Abd al-Wahhab deflected attention from the taking up of the sword (a physical act of defense) in favor of attention to the recognition and realization of the truth that Muhammad had demanded from the people. This latter point was the ultimate purpose of Muhammad's actions, not the undertaking of military action.

Ibn Abd al-Wahhab also pointed out that Muhammad's taking up of his sword had been a defensive move, having as its express purpose the saving and protection of the early Muslims, who were under siege by their opponents. It was not an offensive attack designed to aggrandize or enrich the Muslim community. Furthermore, he asserted that God, in His wisdom, had deliberately set this incident up so as to establish a *hadith* that was to serve for future generations as a guide for behavior toward those who are hostile to God and hate monotheism.[39] The critical issue at stake in this *hadith* was the defense of monotheism, suggesting that one can claim to be fighting in defense of God only when God's omnipotence is under threat.

Ibn Abd al-Wahhab then noted three possible responses to the preached message of monotheism that would indicate to his followers how they should proceed: (1) acceptance of Islam as expressed in joining the movement, making themselves subject to Islamic law, and fighting on the Muslim side in war; (2) payment of the poll tax (*jizyah*) in recognition of Muslim hegemony and in exchange for protected status, which did not entail conversion to Islam; or (3) fighting. If the unbelievers chose to fight (rendering them the aggressors in the conflict), fighting for the Muslims was limited to engaging those capable of conducting fights.[40] He admonished his followers that, like the early Muslims, they were not to engage their unbelieving enemies in a spirit of hatred or deception; rather, prior to engaging in military conflict they should offer peaceful alternatives to their opponents.[41]

It is very important to note that Ibn Abd al-Wahhab did not support the approach of the medieval Hanbali scholar Ibn Taymiyya of simply declaring anyone who did not adhere to his teachings to be an unbeliever (*kafir*) who had to be fought.[42] Ibn Abd al-Wahhab was far more selective about the use of the term *kafir*, limiting it to cases in which a person claimed to be a Muslim, had accepted the authority of the Word of God, and had been properly instructed in the faith yet continued to engage in associationism. In support, he cited Q 9:66, which states, "You are not forgiven/excused if your unbelief (*kufr*) is after your faith."

For Ibn Abd al-Wahhab, the chronological order was of critical importance. Charges of unbelief and apostasy could only be made fairly in cases in which the individual in question was deliberately choosing to engage in disobedience. Someone who did so accidentally or out of ignorance of correct practice should not be charged with such a serious crime.[43] It was for this reason that he taught that the appropriate response to such a situation was to read to the erring individual the Quranic verses appropriate to the situation, so as to provide concrete evidence as to why the behavior was wrong. Only if the person then refused to behave appropriately did fighting become appropriate.[44]

Thus, rather than engaging in name calling and exclusionism by dividing the world into two opposing spheres in order to justify fighting and killing, Ibn Abd al-Wahhab engaged in a more positive and inclusive approach of dialogue and discussion geared toward reconciliation and cooperation whenever possible. Fighting became an option only if the enemy refused both conversion and a treaty relationship with the Muslims. It is within this context that Ibn Abd al-Wahhab's writings on jihad must be analyzed.

The Jihad Factor

Although historical and contemporary discussions of Wahhabis and the Wahhabi movement tend to assume that whatever violence Wahhabis have engaged or currently engage in is due to an interpretation of Islam that emphasizes jihad as holy war, this vision is inconsistent with both the historical record and Ibn Abd al-Wahhab's writings.[45] Rather than proclaiming the responsibility of Muslims to fight permanently and continuously against ungodliness and evil in this world and to consider all non-Wahhabis as unbelievers, Ibn Abd al-Wahhab's writings reveal a worldview in which education and dialogue play a more important role in winning converts and establishing justice than does violence. Because this vision is so at odds with standard images of the Wahhabis, a careful analysis of Ibn Abd al-Wahhab's writings on jihad, as outlined in "Kitab al-Jihad," is in order.

What Is Jihad?

According to Ibn Abd al-Wahhab's understanding, jihad is a *fard kifayah*, or collective duty, required of those who fulfill the requirements established by God: submission to Islam, maturity, financial ability, free (as opposed to slave) status, the intent to remember and serve God in this endeavor, and good moral character.[46] Those possessing these qualifications are expected to carry out the duty of jihad at least once a year, although there is no set period annually when it must occur. Delay of jihad is permissible if one is embarking on the pilgrimage (unless one is on pilgrimage for most of the year) or is in a period of truce.[47]

The purpose of jihad is the protection and aggrandizement of the Muslim community as a whole, not personal gain or glory.[48] Because the emphasis of jihad is on the well-being of the Muslim community, Ibn Abd al-Wahhab did *not* define *jihad* as an individual undertaking—*fard 'ayn*—as contemporary extremists have done. The question of individuality comes into play only with respect to the individual's response to the call to jihad and his intent in fulfilling the duties of jihad. Ibn Abd al-Wahhab excused no individual from the duty to carry out jihad on the basis of following the example of his ancestors, even if it is his father.[49]

Associated with jihad is the act of *hijrah*, or emigration, because the person must leave home in order to participate. The *hijrah* is defined as an act of faith in and of itself because it is the physical expression of one's desire to carry out jihad, thereby adding to the number of Muslims prepared to engage in collective action.[50]

Ibn Abd al-Wahhab's depiction of jihad was clearly intended to set it apart from pre-Islamic military practices, particularly raiding. It is important to recall that in pre-Islamic Arabia tribal affiliation was the critical source of identity. When any clan or kinship group entered into combat, all members of the clan or kinship group were expected to participate. Failure to participate in the military action resulted in the severing of the blood relationship with the clan.

Raiding (*al-ghazw*) was practiced only against groups that were outside of the clan or kinship relationship.[51] The purpose of raiding was the acquisition of booty, the attainment of military glory, control of trade routes, and occasionally official rewards rather than territorial expansion or possession.[52] Practically speaking, raiding provided a means of redistributing resources in pre-Islamic Arabia. Weaker tribes could buy their way out of potential aggressions by paying protection money (*khuwwa*, literally, "brotherhood money") to stronger tribes.[53]

The booty acquired during raiding was to be divided into fourths, with the tribal leader taking one-fourth of the booty for himself. This was not considered to be personal wealth but reflected his role as tribal leader and his responsibility to ransom prisoners and pay restitution for infringements of the accepted rules of engagement incurred by his forces. The remaining three-fourths of the booty was to be divided evenly among the male members of the kinship group.

Bloodshed was not the purpose of raiding and was avoided as much as possible.[54] Massacres of captive troops were rare.[55] Finally, there were no religious or ideological justifications for raiding.[56] In contrast, Ibn Abd al-Wahhab described jihad as an activity that must always have a religious justification and can only be declared by the religious leader (*imam*) and whose intent and purpose must be strictly defensive in nature. He denounced those who used jihad as a means of seeking wealth or personal glory.

Who Is to Carry out Jihad?

The duty of jihad is incumbent on all adult male Muslims according to the Quran. Avoiding this duty is considered a sin that serves to increase the number of unbelievers. However, the Quran provides for exceptions due to weakness, illness, and age.[57]

When Is Jihad Necessary?

Ibn Abd al-Wahhab outlined three scenarios in which jihad is called for: (1) when two opposing divisions or groups meet face to face until the other side retreats, according to Q 8:45, "Whenever you encounter a force, be firm/unshakable," and Q 8:15, "And do not turn [your] backs on them; (2) when the enemy leaves its own territory, beginning with those enemies who are closest geographically;[58] and 3) when the *imam* calls for it.[59] Ibn Abd al-Wahhab emphasized that *only* the *imam* can declare jihad—this is not the prerogative of the political ruler. Furthermore, when the *imam* calls for jihad, it is incumbent on believers to obey him.[60]

In each of these three cases, Ibn Abd al-Wahhab specifically used the verb *fight* (*qaatala* [form III]) rather than *kill* (*qatala* [form I]). While it may be assumed that some killing is likely to occur during the process of fighting, it is important to note that the goal is to fight so as to cause the enemy to retreat or submit, not to annihilate the opposing forces. Thus, the degree of violence here is not as extreme as the Wahhabis are often portrayed to encourage.

To complete his discussion, Ibn Abd al-Wahhab also specified cases in which jihad is *not* called for. These cases involve the personal habits or practices of a given group of people that Muslims may find inappropriate or offensive but do not result in aggression against Muslims. Examples include the drinking of date wine *khamr* and a desire for power.[61] In other words, jihad is not appropriate when conducted as an offensive or preemptive action or to strike down a group whose personal habits or practices may not be in keeping with one's own interpretation of Islam. This is significant because one of the charges typically wielded against the Wahhabis is their supposedly intense opposition to anyone who disagrees with them in any way about a religious matter. Ibn Abd al-Wahhab clearly did not sanction such a position and in fact deplored it.

Likewise, jihad against people with whom one has either a treaty relationship or business relations is not permissible because in both cases a formal relationship of protection has been established between the two groups. Thus, anyone who comes as a messenger from a hostile tribe or for the purpose of conducting business is to be placed under Muslim protection as long as he or she remains in Muslim territory, regardless of his or her faith status. If the person dies, the right of personal protection and protection of property is passed on to his or her heirs unless they choose to opt out of it. The only time that protected people can legitimately be fought or arrested is if they come deceitfully claiming to be engaged in business or to deliver a message. Ibn Abd al-Wahhab here established a zero tolerance policy for cheating and deception that results in the loss of the person's protected status.[62]

Ibn Abd al-Wahhab also restricted the *imam*'s right to declare jihad by charging him not to deliberately incite his people to jihad because the motivation for doing so would be questionable.[63] In other words, the *imam*'s main function as a religious leader is not the call to jihad or the quest for circumstances that could justify declaration of jihad as holy war. The intent of the *imam* is an important factor in determining whether the call to jihad is legitimate.

How Is Jihad to Be Conducted?

Ibn Abd al-Wahhab taught that the motivating factors behind jihad must be piety and devoutedness. These qualities are expected to lead to boldness on the field of battle.[64] Faith provides both the intent that makes jihad possible and protection for the Muslim.[65] Consistent with all of his other writings, Ibn Abd al-Wahhab emphasized intent as the critical motivating factor in undertaking jihad. Faith, rather than wealth, power, or individual glory, as the central motivating factor sets jihad apart from other types of military activities and prepares the stage for later discussions about the types of behaviors that are permissible during and after jihad.

Jihad must be preceded by an attempt to call the opponents to Islam.[66] Ibn Abd al-Wahhab wrote, "It is not permitted that one begin with them by killing or invasion prior to their being made aware of the verse."[67] Because jihad can only be carried out against opponents of Islam, the opponents must be given a fair opportunity to convert to Islam and reject that opportunity in order for jihad to be appropriate. If the opponents convert, they are to be welcomed into the fold of the Muslim *ummah* and money may be spent on them freely. This act of generosity is considered to be in the interest and welfare of the Muslims.[68]

Jihad is further governed by specific rules about what types of activities can be conducted during it and against whom. Because only adult male Muslims are required to engage in jihad, those against whom it is waged should also be adult males. The deliberate killing of innocent women and children, whether born or unborn, is strictly prohibited. Ibn Abd al-Wahhab made no gender distinction among children, specifying that boys who have not yet reached maturity are not to be killed. Also exempted from killing are shaykhs, the elderly, the blind, monks, and slaves.

The reasoning behind these prohibitions is quite interesting because there is admittedly no consensus about them in the classical sources, which vary according to different law schools. Ibn Abd al-Wahhab exempted shaykhs from killing, despite their power over and leadership of the enemy community, because they are learned men who are not actively engaged in military activity. The elderly and the blind are exempted because they are incapable of participating in jihad and thus qualify as innocent bystanders. Monks are exempted because of their status as men of God. Rather than killing them, Ibn Abd al-Wahhab charged Muslims to call them to Islam until they either submit or God causes them to die for their errors in faith. In other words, sovereignty over the determination of life and death for the monks is the prerogative of God, not human beings. Slaves who are not actively engaged in military activity are also exempted because they qualify as innocent bystanders who are located within the enemy camp not due to their own volition but due to their status as slaves. Consequently, they cannot be held responsible for their presence unless they are actively engaged in the fighting. Peasants and farmers who do not fight are also exempted from killing, as are those who pay the *jizyah* in exchange for protection by the Muslims.[69]

In all of the exempted cases mentioned above where adult males are concerned, killing is permitted only if they express an opinion about the religious beliefs against which their community is engaged in battle and participate in resisting it, according to Muhammad's saying, "If they understand/perceive what is everlasting and resist it." In other words, for these men only resistance to the religious message constitutes grounds for killing and this only if they also refuse to enter into a treaty relationship with the Muslims. If they belong to a group with whom a treaty relationship is available via payment of the *jizyah*, Ibn Abd al-Wahhab stated that the *jizyah* covenant was preferable to any other arrangement, particularly killing, sacrifice, or enslavement.[70] Clearly, the godfather of Wahhabism did not call for the annihilation of Jews and Christians. He took care to preserve human life whenever possible.

In an interesting twist on the gender question, Ibn Abd al-Wahhab recognized that it was possible for women to be engaged at some level in opposing Muslims engaged in jihad (*mujahidin*). Consequently, women only enjoy their protected status as long as they remain unengaged in military activity. If they assume a male role by participating in battle, they lose their female status and are to be treated as adult males. Specific male activities in which females might engage include praising the *kuffar* and encouraging them in their battle against the Muslim forces, reviling or scolding the Muslims, revealing the location of Muslim forces, threatening the Muslims with arrows, dropping water on them, or provoking boys to engage in battle against them.[71]

In these cases, Ibn Abd al-Wahhab recognized the power not only of physical aggression (in the case of the arrows and dropping of water)—a typically male undertaking—but also the power of words, whether encouraging or discouraging, a typically female activity. In this way, he recognized the capacity of women to exert power and influence over men on the battlefield, rendering them active participants in the fight against Islam. Any woman who did so was subject to otherwise male penalties, making men and women equal parties in opposing Islam because both physical aggression and words can result in harm to Muslims, as well as strength and support for those opposing them.[72] However, the woman's activities must be specifically offensive in nature in order to consider her as an adult male. Ibn Abd al-Wahhab permitted women to give water to those engaged in battle and to tend to the injured, according to the prophetic example. Such actions were not to be considered aggressive or offensive in nature because they have as their intent the preservation of human life, which is a sacred duty.[73]

Prisoners of War

Opponents of Ibn Abd al-Wahhab have claimed that he " 'made no secret' of his opinion that all Muslims had fallen into unbelief, and that if they did not follow him, they should all be killed, their wives and daughters violated, and their possessions confiscated. Shiis, Sufis, and other Muslims he judged unorthodox were to be exterminated, and all other faiths were to be humiliated or destroyed."[74] However, such killing is *not* supported by Ibn Abd al-Wahhab's writings and in fact is even discouraged.

Contrary to classical jurisprudence, which held that killing the captured enemy with a weapon was appropriate at the conclusion of jihad, Ibn Abd al-Wahhab taught that the appropriate treatment of both male and female enemies during and at the conclusion of the battle is not killing but being "set aside" and locked up.[75] What this indicates is that according to his vision the ultimate purpose of jihad is not the elimination of the enemy via the sword but elimination of the enemy via persuasion to submit to Islam. This contention is supported by his subsequent condemnation of killing an enemy who is bound or binding an enemy with the specific purpose of killing him.[76] Ibn Abd al-Wahhab allowed binding of the enemy only to prevent the person from inflicting further harm on the Muslims or fleeing and also to allow the *imam* the opportunity to come to him to discuss matters of faith without fearing bodily harm. He strictly prohibited killing captives prior to the *imam*'s discussion with them.[77]

Ibn Abd al-Wahhab taught that conversion by a captive is to be accepted provided that there is clear evidence of his truthful acceptance of Islam and witnessing of the same by two honorable people.[78] Any captive who does convert to Islam, whether a free man or a slave, cannot be returned to the enemy due to his new protected status as a Muslim.[79] Thus, the emphasis on education and persuasion remains intact even in the midst of jihad, underscoring the belief that jihad, while undertaken as a matter of defense, should still strive to fulfill the more important goals of spreading Islam and expanding the Muslim community.

In a case in which the captive refuses to submit to Islam, Ibn Abd al-Wahhab still did not permit killing unless the person was a polytheist. According to the prophetic example after the Battle of Badr and the Quran, the appropriate way to deal with captives is to first "Kill the *mushrikun*/polytheists" (Q 9:5) and then "Thereafter is benevolence and ransoming" (Q 47:4). However, Ibn Abd al-Wahhab did not take this prescription literally. Even if the person was a polytheist, Ibn Abd al-Wahhab did *not* assert that this means that the person should automatically be killed. Even for polytheists, he instituted a strict set of rules to be followed.

The punishment of killing is, first of all, reserved for adult male participants in battle. Second, these captives must be given a choice: they can either submit to the Muslims and pay the *jizyah*, thereby gaining benevolence, or they can choose death. This granting of choice is justified as being in the public interest, or *maslahah*, and a matter of *ijtihad*. In any case, the choice belongs to the captives, not the captors. In addition, the captive can choose to be enslaved, although the parameters of the enslavement will change if he eventually converts to Islam.[80]

Another means of dealing with prisoners is to conduct an exchange of prisoners of war. This is both permitted and encouraged because it is not permitted to sell Muslims as slaves to *kuffar*. Muslims have a responsibility to recover their own.[81] Furthermore, because Muslims have a special treaty relationship with the *dhimmi*, they are also required to ransom any *dhimmi* taken captive by the enemy.

Similarly, the enemy has the right to recover free men who were captured by the Muslims whenever this is possible.[82] It is noteworthy that this is one case in which the age and gender of the captive are critical to determining his or her fate. Although some classical jurists permitted the ransoming of women and boys to the enemy, Ibn Abd al-Wahhab was opposed to this practice. Citing Q 60:10—"And do not return them [feminine. pl.] to the *kuffar*"—and the teachings of Ahmad ibn Hanbal, he taught that it was more fruitful for them to remain as captives of the Muslims because their captivity would provide them with the opportunity to become Muslims themselves—an assumed greater good for all involved.[83]

In a case in which captives are taken and convert to Islam, whatever property they own remains with the Muslims and is not to be returned to the enemy. For example, Ibn Abd al-Wahhab stipulated not only that women captives should not to be returned to the enemy but that it is forbidden to return the woman's *mahr* to the enemy. His reasoning on the *mahr* is that it is not due to the enemy because the woman did not take it (i.e., steal it) from them, and even if she had it would have been used to subjugate her.[84] Thus, the woman remains entitled to her *mahr*, regardless of her status or location.

Under no circumstances is a Muslim ever to be returned to a non-Muslim enemy. Ibn Abd al-Wahhab stated this clearly and forcefully, even when the enemy includes the person's close relatives, who may create chaos for the Muslims over the refusal of return. In fact, he asserted that Muslims are required to assist any female Muslim who seeks to leave a non-Muslim enemy, regardless of her circumstances, precisely because she is a Muslim.[85]

Ibn Abd al-Wahhab's thoughtful consideration of the question of what to do with captives extended so far as to address the question of what is to be done when more than one member of a family is captured. Specifically, if both the husband and the wife or both parents and children are taken as captives, what are the repercussions of captivity for family relationships? Ibn Abd al-Wahhab broke with the other law schools, most notably the Malikis and Shafiis, in asserting that captivity does not result in the abrogation of marital or parental bonds but rather that such bonds remain intact and must be respected, even in matters of religious upbringing for the children. He cited as evidence the example of Muhammad following the Battle of Badr, when Muhammad did not abrogate the marriage bonds of his captives. He further stipulated, contrary to the Malikis, that the separation of a mother from her child or of a father from his son is strictly prohibited. Children must always be allowed to remain with their families. When the parents are unavailable, the grandparents are to take over.

Ibn Abd al-Wahhab also opposed the Shafiis and the Malikis by insisting that minor brothers should not be separated, according to the prophetic example.[86] Thus, the integrity of the family unit and family bonds are upheld, suggesting that even captives have some rights that must be respected. This places a much more human face on the aftermath of jihad than one might expect. It also underlines Ibn Abd al-Wahhab's emphasis on the importance of the preservation of life and the family unit.

One other "right" of the captive is to remain within a Muslim community once captured. Although the Muslim "owner" technically has the right to sell a slave, Ibn Abd al-Wahhab insisted that this can only be to another Muslim. Sale of any slave belonging to a Muslim to a *kafir* is strictly prohibited according to *ijma'*.[87] In fact, not only does the captive have the right to remain within a Muslim community, but his/her presence there entitles him or her to the protection of the Muslims. Any Muslim who does not provide for the needs of captives is to be held accountable for it.[88]

Captives are entitled to certain stipulations for their release from captivity. Any Muslim entering into such a relationship is required to abide by them. This is particularly important with respect to women and the weak who are taken prisoner. They may not be returned to the *kuffar* for the precise reason that harm will probably come to them.[89] Higher value is placed on human welfare than on property rights.

One further indication of respect for human life and welfare is the prohibition of rampant amputation of enemies' hands and feet. Although tribal custom permitted such practices and even gloried in the beheading of enemies and captives during and after battles, these activities were not encouraged in jihad, according to the prophetic example. Muhammad himself rejected such offerings from his Companions. Ibn Abd al-Wahhab instructed the *imam* is to follow this example.[90]

Property

Ibn Abd al-Wahhab defined the purpose of property as the satisfaction of the legitimate needs of Muslims, including the needs for food and shelter. Although he asserted the right of Muslims to fulfill their needs as being the most primary of all property rights, he did not sanction Muslims simply taking whatever they wanted from whomever they wanted whenever they wanted. Rather, he set up a series of guidelines regarding property.

First, the right to take what one needs is limited to matters of food for the Muslims and fodder for their riding animals and even then only with the express permission of the *imam*. Second, he distinguished between non-Muslim tribes that are friendly to the Muslims, including those with whom they may legitimately have business relations, and those that are not friendly to the Muslims. The territory of a non-Muslim tribe friendly to the Muslims may be entered for the purpose of taking property to fulfill Muslim needs during jihad *only* with the express permission of the *imam*. For property considered to be ownerless, like firewood, Muslims have the right to take whatever they need. For property that is owned, Muslims have the right to only one-fifth. The rest remains the property of the non-Muslim tribe.[91] Thus, participation in jihad does not serve as a license to take whatever property one comes across or wishes. The restrictions placed on acquisition of property serve to maintain some level of respect for what rightfully belongs to another, as well as to place limitations on potential greed.

The deliberate destruction of property not related to the conduct of jihad is forbidden.[92] Ibn Abd al-Wahhab specifically forbade the burning, drowning, or cutting down of date palms; the destruction of honeycombs inhabited by bees; and the wounding of riding animals that are not actively engaged in the war.[93] Even baggage is not to be burned because the people owning it would suffer unduly by its loss. Ibn Abd al-Wahhab further prohibited the burning of books, particularly the Quran, reflecting an interest in the preservation of knowledge.[94] Burning and destruction of arms and weaponry are forbidden because these objects can be used to serve the cause of the *mujahidin*, thus enriching the Muslims. The saddles of riding animals are also to be kept and used by the Muslims.[95]

Killing of animals is generally restricted to cases in which the animals are to be eaten as food, such as birds, game, cattle, and sheep. The skins, however, are to be added to the booty to be divided upon the conclusion of the battle. Ibn Abd al-Wahhab made it very clear that such killing must be absolutely necessary for the nourishment of the *mujahidin* in order to be considered just. Rampant killing of livestock for the purpose of increasing booty or excessive feasting is not permitted.[96] Furthermore, the use of skins or hides of animals killed for the sole purpose of gaining the skins and hides is strictly forbidden, as is the utilization of such skins and hides, as well as any sinews, hair, or veins from the animals.[97] Only what is *absolutely necessary* is to be taken and used. Ibn Abd al-Wahhab noted that this approach, though faithful to the prophetic example, had always tended to be problematic among the *mujahidin* due to their custom of taking possession of such things during tribal raids. He asserted that these prohibitions were sufficiently important that anyone violating them would lose his right to his share of the booty. Only when public interest (*maslahah*) requires it can property be destroyed.[98]

Activities such as burning or razing enemy fortresses, cutting off water supplies to the troops, and cutting troops off from their main groups are permitted because these people and property are militarily engaged. Likewise, shooting fire and water into the fortresses is permitted because these are means of gaining power over the troops. However, this is not permitted in cases in which women and children are known to be present because they would be harmed by such actions. These types of assaults against fortresses are permitted only when military personnel alone are within them.[99]

As for crops and trees, Ibn Abd al-Wahhab noted three categories. The first consists of what is near the fortress and likely to provide sustenance or protection to those within the fortress. Because it is assumed that the fortress is a location used by military troops, it is permissible, and even necessary, to destroy them so as to prevent their use by the opposing forces. The second consists of what Muslims need either for shelter or food because it is forbidden to inflict damage or harm on Muslims. Anything related to the immediate needs of Muslim troops is permitted. The third consists of that which is not required for their use or that serves to protect the opposing forces. Ibn Abd al-Wahhab strictly prohibited the wanton destruction of plant life and property because it serves no legitimate purpose and is an act of willful anger intending harm beyond what is necessary.[100] Furthermore, lands or plants that bear crops are potentially useful in provisioning the Muslims. Their destruction would constitute the destruction of a portion of the booty to which the Muslims are entitled.[101]

Ibn Abd al-Wahhab's breakdown makes clear the Muslim's responsibility for the preservation and protection of both property and innocent life, whether human, plant, or animal. Although the Wahhabis have been portrayed as participating in rampant and wanton destruction in the course of their military activities, this clearly is *not* sanctioned by the writings of their religious guide.

Responsibilities of the Imam

The *imam* is responsible both for issuing the call to jihad and for ensuring that its conduct is in keeping with the appropriate parameters. The *imam* is personally responsible for the preservation of life and property during the undertaking of jihad, as well as the spiritual guidance of the Muslims. The *imam* is supposed to prevent divisions within the *ummah*, whether due to hatred or the pursuit of immoral or corrupt behavior among Muslims.[102] He is responsible for restoring and strengthening the hearts of the Muslims and for shattering the hearts of the *kuffar* because he knows what lies in the hearts of both.[103] The *imam* is also responsible for the well-being of the animals taken into battle so that an injured horse is not left behind to suffer or starve prior to entering the land of the enemy.[104]

According to the prophetic example, an *imam* is to serve as a teacher and mentor to the *mujahidin*, fortifying their souls via discussions of the reasons for their anticipated victories and watching over their condition. The *imam* is bound by oath to serve in this position and to know the opinions of the group.[105]

The *imam* is also responsible for concluding truces and contracting treaty arrangements whereby the enemy attains *dhimmi* status in exchange for paying the *jizyah*.[106] The only stipulation for entering into a *dhimmi* relationship is that the people must be either People of the Book (Jews or Christians) or people who have a similar book or have borrowed from these religions.[107] Thus, the *dhimmi* relationship is a recognition of a commonality of faith that permits a special relationship not available to those who do not share any beliefs in common.

In matters of booty, the *imam* is responsible for ensuring that the portion assigned to the treasury (Bayt al-Mal) is used for public welfare (*maslahah*). Only the *imam* has the right to distribute money or goods belonging to the Bayt al-Mal. Any other withdrawal from the Bayt al-Mal is considered theft, even if the ostensible purpose is for charitable use.[108] Money and property belonging to the Bayt al-Mal includes the *jizyah* paid by *dhimmis* in exchange for protection by the Muslims.

Responsibilities of the Amir

The *amir* is the political-military leader of the jihad expedition, responsible for directing military action and leading the troops. Obedience to the *amir* is required for the purpose of maintaining order and discipline among the troops, but the *amir* is not to serve as a heavy-handed, full-powered autocrat. The *amir*'s actions are always subject to the spiritual guidance of the *imam* and the counsel/advice of the army.[109] Any action by the *mujahidin*, from the collection of fodder or firewood to meeting the enemy in combat, must be approved by the *amir*.[110]

The *amir* is further responsible for the prevention of competition between *mujahidin* during the conduct of jihad, so that they do not kill each other or seek to take what belongs to another. Such disputes are to be settled outside of the context of jihad.[111]

Expenses During Jihad

Generally speaking, Muslims are not supposed to purchase goods or services from *kuffar* during jihad activities. However, according to the prophetic example, a *kafir* may be hired as a guide, if necessary, because this fulfills a need of the *mujahidin*.[112]

When expenses arise during the carrying out of jihad, the portion of the booty belonging to God and Muhammad may be used to purchase what is needed for the *mujahidin*, with the remainder to be divided according to regulations.[113] However, any loot or goods obtained illegally may not be used to purchase necessities for the *mujahidin* due to the illegal nature of their acquisition.[114] Ibn Abd al-Wahhab noted that the taking of booty is not the main purpose of jihad, differentiating it from the tribal custom of raiding and other types of military activity. Consequently, the collection of booty is very different from robbing and plunder.[115] It is clear that, even in matters of collecting booty, jihad is not intended to be used as an opportunity for acquisition of wealth or property.

How Booty Is to Be Divided

After the conclusion of jihad, whatever money and property have been taken as booty are to be divided among the leader and the *mujahidin* according to strict regulations, which vary according to different law schools. Ibn Abd al-Wahhab distinguished between two types of booty. The first, *al-ghanimah*, is the actual spoils of war, meaning that which falls to the Muslim army after military engagement. Four-fifths of the total spoils of this type of booty are to be distributed among those who participated in the military engagement. The second type—*fai*—is that wealth that non-Muslims surrender without engaging in armed conflict. *Fai* is considered to be the common possession of the whole Muslim society and is to be given to nonsoldiers as well as soldiers as the *amir* desires.[116] The booty in the following discussion is of the *ghanimah* type unless otherwise specified.

The gathering and distribution of booty is a highly regulated matter. Ibn Abd al-Wahhab taught that the booty should first be gathered together and presented collectively to the Muslims. Then it should be examined to determine whether any of the contents are either property or money originally belonging to a Muslim or a *dhimmi*. Property of this type is to be returned to its original owner. Next comes the calculation of the major items—camels, the contents of the storerooms of merchants, and so on—followed by the calculation of the minor items. Determination is then to be made of the total value of the booty, which is to be divided into fifths. One-fifth belongs to God and Muhammad. The other four-fifths are to be divided among those entitled to receive shares.[117] The only case in which booty is not to be taken is when both armies are pious.[118] Booty should always be divided in the territory in which it was acquired.[119]

Ideally, only things that are considered necessities for the Muslims should be taken as booty—food for the soldiers and fodder for the animals—making it clear that jihad is very different from the tribal raid, *ghazw*.[120] While the raid is intended to enrich the victorious tribe, the purpose of jihad is to win adherents to Islam. It is not intended to be a get rich quick scheme.

When the property or money in question originally belonged to a Muslim but was stolen by the *kuffar* and then recovered, it reverts to its owner prior to the division of whatever other booty was taken. If the property or money itself is no longer extant, the original Muslim owner is entitled to compensation for its value. Likewise, when Muslims enter into a *dhimmi* relationship with a group of people, they are required to restore whatever they had taken from those people. Furthermore, it is forbidden to make slaves of people with whom Muslims have a treaty relationship.[121]

Generally speaking, Ibn Abd al-Wahhab assigned to the leader the right to no more than a third and then a fourth of the booty.[122] This booty may be used for the leader's own personal needs, as well as for financing specific jihad activities by certain select groups of Muslims such as the horsemen.[123] However, the leader does not have the right to distribute the booty as he wishes— he must follow very specific regulations about its division. In other words, the leader does not have the right to reward specific individuals who desire special items prior to the division of the booty. In fact, Ibn Abd al-Wahhab noted that, although there are examples of Muhammad doing this, this was not intended to be a universal example. Only the *imam*, as the religious leader, can approve such special treatment.[124] However, even the *imam* cannot assign a portion to a tribe hired to participate in the jihad because it has already been compensated by the hiring. The purpose of this prohibition is to maintain equality among the *mujahidin* so that jihad will not become a means of seeking wealth, privilege, or special status. It is also designed to prevent rebellion and resentment among the ranks because special treatment of certain warriors would lead to an unfair distribution of the booty, which all of the *mujahidin* fought together to achieve.

Facing the reality that particularly strong warriors might be tempted to collect followers and head out on their own in battle, Ibn Abd al-Wahhab taught that such people are to be punished and should lose their claim not only to what they have taken in battle but also to any share of the collective booty. Furthermore, the *amir* is to reject any loot brought to him by such a faction and is not to use it even to purchase goods for the army because it was obtained illegally.[125]

The prohibition against special treatment for specific individuals serves as a strong reminder of the nature of jihad as a collective duty (*fard kifayah*) rather than an individual duty (*fard 'ayn*) and the equality of every *mujahid* along the same lines as the equality of every Muslim. If the leader chooses to provide personal rewards to specific individuals out of his own portion of the booty, that is his prerogative, but he may not do so out of the booty collectively belonging to the *mujahidin*.[126]

According to Q 8:41, one-fifth of the booty belongs to God and Muhammad. In Ibn Abd al-Wahhab's time, this portion was assigned for use for public welfare and is supposed to be used to carry out God's work. This portion is to be set aside before any other divisions are made.[127] The remaining four-fifths are to be divided among the leader and the participants. According to the *hadith*, Muhammad set the precedent of giving a portion of his share to the one who was to succeed him as God's gift to the leader of the Muslim community. After the lifetime of Muhammad, it was determined by the Companions that the one-fifth portion belonging to God and Muhammad was to be turned over to the *imam* for deposit into the Bayt al-Mal and used for the sustenance of the orphans, the poor, and "the sons of the path."[128] In other words, the portion belonging to God and Muhammad is to be used for charitable purposes to sustain those Muslims who do not have families to provide for them. Thus, no Muslim is to be left without the means to survive, again emphasizing Islam's broad concern for the welfare of all Muslims, regardless of gender or age.

Ibn Abd al-Wahhab taught that anyone who falls or is killed in battle is entitled to a share of the booty due to his merit in giving his life in the cause of God.[129] Interestingly, a share of the booty is not automatically due to someone who kills an enemy in battle.[130] On the contrary, he taught that such a person is to be not only deprived of his share but also cast out of his rank. Although this pronouncement does not appear to be in keeping with the standard historical image of the Wahhabis, it is in keeping with Ibn Abd al-Wahhab's overall concern for the maximum preservation of life, even in the midst of jihad. After all, if an enemy is killed in the course of battle, the *imam* will not be able to issue the call to Islam. Thus, killing prevents the ultimate purpose of jihad from being accomplished. This is particularly the case if the Muslim kills the enemy out of greed or a desire for revenge or self-aggrandizement, in which case the killer cannot claim to be carrying out any godly purpose. Only if the *imam* authorizes it can the killer take the portion that belonged to the one who was killed.[131]

Ibn Abd al-Wahhab made it clear that booty, by its nature, is very different from other kinds of property. Most specifically, booty is not subject to inheritance laws in the same manner as money or private property. Any booty obtained via jihad is part of the collective booty that is to be distributed to the participants. If a participant is killed or dies prior to the division of the booty, his portion reverts to the leader, who then has the option of delegating all or part of it to the participant's descendants. However, this is the prerogative of the leader rather than the right of the heirs.[132]

Booty can include people, typically those who have been taken captive during the course of battle, both men and women. However, Ibn Abd al-Wahhab was careful to note that the taking of a female captive does not entitle the owner to sexual relations with her—even if the owner is the *imam*. In fact, he stated that, "When the *imam* takes as booty a beautiful woman, fantasizing about her is immoral."[133] Here, again, he broke with the other law schools in his concern for human dignity and welfare rather than the rights of the victor at the cost of the degradation of the captive. His pronouncement here is consistent with his concern for the protection of women and prevention of their sexual degradation.[134]

Also included in the booty discussion is the breakdown of what types of things may be considered booty that is to be assembled and divided collectively versus what types of things are considered the personal property of the person who killed the one who owned them. For example, money and property, such as livestock, riding animals, or land, are considered part of the assembled booty that must be divided. However, clothing, personal jewelry (such as armlets or girdles), and weaponry are considered the property of the individual who took them.[135] Ibn Abd al-Wahhab made it clear, though, that the taking of such possessions is not supposed to be done in such a way as to cast down the enemy by it.[136] Respect for human dignity is to remain the overriding principle of jihad, even when the enemy has been defeated.

As for any type of mineral or treasure that is found buried in the earth, Ibn Abd al-Wahhab considered this to be the collective property of the Muslims, to be divided along with the booty. It is never considered the property of any individual, regardless of who owns the property in which it is found. If, however, the mineral or treasure is not actually buried in the earth but can be picked up with the hands and is found in the land of the enemy, then it is to be considered to be like other property and divided as booty. If it is found in a Muslim territory, the army does not have any right to it. These statutes apply in cases in which the object found has inherent value. When the object itself is not valuable without being either treated or transported, then it is considered the personal property of the person who found it or who owns the property in which it is located because that person can render it valuable only by exerting personal effort to enhance its value. It is not considered part of the booty.[137]

Ibn Abd al-Wahhab consistently cautioned that acquisition of personal property and riding animals should not be the goal of the *mujahidin* because, according to Muhammad's example, these items are permissible only if they are "end of the line" items. He specifically mentioned with regard to clothing that only worn or undesirable robes (*thobes*) captured in battle may be worn. Likewise, confiscation of riding animals is permitted only when they are emaciated.[138] This is in keeping with his prior statement that only that which is necessary for the survival of the Muslim community may be taken. A worn *thobe* cannot be mistaken for a luxury item. One would expect that a Muslim would take care of an emaciated horse, indicating that even the welfare of riding animals is supposed to be given higher consideration by Muslims than non-Muslims.

Portions of booty are not limited to human participants in jihad. Riding animals, both horses and camels, are also entitled to a share of the booty if they have been active participants in the battle.[139] Mules, on the other hand, are not entitled to anything but fodder.[140] Who actually receives a share depends on two factors: who owns the animal and who is riding it. If a slave fights riding a horse belonging to his master, the horse is entitled to a portion of the booty, which goes to the master, and the slave is entitled to a small gift. If the horse has been borrowed or leased/hired, then the portion belongs to the person who borrowed or hired it. If the horse is being held in custody, the portion belongs to the person holding it. If the horse has been taken illegally, its portion belongs to the actual owner.[141]

Full combatants are entitled to a full share of the booty after the battle. Merchants, manufacturers, and artisans who are noncombatants do not receive portions. Likewise, the sick, the elderly, those unable to fight, those who stay behind, and weak horses do not have any claim to a portion of the booty because they did not participate in the jihad. Those who turn away and abandon the Muslim army are particularly looked down on because they have abandoned their people. Anyone who commits such a crime is not entitled to a share of the booty.

However, anyone who participates in the jihad, whether as a combatant or as one who provides assistance or support to the Muslims or who helps Muslim prisoners to escape prior to the end of battle, is entitled to a share of the booty. If such assistance is provided after the battle, no portion is gained. Thus, the critical factor is the timing of the assistance. Portions are also due to those who send people to the *amir* to provide assistance for the well-being (*maslahah*) of the army or who agitate against the enemy in its homeland.[142]

Although it is clear that booty is intended to be a reward for the combatants in jihad, Ibn Abd al-Wahhab did not completely restrict the assignment of booty to the participants. Rightful shares or portions were limited to actual combatants. However, he noted that Muhammad himself provided small gifts, or tokens, to those Muslims who did not have a legal right to a share of the booty. People benefiting from this practice included slaves, women, and children. The justification for this gift is to provide for the necessities of life for all Muslims, not just able-bodied males. This was believed to be appropriate by the early Muslim community because such people typically accompanied the *mujahidin* and were present during the battles. Ahmad ibn Hanbal used this example and Umar's understanding of the same as the basis for his ruling that anyone who witnesses the battle, regardless of his or her state or participation, is entitled to receive some part of the booty.[143]

Treatment of the People of Conquered Areas

In a case in which the people of a conquered area submit to the Muslims after jihad, they are entitled to remain on their property in exchange for paying both the land tax (*kharaj*) and the poll tax (*jizyah*), which places them in a treaty relationship of protection with the Muslims. Ibn Abd al-Wahhab specified that, although these taxes are due to the Muslims, they are not intended to impoverish the inhabitants, nor are they subject to increases over the years. He specifically forbade Muslims from overtaxing their subjects. He further forbade Muslims from purchasing cultivable lands in such areas because it would deprive them of the land tax and prevent those who were conquered from maintaining their property and entering into a treaty relationship with the Muslims.[144] Thus, it remains clear that even the aftermath of jihad is not intended to serve as a means of enriching the Muslims; rather, it is designed to encourage those whom they have conquered either to submit to Islam or to enter into a treaty relationship with the Muslims. This hardly matches the typical historical image of the Wahhabis as bloodthirsty murderers of any and all who disagreed with them.

The Spoils of War Unrelated to Conquest

Ibn Abd al-Wahhab recognized that not all property and money acquired by the Muslims came from jihad activities. For the broader question, then, of what was to be done with such property, including the *jizyah*, the *kharaj*, the one-tenth tax (*'ushr*), and what enemy tribes left behind when they fled out of fear of the approaching Muslim army, Ibn Abd al-Wahhab responded that they were the collective property of the Muslims, with no distinctions to be made in terms of combatants versus noncombatants, age, or social or financial status. The only preference that should be made among Muslims is to be based on observation of what Muslims tend to do with their money and property. While he agreed that the soldiers provide an important service by using their skills in God's cause, Ibn Abd al-Wahhab did not believe that this was the only way in which one can serve God. In fact, he commented that "the most important" Muslims are those who build mosques, bridges, and aqueducts; repair and restore roads; and nourish judges (*qadis*) and widows.[145] The factor that ties these activities together is their contribution to public *maslahah*, and this serves as the only consideration for potentially granting a larger share of the wealth to such persons because it will be used for the benefit of all Muslims, thus maintaining the principle of collective wealth.

A portion of this collective wealth is to go to the leader to be used at his discretion, although it is not clear how much the leader is entitled to because this is not specified in the Quran or *hadith*.[146] Once the leader has claimed his share, the remainder is to be divided into fifths. As with his fifth of the booty, the leader may choose to reward individuals or finance specific causes out of his share of the wealth. However, this is a personal decision rather than a matter of law. Ibn Abd al-Wahhab declared that Muhammad's example of re-warding individuals and causes in such cases was a personal decision, not a binding precedent for Muslims of all ages.[147]

Conversions to Islam Following Jihad

In matters of faith, Ibn Abd al-Wahhab consistently focused on the questions of intent and sincerity. This remained the case in the aftermath of jihad when captives have the opportunity to accept the call to Islam. Although he could have denied any conversions following conquest out of concern that people might claim to believe anything in order to save their lives, Ibn Abd al-Wahhab, following the example of the caliph Umar, taught that the captive's claim to faith deserves consideration. If a captive swears sincerity of belief and does not intend deceit by it, his or her faith should be considered authentic.[148]

As for how faith is to be determined, Ibn Abd al-Wahhab cited the saying of Muhammad that your faith is known through "your work and your belief," and the Quran which instructs Muslims, "Hire him until he hears the words of God," Q 9:6.[149] In other words, a person's faith should be apparent not only in what s/he says, but also in what s/he does. Everyone should be given the opportunity to come to faith, an opportunity that can only arise when the tasks of missionary work and education are fulfilled.

When Is Retreat from Jihad Permitted?

Although retreat is not the desired outcome of jihad, Ibn Abd al-Wahhab ac-knowledged that there are cases when retreat is authorized. If an individual finds himself outnumbered, he may retreat. Likewise, if he fears that he will be taken prisoner he is permitted to surrender. Thus, it is clear that those carrying out jihad are not required to fight to the death or to seek death delib-erately in the course of the battle. There is no "cult of martyrdom" in Ibn Abd al-Wahhab's writings. The preservation of human life is always a guiding prin-ciple.

However, Ibn Abd al-Wahhab noted that there were consequences to re-treat from jihad: if an individual retreats or surrenders during the battle and the battle is won by the Muslims, the person who retreated or surrendered is not permitted to share in the booty.[150] Thus, he taught that adherence to duty is a serious responsibility. Those who approach this God-given duty faintheart-edly will not be rewarded.

Declaring a Truce

Contrary to popular media images of jihad as a quest for suicide or a fight to the death, Ibn Abd al-Wahhab noted that the Quran itself commands the *mu-jahidin* to grant peace to those who no longer wish to fight. He cited Q 9:1, "Withdrawal is from God and His Messenger," and Q 8:61, "And if they are inclined toward peace, then lean toward it," as well as the prophetic example of allowing truces for up to ten years at a time, as evidence that tolerance and peace are the best means of serving *maslahah*. In fact, he particularly took the Shafii law school to task for its lack of tolerance in dealing with truces, ob-serving that al-Shafii's recommended course of action seemed better designed to serve the interests of greed and killing than that of *maslahah*.[151]

Given the standard reputation of the Wahhabis, this denunciation is quite interesting. Ibn Abd al-Wahhab's discussion of truces departed from the clas-sical approach in two ways. First, many classical jurists held that truces were undesirable and should only be entered into as a last resort. Second, where they did address the possibility of a truce they tended to deal with the legal logistics of truces, such as the specifics of entering into treaties or the payment of taxes, rather than their desirability or consequences.[152] Ibn Abd al-Wahhab, on the other hand, believed that entering into a truce was the second most desirable outcome of jihad, with only conversion to Islam being of higher preference. This stance highlights his belief that jihad is intended to serve God and fellow human beings rather than enriching the Muslim community at someone else's expense. For this reason, he taught that tolerance is necessary for the sake of *maslahah* and he allowed Muslims to engage in relatively friendly relationships with nonhostile non-Muslims, such as would be the case in a business relationship. His hope was that such behavior would make a positive impression on non-Muslims, ultimately leading them to embrace Is-lam.[153]

The regulations for declaring a truce are, as with the rest of jihad, very specific in terms of what is to be done and who is to do it. First, only the *imam* or his authorized representative or proxy is permitted to conclude a truce.[154] Truces concluded by anyone else, even the *amir*, are neither legal nor binding. Again, this emphasizes the different roles of the *imam* and the *amir* in jihad activities, distinguishing between religious and political-military authority. Ibn

Abd al-Wahhab's purpose in keeping these positions separate was to prevent any single human being from claiming both types of authority out of concern that this could lead to corruption. The separation of religious and political authority was not designed to remove religion from the public sphere but rather to ensure that religious authority would not be superseded by political interests.

Second, once the *imam* has concluded the truce, it is binding on the Muslims, regardless of whether the *imam* dies or is dismissed from his position afterward.[155] Ibn Abd al-Wahhab cited Q 9:4, "And continue in them [with] their treaties to their time," as support for this contention.

Third, although stipulations may be written into the truce, they must be in keeping with the precepts of Islamic law. Any stipulation violating Islamic law, such as the requirement that female captives be returned to the enemy, renders the stipulation itself void, although the truce remains intact.[156] Ibn Abd al-Wahhab compared this situation to that of a marriage contract, whereby both spouses have the right to insert conditions into the contract provided that they do not violate Islamic law or the purpose of marriage. This comparison suggests that Muslim relationships with other Muslims or non-Muslims should be considered a contractual relationship.

Fourth, once the *imam* has concluded the truce he is responsible for protecting those with whom the truce has been declared. In addition, the Muslims also become responsible for the protection of the property of those with whom they have concluded the truce, even if it is just a leather skin.[157] This is considered to be part of the nature of the truce.

Muslims are bound to abide by the terms of the truce as long as their truce partners do so. However, if the other side violates the terms of the truce, whether by fighting, killing, demonstrating against the Muslims, or taking Muslim property, this violation results in the abolition of the treaty and gives the Muslims the right to fight. Ibn Abd al-Wahhab noted that Muhammad had set this precedent in his relationship with the Jewish community in Medina. As long as the Jews abided by the terms of their treaty relationship with the Muslims, they enjoyed protected status. It was only after repeated violations of that relationship that Muhammad finally allowed warfare against them. For Ibn Abd al-Wahhab, the point of this history was that the action breaking the truce must come from the other side. As long as the other side abides by the terms of the truce, the Muslims are bound to do so also, without exception.[158]

When the truce results in a treaty relationship in which the enemy becomes *dhimmi*, there are two requirements in order for the relationship to exist: (1) the *dhimmi* must agree to pay the *jizyah*, and (2) the *dhimmi* must recognize and accept Muslim jurisdiction.[159]

Violence in the Works of Ibn Abd al-Wahhab

Although one would expect, given the standard depictions of Wahhabis, that violence would be abundantly present in the written works of Ibn Abd al-Wahhab, the reality is that violence is largely and notably absent. Although there are some calls for fighting those who are labeled *kuffar*, the use of this term is much more limited than has traditionally been assumed. According to Ibn Abd al-Wahhab, a person can only be fairly labeled as a *kafir* after the person has been called to and accepted Islam and provided with instruction in the Quran and *hadith* and, after all of this, chooses to reject it. In other words, the label *kafir* is reserved for a person who has reneged in both word and faith. Only in the face of such a failure to adhere to one's promises can fighting be legitimated.[160]

Ibn Abd al-Wahhab's stance did not, however, prevent some of his more enthusiastic followers from actively seeking an excuse to label someone a *kafir* because he or she refused to join the movement. The desire of such followers was clearly to engage such people in military action that could potentially result in their deaths. Ibn Abd al-Wahhab's writings indicate that he was aware of such distortions of his teachings even during his own lifetime. What is significant is that, not only did he not endorse them, but he also chastised as ignorant those who pursued this path. The purpose of "Kitab al-Jihad" was to address these actions by providing a clear and specific outline of what kinds of activities were and were not permitted and against whom. Rather than broadening the scope for jihad as holy war, "Kitab al-Jihad" severely limited the cases in which jihad as holy war could appropriately be called for.

When read in the context of his other works, "Kitab al-Tawhid" fulfills the same function. Although this treatise has historically been misunderstood as a manifesto for action rather than a theological treatise explaining the implications of belief in monotheism, calls to violence are largely absent in this work. In fact, "Kitab al-Tawhid" contains only one case in which violence in the path of God is directly addressed: a discussion of the promises of God and Muhammad. This discussion involved the interpretation of Q 16:91, which commands Muslims to fulfill their covenants with God once they have been entered into and not to break oaths once they have been confirmed. The purpose of the discussion is to emphasize the importance of keeping one's word. A *hadith* recorded by Muslim describes the commands given by Muhammad to those commissioned to lead military actions or expeditions:

> Strive/Conquer /Attack/Raid[161] in the name of God, in His path/
> way, fight anyone who disbelieves in God. Strive/Attack and do not
> be filled with rancor/hatred. Do not act treacherously/deceitfully. Do
> not maim/mutilate. Do not kill a child. When you encounter your

enemy from the unbelievers (*mushrikin*), then call them to three qualities—or shortcomings. Whichever of them they agree to accede to you then engage them. Hold back from them and then call them to Islam. If they accede to you then engage them. Then call them to depart from their land to the land of the *muhajirin*. Inform them that if they do this then they will have what belongs to the *muhajirin*, and upon them will be what is upon the *muhajirin*. If they refuse to depart from it then inform them that they are being like the Bedouins of the Muslims, setting upon them the judgment of God Most High, and there will not be anything for them in the booty and spoils of war, except that they fight (*jahidu*) with the Muslims. If they decline this, then ask them for the *jizyah*. If they accede to you, then engage them and hold back from them. If they decline, then ask for help from God, and fight them. When you surround a people who are well fortified and they desire of you that you make them the protected people (*dhimmah*) of God and the protected people (*dhimmah*) of His Prophet, do not make them the protected people (*dhimmah*) of God and the protected people (*dhimmah*) of His Prophet, but make them your protected people (*dhimmah*) and the protected people (*dhimmah*) of your companions. Therefore you are to protect your protected people (*dhimmah*) and the protected people (*dhimmah*) of your companions. It is less important than making them the protected people (*dhimmah*) of God and the protected people (*dhimmah*) of His Prophet. If you surround a well-fortified people and they desire of you that you set out God's judgment, do not set it out for them, but set out your own judgment, and therefore you do not know: Will you be correct in God's judgment of them or not?"[162]

One of the most striking points of this *hadith* is the fact that it provides a wide variety of alternatives to fighting and violence. Fighting is always the method of last resort rather than the point of departure. It also allows for the creation of protective relationships (*dhimmah*) so that the purpose of engaging the *mushrikin* is never killing but rather calling them to Islam at best and establishing treaty relationships and formal alliances at least. It is only in the case of abject refusal to recognize the Muslims as any kind of entity that warfare and violence become acceptable methods of interaction. Ibn Abd al-Wahhab's writings reflect this approach. The discussion that follows the *hadith* emphasizes the difference here between the judgments and promises of God and Muhammad and the judgments and promises of human beings. The implication is that human promises and judgments are inferior to those of God and Muhammad. Of the commands to go forth and fight in the cause of God those who deny God, Ibn Abd al-Wahhab simply noted that they are commands. He did not discuss them any further or specify how they are to be carried out.[163]

One of Ibn Abd al-Wahhab's *fatawa* also addresses the question of fighting those accused of unbelief. He was questioned by a *sharif* who wanted a written justification of the accusation of unbelief lodged against one of his men, along with a justification for Ibn Abd al-Wahhab's followers fighting him. Ibn Abd al-Wahhab complied with the request with a written response. Although the *fatwa* is relatively lengthy, it is worth close examination, as it reveals not only what qualified this man as an unbeliever but also the *process* of conversion that the Wahhabis undertook.[164]

Ibn Abd al-Wahhab began the *fatwa* by instructing the *sharif* in the five pillars of Islam. The man in question had first left and then neglected the pillars, which was what led to the Wahhabis fighting him. Ibn Abd al-Wahhab cited the man's sin as being that he believed in the religion of *shirk*, here defined as the religion of the majority of the people of the area, which included belief in rocks, trees, and human beings on a par with God and his preference of those who committed associationism rather than the monotheists. Clearly, such associationism is a violation of God's *tawhid*. Consequently, although there are five pillars of faith in Islam, the first is the most important in Ibn Abd a-Wahhab's opinion because, as the "two witnessings," it is the declaration of faith that proclaims God's uniqueness and asserts the role of Muhammad as God's Messenger—the primary creed of the Muslim faith. Declaration of the two witnessings is critical to being recognized as a Muslim.

Ibn Abd al-Wahhab then noted that the fact of leaving the five pillars does not necessarily lead to an accusation of unbelief because there could potentially be different intents behind such actions. He cited the possibility of laziness as an excuse for not fulfilling some of the pillars, which is not the same thing as denial, repudiation, or rejection of the pillars. Because of the potential ambiguity, he stated that the critical issue was the two witnessings, which require little effort on the part of the believer other than speaking. Furthermore, the accusation of unbelief occurred—and this was the critical point—*after* the man had been instructed in the faith, so that he did have knowledge of the pillars but either decided or pretended not to know them. This point is critical because it demonstrates the hallmark of the Wahhabi approach to conversions—not the conversion by sword, as is typically described in the unfavorable accounts of the movement in later times, but conversion through instruction in the faith. Suggested by this approach is the giving of the benefit of the doubt to those who have not yet been instructed because it is possible that they might not know the pillars of faith. It is only after instruction has occurred and been adhered to and then subsequently rejected that the declaration of unbelief is made. For Ibn Abd al-Wahhab, only someone who has been properly instructed in monotheism and does not enter it but remains in associationism is to be labeled a *kafir* and fought, according to Q 9:12, which prescribes fighting the unbelievers due to their lack of faith, and the example of Muhammad, who fought his own people until they observed monotheism.[165] However, although the prophetic example made fighting in such cases permissible, it did not make it an immediate or absolute requirement. It was only a potential occurrence.

The other striking point in this account is that the issue of concern is fighting rather than killing. Again, the Wahhabis are often depicted, particularly by their opponents, as being particularly ruthless in killing anyone who does not subscribe to their beliefs. The man in this case, however, is clearly still alive because he apparently went to the *sharif* in search of protection. At no point in his discussion of the man's unbelief, however vehemently denounced, did Ibn Abd al-Wahhab ever call for the man's death. In fact, at the end of the *fatwa* he used this case as an example of the negative propaganda circulating about the Wahhabis, which he decried as being far from the truth. He noted the lies and slander about the Wahhabis that accuse them of charging the general public with unbelief and requiring emigration (*hijrah*) as incumbent on anyone who claimed to be a believer as proof of his religion and charging anyone who did not believe and fight with them of unbelief. He stated, "All of this is lies and slander, which alienate the people from the religion of God and His Messenger. And therefore we did not accuse of disbelief anyone who worships idols for the sake of their ignorance or to deprive them of their nobility. How could we accuse of disbelief anyone who did not associate with God? Therefore do not emigrate to us but do not disbelieve and fight."[166]

Ibn Abd al-Wahhab highlighted two important issues here—one a statement that the Wahhabis did not accuse ignorant people of disbelief, suggesting the educational role of the movement, and the second that accusations of disbelief did not have as their purpose the deprivation of any person of his or her nobility. This must have been a critical issue among the movement's opponents to be mentioned so forcefully. Furthermore, he denied the demand for *hijrah* as being instrumental to adherence to the movement. Rather than calling on people to emigrate, he called on them to end their disbelief and cease fighting the supporters of monotheism.[167] Such an approach certainly does not suggest a movement of violent fanaticism but rather recognizes that education and persuasion are the best and most appropriate means of gaining additional adherents.

Conclusion

Across time and space, the Wahhabis have been depicted as violent fanatics, wreaking havoc, death, and destruction against anyone whom they considered to be unbelievers or associationists. This depiction clearly has no basis in the written works of Muhammad Ibn Abd al-Wahhab. Although he taught that monotheism should always be upheld and associationism must be eradicated, violence and killing were not the prescribed methods for achieving these goals. He always emphasized education and discussion as the appropriate means for calling people to monotheism. Rather than calling for violence and destruction, his writings on jihad were permeated with an emphasis on the importance of the preservation of life, human, plant, and animal, and property, both human and material.

Ibn Abd al-Wahhab's writings reflect a constant emphasis on the importance of individual knowledge to be gained through education and the need for believing Muslims to be engaged in missionary work (da'wah) in order to call others to the faith. The preferred method for carrying out these activities was a process of dialogue, debate and discussion rather than violence and militancy. Ibn Abd al-Wahhab asserted the need for all believers, both male and female, to acquire individual knowledge of the Quran and Sunna not only to strengthen them in their faith but also to help them in the critical duty of evaluating correct religious belief and behavior, as well as to choose appropriate religious and political leaders.

Ibn Abd al-Wahhab's careful and detailed discussion of jihad—how it is defined, who is to carry it out, and under what circumstances and the regulations applying to it both during and afterward—demonstrates a concern for placing limitations of violence and destruction rather than calling for indiscriminate militance against nonadherents to his teachings. His focus on the preservation of life—human, plant, and animal—as well as property reflects his concern for respect for others and the desire to pursue peaceful means of conversion and the establishment of cooperative relationships with others. In keeping with this vision, Ibn Abd al-Wahhab sought to limit violence, particularly applications of the death penalty, because he believed that this was counterproductive and likely only to produce fear, not faith.

Ibn Abd al-Wahhab's overwhelming concern was the winning of adherents through faith of the heart—a goal that he believed could best be achieved through dialogue rather than destruction. According to this vision, jihad has no place as an offensive activity. It is a method of last resort in defending the Muslim community from aggression so that the work of proselytization can continue.

6

The Trajectory of Wahhabism: From Revival and Reform to Global Jihad

Ibn Abd al-Wahhab's narrow and restricted discussion of jihad raises an important question: how do contemporary movements whose proclaimed goal is to carry out unlimited, global jihad against unbelievers derive inspiration from Ibn Abd al-Wahhab? If, as was argued in the previous chapter, Ibn Abd al-Wahhab sought to limit the scope and involvement of the Muslim community in jihad as holy war, how can contemporary extremists like Osama bin Laden use Ibn Abd al-Wahhab's ideology to justify their global jihad against the United States and American interests? Is contemporary extremism part of a long historical tradition or is it a recent phenomenon that has developed due to particular contextual circumstances?

Answers to these questions require a comparison of Ibn Abd al-Wahhab's writings on jihad with writings of other Muslim scholars, both past and present, in order to clarify his context and interests in addressing the topic. The contextualization of his thought on jihad in the broader Islamic tradition combined with an appreciation for the changing environment in which Wahhabism developed over time provides clues as to how his writings have been reinterpreted and even distorted in the contemporary era in order to justify activities that were not part of his world. It also raises the question of whether the militant extremism of contemporary *jihadi* movements truly draws its inspiration from Ibn Abd al-Wahhab or if other Islamic thinkers have been more influential in shaping their worldview.

Jihad: A Historical Perspective

The quest for placement of Ibn Abd al-Wahhab's approach to jihad begins with identification of historical thought on this topic. Although there have been unique thinkers in every age, it is possible to identify and categorize general trends of interpretation chronologically. Rudolph Peters has identified three major categories of writings on jihad: traditionalist-classicist, modernist, and fundamentalist. As he describes them: "The traditionalists copy the phrases of the classical works on *fiqh;* the modernists emphasize the defensive aspect of *jihad,* regarding it as tantamount to *bellum justum* in modern international law; and the fundamentalists view it as a struggle for the expansion of Islam and the realization of Islamic ideals."[1] Where does Ibn Abd al-Wahhab fit with respect to these categories?

The Traditional-Classical Interpretation of Jihad Compared to the Works of Ibn Abd al-Wahhab

The form of Ibn Abd al-Wahhab's treatise on jihad is consistent with the classical *ikhtilaf* tradition of theological treatise writing. *Ikhtilaf* is a genre of literature that presents and juxtaposes the opinions of different schools of Islamic law in order to identify controversies between early legal specialists. Ibn Abd al-Wahhab clearly followed this style in presenting a variety of opinions about topics based on Quranic verses and (sometimes) contradictory or competing *hadith.* He typically cited the opinions of at least two law schools (usually two that were in disagreement with each other) and examined the legal reasoning or evidence on which their opinions were based.

Ibn Abd al-Wahhab also addressed certain themes that fall into the category of classical *ikhtilaf* discussion: the emphasis on the need to summon unbelievers to Islam prior to engaging in battle, jihad as a collective rather than an individual duty, and some of the rules for interactions between Muslims and unbelievers both during and after the battle.[2]

Finally, the organization of the treatise also falls within the classical *ikhtilaf* tradition. Ibn Abd al-Wahhab began with a discussion of the legal qualifications for who is to carry out jihad, under what circumstances, and for what purpose, followed by the legal qualifications of the enemy, permissible damage to both people and property, prerequisites for warfare, and the permissibility of truces.[3]

In addition to these format issues, Ibn Abd al-Wahhab, following the classical exegetes, gave a great deal of attention to Muhammad's example in his discussion of jihad. Reuven Firestone has noted the primal role of the Sunna in classical discussions of jihad so that the main focus of the discussions is on the conduct of warfare rather than on ideas about war. This classical approach tends to focus on the behavior and discourse of Muhammad when he was engaged in jihad and centers on issues like the treatment of noncombatants, prisoners, riding animals, and equipment; the rules for gathering and distributing booty; the role of women; and the practice of praying and calling on God prior to and during battle.[4]

However, it would be a mistake to assume that simply because Ibn Abd al-Wahhab followed a standard classical format this means that: (1) there is nothing original in what he wrote; and (2) he can simply and easily be classified as a scholar in the classical, premodernist tradition. While he generally followed the classical format of discussion, Ibn Abd al-Wahhab nevertheless inserted his personal style into his *ikhtilaf* discussions by offering his own conclusions as to which opinion among the many presented was correct and in some cases explaining why other opinions were incorrect. This personal voice is not part of the classical tradition and represents a newer trend of thought. Thus, with respect to format and methodology, Ibn Abd al-Wahhab does not fit neatly into the classicist category.

Ibn Abd al-Wahhab's methodological approach is not particularly surprising or shocking because his purpose was to return to the most basic sources of Islam, the Quran and *hadith*, in order to reinterpret them directly. Although he rejected the notion of imitation of past scholarship and thought (*taqlid*), this did not excuse him from being aware of this history. Rather than considering his discussion of the thoughts of the founders of the original law schools as simply a traditional format of theological discussion, it is important to recognize that his presentation serves as evidence of his familiarity with, and in some cases acceptance of, a broad body of literature. Ibn Abd al-Wahhab was not an illiterate country bumpkin with no appreciation of Islam's long scholarly history, as some opponents have charged.[5] Neither did he seek to discard or "abandon" the classical tradition altogether.[6] In fact, he was a scholar with a broad base of knowledge who was well versed in the classical tradition. His rejection of imitation of the past was not based on rejection of knowledge but on rejection of blind adherence to the past simply because it was the past. He believed that knowledge of the past was critical to understanding the development of thought over time but should not be considered as a substitute for direct knowledge of the fundamental sources of Islam.

A comparison of Ibn Abd al-Wahhab's writings with classical writings on jihad would be incomplete without an analysis of their content. Ibn Abd al-Wahhab emphasized two major themes: the teachings of the Quran and *hadith* about jihad and a delineation of the purpose and consequences of jihad. Firestone's analysis of the classical tradition also addresses these two themes, providing a comparative context for consideration and classification of Ibn Abd al-Wahhab's writings.

Firestone's analysis opens with the question of why jihad should occur and what it signifies. He finds that most of the classical exegetes point to Q 9: 5, the so-called sword verse, in order to define the purpose of jihad, concluding that its ultimate goal is to bring people to witness God's unity, pray, and pay the alms tax. In other words, jihad clearly has mostly religious goals behind it—conversion and adherence to the pillars of Islam (two of which are mentioned here, witnessing and almsgiving)—so that material gain is not the primary purpose of such an endeavor, although it may result from it.[7]

Ibn Abd al-Wahhab agreed with this interpretation. The major difference in perspective lies in the interpretation of what jihad signifies. In Ibn Abd al-Wahhab's writings, jihad is a special and specific type of warfare, which can be declared only by the religious leader (*imam*) and whose purpose is the defense of the Muslim community from aggression. In other words, it describes a particular type of warfare and the circumstances that surround it. In contrast, in the classical tradition jihad is not the war itself but a statement of the relationship between the Islamic and non-Islamic worlds. In other words, it provides a justification for war rather than the terms of how that war is carried out.[8] Inherent in the classical definition is a division of the world into two absolute categories—the land of Islam (*dar al-islam*) and the land of unbelief (*dar al-kufr*)—a distinction on which Ibn Abd al-Wahhab, surprisingly, did not insist.

As a second tactic, Firestone then breaks the Quran verses addressing conversion and jihad into four categories in accordance with the writings of the classical exegete Ibn Kathir: those that are completely nonmilitant, those restricting warfare, those expressing conflict between God's command and the reaction of Muhammad's followers, and those strongly advocating war for God's religion.[9] His conclusion is that the last category, those strongly advocating war for God's religion, came, in the thinking of the classical exegetes, to abrogate the other three, rendering jihad an aggressive as well as defensive mechanism of war historically. Given the historical reputation of the Wahhabis as one of the most aggressive, militant, and literalist of extremist movements, one would expect to find Ibn Abd al-Wahhab's works in accord with this depiction.

This is not the case. Ibn Abd al-Wahhab did not engage in a broad discussion about abrogated verses when dealing with this topic, nor did he necessarily take a chronological approach to the Quran verses addressing it. Although the argument has been made that the Quran took an increasingly militant view toward non-Muslims over time as the early Muslim community became stronger and had greater military prowess,[10] Ibn Abd al-Wahhab did not use this method of Quranic exegesis in his discussion of jihad. Rather, he held Muhammad's example of establishing treaties and truces with non-Muslims as the general rule, so that formal alliances, rather than violence, tend to be the emphasized goal. It is therefore of great interest to compare Firestone's categorization with Ibn Abd al-Wahhab's usage of the same verses to see if Ibn Abd al-Wahhab adhered to classical interpretations or even supported the most belligerent of the verses as indicating the appropriate interpretation of jihad.

Firestone's first category, that of nonmilitant means of propagating or defending the faith, includes verses 2:109, 5:13, 6:106, 15:94, 16:125, 29:46, 42:15, and 50:39. None of these is discussed, referred to, or used as a proof text in either "Kitab al-Tawhid" or "Kitab al-Jihad."

Similarly, the second category—verses placing restrictions on fighting (2:190, 2:194, 9:36, and 22:39–40), are also absent from these two key works of Ibn Abd al-Wahhab.

Of the verses in the third category, those that express conflict between God's command and the reaction of Muhammad's followers (2:216, 3:156, 3:167–168, 4:72–74, 4:75, 4:77, 4:95, 9:38–39, and 9:42), only 3:168 is discussed in "Kitab al-Tawhid." Ibn Abd al-Wahhab included only a portion of the verse: "Those who said of their slain fellows while remaining behind [not having gone to battle]: 'If they had obeyed us, they would not have been killed.'" He used this verse to demonstrate the prohibition of such a demonstration of lack of faith in God in cases of adversity. It is accompanied in the discussion by Q 3:154, which states, "They say: 'If we had anything to do in this matter, slaughter and death would not have befallen us,'" and a *hadith* by Abu Hurayrah saying that Muhammad related that the Muslim should always pray to God for help and not lament when adversity strikes because God knows best and decrees all that happens on this earth.[11] Thus, rather than using this verse as a justification for jihad, Ibn Abd al-Wahhab used it to demonstrate how faith is to determine every action and thought undertaken by the Muslim.

Verses 4:95 ("Those of the believers who stay at home while suffering from no injury are not equal to those who fight for the cause of God with their possessions and persons. God has raised those who fight with their possessions and persons one degree over those who stay at home; and to each God has promised the fairest good") and 9:39 ("If you do not march forth, He will inflict a very painful punishment on you and replace you by another people, and you will not harm Him in the least; for God has power over everything") are included by Firestone in his discussion of the conflict between what God has commanded and how Muhammad's followers reacted. Ibn Abd al-Wahhab also discussed them in "Kitab al-Jihad."

However, rather than focusing on God's punishment of those who do not participate in jihad, Ibn Abd al-Wahhab mentioned these verses at the very beginning of "Kitab al-Jihad," as part of the exhortation to Muslims to recognize jihad as a collective (*fard kifayah*), rather than an individual (*fard 'ayn*), duty. Although he stated that avoidance of this duty would result in God's punishment, this is not the major point of the passage. Rather, he used these verses, along with Q 9:41 and 9:122, as evidence of the abrogation (*naskh*) of a *hadith* related by Abu Dawud in which Muhammad forbade believers to go out collectively, a *hadith* that Ibn Abd al-Wahhab placed into its probable historical context of referring to the Muslims being called to Tabuk.[12] In other words, the point of the citation by Ibn Abd al-Wahhab was to prove that jihad is a collective duty, not to preach hellfire and brimstone to those who do not wish to participate in military action.

Most important for those arguing for a militant character to Islam would be Firestone's fourth category, those Quranic verses that strongly advocate war for God's religion. Firestone identifies 10 passages typically cited by the classical exegetes in their calls to arms: 2:191, 2:193, 2:217, 8:39, 9:5, 9:29, 9:73, 9:123, 47:4–5, and 66:9. Of these, verse 9:5, the so-called sword verse, is considered to be the most important. Indeed, Firestone notes that verse 9:5 is the most frequently cited of all Quranic verses relating to jihad and that most exegetes claim that this verse abrogates 124 other, less militant verses of the Quran.[13] Of the 10 verses cited by the classical exegetes, Firestone notes:

> These verses nevertheless have been understood by most traditional Muslim legalists and religious policymakers to express the most important and eternal divine message with regard to war in the path of God. They carry the highest authority in all discussions of war and have been cited most often from the days of the earliest exegesis until the present. . . . They have come to represent classic post-qur'anic thinking on holy war and serve as proof texts for the codification of the legal traditions on war in all the legal schools of Islam.[14]

Interestingly, *none* of these ten verses, including 9:5, is cited in "Kitab al-Tawhid," despite the fact that many scholars have assumed over the years that this treatise was intended to serve as a manifesto calling for jihad against anyone not subscribing to Ibn Abd al-Wahhab's interpretation of Islam. Only four out of the ten verses are included in "Kitab al-Jihad"—9:5, 9:29, 9:123, and 47:4. All of these verses appear, on the surface and taken completely out of context, to be a call for bloody warfare against non-Muslims. However, this is not how Ibn Abd al-Wahhab explained or used them as proof texts.

Q 9:5 states, "Then, when the sacred months are over, kill the idolaters wherever you find them, take them [as captives], besiege them, and lie in wait for them at every point of observation. If they repent afterward, perform the prayer and pay the alms, then release them. God is truly All-Forgiving, Merciful." This verse is first mentioned in "Kitab al-Jihad" in a discussion about what is required and what is not permitted in the conduct of jihad. It appears in a discussion of who is *not* to be killed during jihad (women, children, youths who have not reached maturity, and leaders [*shaykhs*]). The context in which the verse is cited is Ibn al-Mundhir's assertion that *shaykhs* may be killed—he cites the verse as proof of the permissibility of killing *shaykhs*—an assertion that Ibn Abd al-Wahhab rejected by citing a more specific proclamation by Muhammad, "Do not kill expert *shaykhs* or children/infants or women."[15]

Contrary to prior scholars, who believed that this verse constituted a call to violence, Ibn Abd al-Wahhab rejected the broad, universal usage of this verse as a license for killing. He noted that the Quranic verse is too general to be used in this way, necessitating the search for a more specific *hadith* to provide guidance. Ibn Abd al-Wahhab then cited several other *hadith* from different sources addressing the specific prohibitions against the killing of monks, the elderly, and the blind as a means of limiting the scope of this verse.[16]

The second mention of verse 9:5 occurs in conjunction with verse 47:4: "So, when you meet the unbelievers, strike their necks till you have bloodied them, then fasten the shackles. Thereupon, release them freely or for a ransom, till the war is over." Both verses are included in a discussion about what is to be done with captives who are either Magis or People of the Book who remain in the treaty (*dhimmi*) relationship with Muslims due to their payment of the poll tax (*jizyah*). Ibn Abd al-Wahhab noted that it is preferable for such people to remain in this treaty relationship rather than killing them or granting them grace via compensation (i.e., ransoming them).

Verse 47:4, which calls for benevolence and ransoming, is used as a counter to verse 9:5, which calls for killing the associationists (*mushrikin*). The context of the discussion is a debate among Muhammad's Companions as to what treatment is appropriate for such captives. Verse 47:4 is cited twice, recalling the example of Muhammad in his benevolence toward the captives taken after the Battle of Badr—specifically toward Thamamah and Abi Uzzat al-Shair—and at Buraydah. The only captives killed in these cases were those who refused to pay the poll tax.[17]

Once again, Ibn Abd al-Wahhab considered verse 9:5 to be too broad of a prescription to be applied universally, particularly because it appears to conflict with 47:4. Thus, he required contextualization of both verses along with a search of the *hadith* to determine Muhammad's behavior in specific instances. His rejection of a broad, universal prescription for killing in favor of a more moderate and less violent outcome demonstrates yet again his concern for the maximum preservation of life.

In a later discussion of Q 9:5, which occurs in the context of a discussion about appropriate treaty relations with *dhimmi*, Ibn Abd al-Wahhab noted that the universal specification to fight the *mushrikin* was not applicable in the case of *dhimmi* because they have the right to enter into a treaty relationship with Muslims. As soon as they indicate a willingness to do so, hostilities must end.[18]

Verse 9:29 states, "Fight those among the People of the Book who do not believe in God and the Last Day, do not forbid what God and His Apostle have forbidden and do not profess the true religion till they pay the poll tax out of hand and submit." Ibn Abd al-Wahhab included this verse in his discussion of the contractual relationship that may be established between the Muslims and *dhimmi*, which is based on collection of the poll tax. However, the only portion of the verse that he discussed was the end—"till they pay the poll-tax"—suggesting that his concern with the verse was once again on limiting the fighting rather than calling for it.[19] The part of the verse that was emphasized addresses the cessation of hostilities, not the commencement of them. This prescription and the verse are reiterated in the two conditions required for the *dhimmi* to enter into contractual relations with the Muslims: payment of the poll tax and recognition of the jurisdiction of Islam.[20]

Verse 9:123 states, "O you who believe, fight those of the unbelievers who are near to you and let them see how harsh you can be. Know that God is with the righteous." It is mentioned early in "Kitab al-Jihad" as part of the instructions regarding how jihad is to be carried out. Rather than serving as a call to war, it is cited as a point of military guidance in requiring that the Muslims begin by fighting the unbelievers (*kuffar*) who are geographically closest to them prior to moving farther out. The verse is intended to support a specific military tactic in this case, not to serve as a general call to war, because its citation is preceded by an exhortation to Muslims to recognize and understand the difference between those who are actually aggressive toward Muslims and those who simply observe personal practices or habits that are of concern to the individual in question alone.[21]

It is clear from this analysis that all of these verses, though apparently used in the classical interpretation of jihad to serve as a call to war, were not used or interpreted by Ibn Abd al-Wahhab in this way. Rather than using them to call Muslims to jihad, he instead placed them in their historical context and interpreted them in light of the Quranic value of the importance of the preservation of life. Thus, in his writings they served to place limitations on the violence of jihad's activities rather than to incite them. While this may not be in keeping with traditional historical interpretations of the Wahhabi movement, this support for the maximum preservation of human life and dignity and the protection of property is entirely consistent with Ibn Abd al-Wahhab's worldview.

It is clear that Ibn Abd al-Wahhab does not fit easily and neatly into the traditionalist-classicist category, although he shares some similarities with classical exegetes in terms of format, style, and methodology. There are significant differences with respect to content and the interpretation of specific Quranic verses.

Comparison of the Works of Islamic Modernists and Ibn Abd al-Wahhab

Because Ibn Abd al-Wahhab does not fit neatly into the traditionalist-classicist category, a comparison with the next major group of thinkers historically is the next logical step in the classification process. Islamic modernism arose in the nineteenth century largely in response to the European colonial era, which strongly affected the Muslim world. Rather than calling for militancy against the European colonial overlords, as some of their more militant counterparts did, modernists tended to be more accommodationist, seeking to build a bridge between Islam and the West.

Islamic modernists taught that jihad should be a purely defensive action. They outlined three causes for jihad: repelling aggression against Muslim lives and/or property where an actual or expected attack has occurred, prevention of oppression and persecution of Muslims living outside of Islamic territory, and retaliation against a breach of a pledged truce or treaty by an enemy. "Without any exception, all authors emphatically state that fighting may never serve the aim of compelling people to conversion."[22] Thus, like Ibn Abd al-Wahhab, modernists emphasized the defensive aspects of jihad and limited the circumstances under which it can take place.[23]

Two of the most important Islamic modernists, Muhammad Abduh and Rashid Rida, both of whom drew inspiration from Ibn Abd al-Wahhab, taught not only that jihad was permissible only as defensive warfare when perfidy or aggression against the Muslim community has occurred but that the normal and desired state between Islamic and non-Islamic territories was one of peaceful coexistence.[24] Likewise, the Islamic modernist Mahmud Shaltut supported jihad only as a defensive action, never as an offensive activity:

> These verses [Q 2:190–94] order the Muslims to fight in the way of God those who fight them, to pursue them wherever they find them and to scatter them just as they had once scattered the Muslims. They prohibit the provocation of hostility and this prohibition is reinforced by God's repugnance to aggression and by his dislike of those who provoke hostility. Then they point out that expelling people from their homes, frightening them while they are safe and preventing them from living peacefully without fear for their lives or possessions is persecution worse than persecution by means of murder and bloodshed. Therefore those who practise or provoke these things must be fought just like those who actually fight.[25]

What Shaltut calls for here is not only a defensive response to aggression but also the right to live peacefully without fear for life, home, or possessions, all of which is consistent with Ibn Abd al-Wahhab's assertion of jihad as a defensive activity designed to restore order and preserve life and property. Shaltut then explained the purpose of such a jihad and its limitations:

> The reason for which the Muslims have been ordered to fight is the aggression directed against them, expulsion from their dwellings, violation of God's sacred institutions and attempts to persecute people for what they believe. At the same time they say that the aim upon the attainment of which Muslims must cease fighting is the termi-

nation of the aggression and the establishment of religious liberty
devoted to God and free from any pressure or force.[26]

Although Ibn Abd al-Wahhab did not use quite the same terminology in his
discussion of the conclusion of jihad, he nevertheless made it clear that the
purpose of jihad was to end aggression against Muslims, whether by vanquish-
ing the enemy or establishing a truce or treaty relationship with them.

Mahmud Shaltut found in the Quran "Its desire for peace and its aversion
against bloodshed and killing for the sake of the vanities of this world and out
of sheer greediness and lust."[27] Ibn Abd al-Wahhab's works reflect a similar
attitude. Furthermore, modernists like Shaltut have emphasized that the mere
fact of unbelief is insufficient cause for declaring jihad against an individual
or group: "Therefore this verse [Q 9:123] does not say that the quality of being
an unbeliever etc. constitutes a sufficient reason for fighting, but mentions the
characteristics peculiar to them in order to give a factual description and as a
further incitement to attack them once their aggression will have material-
ized."[28]

In "Kitab al-Jihad," Ibn Abd al-Wahhab took a very similar approach. The
fact of unbelief, however much outlined and denounced in "Kitab al-Tawhid,"
simply is not sufficient for a declaration of jihad against unbelievers. In fact,
discussions of cases in which fighting the nonbeliever is permitted are limited
in "Kitab al-Tawhid." Ibn Abd al-Wahhab found it preferable for the Muslim
to remove himself or herself from the company of associationists and to sever
relations with them rather than engaging in hostilities.[29]

Even in cases in which he called for fighting, Ibn Abd al-Wahhab noted
that it was legitimate and permissible only when the enemy had been called
to Islam *prior* to engaging in hostilities and had rejected the call.[30] In his opinion, an encounter with unbelief was to be considered an opportunity for missionary work and education, not for a blanket call for aggression against someone. Indeed, rather than focusing on fighting, aggression, and conquest, Ibn
Abd al-Wahhab, like the modernists, emphasized the need for openness to
truces and treaties with the enemy because the ultimate goal of jihad was either
conversion to Islam or formal submission to the Muslims, not annihilation.
As Mahmud Shaltut notes: "As regards treaties and the observance of them,
the Koran gives special attention to the observance of treaties, prescribing to
pay heed to them and forbidding treason and violation of them. It teaches that
the aim of treaties is to replace disorder and war by safety and peace and it
warns against using them as an artful means to deprive the other party of its
rights or to oppress the weak."[31] Shaltut further noted that the historical example of Muhammad and the early Muslim community served to show that
one of three outcomes was desirable when an enemy was hostile: conversion
to Islam; payment of the poll tax, which would place the enemy in a treaty
relationship with the Muslims; or, as a last resort, fighting.[32] Fighting comes

third on the list because it is the least desirable outcome and can hopefully be avoided by presentation of the other two possibilities. Nevertheless, it remains on the list as appropriate behavior so that aggression against the Muslims can be stopped. Ibn Abd al-Wahhab's writings reflect a similar understanding, as he constantly emphasized the importance of treaty relationships and the preservation of social order.

Likewise, Shaltut's prohibition of coercion in matters of faith reflects Ibn Abd al-Wahhab's concern for intent and conviction of the heart rather than for nominal adherence to Islam in order simply to save oneself:

> The use of force as a means of making people believe in this Mission would be an insult to it, would make it revolting and would put obstacles in its way. If a man realizes that he is being compelled, or forced into something, this will prevent him from respecting and esteeming it and from reflecting upon it, let alone that he will be able to believe in it. Employing force as an instrument for conversion means wrapping this Mission in complexity, absurdity and obscurity and withholding it from the grasp of the human mind and heart.[33]

Furthermore, the modernists, like Ibn Abd al-Wahhab, placed a heavy emphasis on education, rather than coercion, as the best means by which to win converts to Islam: "The Koran instructs us clearly that God did not wish people to become believers by way of force and compulsion, but only by way of study, reflection and contemplation."[34] Ibn Abd al-Wahhab's citation of words and arguments as weapons and emphasis on the importance of education strike a similar chord with modernist writings: "The only weapons God has given to His previous messengers in order to communicate His Mission to the people, were clear arguments and calling the attention to God's works."[35] From Ibn Abd al-Wahhab's discussion of the importance of debate with nonbelievers and his emphasis on persuasion as the ideal means of conversion, it appears that he was not only in agreement with but an active supporter of this method.

Like Ibn Abd al-Wahhab, the modernists not only rejected coercion as a means of conversion but also raised questions about the truthfulness of repentance made by those in the position of being coerced or awaiting punishment: "When the Koran asserts, as you see, the futility of faith and repentance aroused by coercion, not having freely and peacefully been accepted by the heart, how then could anyone infer that the Koran would require or enforce coercion in matters of religion?"[36]

Likewise, the modernists, like Ibn Abd al-Wahhab, rejected the notion of using jihad as a means of self-aggrandizement or enrichment:

> These verses point out that God only helps those who help and fear Him and therefore do not use war as an instrument for destruction and corruption, for subjecting the weak and satisfying their own de-

sires and lust, but cultivate the land when it falls into their hands, obey God's orders and summon people to do what is good and reputable and not to do what is disreputable and wicked. God distinguishes between those who act destructively and those who act constructively.[37]

Despite the numerous and important similarities, there are differences between modernist interpretations and Ibn Abd al-Wahhab's works. One example is the modernist emphasis on the use of reason and investigation in matters of faith.[38] Although these words and techniques are not used by Ibn Abd al-Wahhab, it could be argued that the outcome is the same.[39] Ibn Abd al-Wahhab required individual study and interpretation of the Quran and *hadith* as the only means of certifying that what one believes is truly a matter of personal conviction. He also permitted the use of words as weapons in the fight against unbelief. He did not, however, employ the modernist arguments about reason confirming revelation.

Perhaps the most significant difference between Ibn Abd al-Wahhab's writings and those of the modernists is the reasons for which the original works were composed. Ibn Abd al-Wahhab wrote his works in response to indigenous social and religious conditions that he personally observed. In the case of the modernists, the environment was complicated by the presence of the Western colonial powers, which had seized control over Muslim lands. The modernist call to revival and renewal of the faith was thus as much of a response to colonialism as it was an observation of the indigenous condition. Ibn Abd al-Wahhab's works were not written in response to European colonialism, as Europe never colonized Arabia.

One other major similarity between Ibn Abd al-Wahhab's writings and those of the modernists is their approach to the question of what is to be done with polytheists. Classical scholarship argued, on the basis of a literal and uncontextualized interpretation of "the sword verse" (Q 9:5), for unconditional fighting of the polytheists. Ibn Abd al-Wahhab placed this verse in the fuller context of intertribal relations. For example, he discussed the importance of making peace with those who are inclined toward peace regardless of their religious status (Q 8:61) and noted that God and Muhammad both permitted withdrawal from military engagement (Q 9:1). Likewise, Q 9:4 notes the importance of fulfilling treaty terms. Chapter 9 also emphasizes the importance of being correct with those who are correct to Muslims (Q 9:7) and allowing fighting only if the other side breaks the terms of the treaty (Q 9:12).[40] Nowhere did he cite Q 9:5 as a justification for blanket fighting of the polytheists or for killing them. Rather, he said of Q 9:5 and an accompanying *hadith* that supposedly portrayed Muhammad as saying, "I command that the people fight" that, despite Malik Ibn Anas's claim that this was intended to serve as a universal prescription for how Muslims are to treat polytheists, "we did not recall it," meaning that he did not accept this interpretation and considered it erroneous.[41]

It is not insignificant that much of Ibn Abd al-Wahhab's discussion of polytheism occurs in the context of his discussion of appropriate relations between Muslims and *dhimmi*, whom he limited to the People of the Book (*Ahl al-Kitab*). His purpose in treating the topic in this manner was to underline the special relationship between Muslims and *dhimmi*, with the desired relationship being one of treaty relations in which the *dhimmi* pay the poll tax, not one of conflict or aggression on either part. Indeed, he commented that it was the establishment of the treaty relationship, *not* conversion, that was the goal of interaction between the two groups.[42] This is particularly striking in the face of scholarly claims, based upon the content of "Kitab al-Tawhid," that Ibn Abd al-Wahhab considered everyone and anyone who was not a Muslim adhering to his own interpretation of Islam to be a polytheist deserving of death. Clearly, there were more thought, specification, and legal requirements involved in his policy making.

In comparison, modernist writers have also gone to great lengths to contextualize "the sword verse" by citing many of the other Quranic verses, both from Surah 9 and other chapters discussing relationships between Muslims and other communities, in order to argue that only those who have either acted aggressively toward the Muslims or broken their treaty relations with them deserve to be fought. In any case, the fighting is never "unconditional." As Rudolph Peters has concluded: "The modernists deny that this verse contains an unconditional command to fight all People of the Book (Jews and Christians) until they pay poll-tax (*jizya*), but infer from the context that only those Jews and Christians were meant that had violated their pledges and assailed the propagation of the Islamic mission."[43] Furthermore, the modernists, like Ibn Abd al-Wahhab, noted that, "This verse also shows, that unbelief is not the reason for fighting the People of the Book for, if this were the case, fighting ought to be continued until conversion and not to cease when they agree to pay poll-tax."[44] Therefore, they also conclude that, "This verse is to be taken as a tactical instruction, not as a general command to fight the unbelievers."[45]

Clearly, although Ibn Abd al-Wahhab shares some similarities with modernists in terms of content and approach, particularly with respect to the goal of establishing treaty relationships with non-Muslims rather than engaging them in warfare and in emphasizing education and verbal debate as the major means of interacting with non-Muslims, the motivation for his work differs from that of the modernists in the face of European colonialism. In terms of content, he is closer to the modernists than he was to the classicists, but he does not fit neatly into either category.

Comparison of the Works of Twentieth-Century "Fundamentalists"
and Ibn Abd al-Wahhab

The twentieth century brought a resurgence and reinterpretation of Islam to the forefront of Muslim politics. Although there have been many interpretations of Islam in the contemporary period, the most relevant for the purpose of this study is the so-called fundamentalist strain, whose roots are often attributed to Ibn Abd al-Wahhab. In the strictest and most basic sense of the word, a fundamentalist is someone who returns to the fundamental sources of his or her religion. However, in the contemporary period the term *fundamentalist* as applied to Muslims has come to mean not only a return to the primary sources but also a literal interpretation of those sources.

Although Ibn Abd al-Wahhab has often been depicted as being literalist in his interpretation of the Quran and *hadith*, examination of his written works reveals careful attention to the contextualization of the sources prior to their interpretation. Such an approach cannot be considered literalist in its mode of interpretation. Indeed, Ibn Abd al-Wahhab often took to task scholars who promoted a literal interpretation of certain passages precisely because of their failure to consider the context in which the verse was revealed or a particular action was taken. He noted, instead, a difference between general rules that are applicable to all of mankind in all circumstances and rules that are specific to particular situations.

Contemporary fundamentalists do not follow the classical prescriptions for addressing questions like jihad. Contemporary writings on jihad tend to be less legalistic than those of the past because they do not outline legal arguments, differentiate between schools of Islamic law, or propose solutions for all potential situations. Instead, "in presenting the topic, they emphasize more the moral justifications and the underlying ethical values of the rules, than the detailed elaboration of those rules."[46] Fundamentalists are further open to the notion of jihad as an individual duty (*fard 'ayn*) as well as a collective one (*fard kifayah*) and promote both offensive and defensive jihad. They also believe that participation in combat is a requirement and that one's duty to engage in jihad cannot be fulfilled via preaching, propagandizing, or any other type of activity.[47]

In contemporary writings in general, varying types of jihad tend to be discussed, opening the door to considering it to be more than just military action. Other types of jihad identified by contemporary writers include educational jihad (*jihad al-tarbiyyah*); missionary jihad or calling other people to Islam (*jihad al-da'wah*); jihad against oneself, that is, against one's own sinful inclinations (*jihad al-nafs*); and jihad of the tongue or word (*jihad al-lisan* or *jihad al-qalam*); in addition to jihad of the sword (*jihad al-sayf*). Some even argue, on the basis of what many scholars have declared to be an inauthentic *hadith*, that there are two kinds of jihad—the Greater, or Internal (battling sinful inclinations within oneself) and the Lesser, or External (jihad of the sword).

However, the group of contemporary writers that concerns us here, the fundamentalists, tend to ignore the distinction between Greater and Lesser jihad because it detracts from the development of the combative spirit they believe is required to rid the Islamic world of Western influences.[48] Similarly, none of these other types of jihad is recognized or defined as jihad by Ibn Abd al-Wahhab, although their importance in his works is clear. Ibn Abd al-Wahhab's definition of jihad is restricted to a defensive military action designed to protect and preserve the Muslim community and its right to practice its faith. He classified the preconditions that must be fulfilled prior to engaging in jihad, such as calling the enemy to Islam and presenting opportunities for conversion or entrance into a treaty or truce relationship, as missionary (da'wah) activities. He clearly distinguished between jihad and missionary work, believing that missionary work is ultimately far more important than jihad.

Rudolph Peters has noted that contemporary writers have several themes that they tend to emphasize: the definition of *jihad* (which includes both moral and spiritual jihad—concepts that are not addressed in classical jurisprudence), the principle of peaceful relations between Islam and all other states, the legal aims of jihad (such as ridding the earth of unbelief and making God's Word prominent), a survey of early Islamic military history, the participation of women in jihad (generally geared toward showing historical precedents for female participation in jihad and emphasizing a supposed historical pattern of equality between the sexes), and the strategic and tactical lessons of the Quran.[49] The issues of early Islamic military history and the strategic and tactical lessons of the Quran are the most strikingly different from the writings of Ibn Abd al-Wahhab because he tended to use historical examples as a means of determining correct legal solutions to problems rather than intending them to stir up passion for fighting or the re-creation of the early Islamic community (ummah). Furthermore, he did not draw any strategic or tactical lessons from the Quran in terms of how armies ought to be positioned or specific methods of using different types of weaponry. Rather, his purpose was to define the limits of what constitutes legal behavior and what does not.

Another striking difference in the discussion of jihad by Ibn Abd al-Wahhab and contemporary fundamentalists has to do with how it is defined. For Ibn Abd al-Wahhab, jihad is always a defensive military action. Here he is synchronous with Islamic modernist writers, who narrow the confines of jihad to defensive action in support of either defending the Muslim community or preventing further aggression against Muslims.[50] Contemporary fundamentalists, on the other hand, tend to emphasize jihad as a means of expanding the territories of Islam and Muslim control.[51] In their view, jihad is intended to be an ongoing, permanent duty of the Muslim community to be carried out both individually and collectively with the purpose of completely eradicating unbelief by the use of force. Contemporary fundamentalists typically describe jihad as an individual obligation (*fard 'ayn*) resulting from the enemy's invasion of Islamic territory.[52] They blame the ruling government for this state of affairs because the government is perceived to be in complicity with the enemy, that is, non-Muslim powers, which they believe is a violation of Islamic public order. Therefore, the target of contemporary fundamentalists is typically the ruling government, which they believe should be overthrown in favor of an "Islamic" state, usually defined as one in which the Sharia is applied as law. According to this interpretation, it is only by "restoring" Islam to power that Muslims can truly live in accordance with their faith and be restored to their rightful position of power. Therefore, jihad is intended to be as much offensive as defensive in nature.

Ibn Abd al-Wahhab does not fall into this category of thought, as his discussions of jihad clearly identify it as a defensive measure to be put into action only when aggression against the Muslim community has been committed. It is not intended to serve as a venue for expansionism or state formation outside of winning new converts. This is far more in keeping with the modernist interpretation of jihad as a purely defensive action.

Contemporary fundamentalists have also taken a new approach to defining who qualifies as a "true Muslim." In classical scholarship, the label of apostate could only be applied when a person either expressly abjured Islam or denied axiomatic articles of faith in either word or deed. Lack of adherence to Islamic law did not constitute sufficient grounds for accusations of apostasy for classical scholars other than Ibn Taymiyya.[53] Contemporary fundamentalists, on the other hand, citing Ibn Taymiyya, argue that any ruler who does not apply Islamic law in its entirety has committed apostasy and therefore deserves to be overthrown. This formulates their basis for antigovernmental action.[54] In contrast, Ibn Abd al-Wahhab was much less violent in his approach to jihad, constantly stressing the need for restraint and protection of both life and property. In this, he is again far more in sync with modernist scholarship than with contemporary fundamentalism and *jihadi* culture.

It is clear from the above discussion that, at least where the topic of jihad is concerned, Ibn Abd al-Wahhab has far more in common with the modernists than he does with contemporary militant extremists. His definition of *defensive* is much narrower than that of contemporary fundamentalists, who, although they claim that their interpretation of jihad is also defensive in nature in that it is the preferred means of "defending Islam," nevertheless believe that jihad must consist of a permanent revolutionary struggle on behalf of all of mankind in order to end the dominion of man over man and of manmade laws in favor of recognition of God's sovereignty and the acceptance of Islamic law as the only law.[55]

In the specific case of the Quranic call to fight polytheists until there is no persecution and the religion is entirely God's (Q 2:193 and 8:39), while modernists emphasize the first part of the verse, which asserts the action as defensive, fundamentalists stress the second part about fighting as a command to fight unbelievers until a universal Islamic order ruled by God's Law is established. Furthermore, contemporary fundamentalists reject the distinction between offensive and defensive jihad because they believe that by its very nature it is a universal revolutionary struggle. Along similar lines, they do not look for moral justifications for or limits on jihad because they interpret Quranic verses to be universal prescriptions for behavior, regardless of the context in which they were revealed or appear.

For the fundamentalists, there can be no truces or treaty relationships—peace can only occur when the entire world has submitted to Islam. The modernists, on the other hand, consider it obligatory, on the basis of the Quran, to live in peaceful coexistence with the rest of the world when it requests peace.[56] Clearly, Ibn Abd al-Wahhab has far more in common with the more balanced and nuanced approach of the modernists than he does with the more literal and aggressive interpretations of contemporary fundamentalists.

From Whence the Violence?

It is clear that unlimited violence and jihad on a global scale are not inherent to Ibn Abd al-Wahhab's writings and that his writings vary significantly, in terms of both methodology and content, from those of contemporary militants. However, the reality also remains that militant extremism and violence have been associated with Wahhabism from the early years of the movement. To what should this disconnect be attributed? Where does the violence come from?

Two important factors must be recalled in coming to terms with the violence question: the environment in which Wahhabism was first preached and spread and the historical development of the movement. As was mentioned in chapter 1, it is important to recall that the theological message preached by Ibn Abd al-Wahhab—that every individual has both the right and the responsibility to encounter and study the Quran and *hadith* directly—represented a threat to the power bases of both the political and religious leaders of his day. Much of the negative imagery of Wahhabism can be traced to those who stood to lose the most with its victory.

Historically, Wahhabism has been viewed mainly through the eyes of its opponents. Particularly prominent in the opposition writings were claims that the Wahhabis killed anyone who did not subscribe to their purportedly austere and puritanical interpretation of Islam. Opponents claimed that the Wahhabis, like the extremist Kharijites before them,[57] divided the world into two spheres, the land of Islam (*dar al-islam*), which was the exclusive realm of the Wahhabis, and the land of unbelief (*dar al-kufr*), which was the domain of everyone else, in order to declare jihad against all non-Wahhabis, who were categorized as unbelievers (*kuffar*).[58] The result was a portrayal of militant Wahhabism in conflict with Muslims, particularly Sufis and Shiis, and non-Muslims alike.

These negative reports about the Wahhabis spread quickly through the grapevine, instilling fear and horror in those who heard about them and becoming part of the historical narrative about Wahhabis. However, not all contemporaries simply recorded these impressions and let them stand. Some took the time to investigate the claims and came to different conclusions about the Wahhabis. Of these contemporary investigators, two—Ali Bey and al-Jabarti—particularly stand out.

Ali Bey was in Mecca in 1803, shortly after the Wahhabi conquest of the Hijaz. Popular hysteria about the Wahhabis led him to expect violence, fanaticism, intolerance, and ignorance on their part. During his own first encounter with them, he noted that those surrounding him literally "fled at the sight" of the incoming Wahhabis out of fear. Curious to see for himself what the notorious Wahhabis were really like, Ali Bey, rather than fleeing with the masses, climbed atop a pile of rubbish "to observe them better."[59] He was surprised to find that the Wahhabis were actually quite moderate, reasonable, and civilized. He described his expectations and experiences as follows:

> When we represent to ourselves a crowd of naked armed men, without any idea of civilization, and speaking a barbarous language, the picture terrifies the imagination, and appears disgusting; but if we overcome this first impression, we find in them some commendable qualities. They never rob either by force or stratagem, except when they know the object belongs to an enemy or an infidel. They pay with their money all their purchases, and every service that is rendered them. Being blindly subservient to their chiefs, they support in silence every fatigue, and would allow themselves to be led to the opposite side of the globe. In short, it may be perceived that they are men the most disposed to civilization, if they were to receive proper instruction.[60]

He further observed that, rather than engaging in rampant violence and destruction, the Wahhabis were actually quite orderly and peaceful—a fact that he found relatively surprising given the large number of guns and women in the Wahhabi contingent:

> I must praise the moderation and good order which reigned amidst this number of individuals, belonging to different nations. Two thousand women who were among them did not occasion the least disorder; and though there were more than forty or fifty thousand guns, there was only one let off, which happened near me. At the

same instant one of the chiefs ran to the man who had fired, and reprimanded him, saying, "Why did you do this? Are we going to make war here?"[61]

Puzzled by the contradiction between popular image and reality, Ali Bey examined the historical record for clues. He found an important difference between the lifetime of Muhammad Ibn Saud, when Ibn Abd al-Wahhab was active in the political life of the Saudi-Wahhabis, and the accession of his son, Abd al-Aziz Ibn Muhammad Ibn Saud, when Ibn Abd al-Wahhab withdrew from active political activity. Ali Bey noted that Muhammad Ibn Saud had supported the teachings of Ibn Abd al-Wahhab but did not use a "convert or die" approach to gaining adherents. This practice was used only during the reign of Abd al-Aziz, who made selective use of Ibn Abd al-Wahhab's teachings for the express purpose of acquiring wealth and property through a convert or die approach to state consolidation—a contention supported by Ibn Bishr's chronicle.[62] Thus, it can be argued that the violence and militancy associated with the Saudi-Wahhabis during this time period had more to do with the political concerns of the state than it did with Ibn Abd al-Wahhab's theological teachings.

The question of Ibn Abd al-Wahhab's theological teachings formed the heart of the critique of Wahhabism. Opponents claimed that the Wahhabis subscribed to a literal and extremely narrow interpretation of Islam that deviated from the broader teachings of the Quran and *hadith* and rejected classical scholarship in its entirety. However, those who had contact with the Wahhabis found them to be scholars in their own right. Although he found their doctrine lacking in some respects, Ali Bey nevertheless declared that he "discovered much reason and moderation among the Wehhabites to whom I spoke, and from whom I obtained the greater part of the information which I have given concerning their nation."[63]

The Egyptian historian Abd al-Rahman al-Jabarti, who encountered Wahhabis in Egypt ten years later, in 1814, was similarly impressed by the knowledge of the Wahhabi scholars he encountered, despite all of the negative things he had heard about them. The two Wahhabis with whom al-Jabarti met had come to Egypt in search of *hadith* collections and Hanbali exegetical discussions of the Quran (*tafsir*) and jurisprudence (*fiqh*): "I myself met with the two Wahhabis twice and found them to be friendly and articulate, knowledgeable and well versed in historical events and curiosities. They were modest men of good morals, well trained in oratory, in the principles of religion, the branches of *fiqh*, and the disagreements of the Schools of Law. In all this they were extraordinary."[64]

A British observer, Harford Jones Brydges, who was stationed in Basra, Iraq, in 1784, also noted popular hysteria about the Wahhabis, although he attributed it to a different cause. Brydges believed that the Ottomans were well aware that the Wahhabi interpretation of Islam was in keeping with the teachings of the Quran and feared its spread on precisely that basis. The Ottoman Empire had worked to stir up popular fear and hatred of the Wahhabis, including the coining of the term *Wahhabi*, claiming that their interpretation of Islam was innovative and therefore heretical.[65] Brydges noted: "When I arrived at Bassora in the year 1784, his [the Wahhabite commander's] proceedings and marauding marches caused great anxiety and alarm to the pacha of Baghdad, to his governor at Bassora, as well as to the best informed Turks. For these last were aware that his doctrines, when examined by the simple text of the Koran, were perfectly orthodox, and consonant to the purest and best interpretations of that volume."[66]

That the Ottomans felt threatened by the spread of Wahhabism was not surprising given that the Wahhabis, having conquered Najd, next set their sights on the Hijaz, ostensibly because the Ottoman sultan had failed to fulfill his religious duties as the overlord of the holy cities of Mecca and Medina. It is also not surprising that the Ottomans would have chosen to attack the Wahhabis on religious grounds because this was the source of the Wahhabi charges of heresy against the Ottomans that justified their conquest of Ottoman territories.

The Ottomans and the Wahhabis

The Hijaz had been claimed as Ottoman territory since 1517. The Ottoman sultan served as the protector of the holy cities and had taken the title of Protector of the Two Holy Sanctuaries, signifying his political role as sovereign of the empire and his religious role as the protector of Islam.[67] As the Protector of the Two Holy Sanctuaries, the sultan was responsible for ensuring the right of Muslims to make the Hajj pilgrimage in safety by providing protection and security along the caravan and pilgrimage routes,[68] guaranteeing the right of all Muslims to worship; protecting and preserving the holy sites in Mecca and Medina; and ensuring justice, such as fair prices in the markets and fair currency exchange rates.

In practice, these duties were carried out on the ground by local officials—the *sharifs* of Mecca, who owed their positions to their claimed status as descendants of Muhammad. By the beginning of the nineteenth century, the *sharifs* had acquired almost unrestricted local power within the Hijaz and had usurped the financial benefits of the pilgrimage—collection of customs duties from pilgrimage caravans—and the dispensation of justice.[69] However, the sultan remained the head of the empire and was held responsible for the actions of his officials.

Corruption, greed, violence, and insecurity were rampant in the Hijaz by the late eighteenth century, yet this territory remained under the sultan's jurisdiction.[70] Appalled by the failure of the sultan to provide the security and justice that served as the sources of his religious legitimacy and political claims to the region, the Wahhabis decided to conquer the Hijaz and restore order themselves. However, this goal presented a major quandary: Islam forbids Muslims fighting Muslims. The Wahhabis therefore turned to religion for justification of their actions.

The Wahhabis charged the Ottomans with a series of violations of Islamic principles: neglect of alms for the poor (zakat, one of the five pillars of Islam); failure to adhere to the sumptuary regulations established by Muhammad; lenient and partial rendering of justice; failure to fight corruption; infidelity to Islam; consumption of alcoholic beverages; unlawful commerce with women; failure to control or punish the scandalous conduct of the pilgrims, who polluted the holy cities with their lust and debauchery; pursuit of pride and selfishness; and numerous other acts of treachery and fraud.[71] They also objected to the Ottoman practices of wearing silk, gold, and silver in large quantities; smoking tobacco; decorating mosques; kissing the hands of *imams* and sultans; and using prayer beads because these were not part of Muhammad's example.[72]

All of these violations proved to the Wahhabis that the sultan had failed to act like a Muslim—a critical point, as Ibn Abd al-Wahhab had always emphasized the importance of actions matching words. However, Ibn Abd al-Wahhab had also taught that only God knows what is in the hearts of human beings and is capable of judging them and that public welfare and the preservation of the social order were of critical importance to the survival of the Muslim community. Although Ibn Abd al-Wahhab had recognized the possibility of a Muslim leader failing to fulfill his duties, he had limited the response to such failure to discussion and debate with the leader about where those errors lay. Following the teachings of Ahmad ibn Hanbal and the general stance of classical Muslim scholarship, he did not allow for the removal of such a leader from power.[73]

It was therefore at this critical juncture that Wahhabi scholars incorporated the writings of the medieval Hanbali scholar Ibn Taymiyya into the main body of the Wahhabi tradition. Ibn Taymiyya provided a worldview and ideology that allowed for revolution against an unfaithful ruler by denying him his status as a Muslim on the basis of his failure to fulfill his responsibilities to Islam.[74]

The Ibn Taymiyya Connection

Ibn Taymiyya (1263–1328) wrote at a time when his homeland—Damascus, Syria—was experiencing the aftermath of the Mongol invasions, which had brought a forcible end to the Abbasid caliphate (750–1258 C.E.), and the ongoing militant threat of Christianity brought about by the Crusades. These two events were critical influences in constructing Ibn Taymiyya's worldview and the religious ideology he developed to combat them. Although many in the West have been more concerned with his refutations of Christianity and Judaism as heretical religions, his more lasting and significant influence has been his espousal of the division of the world into two absolute and mutually exclusive spheres—the land of Islam (dar al-Islam) and the land of unbelief (dar al-kufr)—which for him described both a status (Muslim versus unbeliever) and a necessarily hostile relationship between the two.

The Mongol overthrow of the Abbasid Empire was an event of monumental proportions for the Muslim world. Not only did it bring to an end the most glorious and advanced Islamic civilization in history, but it placed formerly non-Muslim rulers in the position of rulers of Muslim lands. In order to render themselves more legitimate in the eyes of their subjects, the Mongols had claimed conversion to Islam. However, they continued to apply their own customary law rather than adhering to or enforcing Islamic law. Their failure to uphold and enforce Islam in the public sphere raised questions not only about whether they could be considered "true" Muslims but also what the ramifications of their actions were.

Classical scholarship taught that the preservation of the social order had a higher priority than the retention of the ruler. No matter how "bad" of a Muslim a ruler was or how insincere, classical scholars believed that he should remain in power so as to avoid the social chaos and disruption that were bound to occur with his removal.[75] Consequently, the majority of Muslims felt obligated to tolerate and submit to their new Mongol rulers for the sake of the public welfare.

Ibn Taymiyya disagreed. In his opinion, the character of the ruler—specifically, whether he was a faithful and sincere Muslim—was the defining and decisive factor in determining whether he should remain in power. Ibn Taymiyya believed that a legitimate Islamic government had two major responsibilities: governance by Islamic law and the military defense of Muslim lands against invaders. Failure to fulfill either one of these indicated that the ruler could not be considered a Muslim. In the case of the Mongols, Ibn Taymiyya pointed to the fact that they favored their own customary laws over Islamic law. In his opinion, this served as evidence that, however much they might claim to be Muslims, the Mongols were really unbelievers (kuffar).[76] In other words, the mere use of Islamic rhetoric or the claim to be a Muslim was not sufficient for making a person a "true" Muslim. Similar to Ibn Abd al-Wahhab, Ibn Taymiyya believed that words and actions must be consistent. However, Ibn Taymiyya differed in his willingness to label anyone claiming to be a Muslim but not acting like one according to his specifications as an unbeliever (kafir).

Ibn Taymiyya's worldview was not without historical precedent. He drew his inspiration from the militant interpretation of Islam developed by the seventh-century extremist Kharijite movement. The Kharijites had espoused a strict and literal interpretation of the Quran and Sunna that promoted an activist implementation of their teachings. They understood the Quranic injunction to "command good and prohibit evil" to be a religious mandate that was to be implemented absolutely and without compromise at the political level. According to this vision, jihad, as the literal physical struggle against unbelief, was an absolute religious requirement for all Muslims. They defined *unbelief* as any deviation from their interpretation of Islam and Islamic law. The degree of the deviation was irrelevant. What mattered was the fact of the deviation. Thus, even a very pious person who had generally adhered to Islamic law could be declared an unbeliever on the basis of a minor infraction.

The Kharijites' worldview divided the world into *dar al-Islam* and *dar al-harb*. They recognized only two types of actions, either good and permissible or bad and forbidden, and two possible statuses, Muslim or *kafir*. There were no in-between categories. Any engagement in an action that they considered to be bad and forbidden resulted in the person being labeled a *kafir*, who was to be considered guilty of treason to Islam and therefore subject to punishment—jihad as holy war.

The Kharijites viewed themselves as "soldiers of God" engaged in a cosmic battle against evil. As God's instruments of justice and righteousness, they believed that their use of all methods of warfare, including violence, revolution, and guerrilla warfare, was legal, legitimate, and obligatory.[77]

Ibn Taymiyya, interpreting his own context to be nothing less than the usurpation of Islam by apostates, turned to the Kharijites for legitimacy in calling for the overthrow of the Mongols. His adoption of this perspective and interpretation had far-reaching consequences. Unlike the Kharijites, who were a splinter group of extremists, Ibn Taymiyya was a renowned scholar and jurist. His endorsement of a legal and religious justification for the obligatory overthrow of unjust and non-Muslim rulers not only set a stronger historical precedent for extremist movements seeking religious legitimation to overthrow "illegitimate" and "un-Islamic" regimes by revolution, but it also led to Ibn Taymiyya being labeled the most extreme example of "fanaticism" and "exclusivism" in Islamic history because of his role as a "zealous Hanbalite."[78]

The fact that Ibn Taymiyya was considered to be the greatest Hanbali jurist historically led to the assumption, particularly by Western scholars, that Hanbalism, fanaticism, intolerance, militancy, extremism, and radical revolution were all inextricably linked.[79] According to this vision, Ibn Taymiyya was the spokesperson of the militant medieval Hanbali tradition that had later been adopted by the Wahhabis.[80] Thus it was that Hanbalism, Ibn Taymiyya, and Ibn Abd al-Wahhab came to be considered fanatical, intolerant, and outside of mainstream Muslim thought.[81]

While this linear vision of the development of militant Hanbalism makes for a clean and neat analysis, this negative characterization is based on stereotypes and a piecemeal approach to Hanbali texts designed to prove certain negative points rather than a comprehensive analysis of those texts.[82] Most importantly, it overlooks the differences between Ibn Taymiyya's writings and those of Ibn Abd al-Wahhab, particularly with respect to the issue of jihad as

holy war. Ibn Taymiyya and Ibn Abd al-Wahhab differed significantly over issues such as the purpose and justification of jihad and the intent and goals of
those carrying it out, the *mujahidun*.

Ibn Taymiyya and Jihad

Ibn Taymiyya's discussion of jihad was written to justify the overthrow of Mongol rule in Muslim lands.[83] The predetermination of the need to overthrow by
force an unpalatable political regime necessarily lent a militant flavor to the
discussion. Violence and coercion therefore occupy a prominent place in Ibn
Taymiyya's writings.

Ibn Taymiyya had stated that the two purposes of an Islamic government
were the upholding and enforcement of Islamic law and the military defense
of Muslim lands against invaders. In his opinion, both of these responsibilities
were to be enforced by coercion if necessary. He wrote, "Since lawful warfare
is essentially *jihad* and since its aim is that the religion is God's entirely and
God's word is uppermost, therefore, according to all Muslims, those who stand
in the way of this aim must be fought."[84] Thus, he taught that government
enforcement of Islamic law by coercion was permissible because this fulfilled
the greater good of maintaining public order.[85] Although he believed that killing
was both "evil" and "abominable," he believed that government enforcement
of an Islamic order even by violent means was a lesser evil and abomination
than the persecution of Muslims by unbelievers.[86] Thus, coercion as a means
of enforcing religious law and practice was a consistent theme in Ibn Taymiyya's writings.

Ibn Taymiyya's support for coercion stands in marked contrast to Ibn Abd
al-Wahhab's assertion that intent and conviction of the heart are the critical
factors of faith and that coercion has no place in this. Whereas Ibn Taymiyya
believed that anyone who had been called to Islam and had not immediately
accepted it was to be fought, thus rendering jihad offensive as well as defensive,[87] Ibn Abd al-Wahhab restricted jihad to cases in which the enemy in
question had behaved aggressively toward the Muslim community first and
then rejected the call to Islam. Ibn Abd al-Wahhab's treatise on jihad does not
allow for blanket jihad activities directed against unbelievers.

Classical discussions of jihad assumed that the struggle against unbelievers would take place outside of *dar al-Islam*. Ibn Taymiyya departed from this
perspective by recognizing the possibility of a jihad against "heretical" and
"deviant" Muslims within *dar al-Islam*.[88] He identified as heretical and deviant
Muslims anyone who propagated innovations (*bida'*) contrary to the Quran
and Sunna, noting that public support for such practices has the potential to
lead others astray.[89] He therefore legitimated jihad against anyone who refused
to abide by Islamic law or revolted against the true Muslim authorities.[90] In
his opinion, the Mongol rulers were clearly at fault on both counts because

they had overthrown the legitimate Abbasid caliphate and had favored their own customary law over Islamic law once in power.

Past scholarship on Ibn Abd al-Wahhab has assumed a similar approach. Because "Kitab al-Tawhid" specifically details what adherence to absolute monotheism means in practice and what practices and beliefs can be considered innovative (bida'), past scholars have understood this treatise as a justification for excluding people who claim to be Muslim from the "true" Muslim community on the basis of their erroneous ways or beliefs. The assumption was that exclusion of such people from the Muslim community necessarily justified jihad against them in the same way that Ibn Taymiyya had taught.

However, "Kitab al-Tawhid" was not intended to be used in this fashion. When read in the context of Ibn Abd al-Wahhab's full body of writings, it is clear that it was not a blanket prescription for violence, even against unbelievers or those who violated the key theological concept of absolute monotheism by committing associationism. Nor was it designed as a blueprint for exclusion from the Muslim community. Rather, its purpose was to detail erroneous practices and beliefs, both within and outside of the Muslim community, in order to help the Muslim discern what constitutes correct belief and behavior and why. Significantly, although "Kitab al-Tawhid" repeatedly condemns certain practices, it does not call for violence against their perpetrators. Discussions about beliefs and practices are not followed by prescriptive actions to be taken against the person knowingly and willingly engaging in them, other than to allow the "threatening" or "menacing" (wa'id) of and departure from such a person.[91] In all cases, the noun format, rather than the command tense, of verbs is used. Most importantly, at no time is the killing of anyone permitted outside of divinely sanctioned punishments, such as in cases of sorcery (defined as the performance of black magic, divination, or astrology), the intent to spread falsehood and evil, and, in cases of particularly beautiful language, literary eloquence,[92] where "beating/striking him by the sword (darabahu bi-al-sayf)" is prescribed.[93]

The case of the sorcerer/sorceress is the only case discussed by Ibn Abd al-Wahhab in which the perpetrator is to be put to death without an opportunity for repentance because of the unbelief (kufr) committed in such an instance.[94] Not only was he careful to specify that idolatry (al-taghut), while forbidden, was not included in the definition of sorcery and therefore was not punishable by death, Ibn Abd al-Wahhab also distinguished between the sorcerer and the person seeking the sorcerer's assistance. This distinction is important because only the sorcerer is subject to the death penalty. The person seeking assistance is subject to a verbal reminder to "recall God (dhikr)."[95] Ibn Abd al-Wahhab believed that the punishment of human beings was the prerogative of God rather than being subject to the judgment of other human beings.

Violence as destruction of property was also limited by Ibn Abd al-Wahhab to objects that could potentially lead people away from adherence to monotheism. He included in this category talismans, sacred trees, and tombs of holy people, although he acknowledged as "wise moves" the practice of simply removing them from sight or prohibiting their construction in the first place.[96] The reasoning behind the permissibility of such destruction is that ultimately the creation of images can lead people away from belief in monotheism and the creation of images, whether in painting or in sculpture, is considered to be an attempt to imitate God's creative capacities. The major difference is that the human artist cannot give his or her image a soul—only God can provide life and souls. However, although Ibn Abd al-Wahhab thus condemned the image-makers and their images, he permitted—indeed, commanded—the destruction *only* of the images. For the artist, only condemnation by the Muslim was permitted. He consistently upheld punishment of the individual as the prerogative of God in the Afterlife.[97]

The limitations on violence, killing, and destruction of property detailed in "Kitab al-Tawhid" stand in marked contrast to Ibn Taymiyya's calls to jihad over any infraction of Islamic law or perceived offense against the Muslim community. Ibn Abd al-Wahhab did not seek to condemn people—whether Muslim or non-Muslim. He clearly disallowed anything that had as its purpose the deliberate exclusion of people from the Muslim community in order to justify killing them. His worldview and goals are not at all in keeping with the writings of Ibn Taymiyya.

The question of permissible violence and killing during jihad is another point of contrast between the writings of Ibn Taymiyya and those of Ibn Abd al-Wahhab. Ibn Abd al-Wahhab continued his theme of the importance of the maximum preservation of life—human, plant, and animal—and property in his treatise on jihad. Ibn Taymiyya's reading of the Quran, Sunna, and early Islamic history was far more militant. For example, although he required the *imam*'s permission to do so, he permitted the killing of captives. He also offered a broad definition of what constitutes "aggression" against Muslims, allowing even the refusal to give a Muslim something that he desires, such as a goat, to serve as a "rebellious" act, making jihad not only permissible but necessary.[98] The examples cited serve to justify jihad in just about every imaginable interaction with unbelievers, lending Ibn Taymiyya's interpretation a combative spirit. He declared:

> It is allowed to fight people for [not observing] unambiguous and
> generally recognized obligations and prohibitions, until they under-
> take to perform the explicitly prescribed prayers, to pay *zakat*, to fast
> during the month of Ramadan, to make the pilgrimage to Mecca
> and to avoid what is prohibited, such as marrying women in spite of
> legal impediments, eating impure things, acting unlawfully against
> the lives and properties of Muslims and the like. It is obligatory to
> *take the initiative* in fighting those people, as soon as the Prophet's

summons with the reasons for which they are fought has reached
them. But if they first attack the Muslims, then fighting them is
even more urgent, as we have mentioned when dealing with the
fighting against rebellious and aggressive bandits.[99]

Thus, not only did Ibn Taymiyya open the floodgates for any infraction of
Islamic law, belief, or practice to justify jihad, he also allowed Muslims to "take
the initiative," that is, engage in offensive jihad. According to this vision, sum-
moning the enemy to Islam is a matter of format rather than a genuine attempt
at missionary work. He assumed that the intent behind any action not favorable
and immediately submissive to the Muslims was aggression.

By contrast, Ibn Abd al-Wahhab's writings restrict jihad to situations in
which clear military aggression has been directed against the Muslim community. Rather than seeking legalistic ways to try to turn every noncooperative
action into a act of aggression, Ibn Abd al-Wahhab focused on the critical issue
of whether or not actual harm was intended to the Muslims by the enemy as
the criterion for determining whether or not jihad is permissible or necessary.
If no harm was intended or occurred, Ibn Abd al-Wahhab believed that jihad
was not appropriate. For example, in a case in which a person is engaged in
an activity that violates monotheism, such as wearing a talisman (thus placing
his or her confidence in an object or the spirit it is supposed to represent rather
than in God), Ibn Abd al-Wahhab allowed for social ostracism and religious
condemnation. Although he taught that God would leave such a person—the
worst punishment possible—he did *not* call for the person to be put to death
or otherwise physically harmed by the Muslims.[100] The only violence permitted
in such a case was the destruction of the talisman. No harm was permitted to
come to the person making use of it. Consistent with his other writings, punishment of such an act is left to God alone.[101]

Ibn Abd al-Wahhab also restricted the use of violence in cases in which
someone violates monotheism by committing an illegal act, such as cursing
one's parents; sheltering a person who has committed a crime carrying a divinely sanctioned punishment for the express purpose of helping that person
to escape punishment; or unjustly altering the boundaries of personal land. In
these cases, he taught that the appropriate response is neither violence nor
retribution but cursing such a person.[102] Although socially such a response was
considered a humiliation for the person cursed, it nevertheless represents a
verbal, rather than physical, response to the infraction.

Even where the critical theological issue of associationism was concerned,
Ibn Abd al-Wahhab did not seek to exclude people from the Muslim community and label them as *kuffar*. The commission of an act of associationism—
whether greater or lesser—did not automatically serve to exclude a person from
the Muslim community in Ibn Abd al-Wahhab's opinion. He cited the example
of Meccan converts to Islam during the time of Muhammad, who requested

that he establish a sacred tree for them. Muhammad refused the request because it violated monotheism. He then instructed his followers about correct belief in this case.[103] Ibn Abd al-Wahhab believed that the lesson of this *hadith* was the permissibility of condemning a practice without condemning the people involved in it. Rather than responding with condemnation, violence, or exclusion, Ibn Abd al-Wahhab noted that Muhammad's example showed the correct response to such a situation to be the offering of instruction about correct belief.

The citation of this *hadith* also highlights another important difference between Ibn Abd al-Wahhab and Ibn Taymiyya: consideration of historical context. Ibn Abd al-Wahhab was always careful to provide contextualization for Quranic verses and *hadith* when used as proof texts for a particular point. He rejected the literal interpretation of scripture as failing to understand the intent behind the passage or incident in question. Ibn Taymiyya, on the other hand, believed in a more literal interpretation of the Quran and *hadith*. He did not include contextualization of his proof texts, believing that the words of the texts were intended to serve as literal prescriptions for action.

One final major difference between the writings of Ibn Taymiyya and Ibn Abd al-Wahhab is Ibn Taymiyya's discussion of topics that are absent from Ibn Abd al-Wahhab's works. The most important of these is the issue of martyrdom.

Ibn Taymiyya's treatise on jihad pays careful and lengthy attention to the questions of martyrdom and the reaping of benefits to be had via jihad. He asserted that martyrdom and eternal rewards and blessings are the goals that the Muslim should bear in mind and should form the intent behind the *mujahid*'s participation in jihad. He commented that, "It is in *jihad* that one can live and die in ultimate happiness, both in this world and in the Hereafter. Abandoning it means losing entirely or partially both kinds of happiness."[104] He cited as evidence numerous Quranic verses and *hadith* discussing the glories to be had in carrying out jihad and reaping its rewards.

Ibn Taymiyya's discussion of martyrdom is not unique. Classical exegetes also typically focused on issues of martyrdom and the promises of reward for participation in jihad:

> Those who engage in sanctified war receive great benefits for their
> involvement. They will gain deserved material spoils and rewards
> when successful in the campaigns, and if they are killed or even
> wounded while warring in the path of God, they will be admitted to
> paradise. . . . The reward for martyrdom while engaging in war in
> the path of God is stressed greatly, even if the victim dies while not
> actually engaged on the battlefield, and as many as seventy members of one's family who would have been doomed to hellfire will be

ensured entry into paradise because of the intercession of the mar-
tyr in the path of God.[105]

The classical exegetes made it clear that the *mujahidin* will always gain something from the experience: either they will acquire personal wealth through a
share of the booty or they will gain Paradise if they are killed.[106]

This heavy reliance on the Quran and *hadith* in the writings of both classical scholars and Ibn Taymiyya makes it even more significant that these
discussions are *completely* absent from Ibn Abd al-Wahhab's written works. Ibn
Abd al-Wahhab *never* discussed martyrdom, Paradise, or heavenly rewards in
his discussion of jihad. The *hadith* about intercession by martyrs is glaringly
absent from his writings. Why?

The answer lies in the broader worldview that Ibn Abd al-Wahhab had of
faith in general and the purpose of jihad in particular. Although he, like Ibn
Taymiyya, taught that jihad is the responsibility of the believing Muslim, Ibn
Abd al-Wahhab differed in his opinion about what intent should drive the
Muslim to participate in it. In Ibn Abd al-Wahhab's opinion, the only worthy
intent in any matter of faith is strictly that—adherence to faith for the sake
of faith alone. Religion is never to be used as a justification for self-
aggrandizement, the accumulation of wealth, or even the protection of one's
own life. This is why he rejected the notion of conversion by the sword—how
could such conversions truly be a matter of conviction of the heart when one
faces the death penalty for refusing to verbally adhere to Islam?—and why he
insisted on the importance of missionary work via education in the primary
sources of Islam.

This attitude is clearly reflected in the absence of his discussion of martyrdom and the glories of Paradise because seeking such things would essentially be the same as seeking wealth or glory in the act of jihad. The *intent*
behind such actions would be a focus on oneself and what one could personally
gain from participation in jihad, rather than a focus on pure service to God in
God's cause. This is why he regulated so strictly even the distribution of booty
after jihad, ruling out altogether certain types of property, so that self-
enrichment never comes into play. Such goals are left to the more mundane
realm of standard tribal welfare, which served a different purpose.

It is therefore not surprising that Ibn Abd al-Wahhab's mentions of Paradise and heavenly rewards occur in his discussions of adherence to monotheism rather than in his discussions of jihad. He believed that it is adherence
to monotheism alone that atones for sins and permits the Muslim to enter
Paradise without reckoning.[107] His failure to mention the *hadith* about martyrs
interceding with God is due to the fact that he rejected the notion of anyone
other than Muhammad interceding with God on behalf of anyone.[108]

The differences between Ibn Abd al-Wahhab's writings and those of Ibn

Taymiyya with respect to jihad are numerous and striking. Ibn Taymiyya was clearly a more literal interpreter of the Quran and *hadith* and took a far more extremist approach to the questions of violence and killing than did Ibn Abd al-Wahhab.

While there is no validity to the claim that Ibn Abd al-Wahhab was simply a copier and imitator of the works of Ibn Taymiyya,[109] the reality remains that scholars and activists commonly identified as Wahhabis have drawn significant inspiration from some of Ibn Taymiyya's hallmark themes, particularly the permissibility of overthrowing a ruler who is classified as an unbeliever due to a failure to adhere to Islamic law, the absolute division of the world into *dar al-kufr* and *dar al-Islam*, the labeling of anyone not adhering to one's particular interpretation of Islam as an unbeliever, and the call for blanket warfare against non-Muslims, particularly Jews and Christians. It is important to recall that the conscious adoption of Ibn Taymiyya's writings into the Wahhabi tradition occurred in the early nineteenth century when the Wahhabis had a theological and legal need for the strict division of the world into Muslims and unbelievers and the overthrow of rulers who were labeled as unbelievers as a result. It was precisely because these themes are missing from Ibn Abd al-Wahhab's writings and worldview that Ibn Taymiyya's teachings were consciously adopted by the Wahhabis. This fusion of the two has been passed down by other Wahhabis since then, most notably Osama bin Laden and his Al-Qaida network. However, one final element is critical to understanding bin Laden's worldview: the writings of the Egyptian radical Sayyid Qutb, who reinterpreted Ibn Taymiyya's worldview for application to the contemporary world.

Sayyid Qutb and Contemporary Islamic Radicalism

Sayyid Qutb (1906–66) was neither a Wahhabi nor a Hanbali jurist. He did not draw his theological or ideological inspiration from the writings of Ibn Abd al-Wahhab. His influence in the contemporary era is neither geared toward nor limited to Wahhabism but rather is visible in militant Islamic movements around the globe. What similarities exist between Wahhabism and the writings of Qutb are due to two main factors: his insistence on a return to the Quran and *hadith* for direct interpretation and his conscious adoption of Ibn Taymiyya's radical interpretation of Islam through the teachings of his most dedicated and ardent student, Ibn al-Qayyim al-Jawziyyah.

Like Ibn Taymiyya, Qutb lived in an era of turbulence. His lifetime spanned the European colonial era in the Middle East and North Africa; World War I, which resulted in the division of the Middle East and North Africa into mandates and spheres of influence for the Europeans; the rise of secular ideologies—most important, Arab nationalism and communism—the creation of the state of Israel and the resulting displacement of the Palestinians; and the struggle for full Egyptian independence in the early years of the Cold War between the United States and the Soviet Union. His life also reflected the bifurcated education of many of his generation—traditional Islamic instruction, including Quranic memorization, combined with a Western-style education that involved study not only in Egypt but also in Great Britain and, more important, the United States.

Although he had departed for his studies abroad in the late 1940s with admiration for the West and the accomplishments of Western civilization, Qutb returned to Egypt disillusioned with what he perceived to be the vices of American society: the combination of secularism and materialism that in his opinion had resulted in moral laxity, exploitation, oppression, and racism. He attributed these factors to the lack of religion as a guiding moral factor in American public life and to the fact that Americans granted precedence to human laws and thought over divine revelation and law.[110]

Concerned that this same secular ideology and approach had also been implemented in Egypt, Qutb joined the Muslim Brotherhood—an Islamist organization dedicated to the Islamization of Egyptian society from the grassroots level on up. The Brotherhood's belief in the need to engage political issues in order to achieve social change led it to join forces with other organizations to demand full independence for Egypt from Britain following World War II. The most important of these alliances was with a group known as the Free Officers, led by Gamal Abd al-Nasser, which overthrew the pro-British Egyptian monarchy in 1952.

Because they had provided support for the Free Officers' revolution, the Brotherhood expected to play a role in the new government. However, there was a major ideological difference between the officers and the Brotherhood. While the Brotherhood was an Islamist organization, the Free Officers were avowedly secular in orientation, proclaiming the ideology of Arab nationalism. In Nasser's opinion, the key to Egyptian strength lay in its assertion of its Arab, rather than its Islamic, identity and construction of an alliance with other Arab countries on the basis of their shared ethnicity. Like other Arab nationalists, he blamed religion for Egypt's backwardness in the contemporary period and sought to remove it from the public sphere. This goal was at odds with the Brotherhood's goal of the Islamization of society and eventual establishment of an Islamic state with Islamic law as the law of the land.

The tension between Nasser and the Brotherhood came to a head in 1954 after a failed assassination attempt that was blamed on the Brotherhood. Although the charges were never proven, Nasser used the attempted assassination as justification for crushing the Brotherhood. He thereafter engaged in open persecution, oppression, imprisonment and even execution of those affiliated with it. Because Qutb was one of its major leaders and its most influential ideologue by this point, he was particularly singled out by Nasser for harassment, incarceration, and ultimately execution.

Qutb's experiences of repression, authoritarianism, imprisonment, and torture by his own government led to his radicalization. During his ten years in prison, he wrote prolifically. While some of his works, particularly his Quranic commentary, were spiritually attractive to mainstream Muslims, the most influential and widely read of these prison writings for radicals was *Milestones*. This book was dedicated to the exposition of his vision of the necessity for revolution in order to create a truly Islamic society ruled by Islamic law. This revolution was to be carried out via jihad as holy war, which was declared to be the ongoing, permanent duty of Muslims as they engaged in the cosmic battle of good versus evil, played out in everyday life in the struggle of Muslims against non-Muslim governments and ideologies.

Qutb's writings are a combination of the adoption of past militant scholarship justifying jihad against non-Muslims in general, as well as non-Muslim rulers and governments, and a denunciation of contemporary secular ideologies, particularly Arab nationalism, which he held responsible for the removal of religion, and as a result God, from the center of public life. It was the denial of a public role for religion that he believed was the hallmark of ignorance (*jahiliyyah*) such as that which existed during the time of Muhammad, necessitating jihad until such ignorance was vanquished. According to his vision, only Islam was capable of uniting people. He rejected ethnicity, nationalism, and economic ideologies as the cement for community building because they were rooted in commonalities based on birth factors, geographical borders, and human ideas. As such, he believed that these ideologies were artificially designed to promote the exclusion of "others" rather than inclusion of all within a faith community united by belief in a transcendent God.[111]

Because all of these ideologies were secular, rather than divine, in orientation, Qutb believed that none of them were capable of delivering the social justice so desperately needed in Egyptian society. Believing that God is the source of all authority and justice, he held that only a God-centered society would be capable of delivering social justice.[112] He therefore called on Muslims to recognize the revolutionary character of their religion and to fight against any and all human ideologies so that an Islamic order might be implemented:

> This means that religion is an all-embracing and total revolution
> against the sovereignty of man in all its type, shape, system, and
> state, and completely revolts against every system in which authority
> may be in the hands of man in any form or in other words, he may
> have usurped sovereignty under any shape. Any system of gover-
> nance in which the final decision is referred to human beings and
> they happen to be the source of all authority in fact deifies them by
> designating "others than God," as lords over men. . . . In short, proc-
> lamation of the sovereignty of Allah and declaration of His Author-
> ity connotes the wiping out of human kingship from the face of the

earth and establishing thereon the rule of the Sustainer of the world.[113]

Milestones is not an exercise in Quranic exegesis or a consideration of legal doctrine and debates in the *ikhtilaf* tradition. It is precisely what "Kitab al-Tawhid" is not: a manifesto for action. *Milestones* is a sweeping ideological tract describing the cosmic battle between good and evil and the requirement for Muslims to participate in the fight against evil rather than a legal discussion of the implications of faith in monotheism and how this is played out in daily life. While "Kitab al-Tawhid" is largely a collection of Quranic verses and *hadith* with some explanation of their meaning, *Milestones* is the outline of a global order and how it is to be achieved, with Quranic verses and *hadith* serving as literal proof texts for points raised. "Kitab al-Tawhid" cites the Quran and *hadith* far more extensively and frequently than *Milestones* does. In addition, whereas "Kitab al-Tawhid" limits its choice of topics to issues addressed in the Quran and *hadith*, *Milestones* engages a variety of non-Quranic ideas and ideologies, particularly those most prominent in Qutb's lifetime—Arab nationalism, socialism, communism, and democracy.

This is not to say that Qutb downplayed the importance of the Quran in his writings. The importance that he assigned to the Quran is reflected in his completion of a popular and highly influential eight-volume exegetical work on the Quran during his prison years—*Fi Zilal al-Quran* (*Under the Shade of the Quran*). Where he differed most significantly from Ibn Abd al-Wahhab in his use of the Quran was with respect to the contextualization of the verses cited. Qutb tended to interpret Quranic verses literally rather than contextually. The main instance in which he addressed context was when the verses dealt with jihad. His purpose was to explain why jihad had been a limited enterprise during Muhammad's lifetime yet was actually intended to be the modus operandi of Islam afterward. As a result, his use of context was to prove exactly the opposite point of Ibn Abd al-Wahhab's.

Ibn Abd al-Wahhab interpreted the Quran and *hadith* to render engagement in jihad a limited, geographically localized activity that could only occur under specific circumstances and conditions. While participation in jihad was required in defense of the Muslim community, it was neither the hallmark theme of Ibn Abd al-Wahhab's writings nor the preferred method of gaining converts or building an Islamic society. Ibn Abd al-Wahhab placed a much higher importance on education, dialogue, and discussion as the appropriate "weapons" of faith. According to his vision, jihad was to be used strictly for defending the Muslim community. It was not intended to be a primary means of expanding it. While the hope was that the conclusion of jihad would result in the conversion of the enemy to Islam, this was to be carried out via education and discussion rather than death threats.

Sayyid Qutb differed in his perspective. While he recognized preaching and persuasion as important methods of conversion, he did not believe that they were sufficient to impose an Islamic order on society. The political, social, economic, and racial human forces blocking recognition of God and faith in the public sphere were too powerful for preaching and persuasion alone to conquer. In addition, the likelihood that those in power would abdicate their positions in favor of Islam was very slim.[114] Qutb therefore turned to armed struggle as the only hope for freeing humanity to accept Islam's message.[115]

Qutb taught that preaching must be accompanied by "movement." Only this combination could offer a measure of success in "wiping off the tyrannical powers from the face of God's earth whether they may be of a purely political nature cloaked in the form of racialism or class distinctions within a race."[116] Although Qutb did not believe that conversion could only occur by the sword, he did believe that human beings had to be pushed to accept Islam. For Qutb, Islam was more than a mere belief; it was a "way of life" whose purpose was "to put an end to all such systems which serve as obstacles in the way of complete freedom of mankind."[117] He therefore taught that "force and coercion" had to accompany preaching and persuasion in the quest for conversion.[118]

According to this vision, the purpose of jihad was not the defense of the Muslim community, as preached by Ibn Abd al-Wahhab and the Islamic modernists of the nineteenth and early twentieth centuries, in which great attention was given to the mechanics of how jihad was to be declared, undertaken, and concluded. Rather, Qutb believed that the purpose of jihad was to create an atmosphere in which people would be free to exercise their choice of faith.[119] Qutb assumed that people would choose Islam.

> "Islam" (submission to God) is a universal truth, acceptance of
> which is binding on the entire humanity. If it does not incline to-
> wards Islam or accept the same, it should then adopt an attitude of
> total compromise and should not impose any impediment in the
> shape of a political system or material power forestalling the way of
> Islam's message and persuasion. It should leave everybody to his
> free will to accept or reject it. If he does not wish to accept the same
> he should not at the same time oppose it or hinder the way of oth-
> ers. If anyone adopts the attitude of resistance, it would then be
> obligatory on Islam to fight against him until he is killed or he de-
> clares his loyalty and submission.[120]

According to this vision, freedom leaves a person with two choices—conversion or submission to Islam. Any other choice implies resistance to Islam, rendering the person subject to conversion by the sword or the death penalty. Although it would appear that a person would have no other choice but to accept Islam, Qutb denied that Islam intended to "thrust its faith upon people." At the same time, he noted that Islam was not a "mere 'belief.' "[121] Qutb's use of the term *freedom* was not the equivalent of Western understandings of this concept, which imply that an individual is free to make any choice he or she desires. For Qutb, freedom was limited to choices recognizing God's sovereignty and law.

> This freedom does not mean that they can make their desire their
> god or may themselves decide to remain under the servitude of
> other men, making some men lords over others. Whatever system
> of governance may be established in the world, it should be based
> on the worship of God, and the source of authority for the laws of
> life should be God alone, so that under the shade of this universal
> system every one may be free to embrace any faith one likes. This is
> the only way under which religion-that-is-laws, submission, obedi-
> ence and servitude could be purified for God alone.[122]

It is clear that, similar to Ibn Abd al-Wahhab, Qutb supported adherence to absolute monotheism. However, Ibn Abd al-Wahhab believed that this adherence should be a matter of personal conscience and conviction of the heart rather than a belief enforced by the state. In Ibn Abd al-Wahhab's vision, the purpose of the state was to protect Muslims and implement Islamic law. The interpretation of religion was to be left to scholars and individuals, who were responsible for advising the state on religious matters. Qutb insisted on a far more powerful role for the state in determining and enforcing beliefs because only the power and authority of the state could successfully implement and enforce Islamic law and an Islamic order, which were the ultimate purpose of jihad.[123]

For Qutb, jihad as holy war was the tool of "Quranic Revolution."[124] It was intended to be a global enterprise applicable to all situations and circumstances as the ultimate activist means of carrying out professed faith. Because Islam presented a "program of practical life," it was intended to be enforced in the world of action. It was not to be restricted to theological discussions or intellectual speculations because its purpose was to create "an organised and embattling army which had to fight the *jahiliyah*.[125]

This vision of Islam in constant conflict with ignorance was based on Qutb's sharp division of the world into two absolute spheres—*dar al-Islam* and *dar al-jahiliyyah*.[126] Like Ibn Taymiyya before him, Qutb believed that this division of the world was not simply a statement of ideology but the necessary relationship that should exist between the two. The very existence of *dar al-jahiliyyah* necessitated jihad as a permanent state of being rather than a specific type of warfare to be engaged in under limited circumstances in order to prevent Muslims from being led astray.

Qutb's division of the world was based in part on his interpretations of Judaism and Christianity. Ibn Abd al-Wahhab had respected the Quranic recognition of Jews and Christians as People of the Book, who were entitled to a protective relationship with Muslims. His treatise on jihad protected the right of captured Jews and Christians to continue to practice their religion and instruct their children in it, although the call to Islam was to be issued to them simultaneously. Ibn Abd al-Wahhab had also been careful to preserve Muhammad's example of engaging in commerce with Jews and Christians, citing the public good of the benefit brought to the Muslims by such relations.

Qutb rejected outright any kind of relationship with Jews and Christians other than that of jihad. He held "Zionist Jews" and "Christian Crusaders" responsible for the ills of contemporary society as he saw them because of their purported long historical conspiracy to annihilate Islam—a vision consistent with his belief in the ongoing cosmic battle between good and evil. He accused the "poisonous" Jews of being overly focused on ritual to the exclusion of spirituality, eternally ungrateful to God, and vicious and arrogant when in power, as evidenced by their perfidy, greed, and never-ending conspiracies and plots against Muhammad and the early Muslim community. For Qutb, Zionism was merely the logical conclusion of Jewish history and the centuries old campaign by the Jews to destroy Islam.[127]

Christians, on the other hand, were blamed for the separation of existence into two mutually exclusive spheres—the sacred and the secular—and the removal of divine law from religion. The result for Qutb was a worldview in which spiritual existence was completely separate from physical existence, rendering "religion" and "faith" individual exercises rather than a blueprint for life. Furthermore, without divine law Christianity had no structure for human life in the physical world. This led to what Qutb dubbed a "hideous schizophrenia" in the Christian approach to life—the absolute and complete separation of the spiritual from the physical—which was the hallmark of ignorant (*jahili*) societies.[128]

Because of his bipolar understanding of the world, Qutb rejected the concept of jihad as a passive mechanism to be used only in response to physical aggression. Instead, he asserted that jihad by its very nature was a dynamic and activist force that Muslims have the right and the responsibility to initiate.[129] He noted that, "Islam is not prepared to abdicate this right at any cost."[130] He therefore expanded the definition of *defense* from that of self-protection against military action to "defense of man against all the factors and motives which demolish the freedom of man or serve as impediment in the way of his real freedom," particularly when that factor is a political system.[131] Defense of Islam as a faith necessarily carried over to defense of a way of life and the society that made that way of life possible. Thus, the defense of the Muslim community was not to be determined by geographical location, ethnicity, or national interest but by whether a society supporting God's sovereignty and law was under physical or ideological attack.[132]

Expansion of the definition of *defense* resulted in the expansion of the call and need for jihad. Qutb embraced the concept of global jihad precisely because he viewed the conflict between good and evil as one of cosmic proportions. He rejected the classical and modernist interpretations that limited it to "defensive" activities because he found their definitions of *defensive* to be too narrow and confined in scope. Following instead the teachings of Ibn Taymiyya and Ibn al-Qayyim al-Jawziyyah, he used a more activist interpretation of the Quran and *hadith* to justify his vision of global jihad.

Qutb did not cite any of the verses typically used by classical scholars to describe the undertaking of jihad via nonmilitant means. He believed that the more peaceful methods of persuasion and discussion for winning converts were not applicable to his context because Islam itself was under attack. Consequently, an armed response was required.

He cited three out of the four verses typically used by classical scholars to restrict fighting (Q 2:190, 9:36, and 22:39–40),[133] three out of the nine verses referring to a conflict between God's command and the reaction of Muhammad's followers (Q 2:216, 4:72–74, and 4:75),[134] and three out of the ten verses interpreted by classical scholars as a call to arms (Q 2:217, 8:39, and 9:29).[135] Qutb interpreted these verses to demonstrate God's progressive granting of permission to Muhammad to engage in jihad of the sword. According to this interpretation, which cites the authority of Ibn al-Qayyim al-Jawziyyah, Muslims were initially restrained from fighting (Q 3:77). Then, they were permitted to fight (Q 22:39–41). Next they were commanded to fight those who fight them (Q 2:190). And, finally, war was declared against all polytheists (Q 9:36 and 9:29).[136] Only in his interpretation of Q 2:190 did Qutb stick to the classical use of these verses, using it to restrict fighting to cases in which Muslims were attacked first. The other verses were used by Qutb to justify total and permanent warfare against polytheists.

Qutb believed that jihad had been restricted during the time of Muhammad for strategic reasons, namely, the survival of the early Muslim community. While other scholars have argued that jihad is intended to be restricted in scale and scope, Qutb believed that it is the inherent responsibility and right of all Muslims. Thus, he believed that the early Meccan period, in which Muhammad was free to preach, teach, and work to form alliances and during which he did not engage in fighting, was to be understood as a "temporary phase of the long term planning" rather than a universal paradigm for Muslims:[137] "If God restrained the Muslim community from Jihad for a specified period, it was so by way of planning, and not by way of educating any principle and regulation. It was a matter of needs and requirements of the movement at a particular stage, and not related to the fundamental faith and concept of Islam."[138]

He pointed out that the Muslim community was quite small at this time, so that engagement in military action would have been more likely to result in the annihilation of the early Muslims than it would have in their conquest of the unbelievers, potentially resulting in the unacceptable victory of unbelief over Islam.[139] Qutb also believed that the Meccan period served to give the Arabs time to achieve the proper mind-set for the jihad to come: the ability to withstand oppression and repression; the discipline to follow the orders of their leader, even when such orders are unpalatable; and recognition of and preparation for potential martyrdom in the cause of God.[140] According to Qutb's interpretation, the "martyrdom complex" of fighting either until martyrdom or "God's victory" has occurred began with Muhammad and the early Muslims and remains the duty of Muslims today.

Although jihad remained restricted in the early Medinan period, Qutb believed that this was because of the need to stall for time until Muhammad was able to establish the necessary alliances to conquer the unbelievers. However, once the alliances were in place, aggressive military action began in earnest.[141] It was at this point that the full scope and purpose of jihad were revealed, making jihad for the establishment of God's sovereignty and authority on earth and the "extermination" of "all the Satanic forces and their ways of life" the permanent and universal paradigm for Muslims of every time and place.[142] It was at this point that he cited Q 4:74–76, 8:38–40, and 9:29–33 as calls to arms.[143]

Notably absent in Qutb's justifications for jihad are the defense of country, checking the aggressive designs of other empires against Muslims, expansion of Muslim territory, and amassing wealth. Similarly, he did not address specific conflicts or hot spots—not even that of his contemporary Egypt—in anything but the broadest of terms in his ideological discussions. The reason was that his vision of the inherent conflict between Islam and every other faith and ideology was global in perspective. Consequently, he was not caught up in details justifying positions on particular conflicts. Although contemporary global *jihadi* movements drawing inspiration from Qutb tend to pinpoint specific grievances that they wish to resolve, Qutb shied away from such an identification because he believed that it would have restricted and narrowed the cause of jihad by focusing on specific minor grievances rather than the major, ongoing, cosmic battle between good and evil. He rejected the interpretation of jihad as a "temporary injunction, related to changing conditions and transient circumstances," particularly the defense of geographic borders, in favor of a vision of jihad that recognizes no boundaries, physical or temporal:[144] "This struggle is not a temporary phase but a perpetual and permanent war. . . . Jihad for freedom cannot cease until the Satanic forces are put to an end and the religion is purified for God in toto."[145]

Qutb recognized that there were many Muslims who would not subscribe to this absolutist, global vision of jihad. He was pragmatic enough to realize that it was also likely to earn the enmity of governments already in power because of the threat it represented to their control over society. He reminded his followers that it was precisely because of this anticipated opposition from "the inexorable might of the state, the system and traditions of the society, the entire human environment," that jihad is required in order to free "the human soul and reason" so that "no curtain" between Islam and human beings remains.[146] He counseled them not to give in to despair or despondency or to revise their vision of jihad to make it strictly a defensive activity, noting that, "Jihad is continuing and shall continue whether defensive or temporary factors and conditions are obtaining or not."[147]

Consistent with this vision of jihad as a global enterprise to be undertaken until the entire world either converts or submits to Islam, Qutb's vision differs from definitions of peace that specify the absence of military conflict. For Qutb, it is impossible to have an absence of conflict as long as God's order and law have not been unconditionally implemented across the globe because the cosmic conflict between good and evil continues. Thus, his vision of peace is one in which Islam is "established in its entirety in the world" and all people bow in submission before God rather than before human beings.[148] According to this vision, treaty relationships are irrelevant, unless they recognize the sovereignty of Islam, because they otherwise serve to provide only temporary suspensions of military engagements rather than true peace. Similarly, cease-fires with non-Muslim governments were absolutely prohibited unless those governments accepted the sovereignty of Islam and the implementation of an Islamic order—acts that would render them Muslim.[149]

Qutb's vision of global jihad was developed at a time of conflict within a specific environment—Nasser's secular Egypt and its persecution of the Muslim Brotherhood. Yet it was precisely because of this context that his work has been taken as an inspiration for contemporary jihad-oriented organizations that see themselves in similar battles against secular ideologies and repressive, authoritarian governments, from North Africa to the Middle East to Central and Southeast Asia. As they struggle with the apparent weakness of Muslims in the face of powerful, secular societies, particularly in the West, Qutb's absolute vision of right and wrong and what is to be done about it provides a prescription for active resolution of the problems facing the contemporary Muslim world—a return to religion in which the sovereignty of God alone is recognized and all-out, permanent warfare is waged against any and all who fail to recognize that sovereignty. The experiences of many of the adherents of these movements fighting for the *mujahidin* against the Soviet Union in Afghanistan during the 1980s resulted in practical experience and victory in the cosmic battle of good (Islam) versus evil (atheist communism). Osama bin Laden has emerged as the most prominent warrior of this type, and it is within this environment, rather than the Wahhabi tradition, that he can be properly understood.

Wahhabism in the Contemporary Era: Osama bin Laden and Global Jihad

Osama bin Laden (b. 1957) emerged as the prototype of the "Islamic terrorist" following the 9/11 attacks on the Pentagon and World Trade Center. Because he was previously a Saudi citizen (he was stripped of his citizenship in 1994) and advocates a militant, religiously based worldview, many have assumed that his extremist tendencies are due to his affiliation with Wahhabi Islam.

However, as the previous discussions have made clear, bin Laden's absolute division of the world into two mutually exclusive spheres and his declaration of permanent global jihad against unbelievers are not Wahhabi in origin. Their roots lie in the teachings of Ibn Taymiyya, Ibn al-Qayyim al-Jawziyyah, and Sayyid Qutb rather than in the teachings of Ibn Abd al-Wahhab. Although Ibn Abd al-Wahhab is occasionally cited, the writings of Ibn Taymiyya, Ibn al-Qayyim al-Jawziyyah, and Sayyid Qutb figure far more prominently in bin Laden's worldview and ideology.

Like Ibn Taymiyya and Sayyid Qutb, bin Laden has been strongly influenced by a context of turbulence. His worldview reflects two major events in his life: his experiences fighting in Afghanistan, first with the *mujahidin* and later with the Taliban, and his increasingly critical role as a Saudi dissident. These two events have been defining factors in his ideological outlook.

Bin Laden's involvement in Afghanistan began in 1980 when the Afghan *mujahidin* pressed the Saudi royal family to send one of their members to lead the Saudi contingent, consisting of lower-class Saudis and political dissidents and militants, in the jihad against the Soviet Union. The Saudis, along with the United States and Pakistan, had long been supporters of the *mujahidin*, providing financing, weaponry, and intelligence. For the supporters, the jihad in Afghanistan was a powerful means of showing the Soviet Union that the entire Muslim world was opposed to its atheistic communism and was willing to fight with the Americans against it. Because the United States at this time was focused on the Cold War, rather than the rise of Islamic radicalism in Central Asia, it was willing to overlook the radical, extremist indoctrination of the *mujahidin* in training camps and religious schools (*madrasas*)—an indoctrination that affected more than one hundred thousand radicals from forty-three countries over the years.[150]

Because no one from the Saudi royal family was willing to go to Afghanistan to participate physically in the jihad there, the royals turned to bin Laden. Bin Laden's close relationship with the royal family made him an ideal second-tier candidate. More important, his willingness to place himself and his considerable financial assets at the disposal of the *mujahidin* guaranteed strong Saudi representation in the jihad against the communists.

It was during his tenure with the *mujahidin* that bin Laden became somewhat of a folk hero to the Afghans—and to Arabs and Muslims from other countries who had also come from abroad to fight in the jihad against the Soviet Union. As one fellow volunteer described him: "He was a hero to us because he was always on the front line. He not only gave his money, but he also gave himself. He came down from his palace to live with the Afghan peasants and the Arab fighters. He cooked with them, ate with them, dug trenches with them. That was bin Laden's way."[151]

Based in Peshawar, Pakistan, from 1982 until he returned to Saudi Arabia in 1990, bin Laden's contributions to the jihad in Afghanistan were considerable and varied. He brought in engineers from his construction company to build roads, a medical center, training facilities, and arms depots. He is believed to have been an active participant in the fighting against the Soviets and has worked to cultivate this image of himself by insisting that he always be photographed holding a Kalashnikov rifle that he claims to have taken from a Soviet soldier he killed. His experiences during the Afghan jihad had a profound impact on him:

> To counter these atheist Russians, the Saudis chose me as their rep-
> resentative in Afghanistan. . . . I settled in Pakistan in the Afghan
> border region. There I received volunteers who came from the Saudi
> Kingdom and from all over the Arab and Muslim countries. I set up
> my first camp where these volunteers were trained by Pakistani and
> American officers. The weapons were supplied by the Americans,
> the money by the Saudis. I discovered that it was not enough to
> fight in Afghanistan, but that we had to fight on all fronts, commu-
> nist or Western oppression.[152]

It was in Afghanistan fighting the Soviets that bin Laden heard the call to global jihad because it was there that he, along with his Arab Afghans, experienced firsthand the battle between Islam and atheism, making the cosmic conflict of good versus evil so often discussed by Sayyid Qutb a practical reality rather than a theoretical idea. It was in Afghanistan that bin Laden came to believe that "the acme of this religion is *jihad*."[153] For him, as for many of the *mujahidin* who fought there, Afghanistan was not about geopolitics. It was about Islam fighting against unbelief.[154]

The fact that the Soviet Union was ultimately defeated by forced withdrawal in 1989 led the Arab Afghans to interpret their victory as a sign of God's favor and the righteousness of their struggle. They believed that the victory over the Soviets was due to their efforts alone and ignored the other international and domestic issues that contributed to the collapse of the Soviet Union in 1991. The result was a sense of vindication—and the belief that this jihad against atheism and the forces of evil had to move next onto the global scene in order to establish a truly global community of the faithful.[155]

It was therefore in 1989 that Al-Qaida was founded in order to continue the *"jihad* against infidels" beyond the borders of Afghanistan, as well as to provide services for Arab Afghan veterans and their families. However, the members of the fledgling organization were not able to agree on anything beyond this purpose, such as where the next jihad should occur or who was to lead it. Because the Arab Afghans represented a variety of ethnicities and nationalities, as well as religious orientations, consensus on the next step in the global jihad against infidels was impossible to reach.

The Arab Afghans and other *mujahidin*, most notably those from Central Asia, therefore returned to their respective homes with their own agendas. Global jihad continued to provide ideological and religious inspiration, but each society had its own specific issues that had to be addressed. The common points were the goals of overthrowing existing infidel governments via armed jihad and creating Islamic states to take their places. It was this global vision, not the missionary activities of Saudi Wahhabis, that resulted in the civil wars and armed insurrections ranging from Algeria to Uzbekistan and Chechnya. These wars have at their roots the common perception of unjust, un-Islamic governments repressing religion in the public sphere. This, combined with the dire socioeconomic conditions and repressive and authoritarian governments in these societies, is at the root of the rise of radicalism in these countries.

Like other Arab Afghans, bin Laden returned to his native Saudi Arabia following the jihad in Afghanistan. He initially engaged in charity work, founding a welfare organization providing financial support to veterans and the families of those killed in the war. Because he had faithfully fulfilled the royal family's expectations and because of the heady experience of the defeat of atheist communism at the hands of Islam, bin Laden and his fellow Saudi Afghans expected a heroes' welcome upon their return to Saudi Arabia. However, the reality at home was that the Saudi public did not share the euphoria of the Arab Afghans or treat them as sources of inspiration. The result for the Arab Afghans was frustration, anger, disillusionment, and a sense of betrayal. They were turned from self-labeled heroes to shell-shocked and angry has-beens in need of another war to fight.[156] Saddam Hussein's invasion of Kuwait in 1990 seemed to offer the perfect outlet for their energies.

Believing that this was an appropriate time and place to reunite the Saudi Afghans for jihad in defense of the homeland and particularly the holy cities of Mecca and Medina, bin Laden offered the services of the Arab Afghans to the royal family. However, the royal family turned down his offer and invited American troops to protect Saudi Arabia instead. Bin Laden was furious.

Bin Laden was angry over the invitation to the Americans for two reasons. First, he believed that the defense of the homeland of Islam was rightfully the prerogative of Muslims, not infidels. Second, the conflict at hand was one between Muslims, rather than one between Muslims and infidels. However unpalatable the Saddam Hussein regime was, the bottom line for bin Laden was that Iraq was a Muslim majority country and Saddam's soldiers were

Muslims. For the Muslim Saudi monarchy to invite non-Muslim American troops to fight against Muslim Iraqi soldiers was a serious violation of Islamic law. An alliance between Muslims and non-Muslims to fight Muslims was also specifically forbidden by the teachings of Ibn Abd al-Wahhab.

For bin Laden, the consequences were clear. By setting aside its faith in favor of political considerations, the royal family had abandoned its support for Islam and its claims to legitimacy as rulers. Bin Laden therefore ended his support for and service to the Saudi regime at this time and declared himself an opponent to and critic of its rule.

The aftermath of the Gulf War also made clear to bin Laden that the failure of Muslims to continue the jihad against infidels begun in Afghanistan had resulted in a new victory for the infidels. Although the Muslims had stopped fighting, the infidels had not. Qutb's vision of the ongoing cosmic conflict between good and evil could not have been handed stronger evidence: when the Muslims were strong in their fight against the infidels, they were victorious. As soon as they laid down their arms, the infidels had struck back—harder and stronger. The only means of checking infidel power and expansion was to continue the global jihad at all costs. Laying aside armed conflict was not an acceptable option because the infidels would never cease their aggression against Muslims.

Consequently, following his exile to the Sudan in 1992, bin Laden began to regroup Arab Afghan veterans who were disgusted with both the American victory over Iraq and the support of Arab governments for the Americans in this inter-Muslim conflict. He also continued his critique of the royal family.

Bin Laden's opposition to the royal family led him to create the Advice and Reform Committee (ARC) as an umbrella organization for several opposition groups in Saudi Arabia. The ARC was founded neither as a revolutionary organization for global jihad nor in opposition to the United States. It was founded to call for domestic change.

In its early years, the committee was dedicated to reform through education and reinterpretation of the Quran, the Sunna, and the teachings of "our Sunni predecessors," namely, Ibn Taymiyya, Ibn al-Qayyim al-Jawziyyah, and Ibn Abd al-Wahhab. The proclaimed goals of the organization were: "(1) to eradicate all forms of Jahiliya [pre-Islamic or non-Islamic] rule and apply the teachings of God to all aspects of life; (2) to achieve true Islamic justice and eradicate all aspects of injustice; (3) to reform the Saudi political system and purify it from corruption and injustice; and (4) to revive the hezba system [the right of citizens to bring charges against state officials], which should be guided by the teachings of the top 'ulama."[157]

These goals were, on the surface, consistent with Ibn Abd al-Wahhab's teachings.[158] Yet the repeated use of the word *eradicate* left open to interpretation how these goals were to be achieved. Although the goals proclaimed the desire to reform and purify the Saudi system, the use of terms and concepts associated with more radical interpreters of Islam—the eradication of ignorant (*jahiliya*) rule espoused by Sayyid Qutb and the right of citizens to bring charges against state officials, reminiscent of Ibn Taymiyya's call for the overthrow of un-Islamic governments—suggested that the committee was not dedicated to the use of peaceful methods alone to achieve its goals. The increasingly militant stance of the committee over time, particularly its calls for war against the "American-Israeli alliance and its local supporters," suggests that it always recognized the eventuality of armed rebellion.[159]

Bin Laden's main criticisms have targeted the Saudi royal family. In the early years, he criticized its inability to defend the Saudi state (proven by the presence of American troops there), complicity with *kuffar* (proven by rampant corruption in both the government and broader society), forsaking its duty to enjoin what is right and forbid what is wrong (proven by its various alliances with and support for *kuffar*), and its general refusal to abide by God's teachings.[160]

By 1995, this criticism was expanded to include the "lack of commitment of the regime to the teachings of Sunni Islam"; fiscal mismanagement; failure to uphold Islam; the use of Islam as a tool of the royal family to support its policies, no matter how un-Islamic; and the co-optation of the religious scholars (*ulama*), most notably Shaykh bin Baz, to serve as spokespeople for the royal family's policies, rather than as the spokespeople of Islam.[161] In the process, a younger, more critical, and more "honest" generation of religious scholars had been marginalized.[162] In bin Laden's opinion, the role of the religious scholars was to interpret Islamic law, not to mask the degree to which Saudi policy had strayed from it.[163]

It is precisely because the royal family's legitimacy lies in its adherence to and protection of Islam that the religious issues struck such a nerve. Bin Laden's attacks on its supposed failure to adhere to Islam made him a major ideological threat. The most important issue in his critique with respect to Islamic law was his claim that the royal family had abdicated its claim to religious legitimacy by turning over the defense of the country to non-Muslims. According to even the most limited definitions of jihad, self-defense is the absolute right of the Muslim community. The royal family's failure to defend the country against an outside aggressor—its abdication of the right to defensive jihad—in favor of infidels could not possibly be interpreted by bin Laden as anything but abandonment of Islam. His conclusion was blunt: "We have proven that your regime is un-Islamic. It is mired in corruption and applies non-Islamic laws to certain aspects of the human dealings such as commercial law. It also has failed in the areas of the economy and defense. Thus, you should resign."[164]

It is significant that the recommended course of action at this point was the resignation of the current king, on the model of King Saud's resignation in favor of King Faisal, rather than the overthrow of the monarchy altogether.[165]

However, by 1997 bin Laden was no longer calling for a resignation. He was calling for an end to the rule of the royal family.

Between 1995 and 1997, bin Laden shifted his focus from domestic Saudi issues to broader international concerns, particularly American foreign policy in the Middle East and issues of concern to the broad Muslim community, most notably the ongoing devastation of Iraq and the never-ending plight of the Palestinians. Bin Laden's critiques changed from targeting the Saudi royal family to targeting the United States and Americans everywhere. The reason for the shift was the growing scrutiny and criticism of bin Laden by both the royal family and the United States.

American and Saudi concerns about bin Laden's bankrolling of terrorist training and the potential threat to the Saudi monarchy led to joint American and Saudi pressure on Sudan to expel bin Laden. Although they had provided a safe haven for bin Laden since 1992 and had enjoyed his considerable financial assets and business expertise, the Sudanese gave in to these demands in 1996. Bin Laden returned to Afghanistan.

By this point, American influence in the Muslim world was clear to bin Laden. Not only had the Saudi monarchy fallen under American control, but Sudan had also given in to American pressure. Furthermore, bin Laden himself had fallen out of American favor. During the Afghan jihad, he had enjoyed American support because he was a necessary ally in the fight against the Soviets.[166] However, once the Soviets departed and the Soviet Union collapsed a short time later, bin Laden was no longer a useful tool to the Americans and in fact had become a threat to them, for the exact reasons for which he had been considered such an important ally during the Afghan jihad: his military experience, his experience in and facilities for training guerrilla warriors in both conventional and unconventional methods of warfare, and the arms he now possessed.

Because the Afghan jihad had been his only practical experience in dealing with the United States, bin Laden saw the change in American policy toward him as reflective of the broad hypocrisy and hostility toward Muslims that he believed was inimical to American foreign policy in general. He pointed as evidence to the major change in American policy in Afghanistan following the jihad in which former allies became enemies; the support of the supposedly democratic and freedom-loving United States to the weak, corrupt, and power-hungry Saudi royal family; and unconditional American support for Israel despite its atrocities against the Palestinians.

It was at this point, in 1996, that bin Laden first called for jihad against the United States. This initial call for jihad was limited in scope. Its goal was the removal of the American presence from Saudi soil, which he referred to as "the walls of oppression and humiliation." He believed that this could be accomplished only "in a rain of bullets"[167]—an image brought to life by the 1996 bombings of the Khobar Towers attributed to bin Laden and his followers.

The Americans responded to bin Laden's declaration of jihad by freezing his financial assets, an estimated 250 to 300 million dollars.

Because of its cooperation with the Americans, bin Laden's critique of the Saudi royal family also became harsher and less open to forgiveness. In a 1997 interview with the news network CNN, bin Laden criticized the Saudi monarchy for serving as a mere "branch" or "agent" of the United States—a country whose "occupation of the land of the holy places," support for the "Israeli Occupation" of Palestine, and responsibility for the deaths of Muslims in Palestine, Iraq, and Lebanon (due to a 1996 bomb explosion) rendered it "unjust, hideous, and criminal."[168] Bin Laden also lay at the door of the United States the squandering of Saudi oil revenues on "expensive" and "useless" arms, all the while maintaining an artificially low price for oil.[169]

In bin Laden's eyes, this constituted nothing less than an alliance with *kuffar*. Even worse, this was not the only alliance the monarchy had entered into with *kuffar*. He lambasted the Saudi monarchy in a letter:

> In its foreign policy, your government ties its destiny to that of the crusader Western governments. It is shameful that a government that claims the protection of the Two Holy Mosques pays $4 billion in 1991 to help the Soviet Union before the Soviets washed their blood from killing Muslims in Afghanistan. In 1982, your government also aided the infidel regime in Syria with billions of dollars as a reward for killing tens of thousands of Islamists in the city of Hama. Your government also aided with millions a tyrannical regime in Algeria that kills Muslims. And finally your government aided the Christian rebels in southern Sudan.[170]

For bin Laden, the implications of such actions were clear. The royal family had abdicated its religious legitimacy by entering into relationships with *kuffar* against Muslims and Muslim interests. Saudi financial support for governments and rebel groups opposed to Muslims was such a clear violation of two of the basic tenets of Islam—the solidarity of the Muslim community and the prohibition of Muslims fighting Muslims—that the Saudi monarchy could no longer reasonably claim to be Muslim. He therefore called for the overthrow of the monarchy altogether. It was at this point that bin Laden was transformed from mere Saudi dissident to major proponent of global *jihad*.

Bin Laden and Global Jihad

Although bin Laden is supposed to be representative of the worst of what Wahhabism has to offer, the writings of Ibn Abd al-Wahhab play a surprisingly minor role in his ideology and worldview. Ibn Abd al-Wahhab's influence is most apparent in the early approach of the ARC, which cited education and reinterpretation of the Quran and Sunna as the keys to reform in Saudi Arabia.

Ibn Abd al-Wahhab's influence can also be seen in bin Laden's tendency to cite the Quran and *hadith* in order to demonstrate the ongoing relevance of the experiences of the early Muslims to the situations in which contemporary Muslims find themselves. However, when it comes to bin Laden's trademark global jihad, the writings of Ibn Abd al-Wahhab are absent. Bin Laden's vision of global jihad is rooted in the teachings of Ibn Taymiyya, Ibn al-Qayyim al-Jawziyyah, and Sayyid Qutb.

Bin Laden has given the most prominence to Ibn Taymiyya in his writings on jihad because in his words Ibn Taymiyya was "the original inspiration of jihad against a corrupt regime."[171] This foundation in the past is important because bin Laden sees himself as carrying on an important Muslim historical tradition. He rejects the charge that his worldview is anything "new" or "innovative."[172] Evidence of Ibn Taymiyya's influence is also prevalent in bin Laden's statements and the legal rulings (*fatawa*) to which he is a signatory, which typically include citations from Ibn Taymiyya and his disciple, Ibn al-Qayyim al-Jawziyyah, making it clear that his radical stance can better be traced to their influence than to Ibn Abd al-Wahhab's.

A case in point is bin Laden's criticism of a legal ruling (*fatwa*) issued by Shaykh Bin Baz, the former head of the Saudi religious establishment, supporting peace talks between Arab states and Israel. Bin Laden criticized this *fatwa* for five reasons, which he believed demonstrated its invalidity: (1) the peace talks did not meet the requirements of Islamic law for a legitimate contract between Muslims and their enemies because the parties must be recognized as legitimate leaders by the consensus of the nation—a consensus that bin Laden maintains did not exist; (2) the Saudi leadership could not legitimately approve engagement in such peace talks because it is not truly Muslim—"They are a group of secular leaders who have abandoned the faith (*murtadoon*)"; (3) the agreement is based on international rather than Islamic law and agrees to the right of a non-Muslim country (Israel) to land claimed by Muslims, including Jerusalem; (4) Bin Baz was not qualified to issue a *fatwa* on this topic because he had not even read the treaties in question and had a limited understanding of the issues involved and the international legal framework in which the agreement was made; and (5) the purpose of the *fatwa* was to please the Saudi king at the expense of Muslim interests, without the support of the Quran and Sunna, and without the consensus of religious scholars.

Significantly, bin Laden cited the authority of both Ibn Taymiyya and Ibn al-Qayyim al-Jawziyyah, rather than Ibn Abd al-Wahhab, in support of his contentions, concluding that Bin Baz should resign from his position and repent.[173] The classification of the Saudi monarchy as "not truly Muslim" was a particularly prominent theme in Ibn Taymiyya's works but one that was absent from Ibn Abd al-Wahhab's.

Sayyid Qutb's influence on bin Laden's thought is not stated as directly, but it is a known factor in bin Laden's worldview due to his studies with Sayyid

Qutb's brother, Muhammad Qutb, in Saudi Arabia.[174] Sayyid Qutb's influence on bin Laden is clear in his major themes: rejection of all secular ideologies, concern that secular principles should neither influence nor dominate Muslim societies, and the vision of an ongoing cosmic conflict between good and evil that requires permanent and unconditional jihad in response.

Bin Laden also echoes Qutb's theme of the global Christian, Crusader-Zionist, Jewish conspiracy to destroy Islam. Whereas Ibn Abd al-Wahhab never referred to Jews or Christians in any terms but as *dhimmi*, or "People of the Book," reflecting his worldview of the desired relationship among Muslims, Jews, and Christians as that of a treaty relationship, bin Laden's vehement denunciations of "Christian Crusaders" and "Zionist Jews" reflect his concerns about the globalization of culture and his intense opposition to the existence of Israel because of its displacement of Palestinian Muslims. Thus, for bin Laden the only possible relationship among Muslims, Christians, and Jews is a hostile one.

Like Qutb, bin Laden's justification of violence lies in the need to create a righteous society through activism. According to this vision, preaching and persuasion are insufficient. The command to "enjoin what is right and forbid what is wrong" necessarily entails a willingness to take up arms to accomplish that goal.[175]

The influence of both Sayyid Qutb and Ibn Taymiyya is apparent in bin Laden's absolute division of the world into Muslims and *kuffar* with no in-between category. This vision was clear in his statement following the bombings in Riyadh and Khobar that, "What matters is that in Riyadh and Khobar no Saudi was hurt, only Americans were killed."[176]

Like Sayyid Qutb, bin Laden provides no blueprint for life beyond the cosmic battle between good and evil and no political or social vision for the state outside of jihad. He does not address details of minor infractions of Islamic law that, in Ibn Taymiyya's worldview, could result in a person being declared a *kafir*. Bin Laden's vision, like that of Sayyid Qutb, looks only toward jihad. His writings and speeches lack the detailed vision of Ibn Abd al-Wahhab of how belief is to inform every aspect of life.

In addition to these influences, there is also a suggestion of Sufi influence in bin Laden's recitations of his experiences in jihad, particularly in Afghanistan. Although it is not what one might expect from a Wahhabi, the fact that Al-Qaida's ideologue, Ayman al-Zawahiri, is a major Sufi *shaykh* makes the suggestion of Sufi influence plausible.[177] For example, bin Laden often speaks of the "great peace" (*sikina*) that filled him in battle. " 'Once I was only 30 meters from the Russians and they were trying to capture me. I was under bombardment but I was so peaceful in my heart that I fell asleep.' "[178] The message is clear: those who are intent on carrying out God's Will experience no fear in their hearts, regardless of the circumstances surrounding them.

Thus, even in the midst of jihad, it is possible to experience the peace of God if one's cause is righteous. This kind of glorification of military action is completely absent in Ibn Abd al-Wahhab's works.

The other major theme of bin Laden's works that is comparable to the writings of Ibn Taymiyya, Ibn al-Qayyim al-Jawziyyah, and Sayyid Qutb, but not Ibn Abd al-Wahhab, is the glorification of martyrdom. Martyrdom plays an important role in bin Laden's ideology. He has noted that, "There is a special place in the hereafter for those who participate in jihad" and "Being killed for Allah's cause is a great honor achieved by only those who are the elite of the nation."[179]

In the weeks following the 9/11 attacks, bin Laden praised the activism of Pakistani militants in opposing the "American crusade forces and their allies on Muslim lands in Pakistan and Afghanistan." He indicated his prayer to God to accept those killed as martyrs in the "next step" in the fight against the Crusaders and to make the faithful victorious over the "forces of infidels and tyranny" so as to "crush the new Christian-Jewish crusade."[180] He continued: "We hope that these brothers are among the first martyrs in Islam's battle in this era against the new Christian-Jewish crusade led by the big crusader Bush under the flag of the Cross; this battle is considered one of Islam's battles."[181]

Bin Laden's statement makes it clear that those who engage in the jihad against infidels and tyranny have nothing to fear. He even pledged to care personally for any children left behind by martyrs, so that concerns for fellow human beings are not to override duty to God. Thus, according to bin Laden, every believer should enter into jihad without fear, even where death is concerned, because of the rewards that will follow. This glorification of martyrdom is typical in the writings of Ibn Taymiyya, Ibn al-Qayyim al-Jawziyyah, and Sayyid Qutb but is completely absent from Ibn Abd al-Wahhab's.

One of the major differences between bin Laden and Ibn Abd al-Wahhab, Ibn Taymiyya, Ibn al-Qayyim al-Jawziyyah, and Sayyid Qutb is the fact that all but bin Laden were highly educated scholars and jurists with a profound knowledge of the Quran, Sunna, and Islamic law. Bin Laden, in contrast, is neither a scholar nor a teacher. He is a businessman by education and profession. He lacks the scholarly credentials and moral weight to issue *fatawa* on his own, which explains why there are always several signatories to his declarations.

A case in point is the famous *fatwa* declaring jihad against the United States, which was signed not only by bin Laden but also by Yasir Rifa'i Ahmad Taha, leader of the Egyptian Islamic Group (al-Gamaa al-Islamiyyah); Shaykh Mir Hamzah, secretary of the Jamiat-ul-Ulama-e Pakistan; and Fazlul Rahman, amir of the Jihad Movement in Bangladesh, reflecting its international scope and support. Bin Laden's thought and actions are also informed by Al-Qaida's ideologue. Ayman al-Zawahiri, who is both a Sufi *shaykh* and the amir of Egypt's Islamic Jihad movement. This *fatwa* is important not only because of its supporters but because of the reasoning it provides in its declaration of jihad against the United States, reasoning that is used to support the ideology of global jihad.

The *fatwa* outlines Al-Qaida's three major grievances against the United States: the continued American military presence in Saudi Arabia, which is called an "occupation" that has been "plundering its riches, dictating to its rulers, humiliating its people, terrorizing its neighbors, and turning its bases in the Peninsula into a spearhead through which to fight the neighboring Muslim peoples"; the devastation of the Iraqi people; and American subservience to Israel.[182]

The first point is very telling for bin Laden. It lays the blame for the American "occupation" of Saudi Arabia at the doorstep of the United States, not of Iraq or even of Saudi Arabia. According to this vision, the Gulf simply serves as "a staging post" that its rulers are "helpless" to resist because of the strength of "the Americans' continuing aggression."

The second and third grievances point to the roles of the United States and Israel in the "great devastation inflicted on the Iraqi people," which has resulted in more than a million lives lost. No mention is made of Iraq's invasion of Kuwait. Rather, the United States is portrayed as a greedy, bloodthirsty country. Apparently unsatisfied with the fragmentation and devastation of Iraq following the Gulf War and the economic sanctions imposed on it afterward, the Americans are portrayed as coming "to annihilate what is left of this people and to humiliate their Muslim neighbours." The *fatwa* posits that the reason the Americans are doing this is to distract world attention from the plight of the Palestinians so as to "serve the Jews' petty state" and support the Jewish occupation of Jerusalem.

These grievances serve to demonstrate definitively the American-Zionist conspiracy against Islam and the Muslim world, much as Sayyid Qutb saw it. According to this vision, specific examples are mentioned to demonstrate the broader global threat to the Muslim world represented by the "Crusader-Zionist alliance." This global conspiracy is, in the opinion of the signatories, most evident in its "eagerness to destroy Iraq, the strongest neighbouring Arab state, and their endeavour to fragment all the states of the region such as Iraq, Saudi Arabia, Egypt, and Sudan into paper states through their disunity and weakness to guarantee Israel's survival and the continuation of the brutal crusade occupation of the Peninsula."[183]

The proof of the global conspiracy and aggression against Muslim countries is critical because it justifies the call to jihad according to both contemporary and classical scholarship. Jihad is always justifiable when its purpose is to defend Islam. However, the drafters of the *fatwa* make it clear that the issue remains that of cosmic conflict—the "crimes and sins" committed by the United States are nothing less than "a clear declaration of war on God, His Messenger, and Muslims." Thus, the undertaking of jihad is not simply for the sake of the defense of human beings but of God Himself. The resulting jihad must therefore also be a "defense" of global proportions. The killing of Americans that constitutes this defense cannot be restricted in geographic terms.

The jihad to which Muslims are incited in this *fatwa* is one of individual rather than communal responsibility, reflecting the contemporary preference for individual engagement. It is likely that this assignment of jihad as an individual duty also reflects Al-Qaida's preferred modus operandi—a core group of a few people carrying out a series of attacks simultaneously. This military tactic has more in common with guerrilla warfare than standard methods of battlefield warfare, reflecting again the experiences of the Afghan Arabs in the war in Afghanistan. The only "collective duty" recognized in this *fatwa* is that the entire Muslim community should undertake this individual jihad.

This jihad differs from classical interpretations in many respects. Unlike classical interpretations and that of Ibn Abd al-Wahhab, which legitimate only jihad that is proclaimed in response to direct aggression and is carried out in a limited fashion against the direct aggressors, the grievances and demands in bin Laden's jihad are broader and more global in perspective. The goals are broad: liberation of the Al-Aqsa Mosque in Jerusalem and the Holy Mosque in Mecca from American-Jewish control and the removal of American-Jewish armies from all Muslim lands in such a way that they are "defeated and unable to threaten any Muslim." In other words, forcing the enemy to retreat is insufficient. The enemy's military capacities must also be emasculated so that the enemy cannot return at a later date to reengage in aggression against Muslims. In bin Laden's opinion, "pushing out this American occupying enemy is the most important duty after the duty of belief in God."[184]

Winning converts, spreading Islam, and educating non-Muslims are not mentioned anywhere in this *fatwa*. It is a call for fighting until the enemy is killed or defeated. Finally, this jihad is not limited to strictly military warfare. Similar to the Americans and Saudis freezing bin Laden's financial assets and attempting to assassinate him, the *fatwa* encourages Muslims to "kill the Americans and plunder their money wherever and whenever they find it."[185] Bin Laden has justified his attempts to acquire weapons of mass destruction along similar lines. " 'It would be a sin for Muslims not to try to possess the weapons that would prevent infidels from inflicting harm on Muslims. Hostility towards America is a religious duty and we hope to be rewarded for it by God.' "[186]

Thus, bin Laden's jihad seeks to destroy the power of the United States, both militarily and financially. It also fails to respect the classical prohibition against killing noncombatants. The call to global jihad advocates the wholesale destruction and demolition of perceived enemies, both men and women, adults and children, soldiers and civilians. No one is to be spared in the global jihad because all are implicated in the cosmic conflict between good and evil.

Bin Laden's anger over American atrocities against and "humiliation" and "degradation" of Muslims is most evident in the remarks he sent to the al-Jazeerah television network in October 2001, just prior to the U.S. attacks on Kabul. He posited the 9/11 attacks as justice for Muslims and righteous punishment for the United States, thanking God for the destruction of America's "greatest buildings" and for filling America with fear because this is the first time that Americans have had to suffer a little of what the Muslim world has been experiencing for "more than 80 years." He lists the deaths of "millions of innocent children" in Iraq and Palestine, which are protested and condemned by none of the ruling powers or religious establishments in the Muslim world. He notes the hypocrisy of the United States in turning a blind eye to these atrocities while attacking Iraq and Afghanistan after a few dozen deaths occurred in Kenya and Tanzania following the U.S. embassy bombings. At the same time, he notes, the United States has denied that retaliatory measures by Iraq after the Gulf War or Japan following the atomic bombings would be "something that has justification." He concludes that, "Hypocrisy stood in force behind the head of infidels worldwide, behind the cowards of this age, America and those who are with it." Such hypocrisy, says bin Laden, demonstrates the desire of "infidels" worldwide to "wag their tail at God, to fight Islam, to suppress people in the name of terrorism."[187]

For bin Laden, it appears that 9/11 was the defining point in declaring to the world the necessity of global jihad, making the stark division of the world into two mutually exclusive spheres clear once and for all. "These events have divided the whole world into two sides: the side of believers and the side of infidels. . . . Every Muslim has to rush to make his religion victorious."[188] The call to participate in the cosmic battle between good and evil is clear.

Conclusion

The global jihad espoused by Osama bin Laden and other contemporary extremists is clearly rooted in contemporary issues and interpretations of Islam. It owes little to the Wahhabi tradition, outside of the nineteenth-century incorporation of the teachings of Ibn Taymiyya and Ibn al-Qayyim al-Jawziyyah into the Wahhabi worldview as Wahhabism moved beyond the confines of Najd and into the broader Muslim world.

The differences between the worldviews of bin Laden and Ibn Abd al-Wahhab are numerous. Bin Laden preaches jihad; Ibn Abd al-Wahhab preached monotheism. Bin Laden preaches a global jihad of cosmic importance that recognizes no compromise; Ibn Abd al-Wahhab's jihad was narrow in geographic focus, of localized importance, and had engagement in a treaty relationship between the fighting parties as a goal. Bin Laden preaches war against Christians and Jews; Ibn Abd al-Wahhab called for treaty relationships with them. Bin Laden's jihad proclaims an ideology of the necessity of war in the face of unbelief; Ibn Abd al-Wahhab preached the benefits of peaceful coexistence, social order, and business relationships. Bin Laden calls for the killing of all infidels and the destruction of their money and property; Ibn Abd al-Wahhab restricted killing and the destruction of property. Bin Laden calls for jihad as a broad universal prescription for Muslims of every time and place; Ibn Abd al-Wahhab confined jihad to specific and limited circumstances and contexts. Bin Laden issues calls to violence and fighting; Ibn Abd al-Wahhab sought to curtail violence and fighting. Bin Laden provides an ideological worldview based on jihad; Ibn Abd al-Wahhab provided legal justifications for the mechanics of jihad. Bin Laden calls for jihad as an individual duty; Ibn Abd al-Wahhab upheld jihad as a collective duty. Bin Laden requires no justi-fication for jihad outside of the declaration of another as an infidel; Ibn Abd al-Wahhab limited justifications for jihad and restricted the use of the label infidel. Bin Laden's vision of jihad clearly belongs to the category of contem-porary fundamentalists; Ibn Abd al-Wahhab's vision of jihad contains elements of both classical and modernist interpretations of Islam.

Wahhabi Islam is neither monolithic nor stagnant. Changes in thought, topics addressed, and emphases on different themes have clearly occurred over the past 250 years. The militant Islam of Osama bin Laden does not have its origins in the teachings of Ibn Abd al-Wahhab and is not representative of Wahhabi Islam as it is practiced in contemporary Saudi Arabia, yet for the media it has come to define Wahhabi Islam in the contemporary era. However "unrepresentative" bin Laden's global jihad is of Islam in general and Wahhabi Islam in particular, its prominence in headline news has taken Wahhabi Islam across the spectrum from revival and reform to global jihad.

Conclusion

Muhammad Ibn Abd al-Wahhab clearly is an important figure in terms of both his representation of broad trends in eighteenth-century Islamic thought and his influence and impact on contemporary Islamic thought and activism. The breadth of his scholarship and the importance of the themes he emphasized—theology and worldview, Islamic law, education, missionary work (*da'wah*), jihad, and women and gender—were relevant not only for reforming and rejuvenating his own society, but also for the revival and reinterpretation of Islam in the twenty-first century as Muslims seek methodologies for the rejuvenation of Islamic practice and the Islamization of modernity. Ibn Abd al-Wahhab's emphasis on the importance of Islamic values and the intent behind words and actions, as opposed to concern for ritual perfection, has opened the door for reforms in Islamic law, the status of women and minorities, and the peaceful spread of Islam and the Islamic mission in the contemporary era.

As an eighteenth-century activist, Ibn Abd al-Wahhab reflected some of the most important intellectual trends of his time, notably a new methodology of *hadith* criticism that was driven by content rather than form. While he acknowledged the importance of verifying that the chain of transmission (*isnad*) was viable, he did not consider this issue of form to be as substantial or important as the more complex task of reviewing the content of the *hadith* in order to determine whether its values and interpretations of issues, whether legal, religious, social, economic or political, were in keeping with the broader values taught by the Quran and other *hadith* already accepted as being authentic. Ibn Abd al-Wahhab did not invent this method of *hadith* criticism. Rather, he, like other contemporaries, such as Shah Wali Allah, learned it from his teachers in Mecca and Medina. It was this contact with the methodology of content-driven *hadith* criticism that sparked his concern with directly returning to the scriptural sources of Islam—the Quran and *hadith*—for interpretation rather than relying on classical jurisprudence.

Ibn Abd al-Wahhab's dissatisfaction with and ultimate rejection of adherence to past interpretations of Islam (*taqlid*) grew out of his encounter with *hadith* criticism. Recognizing the importance of returning directly to scripture, rather than relying on secondhand interpretations, led him to call for the rejuvenation of the practice of independent reasoning (*ijtihad*). His rejuvenation of *ijtihad* involved the clear and unequivocal assertion of the Quran and *hadith* alone as authoritative sources of revelation, taking precedence over human interpretations whether theological or juridical.

This is not to say that Ibn Abd al-Wahhab rejected familiarity with theological or juridical writings, however. Having received a broad education in jurisprudence (*fiqh*) from his father and having had contact with the judicial system in which his father, grandfather, and uncle held prominent positions, Ibn Abd al-Wahhab was familiar with a broad base of classical jurisprudence. This familiarity is clear in the numerous references to a variety of jurists in his writings. By placing himself well within the context of classical Islamic jurisprudence, he was able to declare subtly his continuity with the Islamic intellectual tradition, exonerating him from the charges of his critics that he was engaged in innovation (*bid'a*).

Yet his own personal and direct encounters with scripture led him to question the interpretations of those same scholars and jurists, particularly in cases in which he felt more attention was being paid to matters of ritual and form than to values, intent, and purpose. His rejection of *taqlid*, therefore, was not so much a matter of rejecting the past as it was a desire to break away from a mentality insisting that only people who had lived in the past were capable of correct interpretation of scripture.

Ibn Abd al-Wahhab believed in the importance of reinterpretation of scripture in one's own time and place as a means of demonstrating the ongoing relevance of God's revelation in the daily personal and communal lives of Muslims. By stripping *taqlid* of its authority and returning that authority to God alone through His revelation, he sought to push Muslims into their own personal encounters with God by direct reading and interpretation of scripture.

At the same time, he was mindful of the need to contextualize revelation—both in terms of why it had occurred and what it would have meant to the people hearing it—in order to interpret it accurately. By insisting on historical contextualization, Ibn Abd al-Wahhab rejected literal interpretations of scripture. He did not believe in simply reading part of a verse of the Quran and making a broad proclamation about its meaning without understanding the context in which it had been revealed because he believed that such a method would lead, and, indeed, had led, to errors in interpretation.

Ibn Abd al-Wahhab further insisted on the broader contextualization of scripture within scripture—that is, allowing scripture to interpret scripture—in order to verify that the value being expressed was consistent with the teachings of the rest of scripture. Thus, for example, he decried the practice of sexual relations with slave women as supposedly justified by the Quran verse permitting men to have sex with "what their right hands possess" because the Quran also teaches that women are not to be forced into sexual relationships and that sex is to be reserved for the marriage relationship alone.

Ibn Abd al-Wahhab's insistence on the recognition of a broad Quranic worldview and its inherent values lent a consistency and logic to his interpretations of scripture that would not have been possible for a literalist. His emphasis on Quranic values, rather than detailed prescriptions, has been adopted by many contemporary Muslim scholars as a guideline for implementing reforms.

Unlike many Muslim scholars and jurists, who have tended to emphasize Islamic law as the defining characteristic of Islam, Ibn Abd al-Wahhab taught a more balanced perspective involving the need for the Muslim to express both correct belief (orthodoxy) and correct practice (orthopraxy). He recognized the symbiotic relationship between the two—correct belief is the necessary foundation from which correct practice stems, so that correct practice cannot exist without correct belief. Consequently, he emphasized the importance of both theology and Islamic law as being the dual defining characteristics of the Muslim.

Theologically, Ibn Abd al-Wahhab believed that all correct beliefs can be determined and elaborated on the basis of two major themes—monotheism (*tawhid*) and associationism (*shirk*). He defined *tawhid* as a broad concept encompassing the requirements of recognizing God alone as the Creator and Sustainer of the universe and recognizing God's uniqueness, so that He cannot be compared in any way to any of what He has created. *Shirk* is comprised of any word or deed that would violate either monotheism or God's uniqueness, whether by worshiping or considering another being or object as God or by comparing it to God.

Ibn Abd al-Wahhab used these themes, which he believed constituted the essential and most important message of the Quran, to define what the Muslim should and should not believe and how the Muslim should and should not behave, as well as to discuss why certain practices associated with non-Muslims, the pre-Islamic past, and even other Muslims, notably Shiis and Sufis, constituted *shirk* and thus could not be considered true Islamic practices. It is important to recall that Ibn Abd al-Wahhab did not exclude such people as unbelievers (*kuffar*) who were necessarily outside of the Muslim community but rather sought to point out where certain of their practices conflicted with the central theological principle of *tawhid* in the hope that they would recognize the error of their ways and correct them accordingly. Thus, his most important work, "Kitab al-Tawhid," was not written as a manifesto for action but as a work of instruction for his followers so that they would understand not only what *tawhid* and *shirk* are but also what the implications of these principles are for thoughts, words, and deeds.

Similarly, Ibn Abd al-Wahhab's interpretation and discussion of Islamic law is based on the theological principles of *tawhid* and *shirk*, so that scripture alone enjoys authoritative status not only in the establishment of Islamic legal principles but also in the determination of the values inherent in those principles, which can then be extracted and applied to other cases.

Most prominently, Ibn Abd al-Wahhab emphasized the legal principle of public welfare or interest (*maslahah*) as a guiding factor in the interpretation of Islamic law because this principle established the right and responsibility of the Muslim leadership to consider the welfare of the people as being of greater importance than strict and literal adherence to ritual. He was careful to emphasize that, while the principle of *maslahah* is in some cases to be restricted to cases of extreme necessity, such as delaying almsgiving (*zakat*) during a period of severe drought because it would represent too great of a hardship, at other times it can be used to restore Quranic values to the actual practice of Islamic law, such as the broad protection of women, the poor, and orphans from exploitation. Behind his use of this principle lay a broader theme in Ibn Abd al-Wahhab's writings, that of the importance of intent.

In Ibn Abd al-Wahhab's understanding of faith and law, intent is the driving force that determines the permissibility of any statement or action. He was not so much concerned with ritual perfection as he was with the more critical matter of the heart—intent—behind that perfection. Likewise, in legal matters, he was more interested in the intent behind a particular transaction or undertaking than he was in its form because he recognized that there were cases that adhered to the letter of the law in outward appearance yet had as their ultimate goal the circumvention of the law.

Ibn Abd al-Wahhab's rejection of literalism in favor of the recognition of broad Quranic values is nowhere more apparent than in his teachings about women and his construction of gender. His vision of gender balance defies standard stereotypes of Wahhabis as misogynists by placing women on a balanced footing with men.

Ibn Abd al-Wahhab wrote extensively on the topics of marriage and divorce and the woman's place within those transactions. Rather than excluding her from the process as simply a party to be bargained for and sold, Ibn Abd al-Wahhab emphasized the right of the woman to participate throughout the process of contracting and negotiating the marriage. Although he did not permit women to carry out the administrative drafting of the marriage contract, he insisted that they be allowed to propose prospective husbands, stipulate favorable conditions in the marriage contract (such as limitations on polygyny and situations that would result in divorce), receive her dower in full as her own property to manage, and be paid maintenance for the duration of the marriage. He further required the woman's consent to the marriage in order for it to be recognized as valid.

Ibn Abd al-Wahhab's prescriptions for the woman's role and participation in the process of contracting the marriage were based on recognition of the girl/woman as a legal person with a vested interest in the marriage. The only distinctions he made, therefore, with respect to the issue of consent were between virgins and deflowered women in the manner in which their consent was to be indicated. He made no distinctions on the basis of age, other than to indicate where classical jurisprudence on this topic fell short with respect to the minor girl. His granting of even a minor girl the right to consent in order for the marriage to be valid was a major and important reform. Ibn Abd al-Wahhab further decried the practice of child marriage and set limitations on ages and maturity levels accordingly because he recognized the potential for literalism to allow for legal circumvention of the intent behind this prohibition.

Although divorce via repudiation (talaq) has historically been the prerogative of the man—and, indeed, this practice has continued into the present era in the Muslim world—Ibn Abd al-Wahhab sought to redress this violation of what he considered to be the Quranic order of balanced rights in divorce by emphasizing the woman's absolute right to demand a divorce via compensation (khul'). Noting that the man has the right to unconditional divorce by talaq, with no requirement for justification, Ibn Abd al-Wahhab granted the woman the reciprocal right by allowing her to cite vague concerns that she would not be able to fulfill her marital duties as the justification for khul' divorce. Recognizing the abuse of power often exercised by men in such cases, he required that the woman return the amount of her dower in exchange for her freedom, comparing this type of divorce to a business contract in which the return of the amount that was paid in order to enter into the relationship symbolizes its end. Ibn Abd al-Wahhab did not allow the man to deny his wife her right to divorce either by refusing her request or by setting the amount at such an excessive rate that she could not possibly pay it. By placing checks on the man's power to deny the woman her right to divorce, he made divorce by the woman a real possibility rather than a theoretical right with no means of being enforced.

Ibn Abd al-Wahhab's writings make clear his broad respect for and protection of women. Recognizing a woman's vulnerability, Ibn Abd al-Wahhab not only sought to grant her power in matters directly related to her family status—marriage, divorce, childbearing, and inheritance—but also in the most personal of matters, sexual relations. On the one hand, he assured women that they, as well as men, were entitled to sexual relations and satisfaction in their marital lives. He underlined the importance of respecting a woman with whom one is engaged in sexual relations by protecting her right to privacy in the marriage bed, as well as making even the most intimate matter of sexual intercourse a matter for negotiation between husband and wife rather than a position in which the man was all powerful. Further, he insisted that husbands treat their wives respectfully and with dignity and forbade husbands to beat their wives.

Ibn Abd al-Wahhab also sought to protect women from male sexual aggression by condemning the practices of rape and sexual relations with female slaves and servants. This, again, marked a major departure from classical interpretations of permissible sexual relations, which included concubinage as a legally recognized and approved activity. Ibn Abd al-Wahhab, however, noted the broad Quranic value of sexual relations occurring legally only within the state of marriage so that all other activities are illicit (zina'). By emphasizing the appropriate place of sex only within marriage, he not only denounced the practices of fornication and adultery but squarely placed the responsibility for both on both genders. In cases in which a woman was a willing partner to sexual relations outside of marriage, he taught that both the man and the woman should be punished if they either confessed to the act or there were viable witnesses to the action itself. However, he also recognized that there were cases in which a woman might not be a willing participant. In such cases, he laid the blame entirely on the man in question. It is significant that Ibn Abd al-Wahhab not only recognized rape as a type of sexual relations, but he also declared it to be a punishable act for the man involved. He did not prescribe punishment for the woman or charge her with having engaged in zina'.

Similarly, Ibn Abd al-Wahhab did not hold women responsible for men's failure to control their sexual desires. He never equated women with chaos (fitnah) or accused them of inciting male desire. Rather, he held men responsible for controlling themselves, much as he held women responsible for controlling themselves. It was for this reason that, although he believed that both men and women should dress modestly, he did not require women to wear the full abaya, including a veil to cover the face. Instead, he taught that women could expose their hands, feet, and faces in public. He further granted couples contemplating marriage the right to meet and view each other more extensively in a more relaxed setting because he believed that this would spare the couple the unpleasant surprise of finding themselves incompatible after agreeing to the marriage contract. His permission granted to unrelated men and women to meet for business and medical purposes and to engage in commercial partnerships also served to create and protect women's access to public space.

Ibn Abd al-Wahhab believed that women have important roles to play in both the private and public spheres and sought to guarantee their access to both by enforcing their rights. He particularly guaranteed their right to education so as to be able to fulfill their religious responsibilities—a task that could not be completed without knowledge of both correct beliefs and practices.

Ibn Abd al-Wahhab's worldview focused heavily on the theme of education. He believed that acquiring and sharing religious knowledge with others was the most important responsibility of Muslims, both male and female. He held both men and women responsible for correct belief and practice, the heart of which was a solid foundation of knowledge. He encouraged all of his followers to study the Quran and *hadith* directly for guidance in their personal lives, as well as in their interactions with God and others.

Ibn Abd al-Wahhab taught that knowledge was also necessary for public order. He charged people to become educated so that they will be able to select appropriate leaders and verify that they are worthy of their jobs. He described those fit for leadership as being, first and foremost, knowledgeable about the sources of scripture so that their actions as public figures will be in accordance with the precepts of Islamic belief and law. He charged his followers with the responsibility of recognizing and being able to distinguish between truth and falsehood on the basis of their own knowledge so that they will know for themselves whether a leader is fit to lead.

Because of the importance he placed on knowledge, Ibn Abd al-Wahhab emphasized not only the personal pursuit of education but also the responsibility of Muslims to engage in debate with others about their beliefs in order to educate them. His concern for the need to educate was based on his recognition of the command to spread Islam. That he chose to do so by educational means—dialogue, discussion, and debate—rather than more militant methods, such as conversions of the sword, is particularly noteworthy in the light of standard stereotypes of Wahhabis as militant, violent, and destructive.

In Ibn Abd al-Wahhab's vision, education and debate were the preferred methods of gaining adherents. Thus, education was to be an integral part even of jihad as holy war. He did not support a "convert or die" mentality or encourage conversions at sword point because he recognized that a true conversion to Islam must come from the heart and mind rather than as an expedient alternative to the threat of immediate death. Consequently, he did not insist on conquering towns or villages by military action first, with only a perfunctory attempt at education afterward, but rather he engaged in letter-writing campaigns and the sending of missionaries, often over extended periods of time, in order to try to peacefully gain adherents through persuasion rather than coercion. The conversions of the towns of Washm and Riyadh are representative of these attempts.

Ibn Abd al-Wahhab's insistence on peaceful calling to Islam reflected his broad worldview, in which the ultimate dual goal of every action undertaken by the Muslim should be personal belief in and adherence to monotheism while calling others to the same. He believed that this could be achieved most effectively through education, so that even jihad included as its main goal the winning of adherents or at least placing them in a protective, cooperative relationship with Muslims through the establishment of a protective treaty (*dhimmi*) relationship. Thus, his vision of the world was not one in which Muslims could only coexist peacefully with other Muslims but rather one in which Muslims were expected to co-exist and even cooperate peacefully with others, even though their religious beliefs and practices might differ.

Ibn Abd al-Wahhab's discussion of jihad includes elements of both the classical and modernist traditions. Like the classicalists, he grounded his discussion of jihad in the Quran, *hadith*, and writings of past jurists in order to demonstrate his continuity with an intellectual tradition. He emphasized the mechanics of jihad—how it was to be carried out, by whom, under what circumstances and how it was to end—rather than broad ideas about warfare. He also issued strict regulations about how enemies were to be treated, distinguishing between adult male combatants, who were liable to punishment, and noncombatants, including women, children, the elderly, the handicapped, slaves, and religious leaders, both Muslim and non-Muslim, who were exempted from punishment on the basis of their nonparticipation in battle.

Ibn Abd al-Wahhab's writings on jihad reflect the Quranic theme of the value and sanctity of life. Consequently, he called for the maximum preservation of life—human, animal, and plant—during jihad, rather than their destruction. He limited the collection of booty to items necessary to the Muslims for survival, such as food and fodder for their riding animals, and nonluxury items, such as used clothing, and insisted that the one-fifth of the booty collected for God and Muhammad be put to use for public welfare services. He did this in order to prevent jihad from deteriorating into a tool for state consolidation or enrichment and to refocus the attention of his followers on the ultimate purpose of jihad—defense of the Muslim community, the winning of converts, and the establishment of peaceful, protective, cooperative relationships with non-Muslims.

Like the modernists, Ibn Abd al-Wahhab's vision of jihad was purely defensive in nature. He legitimated jihad only in cases in which Muslims had experienced an actual aggression. He did not glorify martyrdom because he believed that the only intent a person should have in carrying out jihad was defense of God and God's community, not the desire for personal rewards or glory, whether on earth or in the Afterlife. Further, Ibn Abd al-Wahhab did not permit the use of jihad in aggressive activities directed against others. By limiting jihad to cases that were strictly defensive in nature, he precluded the possibility of using it as a means of consolidating political power or forcibly spreading Wahhabi rule on a religious basis.

Ibn Abd al-Wahhab's teachings on jihad stand in marked contrast to contemporary fundamentalists, most notably Osama bin Laden. Although it is often posited that bin Laden's ideology of global jihad has its origins in Ibn Abd al-Wahhab's writings because both are Wahhabis, the reality is that bin Laden's ideology owes far more to the writings of the medieval scholar Ibn

Taymiyya and his contemporary interpreter, Sayyid Qutb, than it does to the writings of Ibn Abd al-Wahhab.

Bin Laden, like Ibn Taymiyya and Sayyid Qutb before him, envisages the world as divided into two absolute and mutually exclusive spheres—the land of Islam (*dar al-Islam*) and the land of unbelief (*dar al-kufr*)—a division that results in a necessarily hostile relationship. For bin Laden, jihad is intended to be the modus operandi of Muslims, not a restricted method of self-defense. Because bin Laden espouses a vision of a world in which good and evil are engaged in cosmic conflict, he believes that jihad must take on offensive, as well as defensive, capabilities and should be a permanent state of being for Muslims. According to this vision, martyrdom should not be feared but actively pursued. The enemy is not to be called passively to Islam but must be actively, physically engaged. Anyone who resists the message of Islam or Muslim domination is to be fought and killed.

There is a serious disconnect between the writings of Ibn Abd al-Wahhab and bin Laden, a fact that is attributable not only to the different contexts in which they have lived and written but also to their approaches to scripture. Ibn Abd al-Wahhab searched for intents and values. Bin Laden's readings are more literal in their approach. Ibn Abd al-Wahhab's quest was for a broad social order in which Muslims could live peacefully and respectfully with both Muslims and non-Muslims. Bin Laden's vision leaves no space for non-Muslims or those who claim to be Muslims but do not act the part. Ibn Abd al-Wahhab's writings have inspired a variety of contemporary reforms, from a context- and value-oriented reading of the Quran to legislation expanding women's rights and access to public space. Bin Laden's social vision is limited to jihad, suggesting a future of violence and destruction rather than peaceful construction.

At the dawn of the twenty-first century, it is clear that there is more than one type of Wahhabi Islam. The vision of Ibn Abd al-Wahhab was one in which Islam was to be revived and reformed in the service of public order and welfare. It especially created public space and a balance of rights for women, as well as a legal methodology for indigenous reform based on Islamic teachings and law. It is a vision that offers hope for the future.

The vision of bin Laden is one in which global jihad is to define relations between Muslims and the rest of the world. Although this vision does not currently possess a mass following, those who do adhere to it are dedicated and determined to carry it out, as 9/11 and subsequent terrorist attacks have proven. Bin Laden's vision is one that seeks to cause fear and discord.

Which vision of Wahhabi Islam becomes definitive in the future will be largely dependent on the global community's response to and support of the issues of most concern to Muslims today. Emasculation of extremist ideologies requires serious and systematic redress of its root causes—poverty, injustice, authoritarianism, repression, and despair—on a global level. This can only occur with the support of the international community, financial as well as political, from Palestine and Iraq to the countries of Central Asia.

The consequences of allowing bin Laden's vision to win are clear. The question for the future is whether the international community is willing to embrace the tough issues that fuel extremism in order to make space for the revival and reform of Muslim societies around the world. The consequences are of global proportions.

Notes

INTRODUCTION

1. The most recent example of this kind of assertion can be found in Stephen Schwartz, *The Two Faces of Islam: The House of Sa'ud from Tradition to Terror* (New York: Doubleday, 2002).

2. On the issue of Wahhabi support for extremism in Afghanistan and Central Asia, see Ahmed Rashid, *Taliban: Militant Islam, Oil, and Fundamentalism in Central Asia* (New Haven: Yale University Press, 2000); and *Jihad: The Rise of Militant Islam in Central Asia* (New Haven: Yale University Press, 2002).

3. See, for example, Khaled Abou El Fadl, *The Place of Tolerance in Islam* (Boston: Beacon Press, 2002), 8.

4. Extracts are from Philippe Aziz, Interview, *Le Point*, 17 August 1996; and "L'arroseur arrose," *Jeune Afrique*, 17 August 1996.

5. Indeed, Saudi Arabia has not engaged in military occupations or holy wars to gain converts. Instead, the Saudis have supported what has been called "aggressive proselytizing," which is carried out through the construction of mosques and distribution of Qurans in local languages, particularly in the Balkans and the former Soviet Union. See, for example, Bruce Pannier, "Wahhabism and the CIS (From Fergana to Chechnya)," RFE/RL Internet document, 19 May 1997.

6. An example of this type of widespread contemporary anti-Wahhabi polemic can be found in Zubair Qamar, "Who Are the Wahhabees ('Salafis')?" Internet document, 31 March 1998.

7. These issues have been raised, and sharply answered in the affirmative, by Schwartz, who subscribes to the belief that Wahhabism is a threat to all who believe in the principles of tolerance and pluralism.

8. The lack of attention to Ibn Abd al-Wahhab's written works is in part due to lack of access to his writings. The research for this book was

made possible by unprecedented access to these source materials generously provided by the King Abd al-Aziz Foundation for Research and Archives in Riyadh, Saudi Arabia, as facilitated by its Director General, Dr. Fahd al-Semmari, and H.R.H. Faisal bin Salman. The author is grateful for their assistance. However, the author alone retains responsibility for the interpretations presented here.

9. This characterization is contained in Schwartz, who goes so far as to refer to Ibn Abd al-Wahhab as a "bumpkin from an obscure village in a distant district nobody had ever heard of" (*Two Faces of Islam*, 133), clearly rendering him incapable of appreciating the greatness of broader Islamic civilization and empires and making him "the first known exemplar of totalitarianism" (74).

10. The most recent critical work making these assertions is Hamid Algar, *Wahhabism: A Critical Essay* (Oneonta, NY: Islamic Publications International, 2002), esp. 2–5. However, the author admits that these impressions are based on only the source materials to which he had access and notes that he did not have access to the full corpus of Ibn Abd al-Wahhab's written works (14–7). Algar's analysis is based on and limited to analysis of three theological treatises, *Kitab al-Tawhid*, *Kashf al-Shubhat*, and *Three Essays on Tawhid* (the latter was translated by Ismail Raji al-Faruqi and includes the previously mentioned treatises); Ibn Abd al-Wahhab's collection of *hadith*, four volumes entitled *Muallafat al-Shaykh al-Imam Muhammad Ibn Abd al-Wahhab*: and Mahmud Shukri al-Alusi's *Masa'il al-Jahiliyya*.

11. Schwartz, *Two Faces of Islam*, 67.

I. MUHAMAD IBN ABD AL-WAHHAB AND THE ORIGINS OF WAHHABISM

1. In this respect, Najd fit into a broad pattern of eighteenth-century reform because it reflected the general tendency toward regional, provincial, and local autonomy and independence from centralized rule. From a political perspective, the eighteenth century is viewed as a period of weakness in the Muslim world because of the deterioration apparent in the great Muslim empires during this time.

2. For an excellent analysis of the eighteenth-century Islamic world, see John O. Voll, *Islam: Continuity and Change in the Modern World*. 2d ed. (Syracuse: Syracuse University Press, 1994), esp. 24–83.

3. This science of *hadith* authentication came under strong academic criticism in the twentieth century. Some scholars, particularly in the West, questioned whether any *hadith* can truly be considered authentic given the lack of verifiable writtern records for the very early period. However, others argued that the system of oral transmission is acceptable given that this was a common means of transmitting information from one generation to another at this time and should not be discarded simply because it was not in written form. For a more detailed discussion of this methodology of *hadith* criticism and the historical development of its literature, see R. Marston Speight, "Hadith," in *The Oxford Encyclopedia of the Modern Islamic World*, ed., John L. Esposito (New York: Oxford University Press, 1995), 2:87; A. A. Duri, *The Rise of Historical Writing among the Arabs*, ed. and trans. Lawrence I. Conrad (Princeton: Princeton University Press, 1983); Tarif Khalidi, *Arabic Historical Thought in the Classical Period* (Cambridge: Cambridge University Press, 1994); and Reuven Firestone, *Jihad: The Origin of Holy War in Islam* (New York: Oxford University Press, 1999). A more detailed discussion of twentieth-century Western criticism of *hadith* can be found in Ig-

naz Goldziher, *Muslim Studies (Muhammedanische Studien)*, ed. S. M. Stern, trans. C. R. Barber and S. M. Stern, vol. 2 (Chicago: Aldine, 1973); and Joseph Schacht, *The Origins of Muhammadan Jurisprudence*, 4th ed. (Oxford: Oxford University Press, 1964).

4. See, for example, the Egyptian historian, al-Jabarti's, observation of his encounter with Wahhabi scholars as found in Abd al-Rahman al-Jabarti, *'Abd al-Rahman al-Jabarti's History of Egypt*, ed. Thomas Philipp and Moshe Perlmann, 4 vols. (Stuttgart: Franz Steiner Verlag, 1994), 3–4:321.

5. The Sudanese Mahdi is a good example of a later movement that sought to recreate literally the early Muslim community.

6. Esposito has noted, "Islamic revivalism is not so much an attempt to reestablish the early Islamic community in a literal sense as to reapply the Quran and Sunna rigorously to existing conditions." See John L. Esposito, *Islam: The Straight Path*, 4th ed. (New York: Oxford University Press, 1998), 117–18.

7. Important research on this practice has been carried out in recent years, most notably by Wael Hallaq. Hallaq's research has revealed that the practice of *ijtihad* never completely ended, as some scholars had claimed. However, the practitioners of *ijtihad* were typically a minority and belonged mostly to the Hanbali and Shafii schools of Islamic law. *Taqlid* was the broad norm historically.

8. A more militant approach was undertaken by nineteenth-century movements that claimed inspiration from the teachings of eighteenth-century reformers but took a more activist political-military approach, typically in the face of European colonialism. In the nineteenth century, Islam served as the inspiration for resistance movements, necessarily lending them a more militant character. The Indian Ocean region and the Sudan are excellent examples of more militant interpretations of the eighteenth-century reform movements.

9. Although this type of religio-political alliance was a characteristic of the eighteenth-century reform movements, it was not unique to this time period. The Hanbali school of Islamic law supported this type of arrangement historically, both during the caliphate and during the medieval era, as recorded in the works of Ibn Taymiyya. See George Makdisi, "The Sunni Revival," in *Islamic Civilisation, 950–1150: A Colloquium Published under the Auspices of the Near Eastern History Group, Oxford, and the Near East Center, University of Pennsylvania*, ed. D. S. Richards (Oxford: Faber, 1977), 164–65; and Joseph A. Kechichian, "The Role of the Ulama in the Politics of an Islamic State: The Case of Saudi Arabia," *Middle East Studies* 18 (1986): 54.

10. Paralleling the life of the individual whose biography is being written with that of the Prophet Muhammad is a literary style often found in biographies that seek to set the individual in question strongly within the Islamic tradition.

11. An example of questionable factual material is the assertion of an anonymous author that Ibn Abd al-Wahhab studied philosophy in Hamadan, Qum, and Isfahan in Iran during the course of his travels. Anonymous. *Lam al-Shihab fi-Tarikh Muhammad bin Abd al-Wahhab*, ed. Ahmad Abu Hakima (Beirut: n.p., 1967). There is no documentation in any other account to support this assertion or mention of his presence in these locations in contemporary Persian chronicles. It is open to question why he would have spent so much time studying in the major Shii centers of learning. However, this has not prevented some historians from accepting the assertion as fact. See, for example, D. S. Margoliouth, "Wahhabiya," in *E. J. Brill's First Encyclope-*

dia of Islam, 1913–1936 (London: Brill, 1987), 8:1086. Margoliouth asserts that Ibn Abd al-Wahhab traveled to Isfahan in 1736 C.E., where he spent four years studying peripatetic philosophy and the Ishrakiya and Sufi systems and even supposedly practiced Sufism for a year. After this, he reportedly went to Qum, after which he became an adherent of Hanbali law. This assertion does not seem credible due to Ibn Abd al-Wahhab's opposition to certain practices of both Shiism and Sufism, as well as the fact that he already had extensive familiarity with Hanbali law prior to these supposed journeys. Algar has also questioned the veracity of this account. Hamid Algar, *Wahhabism: A Critical Essay* (Oneonta, NY: Islamic Publications International, 2002), 12–13. Although some contemporary scholars have suggested that Ibn Abd al-Wahhab was secretly working for the Shah of Iran, this claim does not appear credible either, given his stance.

12. I have only encountered one drawing that was purportedly of Ibn Abd al-Wahhab. Further research revealed that it was mislabeled. It is actually a drawing of Abd Allah ibn Saud following his capture by the Ottomans.

13. Uthman Ibn Bishr, *Unwan al-Majd fi Tarikh Najd*, ed. Abd al-Rahman bin Abd al-Latif bin Abd Allah Al al-Shaykh. 2 vols. (Riyadh: Matbu'at Darat al-Malik Abd al-Aziz, 1402H/1982), 1:62. The adjective *Hanbali* indicates that they followed the Hanbali school of Islamic law. A description of the Hanbali school can be found in chapter 3.

14. Mohamed A. al-Freih, "The Historical Background of the Emergence of Muhammad Ibn Abd al-Wahhab and His Movement," Ph.D. diss., University of California at Los Angeles, 1990, 335.

15. Ibn Bishr, *Unwan al-Majd fi Tarikh Najd*, 1:33.

16. Memorization of the Quran generally precedes other types of religious education and marks the entrance of the memorizer into religious adulthood.

17. Husayn Ibn Ghannam, *Tarikh Najd*, 2 vols, 4th ed. (Beirut: Dar al-Shuruq, 1994), 1:25–26.

18. Ibn Bishr, *Unwan al-Majd fi Tarikh Najd*, 1:33. It is likely that Ibn Abd al-Wahhab's vehement opposition to the imitation of past scholarship (*taqlid*) grew out of his extensive familiarity with the works of numerous *ulama* and jurists. It has been suggested that he did not realize the importance of rejecting *taqlid* in favor of independent reasoning (*ijtihad*) until he had engaged in serious *hadith* studies in the Hijaz, giving him strong personal and direct contact with and knowledge of one of the major sources of scripture in Islam. See, for example, al-Freih, "Historical Background," 335–38.

19. Ibn Ghannam, *Tarikh Najd*, 1:146; Ibn Bishr, *Unwan al-Majd fi Tarikh Najd*, 1:33.

20. Ibn Bishr, *Unwan al-Majd fi Tarikh Najd*, 1:34. This interpretation is based on a variety of passages in the Quran that make this assertion.

21. Ibid., 34–35. See also Ibn Ghannam, *Tarikh Najd*, 1:172. This pattern was also characteristic of Muhammad's teaching and preaching in the early years.

22. Examples of those having encountered actual Wahhabis and examined their teachings include the Egyptian historian Abd al-Rahman al-Jabarti (al-Jabarti, *Aja'ib al-Athar fi al-Tarajim wa-al-Akhbar*, 3–4: 321).

23. Algar (*Wahhabism*, 7 and 11) has asserted that Ibn Abd al-Wahhab made trips to Huraymila prior to traveling to Medina and upon leaving it, ostensibly to visit his

father, who had been exiled from al-Uyaynah due to Ibn Abd al-Wahhab's teachings. Ibn Bishr's chronicle makes no mention of this.

24. al-Freih, "Historical Background," 331.

25. Ibn Bishr, *Unwan al-Majd fi Tarikh Najd*, 1:6. This information is also cited in Ayman al-Yassini, "Ibn 'Abd al-Wahhab, Muhammad," in *Oxford Encyclopedia of the Modern Islamic World*, 2:159–60. John O. Voll has noted that Muhammad Hayat al-Sindi was also the teacher of Shah Wali Allah al-Dihlawi, who is sometimes referred to (incorrectly) as the leader of the Indian Wahhabi movement. John O. Voll, "Muhammad Hayat al-Sindi and Muhammad ibn 'Abd al-Wahhab: An Analysis of an Intellectual Group in Eighteenth-Century Medina," *Bulletin of the School of Oriental and African Studies* 38, no. 1 (1975): 32–38.

26. The assertion of Ibn Abd al-Wahhab's study of and heavy reliance on Ibn Taymiyya has been made for many years, beginning with the works of Henri Laoust and continuing through Algar (*Wahhabism*, 8–10). This assertion is addressed in several places throughout this book, where it is definitively shown that Ibn Abd al-Wahhab did not rely heavily on Ibn Taymiyya's teachings or interpretation of Islam and in fact disagreed with him on numerous points.

27. Ibn Bishr, *Unwan al-Majd fi Tarikh Najd*, 1:35. This story also reinforces the notion of Ibn Abd al-Wahhab as a well-read and learned scholar, an image supported by his writings, which include citations from a wide variety of sources, as opposed to a person with a very limited formal education who was not well read, which is the image typically portrayed by his detractors.

28. Ibid., 36. How exactly he accomplished this is not specified by Ibn Bishr, who appears to be less concerned with the actual methods used than he is with the fact that this event occurred. This is a case in which Ibn Bishr's telling of the story differs from that of the polemicist Ibn Dahlan. Ibn Bishr describes the relationship between Ibn Abd al-Wahhab and Muhammad Hayat al-Sindi as being one of approval, while Ibn Dahlan claims that al-Sindi detected "signs of heresy" in him. See Margoliouth, "Wahhabiya," 1086.

29. Ibn Bishr, *Unwan al-Majd fi Tarikh Najd*, 1:36.

30. This is a repeat of the pattern in which opposition to Ibn Abd al-Wahhab's teachings arises only when a threat to the power structure of the day is perceived.

31. Ibn Bishr, *Unwan al-Majd fi Tarikh Najd*, 1:36. According to Ibn Bishr's chronicle, this was the first instance in which Ibn Abd al-Wahhab was physically driven out of an area.

32. Muhammad Ibn Abd al-Wahhab, "Risalah fi al-Radd ala al-Rafidah," in *Mu'allafat al-Shaykh al-Imam Muhammad Ibn Abd al-Wahhab* (Riyadh: Jamiat al-Imam Muhammad bin Saud al-Islamiyah, 1398H). This treatise was found in Basra, lending support to the contentions that Ibn Abd al-Wahhab spent time living, studying, and preaching in the city and that he came into contact with Shiism there.

33. A full discussion of the Rafidah sect and Ibn Abd al-Wahhab's concerns about certain Shii beliefs and practices follows in chapter 2.

34. It is believed that the purpose of such travels would have been to continue his *fiqh* studies in Damascus, which was a center of Hanbali scholarship. See, for example, George Snavely Rentz Jr., "Wahhabism and Saudi Arabia," in *The Arabian Peninsula: Society and Politics*, ed. Derek Hopwood (Tonawa, NJ: Rowman & Littlefield, 1972), 55.

35. Ibn Bishr, *Unwan al-Majd fi Tarikh Najd*, 1:36–67. No details are provided as to how this loss occurred.

36. Ibid., 37.

37. According to Ibn Bishr, Ibn Abd al-Wahhab's father had been removed from his judgeship in al-Uyaynah by the ruler of the time, Muhammad ibn Muammar, for reasons that are unclear. He notes that Ibn Abd al-Wahhab's father had "changed residence" from al-Uyaynah to Huraymila in the year 1139H, shortly after which a terrible plague hit al-Uyaynah and the town was completely destroyed. The presentation of events suggests that God saw fit to punish al-Uyaynah after Ibn Abd al-Wahhab's father left. See ibid. Algar (*Wahhabism*, 7) asserts that Ibn Abd al-Wahhab's father was forced out of al-Uyaynah due to his son's preaching, but the chronicles are vague on this matter. Ibn Ghannam (*Tarikh Najd*, 1:28), also records Ibn Abd al-Wahhab's conflict with the authorities of Basra, the journey to al-Zubayr, and the return to Huraymila to be with his father.

38. Ibn Bishr, *Unwan al-Majd fi Tarikh Najd*, 1:37.

39. Ibn Ghannam reports that Ibn Abd al-Wahhab had adherents not only in Huraymila but also in al-Uyaynah, al-Dir'iyyah, Riyadh, and Manfuhah. Ibn Ghannam, *Tarikh Najd*, 1:29–30.

40. For this assertion of irrelevance, see Algar, *Wahhabism*, 2–5.

41. Ibn Bishr, *Unwan al-Majd fi Tarikh Najd*, 1:37.

42. al-Yassini, "Ibn 'Abd al-Wahhab, Muhammad," 159. As is noted in chapter 5, there is nothing in Ibn Abd al-Wahhab's writings to support such a vehement stance.

43. Ibn Bishr, *Unwan al-Majd fi Tarikh Najd*, 1:37–38. This continues the pattern of travel, preaching, and rejection mentioned earlier and apparent in the life of the Prophet Muhammad.

44. Ibid., 38. The slaves did not arrive at this plan of action on their own. There was some encouragement, if not a direct order, from at least one of the masters, although Ibn Bishr does not name the person or persons and implies, rather than directly states, that this was the case, presumably since slaves would not be free agents in undertaking such activities. The attempt does not appear to have been very well organized, since it was foiled by people shouting at the group of slaves rather than engaging in any kind of military or violent action.

45. This is the only marriage the chronicles record for Ibn Abd al-Wahhab, probably because of the political alliance that followed it.

46. Algar (*Wahhabism*, 18) confuses the order of these two events, claiming instead that Ibn Abd al-Wahhab's marriage to al-Jawhara was a means of cementing the political-religious alliance. Ibn Bishr, *Unwan al-Majd fi Tarikh Najd*, 1:38, like earlier sources, makes it clear that the marriage came first.

47. Ibn Bishr, *Unwan al-Majd fi Tarikh Najd*, 1:38.

48. Ibid., 39; Ibn Ghannam, *Tarikh Najd*, 1:30–31. Other non-Wahhabi accounts, particularly those of Western travelers, also record these events. It is therefore reasonable to say that they occurred.

49. Ibn Bishr, 39. The destruction of tombs and shrines became a major point of conflict with the Shiis over time and remains an active part of their collective memory today, as evidenced by the uneasy relationship between Iran and Saudi Arabia and between Wahhabis and Shiis in Saudi Arabia today.

50. Elaboration of the principle of *tawhid* and actions that constitute violations of it are presented in chapter 2.

51. Ibn Abd al-Wahhab himself referred to this incident in a *fatwa* to be found in his collection, "Fatawa wa-Masa'il" (see note 56). It is clear from his discussion of the topic that he was very uncomfortable with the outcome of this case and would have preferred that the woman had changed her ways and thus escaped punishment.

52. The topic of women and gender is examined in greater detail in chapter 4.

53. The other three are the consumption of alcohol, theft, and bearing false witness.

54. The assignment of the death penalty for the commission of adultery is not unique to Islam. The Old Testament also prescribes this punishment. See Leviticus 20:10.

55. This circumstance is by no means unusual for its time or place. The historical record of the center of the Ottoman Empire, Istanbul, for example, supports the notion that women of this time period tended to have open access to the *qadi* and court, that the setting was relatively informal, and that whatever norms of segregation did exist were not applicable in this location. See, for example, Fariba Zarinebaf-Shahr, "Women, Law, and Imperial Justice in Ottoman Istanbul in the Late Seventeenth Century," in *Women, the Family, and Divorce Laws in Islamic History*, ed. Amira El Azhary Sonbol (Syracuse: Syracuse University Press, 1996), esp. 85–89; and C. Ronald Jennings, "Women in the Early Seventeenth Century Ottoman Judicial Records: The Sharia Court of Anatolian Kayseri," *Journal of the Economic and Social History of the Orient* 28 (1983): 53–114. What makes these circumstances remarkable here is that they contradict contemporary stereotypes about the lack of women's rights and access to public space under Wahhabi regimes. The historical record of the original Wahhabi regime finds nothing particularly remarkable about the woman's access to the *qadi*.

56. Ibn Bishr, *Unwan al-Majd fi Tarikh Najd*, 1:39. Ibn Abd al-Wahhab's discomfort with the outcome of this case is apparent in his discussion of it in his "Fatawa wa-Masa'il al-Imam al-Shaykh Muhammad Ibn Abd al-Wahhab," in *Mu'allafat al-Shaykh al-Imam Muhammad Ibn Abd al-Wahhab*, (Riyadh: Jamiat al-Imam Muhammad bin Saud al-Islamiyah, 1398H), 3:67. This history again parallels the life of the Prophet Muhammad, who carried out a similar interrogation and reached the same conclusion when dealing with an adulteress. Historically, the assignment of the death penalty for adultery was unusual because the majority of adultery cases were not tried as zina' cases. Other legal jargon was used in order to avoid the death penalty. An excellent study of this phenomenon has been carried out by Elyse Semerdjian. See her "Qadi Justice or Community Interest? Gender, Public Morality, and Legal Administration in Nineteenth Century Aleppo, Syria," Ph.D. diss., Georgetown University, 2002.

57. al-Yassini, "Ibn 'Abd al-Wahhab, Muhammad," 159.

58. Muhammad Ibn Abd al-Wahhab. "Kitab al-tawhid," in *Mu'allafat al-Shaykh al-Imam Muhammad Ibn Abd al-Wahhab* (Riyadh: Jamiat al-Imam Muhammad bin Saud al-Islamiyah, 1398H), 1:137. This was also the methodology used by Ahmad ibn Hanbal.

59. Ibid., 18.

60. Muhammad Ibn Abd al-Wahhab. "Fatawa wa-masa'il," 18.

61. Muhammad Ibn Abd al-Wahhab, "Kitab al-Tawhid," 1:25.

62. Ibn Abd al-Wahhab, "Fatawa wa-Masa'il," 3:19.

63. Ibid., 65.

64. Ibid., 18.

65. Ibid., 25.

66. Ibid., 17.

67. Ibid., 23.

68. Ibid., 19.

69. This reference work was entitled *al-Aqna'* (*Weapons*) and was apparently widely available.

70. The full text of this debate can be found in Ibn Abd al-Wahhab. "Fatawa wa-masa'il," 3:25–26. His teachings here are consistent throughout his writings, including, as will be discussed later, his discussions of jihad.

71. Ibn Bishr, *Unwan al-Majd fi Tarikh Najd*, 1:39-40. Ironically, this incident shows that the *ulama* and local political leaders presented as much of a threat to the established economic and social order as did Ibn Abd al-Wahhab's teachings.

72. Ibid., 40.

73. Ibid., 40–41.

74. Ibid., 41.

75. Ibid.

76. Ibid., 41–42.

77. Ibid., 42. It is here that Ibn Bishr's role as the official chronicler of the first Saudi dynasty becomes apparent, as his emphasis shifts from presenting Ibn Abd al-Wahhab as a man preaching the Word of God to focusing on Muhammad Ibn Saud and his military exploits.

78. This was the first recorded incident of the swearing of *bayah* between Ibn Abd al-Wahhab and a political protector.

79. Ibn Bishr, *Unwan al-Majd fi Tarikh Najd*, 1:42–43.

80. These responsibilities are discussed more fully in chapter 5.

81. Muhammad Ibn Abd al-Wahhab. "Kitab al-Jihad," in *Mu'allafat al-Shaykh al-Imam Muhammad bin Abd al-Wahhab: al-Fiqh* (Riyadh: Jamiat al-Imam Muhammad bin Saud al-Islamiyyah, 1298H), 2:359–60.

82. It is for this reason that a detailed chronology of Ibn Saud's military conquests and exploits is not included in this biography. The events and issues mentioned here are designed to illustrate particular themes, not to provide a comprehensive chronology of events related to state consolidation. Such chronologies can be found in a number of other works, including Alexei Vassiliev, *The History of Saudi Arabia* (London: Saqi Books, 1998); and Christine Moss Helms, *The Cohesion of Saudi Arabia: Evolution of Political Identity* (Baltimore: Johns Hopkins University Press, 1981), and need not be repeated here.

83. al-Yassini, "Ibn 'Abd al-Wahhab, Muhammed," 160. Some of these letters have been collected in Ibn Abd al-Wahhab. "Fatawa wa-Masa'il."

84. Ibn Bishr, *Unwan al-Majd fi Tarikh Najd*, 1:43.

85. Ibn Ghannam, *Tarikh Najd*, 2:6, 83–86.

86. Ibn Bishr, *Unwan al-Majd fi Tarikh Najd*, 1:46.

87. Ibid. The Wahhabis apparently placed great emphasis on the establishment

and maintenance of security along the roads as one of the hallmarks of their social order. Historical literature, particularly Western travel accounts, confirms this achievement. The achievement of security along the roads was no small task in central Arabia at the time, since the bedouins had a habit of targeting and attacking travelers in order to gain booty. The pilgrimage route to Mecca was particularly notorious for these dangers. See Suraiya Faroqhi, *Pilgrims and Sultans: The Hajj under the Ottomans, 1517–1683* (New York: St. Martin's, 1994), for further details.

88. Details of the conquest of Washm are available in Michael Cook, "The Expansion of the First Saudi State: The Case of Washm," in *The Islamic World from Classical to Modern Times: Essays in Honor of Bernard Lewis*, ed. C. E. Bosworth, Charles Issawi, Roger Savory, and A. L. Udovitch (Princeton, N.J.: Darwin Press, 1989).

89. Ibid., 21.

90. Later Wahhabis, most notably in the early twentieth century, made the *hijra* for study a requirement. Although the concept was religious, the purpose was more political—the forcible settling of the nomadic bedouin in order to facilitate state consolidation and formation. See John S. Habib, *Ibn Sa'ud's Warriors of Islam: The Ikhwan of Najd and Their Role in the Creation of the Sa'udi Kingdom, 1910–1930* (Leiden: Brill, 1978).

91. Ibn Bishr, *Unwan al-Majd fi Tarikh Najd*, 1:43.

92. Ibid.; Ibn Ghannam, *Tarikh Najd*, 1:9–14, 2:8, 11–12. Ibn Abd al-Wahhab's anger is consistent with his broad rejection of violence and his conviction that religious beliefs should be held voluntarily, not imposed by force.

93. Ibn Bishr, *Unwan al-Majd fi Tarikh Najd*, 1:43.

94. Ibid., 45.

95. Ibid., 45–46.

96. Ibid.

97. Ibid., 46.

98. Ibid., 44.

99. Ibid.

100. Ibid.

101. Ibn Bishr makes this even clearer with his tone, the volume of space dedicated to each (only about 20 pages for Ibn Abd al-Wahhab and about 450 for the movement after Muhammad Ibn Saud took over leadership), and his admiration for the methods of the Al Saud family. Ibn Abd al-Wahhab appears to be important only insofar as his initial inspiration was concerned.

102. Ibn Bishr, *Unwan al-Majd fi Tarikh Najd*, 1:46–47.

103. See Rentz, "Wahhabism and Saudi Arabia," 57–58.

104. Ibn Bishr, *Unwan al-Majd fi Tarikh Najd*, 1:47. Ibn Bishr's interest in Ibn Abd al-Wahhab ended with his withdrawal from public life in 1773, emphasizing his role as the chronicler of the Saudi dynasty rather than Ibn Abd al-Wahhab's biographer. From there, Ibn Bishr launched into his major work, the chronicle, beginning in the year 1158 H (1747 C.E.), in which he focused on military exploits. Although Ibn Abd al-Wahhab is mentioned at various times in the chronicle, Ibn Bishr is mainly interested in political-military developments rather than religious issues.

105. Rentz, "Wahhabism and Saudi Arabia," 58.

2. THE THEOLOGY AND WORLDVIEW OF MUHAMMAD IBN ABD AL-WAHHAB

1. For a more comprehensive discussion of Islamic law and its impact on politics, see John L. Esposito with Natana J. DeLong-Bas, "Classical Islam" and "Modern Islam," in *God's Rule: The Politics of World Religions*, ed. Jacob Neusner (Washington, DC: Georgetown University Press, 2003).

2. Ibn Abd al-Wahhab, "Fatawa wa-Masa'il," al-Imam al-Shaykh Muhammad Ibn Abd al-Wahhab," in *Mu'allafat al-Shaykh al-Imam Muhammad Ibn Abd al-Wahhab*, (Riyadh: Jamiat al-Imam Muhammad bin Saud al Islamiyah, 1398H), 3:39.

3. The main exception to this rule is his treatise discussing Surah 8, which addresses jihad. Muhammad Ibn Abd al-Wahhab, "Mukhtasar Tafsir Surat al-Anfal," in *Mu'allafat al-Shaykh al-Imam Muhammad Ibn Abd al-Wahhab*, vol. 4. This *tafsir* is consistent with Ibn Abd al-Wahhab's other writings in that the verses are heavily contextualized with relevant *hadith*, gender balance is present, and the interpretation is rarely literal in nature.

4. A purported *tafsir* by Ibn Abd al-Wahhab was compiled from marginal notes found in two different manuscripts by Dr. Muhammad Biltaji, Joint Professor at the College of the Shariah in Riyadh and the Islamic University of Muhammad bin Saud, both in Saudi Arabia. Although authorship of these notes has been attributed to Ibn Abd al-Wahhab, the inconsistency of the content, methodology, interpretation, and language of these notations with Ibn Abd al-Wahhab's broader body of written works leads me to believe that they are not his. These notations do not reflect his themes of gender balance and historical contextualization of Quranic citations and *hadith*. They further include numerous references to classical interpretations of the verses—a practice in which Ibn Abd al-Wahhab did not engage. The interpretation presented in this work is far more in line with twentieth-century interpretations of Ibn Abd al-Wahhab than it is with the contents of Ibn Abd al-Wahhab's works.

5. For example, in his treatise "Kitab al-Tawhid" he cites the Quranic verse first, then *hadith* where applicable. Muhammad Ibn Abd al-Wahhab, "Kitab al-Tawhid," in *Mu'allafat al-shaykh al-Imam Muhammad Ibn Abd al-Wahhab*, vol. 1 (Riyadh: Jamiat al-Imam Muhammad bin Saud al-Islamiya, 1398H). Only after citing these does he offer any commentary on their meaning. Muhammad Ibn Abd al-Wahhab, "Kitab Kashf al-Shubhat," in *Mu'allafat al-Shaykh al-Imam Muhammad Ibn Abd al-Wahhab*. vol. 1 (Riyadh: Jamiat al-Imam Muhammad bin Saud al-Islamiyah, 1398H), follows an opposite format. In this treatise, he gives his theological argument/interpretation first, then uses Quranic verses as proof texts.

6. Ibn Abd al-Wahhab, "Fatawa wa-Masa'il," 38–39.

7. Ibid., 24.

8. Ibid.

9. Ibid.

10. In fact, he was so insistent on the special role of Muhammad that he labeled anyone not granting this place to Muhammad an unbeliever (*kafir*) guilty of committing *shirk*, the first and only instance I have found in his writings of the use of *shirk* in reference to anyone or anything but God. Ibn Abd al-Wahhab, "Kitab Kashf al-Shubhat," 161–62.

11. Ibn Abd al-Wahhab, "Kitab al-Tawhid," 88–90. In fact, he labeled as "ene-

mies of God" those who recognize that one cannot create, sustain, be useful, or grant benefits except through God yet deny any sort of special significance to Muhammad or refuse to grant him priority over other human beings.

12. The prophet who most clearly comes to mind as a comparison is John the Baptist, who was well known for his wanderings in the desert, where he subsisted on locusts and wild honey. His was not an example that many people cared or dared to follow, nor were they encouraged to do so.

13. Ibn Abd al-Wahhab, "Kitab Kashf al-Shubhat," 155. Ibn Abd al-Wahhab's biography of Muhammad, "Mukhtasar Sirat al-Rasul," in *Mu'allafat al-Shaykh al-Imam Muhammad Ibn Abd al-Wahhab*, vol. 3 (Riyadh: Jamiat al-Imam Muhammad bin Saud al-Islamiyah, 1398H), also distinguishes him from other prophets in this way.

14. Ibid. Contrary to popular belief, this biography is not a copy of Ibn Ishaq's *Sirat Rasul Allah*, which is available in English as A. Guillaume, trans., *The Life of Muhammad: A Translation of Ibn Ishaq's* Sirat Rasul Allah (New York: Oxford University Press, 1997). Ibn Abd al-Wahhab's biography differs substantially from Ibn Ishaq's volume in both content and interpretation.

15. Ibn Abd al-Wahhab, "Kitab Kashf al-Shubhat," 155.

16. Ibn Abd al-Wahhab. "Fatawa wa-Masa'il," 57.

17. Ibid., 37.

18. These canonical sources are the collections of al-Bukhari (d. 870), Muslim ibn al-Hajjaj (d. 875), Abu Daud al-Sijistani (d. 888), Ibn Majah al-Qazwini (d. 887), Abu Isa al-Tirmidhi (d. 892), and Abu Abd al-Rahman al-Nasa'i (d. 915). The collections of al-Bukhari and Muslim are considered the most authoritative. Sunnis additionally look to the collections of Malik ibn Anas (d. 795) and Ahmad ibn Hanbal (d. 855).

19. Ibn Abd al-Wahhab, "Fatawa wa-Masa'il," 33.

20. Ibn Abd al-Wahhab, "Risalah fi al-Radd," 15.

21. Ibn Abd al-Wahhab, "Fatawa wa-Masa'il," 21.

22. Ibn Abd al-Wahhab, "Risalah fi al-Radd," 15.

23. Both points are to be found in Ibn Abd al-Wahhab. "Fatawa wa-Masa'il," 31.

24. Ibn Abd al-Wahhab, "Kitab Kashf al-Shubhat," 161.

25. Ibn Abd al-Wahhab, "Fatawa wa-Masa'il," 32.

26. Ibid.

27. Ibid., 36.

28. Ibid., 57.

29. Ibid.

30. Ibn Abd al-Wahhab, "Kitab al-Tawhid," 31.

31. Ibn Abd al-Wahhab, "Fatawa wa-Masa'il," 34.

32. Ibid.

33. Ibid., 12, 33–34.

34. As cited in Ibn Abd al-Wahhab, "Kitab al-Tawhid," 57.

35. Ibid., 59.

36. See, for example, his discussion of contradictory *hadith* used by Sunnis and Shiis in Ibn Abd al-Wahhab, "Risalah fi al-Radd," 8–9.

37. Ibn Abd al-Wahhab, "Kitab al-Jihad," in *Mu'allafat al-Shaykh al-Imam Muhammad bin Abd al-Wahhab: al-Fiqh*, vol. 2 (Riyadh: Jamiat al-Imam Mohammad bin

Saud al-Islamiyah, 1298H), 384. For example, in the discussion of the division of booty, some of the *hadith* are transmitted by men, others by women, with no distinction made on the basis of gender.

38. Muhammad Ibn Abd al-Wahhab, "Kitab al-Nikah," in *Mu'allafat al-Shaykh al-Imam Muhammad bin Abd al-Wahhab: al-Fiqh*, vol. 2 (Riyadh: Jamiat al-Imam Muhammad bin Saud al-Islamiyah, 1398H), 703–4.

39. Ibn Abd al-Wahhab. "Fatawa wa-Masa'il," 40–41.

40. Ibid.

41. The other four are the declaration of the *shahadah* (witnessing that "There is no god but The God and Muhammad is His Messenger"), prayer five times daily, making the pilgrimage (Hajj) to Mecca once in a lifetime, and fasting during the month of Ramadan.

42. Ibn Abd al-Wahhab. "Fatawa wa-Masa'il," 40.

43. Ibn Abd al-Wahhab. "Kitab al-Tawhid," 32.

44. Ibid., 33.

45. Ibid., 33–34.

46. This was standard practice in the Hanbali school of Islamic law. Farhat Ziadeh, "Law: Sunni Schools of Law," in *The Oxford Encyclopedia of the Modern Islamic World*, ed. John L. Esposito (New York: Oxford University Press, 1995), 2:461.

47. R. Marston Speight, "Hadith," in *Oxford Encyclopedia of the Modern Islamic World*, 2:84.

48. Ibn Abd al-Wahhab. "Kitab al-Tawhid," 35, 114.

49. The Zahiri *madhhab* was the most important of a series of short-lived schools of Islamic law that did not survive the centuries. The Zahiri *madhhab*, whose most important jurist was Ali ibn Hazm (d. 1064), tended to be literalist in its interpretation of the Quran and *hadith*. For more information, see Norman Calder, "Law: Legal Thought and Jurisprudence," in *Oxford Encyclopedia of the Modern Islamic World*, 2: 450–56.

50. Speight, "Hadith," 2:84.

51. Three of the instances categorized here under "Hanbali jurists" are from Ahmad ibn Hanbal, who was also a *hadith* collector. In these instances, it seemed more appropriate to cite him as a legal jurist, although he technically belongs to both categories.

52. This pattern is also apparent in Ibn Abd al-Wahhab's treatise on marriage, "Kitab al-Nikah," which is analyzed in its entirety in chapter 4.

53. Colin Imber, *Ebu's-su'ud: The Islamic Legal Tradition* (Stanford: Stanford University Press, 1997), 34–35.

54. Ibid., 34.

55. See, for example, Ignaz Goldziher, *An Introduction to Islamic Theology and Law*, trans. Andras Hamori and Ruth Hamori. (Princeton: Princeton University Press, 1981), 244.

56. For example, he used the case of Muhammad's cursing of bribery and corruption to forbid bribery in general. Ibn Abd al-Wahhab, "Fatawa wa-Masa'il," 16.

57. Ibid., 97.

58. Ibid., 35. One example was the institution of the triple divorce pronounced at a single session (triple *talaq*), which came into practice during the reign of the second

caliph, Umar. Ibn Abd al-Wahhab rejected this practice as an innovation because it contradicts clear guidelines in the Quran.

59. Ibid., 35–36. This is one of the rare instances in which he uses the term *fit-nah*. Given its contemporary use, it is important to note that this situation had nothing to do with women or sexual urges.

60. Ibn Abd al-Wahhab, "Kitab al-Tawhid," 102.

61. Ibn Abd al-Wahhab, "Fatawa wa-Masa'il," 97.

62. Ibid., 32.

63. Ibid., 97.

64. Ibid., 36.

65. Ibid., 40.

66. Ibid., 22.

67. Ibid.

68. Ibid., 22–23. There is a subtle undertone in this discussion suggesting that similar practices were occurring under the Saudi political-military leadership.

69. Ibid., 23.

70. Ibn Abd al-Wahhab. "Kitab al-Tawhid," 22; Ibn Abd al-Wahhab, "Fatawa wa-Masa'il," 64. For Ibn Abd al-Wahhab, the only people who could be compared to Muslims were the righteous ancestors (*hanifs*), who practiced absolute monotheism. The Quran uses this term to describe Ibrahim/Abraham. Ibn Abd al-Wahhab, "Kitab al-Tawhid," 15.

71. Ibn Abd al-Wahhad, "Kitab al-Tawhid, 21–22.

72. Ibid., 24–6.

73. Ibn Abd al-Wahhab, "Kitab Kashf al-Shubhat," 155.

74. Ibid., 157–58.

75. Ibn Abd al-Wahhab, "Fatawa wa-Masa'il," 42.

76. This definition is based on Q 10:31.

77. Ibn Abd al-Wahhab, "Fatawa wa-Masa'il," 42.

78. Ibid., 42–43.

79. Ibn Abd al-Wahhab, "Kitab al-Tawhid," 45.

80. Ibid, 7–8. This is based on Q 51:56, 16:36, 17:23, 4:36, and 6:151–53.

81. Ibid., 138–39.

82. Ibid, 58.

83. Ibid., 128.

84. Ibid., 12–3.

85. Ibn Abd al-Wahhab, "Fatawa wa-Masa'il," 6–8.

86. Ibid., 10. He denounced this as disbelief on the basis of Q 47:9.

87. Ibid., 10–11.

88. Ibn Abd al-Wahhab, "Kitab al-Tawhid," 25.

89. Ibn Abd al-Wahhab, "Kitab Kashf al-Shubhat," 157.

90. Ibn Abd al-Wahhab, "Kitab al-Tawhid," 14.

91. Again this does not necessarily mean that such people are immediately and without qualification subject to warfare.

92. Ibn Abd al-Wahhab, "Kitab al-Tawhid," 25–26.

93. Ibn Abd al-Wahhab, "Kitab Kashf al-Shubhat," 158.

94. Ibid., 155.

95. Ibid.

96. Again there is no call for violence against such unbelievers. Rather, the impression is that God will take care of punishing them and human beings do not share this responsibility.

97. Ibn Abd al-Wahhab, "Kitab Kashf al-Shubhat," 156–57. Muhammad and the early Muslim community fought at different times against people who prayed to entities other than God, demanding that these people call on, be consecrated to, sacrifice to, appeal to, and worship God alone. However, Ibn Abd al-Wahhab was careful not to interpret this example too literally.

98. Such assertions have continued into the present era, most recently and notably in Stephen Schwartz, *The Two Faces of Islam: The House of Sa'ud from Tradition to Terror* (New York: Doubleday, 2002).

99. Ibn Abd al-Wahhab, "Fatawa wa-Masa'il," 24.

100. The one major exception to this is the Rafidah sect of the Shiis, which he addressed in a treaty dedicated to the topic (to be discussed later in this chapter). However, even in that case he focused on the errors of belief among the Rafidah rather than targeting all adherents of the sect for death or destruction.

101. Ibn Abd al-Wahhab, "Kitab Kashf al-Shubhat," 157.

102. Quran 4:48, 116.

103. As cited in Ibn Abd al-Wahhab, "Kitab al-Tawhid," 18.

104. Ibid., 12.

105. Ibid., 19.

106. Ibid., 9. *Taghut* is defined as "generally anything that is served other than God."

107. Ibn Abd al-Wahhab, "Kitab Kashf al-Shubhat," 156–57, 164–65, based in part on Q 13:14.

108. Ibn Abd al-Wahhab, "Kitab al-Tawhid," 25.

109. Ibid., 21.

110. Ibn Abd al-Wahhab, "Fatawa wa-Masa'il," 66–67.

111. Ibid., 18.

112. Ibn Abd al-Wahhab, "Kitab al-Tawhid," 30. Typical means of doing this in Muhammad's time were tying knots in the beard, wearing talismans, and washing oneself with the urine of an animal.

113. Ibid., 40.

114. Ibid., 41.

115. Ibid., 24, 43.

116. Ibid., 43.

117. Ibn Abd al-Wahhab, "Fatawa wa-Masa'il," 70.

118. Ibid., 9–10. This teaching was based on Q 9:12 and the example of Muhammad.

119. Ibid., 13.

120. Ibn Abd al-Wahhab, "Kitab al-Tawhid," 98.

121. Ibid., 19.

122. Ibid., 101.

123. Ibid.

124. Ibn Abd al-Wahhab, "Fatawa wa-Masa'il," 38.

125. Ibid., 70.

126. Ibid.

127. Ibid.

128. The destruction of the tomb of Zayd ibn Umar was one of the three acts for which Ibn Abd al-Wahhab became famous. The other tombs are mentioned in various historical texts. Shaykh Hafiz Wahba, "Wahhabism in Arabia: Past and Present," *Journal of the Central Asian Society* 26, no. 4 (1929): 460–61.

129. Ibn Abd al-Wahhab, "Fatawa wa-Masa'il," 70.

130. Ibn Abd al-Wahhab, "Kitab al-Tawhid," 61.

131. Ibid., 67.

132. Ibid., 138.

133. Ibid., 139.

134. Ibn Abd al-Wahhab, "Fatawa wa-Masa'il," 63.

135. Ibid.

136. Ibid.

137. Ibn Abd al-Wahhab, "Kitab al-Tawhid," 57–58.

138. Ibid., 56–57.

139. Ibid., 64.

140. Ibid., 64–65. I am grateful to John Esposito for this insight.

141. Ibid., 87.

142. Cited in Wahba, "Wahhabism in Arabia," 460.

143. Q 6:51, 39:44, 2:255, 53:26, and 34:22 are all cited as proof texts in Ibn Abd al-Wahhab, "Kitab al-Tawhid," 51.

144. Q 21:28 is cited as a proof text: "And one cannot intercede in anything except after he knows God in this as the High and Mighty said: 'They do not intercede except those who are satisfactory.'" Cited in Ibn Abd al-Wahhab, "Kitab Kashf al-Shubhat," 165–66.

145. Ibn Abd al-Wahhab, "Fatawa wa-Masa'il," 68–69.

146. Ibn Abd al-Wahhab, "Kitab Kashf al-Shubhat," 155.

147. Ibid.

148. Ibn Abd al-Wahhab, "Kitab al-Tawhid," 51–52.

149. Q 39:44 is cited as a proof text: "Say: To God belongs exclusive intercession." Ibn Abd al-Wahhab, "Kitab Kashf al-Shubhat," 165–66.

150. Ibid. This teaching is based upon Q 3:85.

151. Ibn Abd al-Wahhab. "Kitab al-Tawhid," 52.

152. Ibid., 55.

153. Ibid., 54–55.

154. Ibid., 46–47.

155. Ibn Abd al-Wahhab, "Kitab Kashf al-Shubhat," 156.

156. Ibid., 163.

157. Ibid.

158. Based on Q 39:3.

159. Ibn Abd al-Wahhab, "Kitab Kashf al-Shubhat," 164.

160. Ibn Abd al-Wahhab, "Kitab al-Tawhid," 28–30.

161. Ibid., 30–31.

162. Ibid., 73. This denial of an opportunity for repentance and absolution

stands alone in Ibn Abd al-Wahhab's writings. In every other case, he emphasized the need to educate people prior to fighting them. The harsh stance he takes against sorcery shows just how serious the nature of this offense was.

163. Ibid., 84.

164. Ibid., 74–75.

165. Ibid., 70.

166. Ibid., 49–50.

167. Ibid., 76–77.

168. Ibn Abd al-Wahhab, "Fatawa wa-Masa'il," 61.

169. Ibn Abd al-Wahhab, "Kitab al-Tawhid," 81.

170. Ibid., 82–83.

171. Ibid., 86–87.

172. Ibid., 87.

173. Ibid., 84.

174. Scholars are divided on the question of the actual state of Arabia at the time of Ibn Abd al-Wahhab. Although the contemporary chronicles assert the widespread practice of superstitious and un-Islamic practices, many scholars today believe that this was exaggerated in order to create a sharper contrast with Ibn Abd al-Wahhab's interpretation of *tawhid*. The most compelling work analyzing the actual historical circumstances in which the Wahhabi movement arose is Mohamed A. al-Freih, "The Historical Background of the Emergence of Mohammad Ibn Abd al-Wahhab and His Movement," Ph.D. diss., University of California at Los Angeles, 1990.

175. Ibn Abd al-Wahhab, "Kitab al-Tawhid," 79–80.

176. Ibid., 15.

177. Ibid., 17.

178. Ibid., 132.

179. Ibid., 133–34.

180. Ibid., 135.

181. Ibid., 136.

182. Ibid., 108.

183. Ibid., 112.

184. Ibid., 130–31.

185. Ibid., 110, 123.

186. Ibid., 118. Ibn Abd al-Wahhab cited as supportive evidence a *hadith* in which some people were mocking Muhammad. Although the people claimed that they were only joking, Muhammad did not forgive them.

187. The history of Adam and Eve in the Quran holds them equally responsible for their disobedience to God in the Garden of Eden but limits responsibility for that sin to the two individuals involved. The lack of a doctrine of Original Sin in Islam precludes the need for one all-atoning sacrifice for all of humanity. Thus, in Islam there is no theological need for the crucifixion and resurrection of Jesus.

188. Ibn Abd al-Wahhab, "Kitab al-Tawhid," 35–36.

189. Ibid., 72.

190. One of the unusual aspects of this treatise is that it is largely a compilation of Quranic verses and *hadith* without any written commentary. The apparent assumption on the part of the writer was that these sources are self-explanatory and clear, meriting no further discussion.

191. Muhammad Ibn Abd al-Wahhab, "Kitab al-Kaba'ir," in *Mu'allafat al-Shaykh al-Imam Muhammad Ibn Abd al-Wahhab*, vol. 1 (Riyadh: Jamiat al-Imam Muhammad bin Saud al-Islamiyah, 1398H), 3–4.

192. See ibid., 4–65, for a detailed description of these sins. Failing to keep the achievement of puberty a secret is considered sinful because it consists of boasting and pride in a situation that the individual does not and cannot control.

193. Ibid., 60–66.

194. Ibid., 56–58.

195. Ibid., 56, 58–59.

196. Ibn Abd al-Wahhab, "Fatawa wa-Masa'il," 24.

197. Ibn Abd al-Wahhab, "Kitab al-Tawhid," 93–94.

198. Ibid., 95–97. Examples of forbidden expressions of despair are striking one's cheeks, tearing one's garments, and wailing for and lamenting the dead, as was done in pre-Islamic times.

199. Ibn Abd al-Wahhab, "Fatawa wa-Masa'il," 49. This is based on Q 49:13: "Therefore the most noble/honored among you by God is the most pious among you."

200. Ibid., 8, 53.

201. Ibid., 8.

202. Ibid., 5.

203. Ibid., 53. This is an explanation of Q 39:35.

204. Ibid., 45.

205. Ibid., 21–22.

206. Ibid., 51.

207. Ibid.

208. Ibid., 54.

209. Ibid., 51.

210. Another *hadith* asserts that in the final judgment the weight of the heart will indicate the quantity of faith possessed by the believer, determining whether or not he or she should be thrown into the fires of Hell.

211. Ibn Abd al-Wahhab, "Fatawa wa-Masa'il," 57.

212. Ibid., 55.

213. Ibid., 7.

214. Ibid., 50.

215. Ibn Abd al-Wahhab, "Kitab al-Tawhid," 97.

216. Ibid., 9.

217. Ibn Abd al-Wahhab, "Kitab Kashf al-Shubhat," 159.

218. Ibid., 159–60. He specifies calling on idols and denying the special role of Muhammad as the worst possible acts of *kufr* (162).

219. Two of the most important earlier documents making this assertion are George Snavely Rentz Jr., "Muhammad Ibn 'Abd al-Wahhab (1703/4–1792) and the Beginnings of the Unitarian Empire in Arabia," Ph.D. diss., University of California, Berkeley, 1948, esp. 41; and Henri Laoust, "Ibn 'Abd al-Wahhab, Muhammad b," in *The Encyclopaedia of Islam*, ed. B. Lewis, V. L. Menage, Ch. Pellat, and J. Schacht, new ed., vol. 3 (Leiden: Brill, 1971). Muslim interpreters have also made this assertion. See, for example, Shaikh Sulaiman b. 'Abdullah b. al-Shaikh Muhammad b. 'Abd al-Wahhab, *Majmu'at al-Tawhid*, ed. Rashid Rida (Cairo: Al-Manar, 1346H/1927), esp. 1:

178. Similar assertions have been made in more recent works, including Helms, esp. 82.

220. He cited as supportive evidence Q 9:66, which states, "You are not forgiven/excused if your *kufr* is after your faith," meaning that if your unbelief occurs after the person has accepted the Muslim faith, then that person is not forgiven.

221. Ibn Abd al-Wahhab, "Fatawa wa-Masa'il," 66.

222. Although Ibn Abd al-Wahhab's distinction between the two was maintained for a time, it disappeared altogether by the nineteenth century, when the terms came to be used interchangeably. See Ali Bey, *Travels of Ali Bey in Morocco, Tripoli, Cyprus, Egypt, Arabia, Syria, and Turkey between the Years 1803 and 1807*, vol. 2 (London: John Murray, 1881), 131; and David Commins, " 'Wahhabi' Doctrine in an Age of Political Expediency," unpublished paper presented at the 36th Annual Meeting of the Middle East Studies Association, Washington, DC, 25 November 2002, 3, n. 5.

223. Ibn Abd al-Wahhab, "Kitab al-jihad," 379. The legal concept of public welfare (*maslahah*) is discussed in greater detail in chapter 3.

224. A contemporary prophet of Muhammad, although Muslims believe that he was a false prophet.

225. Ibn Abd al-Wahhab, "Fatawa wa-Masa'il," 45.

226. This stance reinforces my contention that not all military activities undertaken by the Wahhabis were religiously legitimated and in fact were not supported by Ibn Abd al-Wahhab. There was a distinction between jihad and military activities designed to consolidate the Saudi state.

227. Ibn Abd al-Wahhab, "Fatawa wa-Masa'il," 63–64.

228. The most important studies of this issue were carried out by George Makdisi, who has noted that some of the most important Hanbali scholars, including Abd al-Qadir al-Jili (the founder of the first and largest Sufi order), the famous medieval scholar Ibn Taymiyya, and his most famous student, Ibn al-Qayyim al-Jawziyya, were themselves Sufis and included some works of the great Sufi masters among the sources they deemed worthy of study. Makdisi's important studies include "The Hanbali School and Sufism," in *Humaniora Islamica*, vol. 2 (The Hague and Paris: Mouton, 1974); "Ibn Taimiya: A Sufi of the Qadiriya Order," *American Journal of Arabic Studies* 1 (1974): 118–29; and "The Sunni Revival," in *Islamic Civilisation, 950–1150: A Colloquium Published under the Auspices of the Near Eastern History Group, Oxford, and the Near East Center, University of Pennsylvania*, ed. D. S. Richards (Oxford: Faber, 1977).

229. Although these events occurred in 1802, more than ten years after Ibn Abd al-Wahhab's death, the destruction was consistent with his teachings.

230. Makdisi, "Hanbali School," 61.

231. Ibid., 66–68. See also Makdisi, "Ibn Taimiya," 118–29.

232. Makdisi, "Ibn Taimiya," 120.

233. Makdisi, "Hanbali School," 65–66.

234. Makdisi, "Sunni Revival," 167.

235. Makdisi, "Ibn Taimiya," 129.

236. Ibid.

237. Ibn Abd al-Wahhab's approach here is similar to that of another important Hanbali scholar, Ibn al-Jawzi, whose treatise *Tablis Iblis* (*The Devil's Delusion*) has been cited as "the most important single factor in keeping alive the notion of Hanbali hos-

tility to Sufism." Makdisi, "Hanbali School," 69. Although Western scholars, beginning with D. S. Margoliouth, believed that this work was a denunciation of Sufism per se, Makdisi's careful analysis concludes that the purpose of the work was to denounce certain Sufi practices, not Sufism itself. Ibn Abd al-Wahhab's approach to the matter continued the trend (71).

238. Makdisi, "Sunni Revival," 156.

239. Ibn Abd al-Wahhab, "Risalah fi al-Radd," 5.

240. Ibid., 8.

241. Ibid. For example, he did not allow anyone to steal or falsely claim their property.

242. These special privileges and powers included their preference, exaltation, conformity to the conditions of the imamate, pledge of allegiance of the people to them, authenticity and genuineness of their affinity, the surplus of the "knowledge of life" that they possess, and the right to unlimited, unrestricted *ijtihad*.

243. Ibn Abd al-Wahhab, "Risalah fi al-Radd," 29.

244. Ibn Abd al-Wahhab, "Fatawa wa-Masa'il," 45. Ibn Abd al-Wahhab's accordance of special status to the descendants of Muhammad is reflected in his response to a request for an example of an evil, lying leader. He cited the example of Muawiyah, who was responsible for the deaths of Husayn (Muhammad's grandson and Ali's son) and Muhammad's other descendants. Ibn Abd al-Wahhab condemned this as an act of atheism.

245. This *hadith* comes from the collection of the Shii scholar Ibn al-Muallim and is cited in Ibn Abd al-Wahhab, "Risalah fi al-Radd," 5–6.

246. Ibid., 6. This is an excellent example of Ibn Abd al-Wahhab's methodology of *hadith* criticism in which he focuses more on the content of the *hadith* than on *isnad*.

247. Ibid., 28–29.

248. Ibid., 9–12.

249. Details of Muhammad's singular perfection can be found in Ibn Abd al-Wahhab, "Mukhtasar Sirat al-Rasul," 8–18.

250. Ibn Abd al-Wahhab, "Risalah fi al-Radd," 7.

251. Ibid., 28–29.

252. Ibid., 8–9.

253. Ibid., 13–15. Shiis historically have claimed that the third caliph, Uthman, left out of the final compilation of the Quran completed under his tenure passages justifying certain Shii theological stances. The Rafidah claimed to have restored these passages to the Quran, thus explaining Ibn Abd al-Wahhab's charge of tampering.

254. Ibid., 13–14.

255. For a more detailed analysis of discussions of Aisha in religious literature, see D. A. Spellberg, *Politics, Gender, and the Islamic Past: The Legacy of A'isha bint Abi Bakr* (New York: Columbia University Press, 1994).

256. Ibn Abd al-Wahhab, "Risalah fi al-Radd," 26.

257. Ibn Abd al-Wahhab also cited Q 24:23–26, which issues similar warnings about punishment for false accusers of chaste women.

258. The *hadith* collections cited were compiled by Abd al-Razzaq, Ahmad ibn Hanbal, Abd bin Hamid, al-Bukhari, Ibn Jarir, Ibn al-Mundhir, Ibn Abi Hatim, Ibn Mardawih and al-Bayhaqi. Companions cited were Umm Ruman, Abi Hurayrah, Ibn

Abbas, Ibn Umar, Abi Iyas al-Ansari, Said bin Jubayr, al-Hakim bin Utaybah, Abd Al-lah bin al-Zubayr, Arwah bin al-Zubayr, Said bin al-Musayb, Ilqimah Ibn Waqqas, Ubayd Allah Ibn Abd Allah bin Utaybah bin Masud, Umarah bint Abd al-Rahman, Abd Allah bin Abi Bakr bin Hazm, Salmah bin Abd al-Rahman bin Awf, al-Qasim Ibn Muhammad bin Abi Bakr, al-Aswas bin Yazid, Abbad bin Abd Allah Ibn al-Zubayr, Maqsam Mawli Ibn Abbas, "and other than them." *Hadith* collections citing the Companions include those compiled by Ibn Mansur, Ahmad ibn Hanbal, al-Bukhari, Ibn al-Mundhir, Ibn Mardawih, al-Bazzar, and al-Tabarani.

259. Ibn Abd al-Wahhab, "Risalah fi al-Radd," 23–24.

260. The Quran records that Noah's wife told his friends that he was crazy. Lot's wife flirted with visitors and guests. Both were therefore guilty of deceiving their husbands, but neither committed adultery.

261. Ibn Abd al-Wahhab, "Risalah fi al-Radd," 25.

262. Ibid., 24.

263. Ibid., 26.

264. See ibid., 34–42, for full texts. Ibn Abd al-Wahhab was particularly puzzled by the case of giving women as co-wives with their paternal and maternal aunts because the prohibition of this practice was based on *hadith*, some of which were narrated by Ali ibn Abi Talib. Ibn Abd al-Wahhab did not understand how it was possible for Shiis to overlook the authority of Ali (39).

265. Ibid., "Risalah fi al-Radd," 38.

266. Ibid., 30.

267. Ibid., 30–31.

268. Ibid., 31.

3. ISLAMIC LAW

1. For an excellent and brief introduction to Islamic law, see Mohammad Hashim Kamali, "Law and Society: The Interplay of Revelation and Reason in the Shariah," in *The Oxford History of Islam*, ed. John L. Esposito (New York: Oxford University Press, 1999), 107–53.

2. For a broader discussion of eighteenth-century Islamic thought, see John O. Voll, *Islam: Continuity and Change in the Modern World*, 2d ed. (Syracuse: Syracuse University Press, 1994); and Nehemiah Levtzion and John O. Voll, eds., *Eighteenth-Century Renewal and Reform in Islam* (Syracuse: Syracuse University Press, 1987).

3. The topic of contemporary movements either claiming or purported to be influenced by Ibn Abd al-Wahhab is addressed in chapter 6.

4. A *qadi* holds an official position and is responsible for investigating and ascertaining the facts of a given case. The judgment of a *qadi* is binding and enforceable. A *mufti* is a respected scholar working in an unofficial capacity. *Muftis* often serve as consultants to *qadis*, but the opinion of a *mufti* is neither binding nor necessarily enforceable.

5. The Hanbali, Hanafi, Shafii and Maliki *madhahib* are the four major Sunni schools of Islamic law. The Zahiri school was a short-lived Sunni school, typically characterized by literal interpretation of the scriptures. The Jafari *madhhab* is the most important of the Shii schools of Islamic law.

6. Works such as "Kitab al-Jihad" and "Kitab al-Nikah" have been classified as

ikhtilaf literature here because they discuss a variety of topics and include numerous legal opinions about them. Unlike his *fatawa*, which respond to specific individual questions, the *ikhtilaf* literature addresses multiple topics in a more general fashion.

7. In this respect, he followed a strong Hanbali tradition of writing *ikhtilaf* and challenging local power holders. See Makdisi, "The Sunni Revival," in *Islamic Civilisation, 950–1150: A Colloquium Published under the Auspices of the Near Eastern History Group, Oxford, and the Near East Center University of Pennsylvania*, ed D.S. Richards (Oxford: Faber, 1977), 165.

8. A standard example of *qiyas* is the extension of the Quranic prohibition of date wine to grape wine and every other kind of alcoholic beverage based on the legal principle that date wine produces an altered state of mind. This same physical reaction is produced by the consumption of alcoholic beverages generally. For a more comprehensive discussion of Islamic legal thought and principles, see Wael B. Hallaq, *A History of Islamic Legal Theories: An Introduction to Sunni Usul al-Fiqh* (Cambridge: Cambridge University Press, 1997), and Norman Calder, "Law: Legal Thought and Jurisprudence," in *The Oxford Encyclopedia of the Modern Islamic World*, ed. John L. Esposito, vol. 2 (New York: Oxford University Press, 1995), 450–56.

9. Farhat Ziadeh, "Law: Sunni Schools of Law," in *Oxford Encyclopedia of the Modern Islamic World*, 2:461.

10. Muhammad Ibn Abd al-Wahhab, "Fatawa wa-Masa'il al-Imam al-Shaykh Muhammad Ibn Abd al-Wahhab," in *Mu'allafat al-Shaykh al-Imam Muhammad Ibn Abd al-Wahhab*, vol. 3 (Riyadh: Jamiat al-Imam Muhammad bin Saud al-Islamiyah, 1398H), 66.

11. Ibid., 27, 32.

12. Muhammad Ibn Abd al-Wahhab, "Kitab al-Nikah," in *Mu'allafat al-Shaykh al-Imam Muhammad Ibn Abd al-Wahhab*, vol. 3 (Riyadh: Jamiat al-Imam Muhammad bin Saud al-Islamiyah, 1398H), 671.

13. For example, he cited *ijma'* in interpretational support of a Quranic passage that declared that anyone who worships idols is an unbeliever (*kafir*) whose blood and money are permitted (*halal*) to Muslims. Ibn Abd al-Wahhab, "Fatawa wa-Masa'il," 25.

14. Ibn Abd al-Wahhab, "Kitab al-Nikah," 670.

15. Ibid.

16. Ibid.

17. Muhammad Ibn Abd al-Wahhab, "Risalah fi al-Radd ala al-Rafidah," in *Mu'allafat al-Shakh al-Imam Muhammad Ibn Abd al-Wahhab*, vol. 4 (Riyadh: Jamiat al-Imam Muhammad bin Saud al-Islamiyah, (1398H), 8.

18. Muhammad Ibn Abd al-Wahhab, "Kitab al-Jihad," in *Mu'allafat al-Shaykh al-Imam Muhammad Ibn Abd al-Wahhab*, vol. 2 (Riyadh: Jamiat al-Imam Muhammad bin Saud al-Islamiyah, (1398H), 401–2.

19. Ibn Abd al-Wahhab, "Fatawa wa-Masa'il," 24.

20. Ibid., 20.

21. Ibid.

22. Ibid.

23. Ibid., 80–81. *Maslahah* is discussed more fully later in this chapter.

24. Ibid., 63.

25. Ibid., 64.

26. Ibid., 25.

27. Hallaq, *History of Islamic Legal Theories*, 76.

28. Ibn Abd al-Wahhab's stance here is typically Hanbali. Susan Spectorsky, *Chapters on Marriage and Divorce: Responses of Ibn Hanbal and Ibn Rahwayh* (Austin: University of Texas Press, 1993), 5.

29. Ibn Abd al-Wahhab, "Fatawa wa-Masa'il," 53–54.

30. John L. Esposito with Natana J. DeLong-Bas, *Women in Muslim Family Law*, 2d ed. (Syracuse: Syracuse University Press, 2001), 8.

31. Bjorn Olav Utvik, "The Modernising Force of Islamism," in *Modernizing Islam: Religion in the Public Sphere in the Middle East and Europe*, ed. John L. Esposito and François Burgat (London: Hurst, 2003), 55.

32. Ibn Abd al-Wahhab. "Fatawa wa-Masa'il," 40.

33. Ibid., 23.

34. Ibid.

35. Ibn Abd al-Wahhab, "Kitab al-Nikah," 643.

36. Ibn Abd al-Wahhab, "Kitab al-Jihad," 367.

37. Ibn Abd al-Wahhab, "Fatawa wa-Masa'il," 40.

38. Ibn Abd al-Wahhab, "Kitab al-Jihad," 375.

39. Hallaq, *History of Islamic Legal Theories*, 69.

40. For an analysis of this reasoning, see Mahmoud Mohamed Taha, *The Second Message of Islam*, trans. and introduced by Abdullahi Ahmed An-Na'im (Syracuse: Syracuse University Press, 1987). Although Taha was executed for his "heretical teachings," his discussion of *naskh* was not innovative. Historically, Muslim jurists were uncomfortable with the notion of God issuing increasingly restrictive commands over time because this conflicted with His attribute of being merciful. Consequently, they were more comfortable with the notion of heavier restrictions being a temporary measure and the more universal and lenient rulings being the desired ultimate goal. Hallaq, *History of Islamic Legal Theories*, 69.

41. Ibn Abd al-Wahhab, "Risalah fi al-Radd," 38.

42. Ibid., 34–35.

43. Ibn Abd al-Wahhab, "Kitab al-Jihad," 359.

44. Ibid., 386–87.

45. Again, this teaching had strong support in the historical record of Islamic legal thought, although there were always scholars who disgreed with it and believed that the *hadith* could abrogate the Quran. See Hallaq, *History of Islamic Legal Theories*, 72–73.

46. The most prominent examples of this assertion are Ignaz Goldziher, *Introduction to Islamic Theology and Law*, trans. Andras Hamori and Ruth Hamori (Princeton: Princeton University Press, 1981) Joseph Schacht, *An Introduction to Islamic Law* (New York: Oxford University Press, 1964); Schacht, *The Origins of Muhammadan Jurisprudence*, 4th ed. (Oxford: Oxford University Press, 1964); and N. J. Coulson. *A History of Islamic Law* (Edinburgh: Edinburgh University Press, 1964).

47. Hallaq's placement of the closing of the gate at a later date is based on his research into discussions of the controversy, the earliest of which dates to a twelfth-century debate between a Hanbali jurist, Ibn Aqil, and an anonymous Hanafi jurist. The Hanafi jurist claimed that the gate of judgeship was closed because there were no qualified practitioners of ijtihad left. Ibn Aqil refuted this argument, believing that

such practioners must exist at all times. See Wael B. Hallaq, "On the Origins of the Controversy about the Existence of Mujtahids and the Gate of Ijtihad," *Studia Islamica* 63 (1986): 129, for this discussion.

48. Ibid., 136–37.

49. Wael B. Hallaq, "Was the Gate of Ijtihad Closed?" *International Journal of Middle East Studies* 16 (1984): 3–41; Hallaq, "Origins"; Hallaq, *History of Islamic Legal Theories*.

50. It is important to emphasize that while this was a broad, general tendency there nevertheless remained individuals affiliated with these law schools who continued to exercise *ijtihad*. However, these individuals were the exception rather than the rule.

51. Hallaq, "Origins," 129–30; Coulson, *History of Islamic Law*, 202–3.

52. For a more detailed study of this phenomenon in the eighteenth century, see Voll, *Islam*, 24–83, esp. 29–31.

53. Ibn Abd al-Wahhab, "Kitab al-Tawhid," 70.

54. Ibn Abd al-Wahhab, "Risalah fi al-Radd," 28.

55. Ibn Abd al-Wahhab, "Fatawa wa-Masa'il," 17, 23.

56. Ibid.; Ibn Abd al-Wahhab, "Risalah fi al-Radd," 29.

57. Ibn Abd al-Wahhab, "Risalah fi al-Radd," 29.

58. Ibn Abd al-Wahhab, "Fatawa wa-Masa'il," 61.

59. Ibid.

60. Ibid., 61–62.

61. Ignaz Goldziher, "Patton's Ahmad ibn Hanbal and the Mihna (Zusammenhang zwischen Ibn Hanbal, Ibn Tejmijja und 'Abdul Wahhab)," cited in George Makdisi. "Hanbalite Islam," in *Studies on Islam*, trans. and ed. Merlin L. Swartz. (New York: Oxford University Press, 1981), 223–24.

62. The collection of Ibn Abd al-Wahhab's writings published by Jamiat al-Imam Muhammad bin Saud al-Islamiyah includes a selection of excerpts of Ibn Taymiyya's writings, with Ibn Abd al-Wahhab's own purported commentary appearing beside them. This work is similar to Ibn Abd al-Wahhab's purported *tafsir*, compiled by the same university, which consists of marginal notes attributed to Ibn Abd al-Wahhab. The notes in the case of the Ibn Taymiyya commentary are taken from two different manuscripts—one located at Maktabat al-Shaykh Muhammad bin Abd al-Latif bin Abd al-Rahman Al Al-Shaykh and the other at al-Maktabat al-Saudiyah bi-Dakhanah. It is important to mention the format because the resulting work is not a treatise or comprehensive discussion of a given topic in the same manner as Ibn Abd al-Wahhab's formal works. Such marginal notes are of limited use because of their highly selective nature and because the commentary in many cases consists of only a few words of opinion rather than systematic comparison with the Quran and *hadith* more broadly representative of Ibn Abd al-Wahhab's writings. The work is therefore of little use for analysis of Ibn Abd al-Wahhab's methodology or themes.

63. Ibn Abd al-Wahhab, "Fatawa wa-Masa'il," 18–19, 38.

64. Ibid., 18.

65. Ibid.; Ibn Abd al-Wahhab, "Risalah fi al-Radd," 29.

66. Ibn Abd al-Wahhab, "Fatawa wa-Masa'il," 21.

67. Ibid., 76.

68. Ibid., 28–29.

69. Ibid., 33.

70. Ibid., 33–34.

71. The closest he came to affiliation with the Hanbali school of Islamic jurisprudence was his denial that he was among those who had strayed from the teachings of Imam Ahmad. Ibid., 25. In a different *fatwa*, he asserted that denial of Imam
Ahmad was a sin (50).

72. No legal scholar was ever absolutely bound by the legal opinions of the
founder of his law school or subsequent jurists. Disagreements and alternative interpretations always existed. Furthermore, affiliation with a given law school did not preclude the possibility of consultation with the rulings of other law schools. For example, although the Ottoman Empire was officially Hanafi in legal orientation, the
rulings of other law schools were applied in selected cases and Ottoman subjects had
the right to consult jurists from a variety of schools until the law was codified in the
nineteenth century. Hanbali law was generally preferred for long-term commercial
transactions because it offered the best protection against economic fluctuations and
speculation. See Amira El Azhary Sonbol, Introduction to *Women, the Family, and Divorce Laws in Islamic History*, ed. Amira El Azhary Sonbol (Syracuse: Syracuse University Press, 1996); Baber Johansen, *The Islamic Law on Land Tax and Rent* (New York:
Croom Helm, 1988); and Mohamed Afifi, *al-Awqaf wa-al-Hayat al-Iqtisadiyyah fi Misr
fi al-'Asr al-'Uthmani* (Cairo: al-Hay'ah al-Misriyyah al-'Ammah li-al-Kitab, 1991).

73. This status as both a theological and a law school was unique to the Hanbalis. Makdisi, "Hanbalite Islam," 238–39.

74. Ibn Abd al-Wahhab. "Kitab al-Tawhid," 22.

75. Makdisi, "Hanbalite Islam," 252–53. Ironically, not only has the Hanbali
school proven to be more flexible and tolerant than the other law schools in interpretation, but it also provided many of the legal methodologies, tools, and practices that
have led to contemporary reforms in the Muslim world, particularly those pertaining
to greater and more equal rights for women. John L. Esposito, *Islam*, 4th ed. (New
York: Oxford University Press, 1998), 192. For more information on the role of Hanbali methodology in contemporary reforms related to women and gender issues, see
Esposito with DeLong-Bas, *Women*.

76. Ibn Abd al-Wahhab, "Fatawa wa-Masa'il," 17.

77. Ibid., 81.

78. Ibid., 42.

79. Ibid., 77.

80. Ibid. The most important example was the use of contradictory *hadith* by
Sunnis and Shiis to support differing theological positions. Both sides claim that their
hadith are authentic, yet the contradictions prove that they cannot be.

81. Ibn Abd al-Wahhab, "Risalah fi al-Radd," 14.

82. Ibn Abd al-Wahhab, "Kitab al-Jihad," 381.

83. Ibid.

84. Ibid.

85. Ibid.

86. See Calder, "Law," 450–56.

87. Ibn Abd al-Wahhab, "Fatawa wa-Masa'il," 78–79.

88. Ibn Abd al-Wahhab, "Kitab al-Tawhid," 39.

89. Ibid., 38–39.

90. Ibid., 39.

91. Ibn Abd al-Wahhab, "Fatawa wa-Masa'il," 54.

92. Ibid., 5.

93. Ibid., 5–6.

94. Ibid., 66.

95. Ibid., 68.

96. Recounted and interpreted in Ibn Abd al-Wahhab, "Kitab al-Tawhid," 35–37.

97. Ibid., 36.

98. Ibn Abd al-Wahhab, "Fatawa wa-Masa'il," 13–14. This denunciation of the Kharijites in such strong terms is particularly interesting in light of the historical assumption that Wahhabis, from Ibn Abd al-Wahhab to Osama bin Laden, have looked to the Kharijites for inspiration and justification of their violent activities. This issue is addressed in greater detail in chapter 6.

99. Ibid., 25.

100. Ibid., 14–15.

101. Ibid., 15.

102. Ibid., 35.

103. An important work that explains and then challenges the classical interpretation of Islamic law is David S. Powers, *Studies in Qur'an and Hadith: The Formation of the Islamic Law of Inheritance* (Berkeley: University of California Press, 1986).

104. Ibn Abd al-Wahhab, "Fatawa wa-Masa'il," 122.

105. Ibid., 72.

106. Esposito with De Long-Bas. *Women,* 64–65.

107. Ibn Abd al-Wahhab, "Fatawa wa-Masa'il," 72. The right of grandchildren to inherit as primary heirs in the place of the deceased parent was adopted by several countries in the twentieth century as a major reform in Islamic inheritance law. Esposito with De Long-Bas, *Women,* 64–65, 85–86, 92.

108. Ibn Abd al-Wahhab, "Fatawa wa-Masa'il," 72.

109. Ibid., 85.

110. Ibid., 89–90.

4. WOMEN AND WAHHABIS

1. One example of the abundant popular literature making such claims is Jean Sasson, *Princess: A True Story of Life behind the Veil in Saudi Arabia* (New York: Morrow, 1992).

2. For example, the Taliban was Hanafi in its orientation to Islamic law, while the Saudis are Hanbali.

3. For example, in the former Soviet republics the ruling regimes have labeled as Wahhabi any Muslim who challenges either the religious or political status quo. Muriel Atkin, "The Rhetoric of Islamophobia," *Central Asia and the Caucasus: Journal of Social and Political Studies* 1, no. 1 (2000): 130.

4. For an analysis of some of his contemporaries in Palestine and Syria, see Judith E. Tucker, *In The House of Law: Gender and Islamic Law in Ottoman Syria and Palestine* (Berkeley: University of California Press, 1998). For coverage of gender is-

sues from the same time period, see the collection of historical essays in Amira El Azhary Sonbol, ed., *Women, the Family, and Divorce Laws in Islamic History* (Syracuse: Syracuse University Press, 1996).

5. Susan Spectorsky, *Chapters on Marriage and Divorce: Responses of Ibn Hanbal and Ibn Rahwayh* (Austin: University of Texas Press, 1993), 7.

6. For a broad contextualization of Muhammad's teachings about women in pre-Islamic Arabia, see John L. Esposito with Natana DeLong-Bas, *Women in Muslim Family Law* 2d ed. (Syracuse: Syracuse University Press, 2001); and Leila Ahmed, *Women and Gender in Islam: Historical Roots of a Modern Debate* (New Haven: Yale University Press, 1992).

7. Al-Shafii is cited a total of forty-four times, thirty-one of which were in disagreement. Malik is cited thirty-six times, twenty-five of which were in disagreement.

8. Ibn Hanbal was cited forty-three times. In two of these instances, Ibn Abd al-Wahhab disagreed with him.

9. Those most frequently cited in agreement are Umar (sixteen), Ibn Abbas (fourteen), and Ali (ten).

10. For a detailed analysis of Abu Hurayrah's *hadith*, and concerns about the misogyny reflected in them, which have been used as a justification for limiting women's rights in some Arab countries, see Fatima Mernissi, *The Veil and the Male Elite: A Feminist Interpretation of Women's Rights in Islam*, trans. Mary Jo Lakeland (Reading, MA: Addison-Wesley, 1991), esp. 70–73, 78–81.

11. Ibid., 72–73 and 78.

12. Muhammad Ibn Abd al-Wahhab, "Kitab al-Jihad," in *Mu'allafat al-Shaykh al-Imam Muhammad Ibn Abd al-Wahhab*, vol. 2 (Riyadh: Jamiat al-Imam Muhammad bin Saud al-Islamiyah, 1398H), 393.

13. This stands in marked contrast to some classical interpretations and even religions, like Judaism, which teach that menstruation places a woman in a state of impurity that renders God inaccessible to her until she has been purified. Muhammad Ibn Abd al-Wahhab, "Kitab al-Nikah," in *Mu'allafat al-Shaykh al-Imam Muhammad Ibn Abd al-Wahhab*, vol. 2 (Riyadh: Jamiat al-Imam Muhammad bin Saud al-Islamiyah, 1398H), 641.

14. Muhammad Ibn Abd al-Wahhab, "Kitab al-Tawhid," in *Mu'allafat al-Shaykh al-Imam Muhammad Ibn Abd al-Wahhab*, vol. 1 (Riyadh: Jamiat al-Imam Muhammad bin Saud al-Islamiyah, 1398H), 46–47.

15. Ibn Abd al-Wahhab, "Kitab al-Nikah," 682.

16. Ibid., 637.

17. I am grateful to Judith E. Tucker for highlighting the importance of the terminology here in making the distinction between declarations of legal doctrine and statements of personal opinion.

18. Other jurists, most notably al-Shafii, taught that celibacy was desirable.

19. Ibn Abd al-Wahhab, "Kitab al-Nikah," 637.

20. Muhammad prescribed stoning if the perpetrator was married and one hundred lashes and temporary exile if he or she was unmarried. Stoning was rarely prescribed due to the legal requirements for evidence. In order to prove a case of *zina'*, either four adult males of sound character had to witness the actual act of penetration or the participants had to bear witness against themselves. Without such evidence, *zina'* could not be proven and the accusers were liable to punishment for false accu-

sations of unchastity against a chaste woman. Court records show that euphemisms were preferred so as to charge the perpetrators with crimes that were easier to prosecute, such as *desertion*. For a discussion of this phenomenon, see Elyse Semerdjian, "Qadi; Justice or Community Interst? Gender, Public Reality, and Legal Administration in Nineteenth Century Aleppo, Syria," Ph.D. diss., Georgetown University, 2002.

21. In the cases of adultery and fornication, the law schools were unanimous in considering *zina'* a *hudud*, a crime necessitating punishment and compensation for both parties. In the case of rape, they held only the man liable for punishment. The second caliph, Umar ibn al-Khattab, established the precedent of allowing the woman claiming the rape to choose the punishment. Either she could marry the man who had raped her, thus entitling her to both a dower and maintenance, or she could refuse to marry the man and accept the equivalent dower as compensation. Amira Sonbol, "Rape and Law in Ottoman and Modern Egypt," in *Women in the Ottoman Empire: Middle Eastern Women in the Early Modern Era*, ed. Madeline C. Zilfi (Leiden: Brill, 1997), 216–18.

22. Ibn Abd al-Wahhab, "Kitab al-Jihad," 405. This teaching was consistent with the teachings of Ahmad ibn Hanbal.

23. The practice of masters having sexual relations with female slaves has a long history globally. For a discussion of this topic in the Ottoman Empire, see Mary Ann Fay, "Women and *Waqf*: Property, Power, and the Domain of Gender in Eighteenth-Century Egypt," in Zilfi, *Women in the Ottoman Empire*, esp. 41–45.

24. Ibn Abd al-Wahhab, "Kitab al-Jihad," 405.

25. Ibid. Although he does not actually use the word *haram* (forbidden), it is nevertheless clear that he believed that these Quranic verses forbade the practice of sexual relations with a female slave.

26. Ibn Abd al-Wahhab, "Risalah fi al-Radd," 38. He clearly considered masters having sexual relations with their female slaves to constitute *zina'*, rendering the men liable to the *hudud*. He did not hold the woman responsible because a female slave would necessarily have been coerced into intercourse due to her slave status.

27. Ibn Abd al-Wahhab, "Kitab al-Nikah," 642.

28. Ibid.

29. Ibid., 650.

30. Ibid.

31. Ibn Abd al-Wahhab, "Risalah fi al-Radd," 40. The prohibition of anal intercourse with both wives and slaves is fairly standard in juridical literature.

32. Ibid.

33. Ibid., 38.

34. Ibn Abd al-Wahhab, "Kitab al-Jihad," 379.

35. Ibn Abd al-Wahhab, "Kitab al-Nikah," 637.

36. Ibid., citing Q 24:33.

37. Ibid., 637–38. Similar reasoning has been followed in the contemporary era in reforms seeking to either severely curtail or prohibit outright the practice of polygyny. See Esposito with DeLong-Bas, *Women in Muslim Family Law*, 136–37, 151–52.

38. Ibn Abd al-Wahhab, "Risalah fi al-Radd," 38–39.

39. Ibn Abd al-Wahhab, "Kitab al-Jihad," 379.

40. These exceptions were made in the Quran because these people are believed

to share revelation from the same source book in Heaven. Not all jurists accepted Zoroastrians as People of the Book.

41. This prohibition is typically explained in classical literature as being due to the fact that the fathers are responsible for the religious upbringing of any children born to a marriage. Consequently, the marriage of a Muslim woman to a non-Muslim man would result in the children being raised as non-Muslims.

42. Ibn Abd al-Wahhab, "Kitab al-Jihad," 379.

43. Ibn Abd al-Wahhab, "Kitab al-Nikah," 642.

44. Ibn Abd al-Wahhab, "Kitab al-Jihad," 379.

45. Ibn Abd al-Wahhab, "Kitab al-Nikah," 642.

46. Ibn Abd al-Wahhab, "Kitab al-Jihad," 379.

47. The definition of *nushuz* in Ibn Abd al-Wahhab's writings is discussed later in this chapter.

48. Cited in Ibn Abd al-Wahhab, "Kitab al-Nikah," 644.

49. Ibid. A subtle critique of concubinage is implied here with the suggestion that the mere existence of a sexual relationship can constitute grounds for the woman to assert her financial marital rights.

50. Ibid., 644–51, for this discussion.

51. Ibid., 644. This case is a variation on the old story of Jacob, Leah, and Rachel from the Old Testament. The "bait and switch" story has deep roots in the Middle East, and this kind of case appears frequently in legal literature discussing marriage. I am indebted to John Voll for this observation.

52. Virginity is given as the legal justification for the woman's right to compensation because the legal literature equates loss of virginity with the loss of a body part.

53. Ibn Abd al-Wahhab, "Kitab al-Nikah," 644, 645.

54. Ibid., 645.

55. All of the law schools required the consent of spouses who were in their majority.

56. Ibn Abd al-Wahhab, "Kitab al-Nikah," 645. Al-Shafii did not allow this practice.

57. Ibid., 646. The exact phrase is, "It is commendable (*yustahibb*) for the father to ask permission of the virgin in the commanding/contracting of it."

58. Ibid., 645. The exact wording of this discussion is, "And the giving in marriage (*tazwij*) is not valid (*lam yusihh*) if the father has married off his minor son or his virgin daughters (*banatihi al-abkar*) by means other than with their permission (*bi-ghayr idhnihim*)." His inclusion of the agreement of the spouses as one of the five conditions/stipulations of the "pillars" of marriage suggests that he considered this to be a requirement, much as the five pillars of Islam are requirements for all Muslims.

59. Ibid., 646. This is a very interesting statement of legal doctrine because Ibn Abd al-Wahhab uses the verb *yustahibb* with respect to *istidhan al-marah*, "the permission of the mother." Muhammad advised men that they should inform mothers of the marriages of their daughters.

60. For a discussion of the general Hanbali approach to the question of consent, see Spectorsky, *Chapters*, 9.

61. Ibn Abd al-Wahhab, "Kitab al-Nikah," 646. He stated with respect to the father (*al-ab*) and grandfather (*al-jad*): "They do not have the right to give in marriage the minor girl according to a condition (*wa-laysa la-hum tazwij saghirah bi-al-hal*)."

62. Ibid., 645. This is one of the relatively rare cases in which he cited the authority of Ahmad ibn Hanbal as being authoritative and supportive of his own stance. He stated, "And according to Ahmad it is not permitted (*la yujawwaz*) to marry a girl of nine by means other than with her permission (*bi-ghayr idhniha*)." He also cited the authority of Ibn al-Mundhir (with whom he generally agreed and who he generally considered to be authoritative as a Companion): "And not the virgin (*bikr*) until she gives permission (*hata tasata'dhin*)." Again, the issue here was one of virginity rather than age. Ibid., 645–46.

63. Ibid., 646. The exact wording is, "Permission is absent (*intifa al-idhn*) for one who is not mature at nine years of age and it is required (*wujub an*) that it be carried/withheld until her maturity (*balaghatiha*)."

64. Ibid., 645. This was according to the saying of Muhammad: "And not the virgin (*bikr*) until she gives permission (*hata tasata'dhin*)." Ibn Abd al-Wahhab interpreted this statement to mean that the issue of concern was the fact of virginity, not age.

65. Ibid. This opinion was based on Ahmad ibn Hanbal's requirement of the permission of a girl who is nine or older. The other law schools, particularly the Malikis and Shafiis, did not require the girl's permission.

66. Ibid., 645–46. These teachings about the mature woman were standard for the Hanbalis and Hanafis, who required that a woman who had reached her majority had to give her consent in order for the marriage to be considered valid, regardless of whether she was a virgin (*bikr*) or a nonvirgin (*thayb*). Amira El Azhary Sonbol, "Adults and Minors in Ottoman Shari'a Courts and Modern Law," in Sonbol, *Women, the Family, and Divorce Laws in Islamic History*, 246.

67. Ibn Abd al-Wahhab, "Kitab al-Nikah," 646.

68. Ibid., 644.

69. Ibid., 641. The other law schools, particularly the Shafiis, permitted the dissolution of an engagement even when the woman had given her consent.

70. Ibid., 646.

71. Ibid., 647. The Maliki school made distinctions on the basis of how the woman came to be deflowered. They taught that a woman deflowered by fornication or immorality was to be treated like a virgin in the contracting of marriage so that her silence was understood to indicate her consent. However, if the woman had "lost" her virginity in a previous marriage, a finger or by jumping, then her direct permission was required.

72. Ibid., 646–47. Only al-Shafi'i dispensed entirely with the virgin's consent if the father had arranged the marriage.

73. Ibid., 647.

74. Ibid.

75. Ibid., 646.

76. Ibid.

77. Ibid., 649. This was a standard Hanbali teaching. Spectorsky, *Chapters*, 10.

78. Ibn Abd al-Wahhab, "Kitab al-Nikah," 647, 649.

79. *Hadith* collections cited include those of al-Shafii, al-Tabarani, al-Daraqatni, Malik ibn Anas, al-Bayhaqi, Ahmad ibn Hanbal, Abu Dawud al-Tirmidhi, Ibn Majah, Abu Awanah, Ibn Habban, and al-Hakim, among others.

80. According to the Shii scholar al-Hilli, guardians and witnesses are not re-

quired in marriage and secrecy and suppression of knowledge of a marriage is allowed because it was not forbidden. Ibn Abd al-Wahhab did not dispute that the practice was permitted at an early point in Islam. However, like temporary marriage (*mut'ah*, to be discussed in more detail later), it was ultimately forbidden and the practice was discontinued. Ibn Abd al-Wahhab, "Risalah fi al-Radd," 36–37.

81. Ibn Abd al-Wahhab, "Kitab al-Nikah," 647, 649.

82. Ibid.

83. Ibid. for the *hadith* citations.

84. Ibn Abd al-Wahhab, "Risalah fi al-Radd," 37.

85. Ibn Abd al-Wahhab, "Kitab al-Nikah," 649.

86. Ibid.

87. Ibid.

88. Ibid.

89. Ibid., 650.

90. Ibid., 647.

91. Ibid., 648. The order of the agnates varies according to the law schools. Ibn Abd al-Wahhab's ordering is consistent with the Hanbali tradition. Spectorsky, *Chapters*, 11.

92. Ibn Abd al-Wahhab, "Kitab al-Nikah," 648–49.

93. Ibid., 649.

94. Ibid., 648.

95. Ibid.

96. Ibid., 650. Muhammad recommended "Nobility for nobility."

97. Ibid. The second caliph, Umar, held that the woman belonged to the second husband because they had consummated the marriage. Ibn Abd al-Wahhab disagreed with this *hadith* because (1) it had not been authenticated by the early *hadith* collectors; and (2) a more direct *hadith*, attributed to Muhammad and narrated by two individuals—Samarrah and Uqbah—existed, claiming that the woman who is married to two men belongs to the one who married her first. Three of the major *hadith* collectors, Abu Dawud, al-Tirmidhi, and al-Nasai, believed that the *hadith* of Samarrah negated the *hadith* of Umar. The fourth caliph, Ali ibn Abi Talib, shared this opinion.

98. Ibid.

99. This approach is consistent with the broad reform brought about by the initial revelation of Islam, which recognized women as parties to the marriage contract rather than objects to be bought and sold by male family members. See Esposito with De Long-Bas, *Women in Muslim Family Law*, esp. 12–14 and 45–46.

100. Ibn Abd al-Wahhab, "Kitab al-Nikah," 643.

101. Ibid.

102. Ibid., 650–51.

103. Ibid.

104. Ibid.

105. Ibn Abd al-Wahhab, "Risalah fi al-Radd," 37–38.

106. Only in the case of women conducting business with other women did Ibn Abd al-Wahhab allow for the discarding of a male witness altogether because the presence of men in such an affair would be inappropriate. Although this was a special case, it set a clear and important precedent and constituted permission for women to engage in business or trade with other women and to set their own terms and

contracts. This discussion can be found in Ibn Abd al-Wahhab, "Fatawa wa-Masa'il," 129.

107. Ibn Abd al-Wahhab, "Risalah fi al-Radd," 37–38.

108. Ibn Abd al-Wahhab, "Kitab al-Nikah," 650–51.

109. Ibid., 651. Quran 49:13 states, "Therefore the most honored/noble of you for God is the most righteous of you."

110. Ibid. Abu Hanifah agreed with this approach, while Malik and al-Shafii allowed it only when the husband was not a relative.

111. Ibid.

112. Ibid., 663.

113. Ibid., 651. Other law schools did not allow women any agency with respect to status issues. For example, Malik maintained that certain tribes could not intermarry with other tribes. Thus, Malik taught that Qurayshi women must be given to Qurayshi men in marriage and Hashemi women to Hashemi men.

114. Ibid., 663.

115. Ibid., 661. Divorce is discussed more fully later in this chapter.

116. Ibid.

117. Although the other law schools theoretically either did not permit the woman to stipulate conditions in the marriage contract or strongly discouraged the practice, the historical reality is that judges (qadis) from all of the law schools permitted the inclusion of stipulations in marriage contracts and considered them binding. Nelly Hanna, "Marriage among Merchant Families in Seventeenth-Century Cairo," in Sonbol, Women, the Family, and Divorce Laws, 147. This observation has also been made in David Pearl, A Text on Muslim Personal Law (London: Croom Helm, 1979), 74; and Colin Imber, "Women, Marriage, and Property: Mehr in the Behcetu'l-Fetava of Yenisehirli Abdullah," in Zilfi, Women in the Ottoman Empire, 101.

118. Ibn Abd al-Wahhab, "Kitab al-Nikah," 661. This methodology, which was the hallmark of the Hanbali law school, has served as the springboard for reforms in the practice of marriage throughout the Muslim world in the contemporary era. See Esposito with DeLong-Bas, Women in Muslim Family Law.

119. Ibn Abd al-Wahhab, "Kitab al-Nikah," 663.

120. Ibid., 664.

121. Ibid., 661.

122. Ibid. This was a standard Hanbali teaching, Spectorsky, Chapters, 183–84. Although the other law schools were theoretically opposed to the stipulation of conditions, the historical record demonstrates that conditions placing limitations on polygyny were often included in non-Hanbali marriage contracts. See, for example, Abdal-Rehim Abdal-Rahman Abdal-Rehim, "The Family and Gender Laws in Egypt during the Ottoman Period," in Sonbol, Women, the Family, and Divorce Laws, esp. 106–8, 110.

123. Ibn Abd al-Wahhab. "Kitab al-Nikah," 661. Historically, some other law schools allowed men, as well as women, to stipulate conditions. See ibid., 110.

124. Ibn Abd al-Wahhab, "Kitab al-Nikah," 661.

125. Ibid., 662.

126. All of the law schools require the payment of mahr as a requirement for a valid marriage to exist. See Esposito with DeLong-Bas, Women in Muslim Family Law, 23–25, and Imber, "Women, Marriage, and Property," 92–93.

127. Ibn Abd al-Wahhab, "Kitab al-Nikah," 661.

128. Ibid., 662.

129. Ibn Abd al-Wahhab here denied the validity of a *hadith* transmitted by Abu Hurayrah, which claimed that the *mahr* is not due to the woman in order for the marriage to be valid.

130. Ibn Abd al-Wahhab, "Kitab al-Nikah," 662. This was according to the saying of the People of Knowledge, a group whose opinion Ibn Abd al-Wahhab considered to be authoritative but not infallible.

131. Ibid. Malik ibn Anas, Abu Hanifah, al-Shafii, and al-Awzai supported this position.

132. Ibid. The issue of *mut'ah* was one of Ibn Abd al-Wahhab's major sources of contention with Shii theology, as evidenced by his discussion in Ibn Abd al-Wahhab, "Risalah fi al-Radd," 34.

133. Ibid., 34–35.

134. Ibn Abd al-Wahhab, "Kitab al-Nikah," 662.

135. This is a standard teaching of all of the law schools.

136. Ibn Abd al-Wahhab, "Kitab al-Nikah," 662, 664.

137. Ibid., 662. Ahmad ibn Hanbal considered this kind of stipulation to be so unfair to the woman that he declared that it made the marriage contract itself invalid if the woman desired to leave.

138. Ibid. This was a standard ruling among all of the law schools.

139. Ibid.

140. Ibid., 664.

141. Ibid., 663. Only the Hanafis allowed the man to stipulate that his wife be a virgin and to fix the amount of *mahr* on that basis. In the event that he found her not to be a virgin, the woman was entitled to only the "fair" *mahr*, but the man had to dissolve the marriage via divorce by repudiation rather than invalidation. Legally, the issue was one of misrepresentation rather than virginity or nonvirginity. See Imber, "Women, Marriage, and Property," 101.

142. Ibn Abd al-Wahhab, "Kitab al-Nikah," 663.

143. Ibid.

144. Ibid. Although some of these causes for the potential loss of virginity, as evidenced by the lack of a hymen, are physiologically unlikely, they are nevertheless typically listed in juridical discussions of marriage and the possibility that the wife be found technically not to be a virgin on the wedding night. For example, see Imber, "Women, Marriage, and Property," 101.

145. The classical sources are in relative unanimity about these imperfections. Ibn Abd al-Wahhab cites Umar, Umar's son, and Ibn Abbas as his authoritative sources.

146. Ibn Abd al-Wahhab, "Kitab al-Nikah," 665.

147. Ibid.

148. Ibid.

149. Ibid. This is based on the saying of Umar that, "If he marries her and is believed to be mutilated or a leper then she has the right to her dower according to the harm done to her."

150. Ibid., 639. A suckling relationship creates a familial bond. For a discussion

of the classical prescriptions about permissible marriage partners, see Esposito with DeLong-Bas, *Women in Muslim Family Law*, esp. chap. 2.

151. Ibn Abd al-Wahhab, "Kitab al-Nikah," 641. This is standard among the law schools.

152. Ibid. A *talaq* is a declaration by the man to his wife that he divorces her. *Li'an* is an accusation of adultery without proof made by the husband before a judge that ends in an irrevocable divorce. Both are addressed in detail later in this chapter.

153. *Khul'* is a form of divorce whereby the wife agrees to pay her husband a sum negotiated by the couple in exchange for him declaring that he divorces her.

154. Ibn Abd al-Wahhab, "Kitab al-Nikah," 641.

155. Ibid., 641–42.

156. Ibid., 638.

157. Ibid.

158. Ibid.

159. Ibid. There are many *hadith* supporting this position.

160. Ibid.

161. Ibid., 638–39. He also cited the teachings of al-Awzai in support of this teaching.

162. Ibid., 639.

163. Ibid., 638–40. The only body parts absolutely and strictly forbidden to any male having reached the age of discernment, whether possessed by carnal desire or not, is what is between the navel and the knee. These body parts are generally prohibited from view, whether it concerns men looking at women, women looking at women, or men looking at men. The only exception is made for children under the age of seven because they are too young to understand what they are looking at and are expected to be with their mothers full time.

164. Thus, it becomes clear that the contemporary insistence of Saudi Arabia on the full veiling of women and their absolute gender segregation does not have its origins in Wahhabism.

165. Ibn Abd al-Wahhab, "Kitab al-Nikah," 638. What, exactly, a woman would wear around her home but not outdoors is not specified, but presumably it would be more revealing than what would be permissible around unrelated males.

166. Ibid., 640. Ibn Abd al-Wahhab specifically mentioned three categories of women—unbelieving (*kuffar*), foreign, and Jewish—as examples of women who did not veil, even when married. Some of Muhammad's wives who were not Muslims did not veil, setting a strong scriptural precedent for allowing women to retain their own faith and traditions.

167. Ibid., 642.

168. Ibid., 640.

169. Ibid., 639. In support, he cited the prophetic example of allowing impotent men to enter among his wives because they represented no threat to them.

170. Ibid., 639–40.

171. Ibid., 640. Evidence of women being considered as the sources of temptation and chaos are abundant in the historical literature. For a broad historical discussion, see Mernissi, *Veil*. For an example contemporary to Ibn Abd al-Wahhab, see the

biographical dictionary of women written by the eighteenth-century scholar Yasin al-'Umari, highlighting the merits and dangers that women represent for men. "They are temptresses, sometimes ruinous, often necessary for sexual pleasure and reproduction, and can bring men good fortune when they are virtuous." Cited in Dina Rizk Khouri, "Drawing Boundaries and Defining Spaces: Women and Space in Ottoman Iraq," in Sonbol Women, the Family, and Divorce Laws, 175.

172. Ibn Abd al-Wahhab, "Kitab al-Nikah," 640. Ibn Abd al-Wahhab cited several hadith in support of this teaching and noted that Muhammad was in the habit of hiding both Aisha and Fatima when male visitors were present.

173. This is in keeping with the Quranic prescription that both believing men and believing women are to maintain their modesty. Neither party is entirely culpable or innocent in questions of desire.

174. Ibn Abd al-Wahhab, "Kitab al-Nikah," 639. He noted a hadith about Abu Tayyibah whereby he withdrew from the company of Muhammad's wives, even though he was only a youth, because he experienced carnal desire.

175. Ibid., 640–41.

176. Ibid., 643. Thus, he cited the case of a "beardless, handsome" man entering into seclusion with a woman and laying down with her as a damnable activity that should be publicized and punished.

177. Ibid., 639.

178. This is particularly striking in comparison with European and even Ottoman medicine of a similar period, when a physician was supposed to ascertain the woman's medical condition by taking her pulse.

179. These questions all appear in a Ibn Abd al-Wahhab, "Fatawa wa-Masa'il," 52–53.

180. Ibid., 55.

181. For further and more detailed discussions of these issues, see Baber Johansen, "Legal Literature and the Problem of Change: The Case of Land Rent," in Islam and Public Law, ed. Chibli Mallat (London: Graham & Trotman, 1993), 29–47; and Judith E. Tucker, " 'And God Knows Best': Fatawa as a Source for the History of Gender in the Arab World." Unpublished paper in the possession of the author.

182. These rulings are not necessarily confined to a single school of Islamic law. In fact, the ikhtilaf genre of legal literature is designed to allow the author to demonstrate familiarity with a wide variety of legal opinions about any given topic. Ibn Abd al-Wahhab's own legal literature reflects this approach, demonstrating his familiarity with the Hanafi, Shafii, Maliki, Zahiri, and Jafari law schools, as well as that of the Hanbalis.

183. This topic is addressed in some detail later, given its importance.

184. Ibn Abd al-Wahhab, "Kitab al-Nikah," 682.

185. Ibid., 671. On this basis, Ibn Abd al-Wahhab taught that anyone claiming to have paid the mahr "in accordance with what the Quran prescribes" is in error.

186. Ibid., 670.

187. Ibid. The most important of these opinions was that of Umar, who declared that the mahr should not be fettered or shackled, meaning that the amount should be a matter of negotiation.

188. Ibid. This agreement is in accordance with Muhammad's saying that the mahr should be sealed in order to protect the woman's rights.

189. Ibid., 674–75.

190. Ibid., 675.

191. Ibid., 671.

192. Ibid., 675. In fact, he felt so strongly about this issue that he lambasted those who taught that the woman was not entitled to her *mahr* in such cases as being hateful in their hearts and charged them with deliberately seeking to deceive and create errors!

193. Ibid., 672.

194. Ibid., 671–72.

195. Ibid., 671. As Umar said, "They cannot seize the dowers of the women."

196. Ibid. Abu Hanifah forbade this practice because it was not specifically permitted by the Quran.

197. Ibid. He stated, "And if the one making the condition is other than the father, then everything belongs to her."

198. Ibid., 671–72. This was a fairly standard teaching. See Imber, "Women, Marriage, and Property," 93–94.

199. Ibn Abd al-Wahhab, "Kitab al-Nikah," 675.

200. Ibid., 673.

201. Ibid.

202. Ibid. Again, this is standard in the legal literature. See Esposito with DeLong-Bas, *Women in Muslim Family Law*, 18; and Imber, "Women, Marriage, and Property," 93–95.

203. Ibn Abd al-Wahhab, "Kitab al-Nikah," 673.

204. Amira El Azhary Sonbol, "Law and Gender Violence in Ottoman and Modern Egypt," in Sonbol, *Women, the Family, and Divorce Laws*, 285.

205. This is a widespread problem in some countries in the twenty-first-century, where rape as a legal category is not recognized, notably Pakistan and Egypt. See Esposito with DeLong-Bas, *Women in Muslim Family Law*, 90, for a broad discussion of the contemporary era.

206. Ibn Abd al-Wahhab, "Kitab al-Nikah," 674.

207. Ibid., 675. This definition is not unique to Ibn Abd al-Wahhab and in fact has a long history in legal literature. See Imber, "Women, Marriage, and Property," 87–88.

208. Ibn Abd al-Wahhab, "Kitab al-Nikah," 674.

209. This remains an important issue today in countries such as India, where large dowers are often specified in marriage contracts but are never paid to the wife. Esposito with DeLong-Bas, *Women in Muslim Family Law*, 113–14.

210. In some cases, Muhammad requested that the husband give something to the wife prior to consummation (as in the case of Ali and Fatima), and in others he did not require it (as in a *hadith* related by Uqbah bin Amir).

211. Ibn Abd al-Wahhab, "Kitab al-Nikah," 672. Ibn Abd al-Wahhab did not divide the *mahr* into *mu'ajjal/muqaddam* and *mu'akhkhal* portions, portions that were payable at the time of the marriage and at the end of the marriage. It is not clear when this practice emerged, but the historical record contains abundant references to disputes over the matter of payment of the deferred portion. See Imber, "Women, Marriage, and Property," 98–99.

212. Other law schools, most notably the Hanafis, apparently did not consider

maintenance to be the absolute right of the wife because they did not consider lack of payment of maintenance to be a valid reason for the wife to seek a divorce. See Hanna, "Marriage," 148.

213. Ibn Abd al-Wahhab, "Kitab al-Nikah," 702. The Malikis did not require payment of maintenance to the man's mother because she is not a paternal relative.

214. This teaching was based on Muhammad's injunction to "Apportion what is necessary for you and your offspring," which does not specify the age of the offspring. The Hanafis and Malikis required maintenance for boys only until they reached maturity and for girls until marriage.

215. Under Islamic law, responsibility for the children falls on the paternal relatives in the event of the absence or death of the father. Ibn Abd al-Wahhab, "Kitab al-Nikah," 702–3.

216. Ibid., 706. This latter inclusion reflected his belief that the relationship between the Muslim master and a slave was intended to be one of responsibility rather than exploitation.

217. Ibid., 701. The Shafii law school required consideration only of the man's status. Other law schools considered only the woman's status prior to the marriage.

218. Ibid.

219. Ibid.

220. Ibid. In contrast, Abu Hanifah upheld the man's rights in marriage and did not allow the woman to seek separation from her husband on the basis of poverty (704).

221. Ibid., 701.

222. Some modern legal codes in the Arab world have also made this argument. See, for example, the case of Egypt discussed in Esposito with DeLong-Bas, *Women in Muslim Family Law*, 59–61.

223. This teaching was based on the practice of Umar, who put this policy into place when he found husbands trying to avoid their maintenance duties by engaging in military service for the state. Thus, not even service to the state excuses the man from his obligations in marriage. Ibn Abd al-Wahhab, "Kitab al-Nikah," 702.

224. Ibid.

225. See, for example, Ibn Hanbal's treatment of the topic in Spectorsky, *Chapters*, 26–27.

226. Ibn Abd al-Wahhab, "Kitab al-Nikah," 676.

227. Ibid.

228. Ibid.

229. Ibid.

230. Ibid., 676–77.

231. Ibid., 677.

232. Ibid.

233. Ibid., 678.

234. Ibid., 679. Drums, on the other hand, were to be reserved for war. The type of instrument played indicated the nature of the message conveyed.

235. Ibid., 678. He specifically stated that, "Publication of the marriage is preferable and should be imposed by him via the tambourine until it is well known, according to his saying about the salutation: 'Prefer what is between what is permitted and what is forbidden, the voice and the tambourine in marriage.' "

236. Ibid.

237. Ibid., 677. This is another case in which Ibn Abd al-Wahhab sided with the *hadith* of Aisha rather than those of Abu Hurayrah. In this discussion, Abu Hurayrah is portrayed as a rather grumpy individual whose extremist views did not allow for any sort of feasting or celebrating. Ibn Abd al-Wahhab clearly disagreed with this approach.

238. Ibid. He cited as evidence Muhammad's entry into the Kaabah, where he found an illustration of Ibrahim and Ismail, and Umar's allowance of Muslim interaction with the *dhimmis*, such as entering churches where walls and gates hold illustrations and representations.

239. Ibid., 678.

240. Ibid. Muhammad stated, "There is no objection to entertainment if there is no representation."

241. Ibid., 679.

242. Ibid., 676.

243. Ibid., 678–79. The extreme attention devoted to ritual detail here is unusual in Ibn Abd al-Wahhab's writings.

244. Ibid., 680.

245. Ibid.

246. Ibid.

247. Ibid., 680–81.

248. Ibid., 681.

249. Ibid., 681–82. Equal treatment does not necessarily translate into equal maintenance. The maintenance owed by the husband to the wife, particularly with respect to housing and clothing, is a negotiated matter that largely depends on the wife's status prior to the marriage.

250. Ibid., 681. All of these teachings are in keeping with classical rulings.

251. This is in keeping with classical teachings. The maximum spacing of four nights is due to the Quranic limitation of four wives per husband.

252. Ibn Abd al-Wahhab, "Kitab al-Nikah," 680–81.

253. Ibid., 680.

254. Ibid., 682.

255. For example, the problem of domestic violence among Muslim couples is so widespread in Malaysia that a grassroots organization, Sisters in Islam, has put together a short pamphlet addressing the question of whether domestic violence is permissible in Islam. They argue along the same lines as Ibn Abd al-Wahhab that it is not. Sisters-in-Islam, *Are Muslim Men Allowed to Beat Their Wives?* (Selangor: Sisters-in-Islam, 1991).

256. Ibn Abd al-Wahhab, "Kitab al-Nikah," 681.

257. This is a strong and significant departure from the traditional interpretation of this term by the Shafii, Maliki, and Hanafi law schools, which tended to consider any act of disobedience on the part of the wife to be *nushuz*, thus depriving her of her right to maintenance for the period of disobedience. Sonbol, "Law and Gender Violence," 280–81.

258. This interpretation stands in marked contrast to traditional interpretations, which permit wife beating on the basis of Q 4:34 as long as no limbs are broken or permanent physical damage is done in the process. Such an interpretation has been

carried over into the modern period, legitimating cultures of domestic violence in some- countries. See ibid., 283.

259. Ibn Abd al-Wahhab, "Kitab al-Nikah," 681–82. According to Q 4:128, the wife need not tolerate abandonment by her husband.

260. Ibid., 686.

261. Ibid., 688. So far this discussion is standard and in accordance with classi- cal jurisprudence.

262. Ibid., 686. Although neither Muhammad nor his Companions permitted the declaration of a *talaq* while in a state of drunkenness, some of the law schools, notably the Hanafis, allowed it to stand simply because it had been spoken. Ibn Abd al-Wahhab rejected this literal intepretation, looking instead to the intent behind it. He declared such a *talaq* to be one of hatred, rendering the husband despicable.

263. Ibid., 687. He also applied this line of thinking to a drunken man who makes a pledge or manumits a slave—the word of the other party is to be accepted as valid and binding.

264. For more detailed information on this practice and reforms, see Esposito with DeLong-Bas, *Women in Muslim Family Law*, esp. 94, 104–5.

265. Ibn Abd al-Wahhab, "Fatawa wa-Masa'il," 28–29.

266. Ibid., 33.

267. Ibid., 35.

268. Ibid.

269. Ibn Abd al-Wahhab, "Kitab al-Nikah," 688.

270. Spectorsky, *Chapters*, 29.

271. Ibn Abd al-Wahhab, "Kitab al-Nikah," 688.

272. Ibid. He denied the need for the two of them to curse each other, as was recommended in other sources.

273. Ibn Abd al-Wahhab, "Risalah fi al-Radd," 41–42. He upheld the necessity of the interim marriage in order for sexual intercourse to be legal for the couple. He declared any sexual relations occurring between the two after the triple *talaq* without an intervening marriage to be nothing less than *zina'*.

274. Ibn Abd al-Wahhab, "Fatawa wa-Masa'il," 29, 36.

275. Ibn Abd al-Wahhab, "Kitab al-Nikah," 686.

276. Ibn Abd al-Wahhab, "Fatawa wa-Masa'il," 125.

277. Ibid., 126. Both Ibn Abd al-Wahhab and Ibn Hanbal emphasized the critical role of intent in declarations of *talaq*. However, whereas Ibn Abd al-Wahhab insisted that the man be clear about his intentions and asked directly for a clear answer in ambiguous cases, Ibn Hanbal allowed the man to "clarify" what he had said after the fact, ostensibly giving him the opportunity to change his mind. Spectorsky, *Chapters*, 32.

278. Ibn Abd al-Wahhab, "Fatawa wa-Masa'il," 126.

279. Ibn Abd al-Wahhab, "Kitab al-Nikah," 690.

280. Ibid., 689.

281. Ibid., 690. This is consistent with Ibn Hanbal's teachings. Spectorsky, *Chapters*, 33.

282. Ibn Abd al-Wahhab, "Kitab al-Nikah," 691.

283. Ibid.

284. Ibid., 693.

285. Ibid., 682.

286. Ibid., 691. This is one of the cases in which Ibn Abd al-Wahhab disagreed with Ahmad ibn Hanbal. Ibn Hanbal discouraged this practice because it upsets the balance of rights between husband and wife. However, he did not declare the practice—or its consequences—to be invalid

287. Ibid., 682.

288. Ibid., 692.

289. Ibid., 692–93.

290. Ibid., 693.

291. Ibid., 699. It is possible that he did not specify the limitation of this regulation to the waiting period because this would have been generally understood. However, it is noteworthy that he did not make this specification, given the absolute time limits generally set in classical interpretations and his broad tendency to be specific in such matters so as to avoid ambiguity. Ibn Abd al-Wahhab tended to interpret issues related to marriage and divorce in such a way as to maximize the benefits for women while minimizing the harm that they could potentially suffer. His stance here, as in many other instances, is similar to those of contemporary reforms, which have extended and expanded the woman's right to both maintenance and housing dependent on her contribution to the marriage and whether the marriage ended due to no fault of hers. See Esposito with DeLong-Bas, *Women in Muslim Family Law*, 96–97.

292. Ibn Abd al-Wahhab, "Kitab al-Nikah," 694–95.

293. Ibid., 697. Again, this ruling has been adopted in contemporary reforms in the Muslim world. See Esposito with DeLong-Bas, *Women in Muslim Family Law*, esp. 102–4.

294. Ibn Abd al-Wahhab, "Kitab al-Nikah," 697; Spectorsky, *Chapters*, 55.

295. Ibn Abd al-Wahhab, "Kitab al-Nikah," 697.

296. Ibid., 698.

297. Ibid., 697.

298. Ibid., 695.

299. Ibid., 697.

300. Ibid., 696–97. The miscarriage scenario is valid only when the fetus is recognizably human, as opposed to the presence of an unusually heavy menstrual flow.

301. Ibid., 694.

302. Ibid., 696.

303. Spectorsky, *Chapters*, 52–54. Classical jurists halved the waiting period for slave women. This same legal reasoning was used to halve the punishment for a slave woman convicted of *zina'*.

304. Ibn Abd al-Wahhab, "Kitab al-Nikah," 696.

305. Ibid., 695.

306. Other law schools, most notably the Shafiis, required the woman to wait four years to see if her menstrual cycle would resume. If it did not, the Shafiis required the woman to wait an additional three months after the four-year period. Other law schools required the woman to wait until either menstruation resumed or she reached a "point of despair."

307. Ibn Abd al-Wahhab, "Kitab al-Nikah," 696.

308. Ibid., 699.

309. Ibid.

310. Ibid.

311. Ibid., 683. He cited as evidence the fact that Muhammad did not ask the woman divorced by *khul'* about her condition.

312. Ibid., 684.

313. Ibid., 685.

314. Of most relevance for comparative purposes is the relative abundance of *khul'* divorces in the Ottoman court records (*sijill*). See Madeline C. Zilfi, " 'We Don't Get Along': Women and *Hul* Divorce in the Eighteenth Century," in Zilfi, *Women in the Ottoman Empire*, 271–81.

315. There are many examples of this practice in the Ottoman court records for this time period because some women chose to countersue their former husbands for divorce by *talaq* (which would leave the woman's financial rights intact) by claiming that the *khul'* agreement had been reached under duress. See, for example, Fariba Zarinebaf-Shahr, "Women, Law, and Imperial Justice in Ottoman Istanbul in The Late Seventeenth Century," in Sonbol, *Women, the Family, and Divorce Laws*, esp. 91–94, and Svetlana Ivanova, "The Divorce between Zubaida Hatun and Esseid Osma Aga: Women in the Eighteenth Century Shari'a Court of Rumelia," in Sonbol, *Women, the Family, and Divorce Laws*, esp. 118–22 and 124–25.

316. This latter difficulty has become particularly problematic in the contemporary era. See, for example, Esposito with DeLong-Bas, *Women in Muslim Family Law*, esp. 79–80, 104–5, for a broad discussion of this issue in the contemporary era; and Sonbol, Introduction to *Women, the Family, and Divorce Laws*, esp. 1–2, for a discussion of Egypt; and Abdal-Rehim, "Family," esp. 104–6. Sonbol, "Law and Gender Violence," 281–82, has further argued that it was sometimes left up to the judge to decide whether the divorce would occur by *khul'* or *talaq*.

317. Ibn Abd al-Wahhab, "Kitab al-Nikah," 683. The exact wording of this statement is, "If she dislikes/despises her husband and believes that she cannot carry out her duties to God in obeying him, *khul'* is permitted (*jaza al-khul'*) by means of compensation (*ala iwadh*)."

318. Ibid., 683–84. The man's refusal does not make a *khul'* divorce impossible. The woman can always seek recourse from the courts.

319. Ibn Abd al-Wahhab's interpretation differed from those of other jurists. Zilfi, in "We Don't Get Along," 274–75, has noted that the court records of the Ottoman Empire reflect a vision that maintains the man's power in both *talaq* and *khul'*.

320. Ibn Abd al-Wahhab's exact wording on this is, "The *khul'* according to a similar *hadith* is to be easy for her (*sahlah*) on the basis of her dislike of the man and she is to give him the *mahr* and this is *khul'*, and this is proven by the fact that other than in this way it is not valid (*la yusihh*)." Ibn Abd al-Wahhab, "Kitab al-Nikah," 683.

321. Ibid.

322. Ibid.

323. Ibid. The exact wording on this issue is, "And therefore her divorcing him as *khul'* by other than this is disliked and despised, but there is not evidence about it that it is forbidden (*tahrim*)," suggesting that there were alternate means by which the wife could seek divorce but that these were frowned upon.

324. Ibid., 683–84.

325. Ibid., 685.

326. Ibid., 684.

327. Ibid. Indeed, he declared it *nahy*.

328. Ibid. Both Malik and al-Shafii freely permitted the man to demand more than the *mahr* in compensation for the divorce, Spectorsky, *Chapters*, 51.

329. Ibn Abd al-Wahhab, "Kitab al-Nikah," 685. The full text of this decision reads, "*Khul'* by a subterfuge is not valid (*la yusihh*) and he chose between the teachings of the two opinions/sides that it was forbidden (*anhu yuharam*)." The use of the terms *valid* and *forbidden* marks this as a statement of binding legal doctrine.

330. Ibid. His legal reasoning in this case likens the declaration of divorce to the annulment of a sales contract by one of the contracting parties—compensation to the other party is always due.

331. Ibid., 688.

332. Ibid., 698. Thus, the color coding of dark green and black was reserved for widows in his thought. Other women were apparently free to wear other colors.

333. Ibid. This teaching was based upon the rulings of the Maliki jurists al-Hasan, and Ata.

334. For more information on this topic, see Esposito with DeLong-Bas, *Women in Muslim Family Law*, esp. the section "Muslim Minorities in non-Muslim Majority Countries," 111–19.

335. Ibn Abd al-Wahhab, "Kitab al-Nikah," 698.

336. Ibid.

337. Ibid., 705.

338. Ibid.

339. Ibid. For a discussion of standard jurisprudence on the topic of custody, particularly in the Hanafi tradition, see Judith E. Tucker, "The Fullness of Affection: Mothering in the Islamic Law of Ottoman Syria and Palestine," in Zilfi, *Women in the Ottoman Empire*, 232–52. This article also contains examples of expanded roles for women as guardians of their children so that Ibn Abd al-Wahhab was not an anomaly but can be seen to fit into a line of thought recognizing the capacity of women to carry out their responsibilities and affection as mothers beyond the age of *hidanah*. See also Margaret L. Meriwether, "The Rights of Children and the Responsibilities of Women: Women as Wasis in Ottoman Aleppo, 1770–1840," in Sonbol, *Women, the Family and Divorce Laws*, esp. 225–34.

340. Here Ibn Abd al-Wahhab differs from Malik, who gives the mother the right of guardianship until the girl is married, and al-Shafii, who allows the girl to choose between her mother and her father. Cited in Ibn Abd al-Wahhab, "Kitab al-Nikah," 705.

341. Ibid. The reasoning is that, while it would be inappropriate for the girl to remain with her mother if she is now married to a man who is not her father, it would be unfair to the mother to turn the girl over to her paternal relatives. This is a case in which Ibn Abd al-Wahhab departs from consensus (*ijma'*) in favor of women's rights.

342. Ibn Abd al-Wahhab, "Fatawa wa-Masa'il," 123.

343. Ibn Abd al-Wahhab's choice of wording was deliberate. Although modern medicine does not recognize the possibility of a pregnancy lasting for a year, Islamic law makes a provision for a "sleeping fetus." A "sleeping fetus" is defined as a fertilized ovum that goes into suspended being for an indeterminate time period. The law schools varied on the length of time that this could occur. The Maliki school was the

most liberal, allowing a "sleeping fetus" to exist for four years. This reasoning was recently used in the Amina Lawal adultery case in Nigeria to overturn the stoning conviction on the basis that Lawal's pregnancy could not convict her of adultery because it could have been a case of a "sleeping fetus."

344. Ibn Abd al-Wahhab, "Fatawa wa-Masa'il," 123.

345. Ibid., 90.

5. JIHAD

1. See, for example, the furor over the address by a Muslim student at Harvard University's commencement ceremonies in May 2002 entitled "My Personal Jihad." Although the content of the speech remained the same, he was ultimately pressured into altering the title because the term *jihad* is offensive to so many.

2. See Bernard Lewis's book by this title: *What Went Wrong: Western Impact and Middle Eastern Response* (New York: Oxford University Press, 2001).

3. See the landmark article by Samuel P. Huntingdon, "A Clash of Civilizations?" *Foreign Affairs* (summer 1993): 22–39.

4. Muhammad Ibn Abd al-Wahhab, "Fatawa wa-Masa'il al-Imam al-Shaykh Muhammad Ibn Abd al-Wahhab," in *Mu'allafat al-Shaykh al-Imam Muhammad Ibn Abd al-Wahhab*, vol. 3 (Riyadh: Jamiat al-Imam Muhammad bin Saud al-Islamiyah, 1398H), 97.

5. Muhammad Ibn Abd al-Wahhab, "Kitab al-Tawhid," in *Mu'allafat al-Shaykh al-Imam Muhammad Ibn Abd al-Wahhab*, vol. 3 (Riyadh: Jamiat al-Imam Muhammad bin Saud al-Islamiyah, 1398H), 47.

6. Ibid., 19.

7. Ibid., 47, 92.

8. Ibid., 22.

9. Ibn Abd al-Wahhab, "Fatawa wa-Masa'il," 5–6.

10. Ibid., 15.

11. Ibid., 17.

12. Ibid., 34.

13. Ibid., 34–35.

14. Ibid., 12.

15. The Kharijites were seventh-century extremists who withdrew from the mainstream Muslim community over frustration with the fourth Sunni caliph Ali's failure to pursue the third Sunni caliph Uthman's assassin. They believed that Ali's failure to pursue justice marked him as a sinner and non-Muslim. They assassinated him in 661 C.E.

16. Ibn Abd al-Wahhab, "Fatawa wa-Masa'il," 21.

17. Ibid., 44. The Mutazilites were twelfth-century extremists who taught that God does not exist independently and that the Quran was created. They emphasized reason over revelation.

18. Ibid., 76–78. This discussion is based on Q 4:165.

19. Ibid., 21. This had been the case historically for Ahmad ibn Hanbal, whose works were discarded by some on the basis of what he wrote about obscure Quranic passages.

20. Ibid., 12.

21. Ibid., 44. This is generally in keeping with the Sunni tradition.

22. Ibn Abd al-Wahhab, "Kitab al-Tawhid," 88–90.

23. Ibn Abd al-Wahhab, "Fatawa wa-Masa'il," 6.

24. Ibid., 20.

25. Ibid., 14–15.

26. Ibid., 6.

27. Ibn Abd al-Wahhab, "Kitab al-Tawhid," 19.

28. Ibid., 20–21.

29. This explains why his followers always referred to themselves as *Muwahhidun* or *Ahl al-tawhid*, meaning "the people of *tawhid*," rather than Wahhabis, reflecting their adherence and faithfulness to monotheism rather than Ibn Abd al-Wahhab.

30. The historical record shows that the Saudi-Wahhabi conquests of various areas occurred over long time periods (twenty-seven years for Riyadh and seven years for Washm). These conquests included letter-writing campaigns geared toward winning adherents to Ibn Abd al-Wahhab's religious teachings. See chapter 1 for more details.

31. Ibn Abd al-Wahhab, "Kitab al-Tawhid," 22.

32. Ibn Abd al-Wahhab, "Fatawa wa-Masa'il," 69.

33. This process is described in full in a *hadith* reported by both al-Bukhari and Muslim, as recorded in Ibn Abd al-Wahhab, "Kitab al-Tawhid," 20.

34. This treatise is also striking for Ibn Abd al-Wahhab's deliberate and strong use of his own personal voice in making statements using the personal pronoun meaning "I"—*ana*,—in statements such as "I remind you," "I witness," and "I say." The use of his own voice typically occurs in cases in which he is issuing directives to his followers about how they are to conduct themselves, about the permissibility of self-defense, or about their responsibilities, always rooted in either Quranic verses or biblical history. This treatise is one of the few instances in which Ibn Abd al-Wahhab asserted his personal authority as leader.

35. Ibn Abd al-Wahhab, "Kitab Kashf al-Shubhat," 160–61. Ibn Abd al-Wahhab claimed that it was this method that permitted the ordinary people of the Muwahhidin to be victorious over a thousand *ulama* of the Mushrikin.

36. Ibid., 160.

37. Ibid. This is likely a reference to the hostility some of his followers encountered while carrying out their missionary work. The chroniclers Ibn Bishr and Ibn Ghannam note that Wahhabi *ulama* were often badly treated, sometimes having their mouths sewn shut or being tossed out on their ears.

38. Ibn Abd al-Wahhab, "Fatawa wa-Masa'il," 69.

39. Ibid.

40. Thus, for example, infants were never to be killed or the dead mutilated. Cited in Ibn Abd al-Wahhab, "Kitab al-Tawhid," 142–43. These are standard options in classical writings on jihad.

41. Ibid.

42. Ibn Abd al-Wahhab, "Fatawa wa-Masa'il," 12.

43. Ibid., 66.

44. Ibid., 37.

45. Even so adamant an opponent of Wahhabism as Ignaz Goldziher had to acknowledge that Ibn Abd al-Wahhab never carried a sword or engaged in violence

against those who chose not to adhere to his teachings. What military activities were undertaken by the Wahhabis were entirely the domain of Muhammad Ibn Saud, whose express goal was state consolidation. Ignaz Goldziher, *An Introduction to Islamic Theology and Law*, trans. Andras Hamori and Ruth Hamori (Princeton: Princeton University Press, 1981), 242.

46. Muhammad Ibn Abd al-Wahhab, "Kitab al-Jihad," in *Mu'allafat al-Shaykh al-Iman Muhammad bin Abd al-Wahhab: Al-Fiqh*, vol. 2 (Riyadh: Jamiat al-Imam Muhammad bin Saud al-Islamiyah, 1298H), 359. This is in keeping with classical interpretations. For a discussion of the classical interpretation, see Rudolph Peters, *Jihad in Classical and Modern Islam: A Reader* (Princeton: Markus Wiener, 1996), 29.

47. Ibn Abd al-Wahhab, "Kitab al-Jihad," 359.

48. Ibid., 359, 361.

49. Ibid., 362.

50. Ibid.

51. Reaven Firestone, *Jihad: The Origin of Holy War in Islam* (New York: Oxford University Press, 1999), 33–34.

52. Ibid., 23.

53. Ibid., 34. Firestone believes that this practice set the precedent for Muslims to accord the protected (*dhimmi*) status to Jews, Christians, and Zoroastrians as "People of the Book." The mechanics of the relationship are the same—in exchange for payment of a special tax (*jizyah*), the *dhimmi* are to be granted protection by the Muslims, even though they have not converted to Islam.

54. Ibid.

55. Ibid., 24.

56. Ibid., 37.

57. Ibn Abd al-Wahhab, "Kitab al-Jihad," 362.

58. The classification of anyone as an enemy presumes that there has already been a conflict, rendering the enemy an aggressor.

59. Ibn Abd al-Wahhab presumes that the *imam*, conscious of his role and knowledge that jihad is intended only as a defensive activity, will adhere to the requirements for declaring jihad. I am grateful to David Commins for raising this issue.

60. Ibn Abd al-Wahhab, "Kitab al-Jihad," 360.

61. Ibid.

62. Ibid., 395–96.

63. Ibid., 361.

64. Ibid., 360.

65. Ibid., 394.

66. Ibid., 372. This is in keeping with the consensus (*ijma'*) of classical scholars, who require the summons to Islam prior to engaging in warfare. Peters, *Jihad in Classical and Modern Islam*, 37.

67. Ibn Abd al-Wahhab, "Kitab al-Jihad," 400.

68. Ibid., 373.

69. Ibid., 363–65.

70. Ibid., 365–66.

71. Ibid.

72. Ibid.

73. Ibid., 371. This interpretation of the gender question in jihad differs slightly from more classical discussions, which prohibited killing women as long as they are not actively engaged in fighting. The classical approach seems to focus more on actual fighting than engaging in encouragement of the enemy. See Peters, *Jihad in Classical and Modern Islam*. 33.

74. Stephen Schwartz, *The Two Faces of Islam: The House of Sa'ud from Tradition to Terror* (New York: Doubleday, 2002), 71.

75. For classical discussions, see Peters, *Jihad in Classical and Modern Islam*, 35.

76. Ibn Abd al-Wahhab, "Kitab al-Jihad," 366.

77. Ibid.

78. Ibid.

79. Ibid., 399.

80. Ibid., 367.

81. Ibid.

82. Ibid., 397.

83. Ibid., 367.

84. Ibid., 399–400.

85. Ibid., 400.

86. Ibid., 368–69.

87. Ibid., 368.

88. Ibid., 396.

89. Ibid.

90. Ibid., 378.

91. Ibid., 379.

92. Classical jurisprudence on this topic varies. Ibn Abd al-Wahhab's approach is consistent with the example of the Rightly Guided Caliphs, who strictly forbade acts of wanton destruction in war. See Peters, *Jihad in Classical and Modern Islam*, 36–37 for classical discussions and 172 n. 7 for the example of the caliphs.

93. Ibn Abd al-Wahhab, "Kitab al-Jihad," 363.

94. This makes it clear that, contrary to the claims of Schwartz (*Two Faces*, 71), Ibn Abd al-Wahhab did not support book burning or the eradication of knowledge.

95. Ibn Abd al-Wahhab, "Kitab al-Jihad," 387–88.

96. Ibid., 363–64.

97. Ibid., 380.

98. Ibid., 388.

99. Ibid., 363–64.

100. Ibid., 364.

101. Ibid., 388.

102. Ibid., 371.

103. Ibid., 376.

104. Ibid., 371.

105. Ibid., 372.

106. Ibid., 398, 401.

107. Ibid., 401.

108. Ibid., 403.

109. This understanding of the intended relationship between the *imam* and the *amir* formed the basis of the alliance between Muhammad Ibn Abd al-Wahhab and

Muhammad Ibn Saud in 1744. There is a great deal of tension between the two in this discussion, indicating that there was likely some conflict between Ibn Abd al-Wahhab and Ibn Saud in the expansion of the movement and the conduct of jihad.

110. Ibn Abd al-Wahhab, "Kitab al-Jihad," 375–76.

111. Ibid., 376.

112. Ibid., 373.

113. Ibid., citing Q 8:1.

114. Ibid., 387.

115. Ibid., 374.

116. Peters, *Jihad in Classical and Modern Islam*, 171 n.4.

117. Ibn Abd al-Wahhab, "Kitab al-Jihad," 383.

118. Ibid., 377.

119. Ibid., 383.

120. Ibid., 380.

121. Ibid., 381–82.

122. Ibid., 373.

123. Ibid., 375.

124. Ibid., 384.

125. Ibid., 387.

126. Ibid., 384.

127. Ibid., 375.

128. Ibid., 384.

129. Ibid., 376.

130. Ibid., 387.

131. Ibid., 377–78.

132. Ibid., 379.

133. Ibid., 374.

134. For a more complete analysis of this topic, see chapter 4.

135. Ibn Abd al-Wahhab, "Kitab al-Jihad," 378.

136. Ibid., 380.

137. Ibid., 382.

138. Ibid., 380.

139. Ibid., 386.

140. Ibid., 389.

141. Ibid., 386.

142. Ibid., 383.

143. Ibid., 385–86.

144. Ibid., 390.

145. Ibid., 391.

146. Al-Shafii asserted that the leader's portion was to be one-fifth, as was the case with booty. Ahmad ibn Hanbal did not specify the amount because it is not specified in either the Quran or the *hadith*.

147. Ibn Abd al-Wahhab, "Kitab al-Jihad," 391–92. This is a clear case of his rejection of literal adherence to Muhammad's example because it separates his actions into two types—divinely inspired and personal. It suggests that, while Muhammad's example as a prophet had to be followed, his example as a political-military leader did not.

148. Ibid., 393. The Shafiis forbade this practice.

149. Ibid., 394.

150. Ibid., 362.

151. Ibid., 398.

152. For a presentation of some of the classical discussions about the permissibility of truces, see Peters, *Jihad in Classical and Modern Islam*, 38–40.

153. Ibn Abd al-Wahhab, "Kitab al-Jihad," 405.

154. Ibid., 398.

155. Ibid.

156. Ibid., 399.

157. Ibid., 400.

158. Ibid., 398.

159. Ibid., 402.

160. Ibn Abd al-Wahhab, "Fatawa wa-Masa'il," 9–11; "Kitab al-Tawhid," 23.

161. The Arabic verb used here is *ighzu*, the command tense of form I of *ghazw* (raid).

162. Ibn Abd al-Wahhab, "Kitab al-Tawhid," 142–43.

163. Ibid., 143.

164. The following discussion is based on the *fatwa* presented as "The Second Case" in Ibn Abd al-Wahhab, "Fatawa wa-Masa'il," 9–11.

165. Ibid., 9–10.

166. Ibid., 11.

167. Muhammad Ibn Abd al-Wahhab, "Kitab Kashf al-Shubhat," in *Mu'allafat al-Shaykh al-Imam Mohammad Ibn Abd al-Wahhab*, Vol. 1 (Riyadh: Jamiat al-Imam Muhammad bin Saud al-Islamiyah, 1398H), 162.

6. FROM REVIVAL AND REFORM TO GLOBAL JIHAD

1. Rudolph Peters, *Jihad in Classical and Modern Islam: A Reader* (Princeton: Markus Wiener, 1996), 150.

2. Ibid., 3–5.

3. This structure is comparable to that of Averroes's chapter on jihad in his legal work *al-Bidaya*. Ibid., 27–42, esp. the outline on p. 29.

4. Reuven Firestone, *Jihad: The Origin of Holy War in Islam* (New York: Oxford University Press, 1999), 99.

5. See, for example, Stephen Schwartz, *The Two Faces of Islam: The House of Sa'ud from Tradition to Terror* (New York: Doubleday, 2002), 133.

6. Ibid., 70–1.

7. Ibid., 62–63.

8. Ibid., 15.

9. Firestone, *Jihad*, 63.

10. Ibid., 54.

11. Muhammad Ibn Abd al-Wahhab, "Kitab al-Tawhid," in *Mu'allafat al-Shaykh al-Imam Muhammad Ibn Abd al-Wahhab*, vol. 1 (Riyadh: Jamiat al-Imam Muhammad bin Saud, al-Islamiyah, 1398H), 143–44.

12. Muhammad Ibn Abd al-Wahhab, "Kitab al-Jihad," in *Mu'allafat al-Shaykh al-*

Imam Muhammad bin Abd al-Wahhab: Al-fiqh, vol 2. (Riyadh: Jamiat al-Imam Mu-hammad bin Saud, al-Islamiyah, 1298H), 359.

13. Firestone, *Jihad*, 63.

14. Ibid., 84.

15. Ibn Abd al-Wahhab, "Kitab al-Jihad," 364–65.

16. Ibid., 365.

17. Ibid., 366–67.

18. Ibid., 402.

19. This citation of only a portion of the verse is typical of his style. Unless he specifically indicates "the verse" when citing a portion of the Quran, the only portion that he intends to consider is that which is specifically stated.

20. Ibn Abd al-Wahhab, "Kitab al-Jihad," 401–2.

21. Ibid., 360.

22. Peters, *Jihad in Classical and Modern Islam*, 121.

23. Although jihad as a purely defensive action is typically associated with Is-lamic modernism, this interpretation is older than the modernist movement, as Ibn Abd al-Wahhab's writings testify. Ibid., 187n. 52.

24. Ibid., 6.

25. Mahmud Shaltut, as translated in ibid., 74.

26. Ibid., 75.

27. Ibid., 62.

28. Ibid., 77.

29. Ibn Abd al-Wahhab, "Kitab al-Tawhid," 21.

30. Ibid., 23.

31. Peters, *Jihad in Classical and Modern Islam*, 93.

32. Ibid., 100. This is in keeping with the classical discussions about appropriate responses by others to the invitation to Islam.

33. Ibid., 64.

34. Ibid., 65.

35. Ibid., 66.

36. Ibid., 69.

37. Ibid., 73.

38. Ibid., 45.

39. See, for example, Samira Haj's article, "Reordering Islamic Orthodoxy: Mu-hammad ibn 'Abdul Wahhab," *The Muslim World* 92 (fall 2002): 333–71, which makes a similar argument about the outcome but distinguishes between the Western liberal tradition of separating reason and religion and the Islamic tradition of reason in-formed by ethics and religion.

40. This discussion occurs in Ibn Abd al-Wahhab, "Kitab al-Jihad," 398–99.

41. Ibid., 402.

42. Ibid., 401–2.

43. Peters, *Jihad in Classical and Modern Islam*, 127.

44. Ibid.

45. Ibid.

46. Ibid., 111.

47. Ibid., 164–65.

48. Ibid., 118.

49. Ibid., 111–15.

50. Ibid., 120.

51. Ibid., 122–23.

52. Ibid., 104.

53. Ibid., 166.

54. Ibid.

55. Ibid., 128.

56. Ibid., 130–31.

57. The Kharijites were members of a seventh-century extremist movement that became notorious for its proclamation of violence against anyone who did not follow its teachings.

58. This assertion is made, for example, in George Snavely Rentz Jr., "Muhammad ibn 'Abd al-Wahhab (1703/4–1792) and the Beginnings of the Unitarian Empire in Arabia," Ph.D. diss., University of California, Berkeley, 1948, esp. 41; and Henri Laoust, "Ibn 'Abd al-Wahhab, Muhammad b," in The Encyclopedia of Islam, ed. B. Lewis, V.C. Menage, Ch. Pellat, and J. Schacht, vol. 3 (Leiden: Brill, 1971). It has also been made by Muslim interpreters of Ibn Abd al-Wahhab's teachings, such as al-Shaikh Muhammad b 'Abd al-Wahhab shaikh Sulaiman b. Abdullah b., Majmu'at al-Tawhid, ed. Rashid Rida, vol. 1 (Cairo: Al-Manar, 1346H/1927), esp. 178. More recent works concerned with this belief and its impact on state formation include Christine Moss Helms, The Cohesion of Saudi Arabia: Evolution of Political Identity (Baltimore: Johns Hopkins University Press, 1981), esp. 82.

59. Ali Bey, Travels of Ali Bey in Morocco, Tripoli, Cyprus, Egypt, Arabia, Syria, and Turkey between the years 1803 and 1807, vols. 1–2 (London: John Murray, 1881), 2:60.

60. Ibid., 62–63.

61. Ibid., 71.

62. Ibid., 133–34; Uthman Ibn Bishr, Unwan al-Majd fi Tarikh Najd, ed. Abd al-Rahman bin Abd al-Latif bin Abd Allah Al al-Shaykh, 2 vols. (Riyadh: Matbu'at Darat al-Malik Abd al-Aziz, 1402H/1982), 1:44.

63. Bey, Travels, 2:69–70.

64. Abd al-Rahman al-Jabarti. Aja'ib al-Athar fi al-Tarajim wa-al-Akhbar, ed. Thomas Philipp and Moshe Perlman, 4 vols. (Stuttgart: Franz Steiner Verlag, 1994), 3–4: 321.

65. The term Wahhabi was offensive to Ibn Abd al-Wahhab's followers because it suggested loyalty and obedience to Ibn Abd al-Wahhab rather than God. Ibn Abd al-Wahhab's followers preferred the terms Muwahhidun (monotheists) and ahl al-tawhid (the people of monotheism).

66. Sir Harford Jones Brydges, An Account of the Transactions of His Majesty's Mission to the Court of Persia, in the Years 180, 7–11, to Which is Appended a Brief History of the Wahauby. (London: J. Bohn, 1834), 2:9.

67. Mouradjea Ignatius d'Ohsson Ignatius, Tableau Général de l'Empire Ottoman, vol. 3 (Paris: Imprimerie de M. Firman Didot, 1790), 3:259.

68. William Ochsenwald, Religion, Society and the State in Arabia: The Hijaz under Ottoman Control, 1840–1908 (Columbus: Ohio University Press, 1984), 131; Louis-Alexandre Corancez. Histoire des Wahabis depuis leur origine jusqu'à la fin de 1809. (Paris: Imprimerie de Crapelet, 1810), 57.

69. Charles Didier, Sojourn with the Grand Sharif of Makkah (New York: Olean-

der Press, 1985), 89; John Lewis Burckhardt. *Travels in Arabia Comprehending an Account of Those Territories in Hedjaz Which the Mohammedans Regard as Sacred* (London: Henry Colburn, 1829; reprint London: Frank Cass, 1968), 46–47, 219–20, and 233.

70. al-Jabarti, *Aja'ib al-Athar*, 3:445, and 4:6; Corancez, *Histoire*, 59; Burckhardt, *Travels*, 143–44, 159, 172–73, 188, 233–34.

71. al-Jabarti, *Aja'ib al-Athar*, 4:5–6, John Lewis Burckhardt, *Notes on the Bedouins and Wahabys Collected during His Travels in the East by the Late John Lewis Burckhardt*, 2 vols. (London: Henry Colburn and Richard Bentley, 1831), 1:110–11.

72. Al-Jabarti, *Aja'ib al-Athar*, 3: 391, 529, 4:6; Burckhardt, *Notes*, 114–15; Corancez, *Histoire*, 4; Jeanne Broucke, *L'Empire Arabe d'Ibn Seoud*. (Bruxelles: Librairie Falk Fils, 1929), 11.

73. For a discussion of classical teachings on this topic, see John L. Esposito with Natana J. DeLong-Bas, "Classical Islam," in *God's Rule: The Politics of World Religions*, ed. Jacob Neusner (Washington, DC: Georgetown University Press, 2003.

74. Commins has found that the conscious citation of Ibn Abd al-Wahhab and Ibn Taymiyya is prevalent in the writings of early-nineteenth-century Wahhabi *ulama*. Ibn Abd al-Wahhab's own writings assert neither his personal authority nor that of Ibn Taymiyya.

75. See Esposito with DeLong-Bas, "Classical Islam."

76. Peters, *Jihad in Classical and Modern Islam*, 7–8.

77. John L. Esposito. *Unholy War: Terror in the Name of Islam*. New York: Oxford University Press, 2002, 41–43.

78. George Makdisi, citing Goldziher, in "Hanbalite Islam," in *Studies on Islam*, trans and ed Merlin L. Swartz (New York: Oxford University Press, 1981), 253.

79. Ibid., 223.

80. Ibid., 256.

81. Ibid., 263; Makdisi, "Ibn Taimiya: A Sufi of the Qadiriya Order," *American Journal of Arabic Studies* 1 (1974): 119. For a detailed and comprehensive study of Ibn Taymiyya's thought and a refutation of the generally negative characterization of him, see Henri Laoust, *Essai sur les doctrines sociales et politiques de Taki-d-Din Ahmad b. Taimiya* (Cairo: Institut Français d'Archéologie Orientale, 1939).

82. George Makdisi, "The Hanbali School and Sufism," in *Humaniora Islamica*, vol. 2 (The Hague and Paris: Mouton, 1974), 62, Makdisi, "Hanbalite Islam," 226–27.

83. Peters, *Jihad in Classical and Modern Islam*, 7–8.

84. Quoted in ibid, 49.

85. Ibid., 43.

86. Ibid., 49.

87. Ibid.

88. Ibid., viii.

89. Ibid., 50.

90. Ibid., 44.

91. See, for example, Ibn Abd al-Wahhab, "Kitab al-Tawhid," 124, which commands shunning ignorant, evil blasphemers and threatening or menacing people guilty of blasphemy yet never mentions any physical violence to be taken against them.

92. Ibid., 74–75.

93. Ibid., 72–73.

94. Ibid., 73. Both genders are specified in the text.

95. Ibid., 78, 84.

96. Ibid., 58.

97. Ibid., 138–39.

98. See Peters, *Jihad in Classical and Modern Islam*, 50–51.

99. Quoted in ibid., 52. I have added italics to emphasize Ibn Taymiyya's call for offensive action.

100. Ibn Abd al-Wahhab, "Kitab al-Tawhid," 28.

101. Ibid., 31.

102. Ibid., 36.

103. Ibid., 33–34.

104. Quoted in Peters, *Jihad in Classical and Modern Islam*, 48.

105. Firestone, *Jihad*, 100.

106. Ibid., 80.

107. Ibn Abd al-Wahhab, "Kitab al-Tawhid," esp. 12–17.

108. Ibid., 47, 49.

109. Haj has suggested that Ibn Abd al-Wahhab's selective use of Ibn Taymiyya's writings reflects a Muslim literary and religious style rather than direct imitation. Haj, "Reordering Islamic Orthodoxy," 340–42.

110. Sayyid Qutb, *Milestones* (Karachi: International Islamic Publishers, 1988), 49–50.

111. Ibid., 67–70.

112. Ibid., 70.

113. Ibid., 114.

114. Ibid., 115–16.

115. Ibid., 122.

116. Ibid., 118–19.

117. Ibid., 142.

118. Ibid., 111.

119. Ibid., 112, 114.

120. Ibid., 113.

121. Ibid., 119.

122. Ibid.

123. Ibid., 80.

124. See ibid., 64–94, for the discussion of Quranic Revolution.

125. Ibid., 86.

126. Ibid., 172.

127. Ibid., 199–200; Paul Berman, "The Philosopher of Islamic Terror," *New York Times Magazine*, 23 March 2003, 3.

128. Qutb, *Milestones*, 200–201; Berman, "Philosopher," 3–4.

129. Qutb, *Milestones*, 140.

130. Ibid., 141.

131. Ibid., 120.

132. Ibid., 136–37.

133. Ibid., 124–25.

134. Ibid., 131–33.

135. Ibid., 124 and 131–33. These categorizations are taken from Firestone, *Jihad*,

following the comparative analysis earlier in this chapter between Ibn Abd al-Wahhab and other scholars.

136. Ibid., 123–24.

137. Ibid., 126.

138. Ibid., 144.

139. Ibid., 130.

140. Ibid., 127–28, 9.

141. Ibid., 131–32.

142. Ibid., 124, 133–34.

143. Ibid., 132–33.

144. Ibid., 135.

145. Ibid., 125–26.

146. Ibid., 137.

147. Ibid., 138.

148. Ibid., 122.

149. Ibid., 139.

150. Ahmed Rashid, *Taliban: Militant Islam, Oil, and Fundamentalism in Central Asia* (London: I. B. Tauris, 2000), 130.

151. Cited in Mamoun Fandy, *Saudi Arabia and the Politics of Dissent* (New York: Palgrave, 1999), 180.

152. Interview with bin Laden cited in Rashid, *Taliban*, 132.

153. Interview with Osama bin Laden, *Al Huquq*, no. 124, 14 May 1997, 3.

154. Fandy, *Saudi Arabia*, 191.

155. Rashid, *Taliban*, 131.

156. Fandy, *Saudi Arabia*, 183.

157. Ibid., 181–82.

158. Ibid., 181. Fandy has claimed that bin Laden believes himself to be the legitimate heir of Ibn Abd al-Wahhab. I have not found evidence to support this claim, as bin Laden cites Ibn Taymiyya and Ibn al-Qayyim al-Jawziyya more frequently in the interviews and statements that I have read.

159. Ibid., 182.

160. Ibid., 193.

161. Advice and Reform Committee, "Open Letter to King Fahd," communiqué 17, 3 August 1995.

162. The letter mentions two of the most prominent by name—Safar al-Hawali and Salman al-Auda.

163. Fandy, *Saudi Arabia*, 187.

164. Advice and Reform Committee, "Open Letter."

165. Fandy, *Saudi Arabia*, 187.

166. Ibid., 182–83.

167. Cited in Rashid, *Taliban*, 133.

168. CNN interview with Osama bin Laden, 7 April 1997.

169. Fandy, *Saudi Arabia*, 189.

170. Ibid., 189–90.

171. Ibid., 191.

172. Osama bin Laden, "I'lan al-Jihad 'ala al-Amrikiyyin al-Muhtalin li-Bilad al-

Haramayn" (Declaration of Jihad against the Americans Who Occupy the Land of the Two Holy Mosques), Afghanistan, 23 August 1996.

173. Fandy, *Saudi Arabia*, 188.

174. Berman, "Philosopher," 2.

175. Fandy, *Saudi Arabia*, 192.

176. Interview with *Al-Huquq*, 1997, cited in ibid., 177.

177. Schwartz, in *Two Faces*, for example, has posited that Sufism and Wahhabism are at the opposite ends of the spectrum, explaining their purportedly different worldviews: "On one side, there was the bright aspect of Sufi traditionalism, ever renewed, happy, filled with love of God and humanity, seeking to embrace believers in the other monotheistic faiths, always committed to the defense of human dignity. On the other was the ugly visage of Wahhabi fundamentalism, narrow, rigid, tyrannical, separatist, supremactist, and violent" (163). Ibid., 163.

178. Cited in Fandy, *Saudi Arabia*, 192.

179. Cited in ibid.

180. Osama bin Laden, fax to the al-Jazeera television news network, Qatar, 24 September 2001, reprinted in *Boston Globe*, 25 September 2001.

181. Ibid.

182. Bin Laden, "I'lan al-Jihad."

183. Ibid.

184. Osama bin Laden, published interview with Robert Fisk, 1996.

185. Ibid.

186. Cited in Rashid, *Taliban*, 135.

187. Osama bin Laden, remarks aired on the al-Jazeerah television network, 7 October 2001, reprinted in the *Boston Globe*, 8 October 2001.

188. Ibid.

Glossary

Ahl al-Kitab   People of the Book
abaya   Islamic dress that covers a woman from head to toe
adab   pre-Islamic literature
'adil   justice
'alim, pl. *ulama*   Muslim scholar
amir   political leader
ashraf,   sing. *sharif* one who claims direct descent from the Prophet Mu-
     hammad
barakah   blessing or capacity to perform miracles. Believed to be possessed
     by Sufi saints.
Bayt al-Mal   treasury
bid'a   innovation
bikr   virgin
burqa'   Islamic dress that covers a woman from head to toe
dar al-harb   land of war
dar al-Islam   land of Islam
dar al-kufr   land of unbelief
dar al-Jahiliyya   land of ignorance
daruriyyat   necessities
da'wah   missionary work, proselytizing
dhikr   remembrance of God. Also used to refer to special devotional prac-
     tices of Sufi orders
dhimmi, Ahl al-dhimmah   person eligible for protective treaty relationship
     via payment of the poll tax. Generally understood to include Jews,
     Christians and Zoroastrians.
fai   wealth surrendered by non-Muslims without engaging in armed con-
     flict
fard 'ayn   individual duty

fard kifayah   collective duty

fasid   an imperfect marriage

fatwa, pl. *fatawa*   juridical opinion

fiqh   Islamic jurisprudence

fitnah   chaos

ghanimah   spoils of war

ghazw   tribal raid

hadith   written accounts of the sayings and deeds of Islam's prophet, Muhammad

hajiyyat   needs

Hajj   Muslim pilgrimage to Mecca. One of the five pillars of Islam.

hakim   judge

halal   legal, permissible

haram   forbidden

hijra   migration

hilf al-talaq   oath of divorce

hudud   crimes punishable by death. These include theft, consumption of alcohol, false witness, and *zina'*.

ibadat   relationship between human beings and God

iddah   waiting period observed by the woman at the end of a marriage

idhn   consent

ightisab   rape

ijma'   legal consensus

ijtihad   independent reasoning in the interpretation of Islamic law

ikhtilaf   genre of literature in which a variety of scholars and interpretations of an issue are cited

imam   religious leader. In the Shii tradition, this title was given to Muhammad's direct male descendants, who were believed to have been infallible interpreters of the Quran and to have had hidden knowledge of it.

iman   faith

irtidad   apostasy

isnad   chain of transmitters of a *hadith*

istishabb   commendable

jahil, jahiliyyah   ignorance

jihad   literally, "struggle," but often used to refer to holy war in defense of Islam and Muslims

jinn   demon or devil

jizyah   poll tax. Payment allows People of the Book to enter into a protective treaty relationship with Muslims.

kaba'ir   major sins

kafir, pl. *kuffar*   unbeliever

khamr   date wine

kharaj   land tax

khul'   divorce initiated by the wife in which she offers the man compensation in exchange for ending the marriage

khuwwa   protection, or "brotherhood," money

kufr   unbelief

li'an   accusation of infidelity

madhhab, pl. *madhahib*   school of Islamic law

madrasa   Islamic school

Mahdi   messianic figure expected to come at the end of time to institute an Islamic society of peace and justice

mahr   dower

manaqib   hagiographical biographies

maslahah   public interest or welfare

muamalat   interpersonal human interactions

mufti   person issuing a *fatwa* (legal opinion)

muhaddith   person who transmits a hadith

muhajir, pl. *muhajirun*   person who emigrates

mujahid, pl. *mujahidun*   one who carries out jihad

mujtahid   one who carries out *ijtihad* (independent interpretation of Islamic law)

munafiq   hypocrites

mushrik, pl. *mushrikun*   person who commits *shirk* (associationism)

mut'ah   temporary marriage

nafaqah   maintenance

naskh   abrogation

nikah   marriage

nushrah   the casting and breaking of magic spells

nushuz   disobedient

People of the Book   people who possess a divinely revealed scripture. Typically understood to include Jews, Christians, and Zoroastrians.

qadi   judge

qital   fighting

qiyas   analogy

Quran   Islam's scripture or holy book, which Muslims believe was divinely revealed to the Prophet Muhammad

Rafidah   extremist Shii sect generally believed to have been heretical

Ramadan   month of the Islamic calendar during which Muslims fast from sunrise to sunset. One of the five pillars of Islam.

ruqyah   spiritual powers

sahh, sahih   valid, true

Salihin   righteous ancestors

shahadah   Muslim declaration of belief in the One God and in Muhammad's prophethood. One of the five pillars of Islam.

Sharia   Islamic law

Shaykh   leader

Shii   person believing that leadership of the Muslim community should be hereditary. About 10% of the world's Muslim population is Shii.

shirk   associationism

Sufi   Muslim mystic

Sunna   Muhammad's example

Sunni   person who believes that leadership of the Muslim community should belong to the person most qualified to carry it out. About 90% of the world's Muslim population is Sunni.

tafsir   Quranic exegesis

taghut   idolatry

tahsinat   improvements

talaq   divorce by a man via repudiation of his wife

tamlik   a husband granting his wife the option of requesting a divorce should he marry additional wives or take a concubine

taqlid   imitation of past interpretations of Islamic law

tawakkul   trust in God

tawhid   absolute monotheism

thobe   robe

ulama, sing. *'alim*   Muslim scholars

ummah   transnational Muslim community

ushr   the one-tenth tax

wakil, pl. *wukala'*   representative

wali, pl. *awliya'*   marriage guardian. Also means "friend of God." Often used by Sufis to describe holy people.

waqf, pl. *awqaf*   charitable endowment

zakat   almsgiving, tithe. One of the five pillars of Islam.

zihar   husband's comparison of his wife to his female relatives, constituting repudiation of his wife

zina'   illicit sexual intercourse, either fornication or adultery

Bibliography

PRIMARY SOURCES

Works by Muhammad Ibn Abd al-Wahhab

"Fatawa wa-Masa'il al-Imam al-Shaykh Muhammad Ibn Abd al-Wahhab."
   In *Mu'allafat al-Shaykh al-Imam Muhammad Ibn Abd al-Wahhab*.
   Vol. 3. Riyadh: Jamiat al-Imam Muhammad bin Saud al-Islamiyah,
   1398H.

Fi Aqa'id al-Islam min Rasa'il al-Shaykh Muhammad Ibn Abd al-Wahhab.
   Edited by Muhammad Rashid Ridda. Beirut: Dar al-Afaq al-Jadidah,
   1983.

"Kitab al-Jihad." In *Mu'allafat al-Shaykh al-Imam Muhammad bin Abd al-
   Wahhab: al-Fiqh*. Vol. 2. Riyadh: Jamiat al-Imam Muhammad bin Saud
   al-Islamiyah, 1298H.

"Kitab al-Kaba'ir." In *Mu'allafat al-Shaykh al-Imam Muhammad Ibn Abd al-
   Wahhab*. Vol. 1. Riyadh: Jamiat al-Imam Muhammad bin Saud al-
   Islamiyah, 1398H.

"Kitab al-Nikah." In *Mu'allafat al-Shaykh al-Imam Muhammad bin Abd al-
   Wahhab: al-Fiqh*. Vol. 2. Riyadh: Jamiat al-Imam Muhammad bin Saud
   al-Islamiyah, 1398H.

"Kitab al-Qawaid al-Arba.'" In *Mu'allafat al-Shaykh al-Imam Muhammad
   Ibn Abd al-Wahhab*. Vol. 1. Riyadh: Jamiat al-Imam Muhammad bin
   Saud al-Islamiyah, 1398H.

"Kitab al-Tawhid." In *Mu'allafat al-Shaykh al-Imam Muhammad Ibn Abd al-
   Wahhab*. Vol. 1. Riyadh: Jamiat al-Imam Muhammad bin Saud al-
   Islamiyah, 1398H.

Kitab al-Tawhid. Translated by Ismail al-Faruqi. Kuwait: al-Faisal Printing
   Co., 1986.

"Kitab Fadl al-Islam." In *Mu'allafat al-Shaykh al-Imam Muhammad Ibn Abd al-Wahhab. Vol. 1. Riyadh: Jamiat al-Imam Muhammad bin Saud al-Islamiyah, 1398H.

"Kitab Kashf al-Shubhat." In *Mu'allafat al-Shaykh al-Imam Muhammad Ibn Abd al-Wahhab*. Vol. 1. Riyadh: Jamiat al-Imam Muhammad bin Saud al-Islamiyah, 1398H.

"Kitab Mufid al-Mustafid fi Kufr Tarik al-Tawhid." In *Mu'allafat al-Shaykh al-Imam Muhammad Ibn Abd al-Wahhab*. Vol. 1. Riyadh: Jamiat al-Imam Muhammad bin Saud al-Islamiyah, 1398H.

"Kitab Thalathat al-Usul." In *Mu'allafat al-Shaykh al-Imam Muhammad Ibn Abd al-Wahhab*. Vol. 1. Riyadh: Jamiat al-Imam Muhammad bin Saud al-Islamiyah, 1398H.

"Kitab Usul al-Iman." In *Mu'allafat al-Shaykh al-Imam Muhammad Ibn Abd al-Wahhab*. Vol. 1. Riyadh: Jamiat al-Imam Muhammad bin Saud al-Islamiyah, 1398H.

Majmu'at al-Fatawa wa-al-Rasa'il wa-al-Ajwibah (Khamsun Risalah fi al-Tawhid). Edited by Abd Allah al-Sayyid Ahmad al-Hajjaj. Cairo: Dar al-Wahi, 1979.

Majmu'at al-Tawhid al-Najdiyah. Cairo: Matba'at al-Manar, 1345H/1926.

"Majmu'at Rasa'il fi al-Tawhid wa-al-Iman." In *Mu'allafat al-Shaykh al-Imam Muhammad Ibn Abd al-Wahhab*. Vol. 1. Riyadh: Jamiat al-Imam Muhammad bin Saud al-Islamiyah, 1398H.

Mu'allafat al-Shaykh al-Imam Muhammad Ibn Abd al-Wahhab. 5 vols. Riyadh: Jamiat al-Imam Muhammad bin Saud al-Islamiyh, 1398H.

Muamalat al-Shaykh al-Imam Muhammad Ibn Abd al-Wahhab: Mulhaq al-Musnifat. Riyadh: Jamiat al-Imam Muhammad bin Saud al-Islamiyah, 1398H.

Muamalat al-Shaykh al-Imam Muhammad Ibn Abd al-Wahhab: Qism al-Hadith. 4 vols. Riyadh: Jamiat al-Imam Muhammad bin Saud al-Islamiyah, 1398H.

"Mukhtasar al-Ansaf wa-al-Sharh al-Kabir." In *Mu'allafat al-Shaykh al-Imam Muhammad Ibn Abd al-Wahhab: al-Fiqh*. Vol. 1. Riyadh: Jamiat al-Imam Muhammad bin Saud al-Islamiyah, 1398H.

"Mukhtasar Sirat al-Rasul." In *Mu'allafat al-Shaykh al-Imam Muhammad Ibn Abd al-Wahhab*. Vol. 3. Riyadh: Jamiat al-Imam Muhammad bin Saud al-Islamiyah, 1398H.

"Mukhtasar Tafsir Surat al-Anfal." In *Mu'allafat al-Shaykh al-Imam Muhammad Ibn Abd al-Wahhab*, vol. 4. Riyadh: Jamiat al-Imam Muhammad bin Saud al-Islamiyah, 1398H.

"Risalah fi al-Radd ala al-Rafidah." In *Mu'allafat al-Shaykh al-Imam Muhammad Ibn Abd al-Wahhab*, vol. 4. Riyadh: Jamiat al-Imam Muhammad bin Saud al-Islamiyah, 1398H.

Three Essays on Tawhid. Translated by Ismail Raji al-Faruqi. Teaneck, NJ: Islamic Publications International, 1979.

Other Contemporary Arabic Accounts

Anonymous. *Lam al-Shihab fi-Tarikh Muhammad bin Abd al-Wahhab*. Edited by Ahmad Abu Hakima. Beirut: n.p., 1967.

Dahlan, al-Sayyid Ahmad bin Zayni. *al-Durar al-Saniyah fi al-Radd ala al-Wahhabiyah*. Cairo: Dar Jawami al-Kalam, 1980.

————. *Khilasat al-Kalam fi Bayan Ahra al-Balad al-Haram*. Cairo: Maktabat al-Kulliyat al-Azhariyah, 1977.

al-Hazimi, Muhammad bin Nasr. *Min Turath Shibuhi Jazirat al-Arab: Munazzimah Bayna 'Ulama Makkah wa-'Ulama Najd*. al-Qahirah: Maktabat Madbuli, 1997.

Ibn Abd al-Wahhab, Sulayman ibn Abd Allah ibn Muhammad. *Taysir al-Aziz al-Hamid fi Sharh Kitab al-Tawhid*. Beirut: al-Maktab al-Islami, 1402H/1983.

Ibn Bishr, Uthman. *Unwan al-Majd fi Tarikh Najd*. Edited by Abd al-Rahman bin Abd al-Latif bin Abd Allah Al al-Shaykh. 2 vols. Riyadh: Matbu'at Darat al-Malik Abd al-Aziz, 1402H/1982.

Ibn Ghannam, Husayn. *Tarikh Najd*. 4th ed. 2 vols. Beirut: Dar al-Shuruq, 1994.

al-Jabarti, Abd al-Rahman. *Aja'ib al-Athar fi al-Tarajim wa-al-Akhbar*. 4 vols. Edited by Thomas Philipp and Moshe Perlmann. Stuttgart: Franz Steiner Verlag, 1994.

————. *Abd al-Rahman al-Jabarti's History of Egypt*. 4 vols. Edited by Thomas Philipp and Moshe Perlmann. Stuttgart: Franz Steiner Verlag, 1994.

al-Tamimi, Hamd bin 'Uthman bin Mu'ammar al-Nadjdi. *al-Hadiyyah al-Sunniyah wa-al-Tuhfah al-Wahhabiyah al-Najdiyah*. Collected by Sulayman bin Sahman and edited by Muhammad Rashid Ridda. 2d imprint. Cairo: Matba'at al-Manar, 1344H/1925–26.

SECONDARY SOURCES

Abdal-Rehim, Abdal-Rehim Abdal-Rahman. "The Family and Gender Laws in Egypt during the Ottoman Period." In *Women, the Family, and Divorce Laws in Islamic History*, ed. Amira El Azhary Sonbol. Syracuse: Syracuse University Press, 1996.

Abou El Fadl, Khaled. *The Place of Tolerance in Islam*. Boston: Beacon Press, 2002.

Advice and Reform Committee. "Open Letter to King Fahd." Communiqué 17. 3 August 1995.

Afifi, Mohamed. *al-Awqaf wa-al-Hayat al-Iqtisadiyyah fi Misr fi al-'Asr al-'Uthmani*. Cairo: al-Hay'ah al-Misriyyah al-'Ammah li-al-Kitab, 1991.

Ahmed, Leila. *Women and Gender in Islam: Historical Roots of a Modern Debate*. New Haven: Yale University Press, 1992.

Ahmed, Mustafa Abdul-Basit. "Impact of the Historical Settings of Ibn Taymiyah on His Program of Reform." Ph.D. diss., Ohio State University, 1997.

Algar, Hamid. *Wahhabism: A Critical Essay*. Oneonta, NY: Islamic Publications International, 2002.

Ali, Abdullah Yusuf. *The Holy Qur'an: Text, Translation, and Commentary*. Bentwood, MD: Amana, 1989.

Arebi, Saddeka. *Women and Words in Saudi Arabia: The Politics of Literary Discourse*. New York: Columbia University Press, 1994.

Atkin, Muriel. "The Rhetoric of Islamophobia." *Central Asia and the Caucasus: Journal of Social and Political Studies* 1, no. 1 (2000): 123–32.

Aziz, Philippe. Interview, *Le Point*. 17 August 1996.

Bari, M. A. "A Comparative Study of the Early Wahhabi Doctrines and Contemporary Reform Movements in Indian Islam." Ph.D. diss., Oxford University, 1953.

Berman, Paul. "The Philosopher of Islamic Terror." *New York Times Magazine*, 23 March 2003.

Bey, Ali. *Travels of Ali Bey in Morocco, Tripoli, Cyprus, Egypt, Arabia, Syria, and Turkey between the Years 1803 and 1807.* Vols. 1–2. London: John Murray, 1881.

Bin Laden, Osama. Fax to the al-Jazeera television news network. Qatar. 24 September 2001. Reprinted in the *Boston Globe,* 25 September, 2001.

———. "I'lan al-Jihad 'ala al-Amrikiyyin al-Muhtalin li-Bilad al-Haramayn" (Declaration of Jihad against the Americans Who Occupy the Land of the Two Holy Mosques). Afghanistan. 23 August 1996.

———. Interview. *Al Huquq,* no. 124, 14 May 1997.

———. Interview. CNN television news network, 7 April 1997.

———. Published interview with Robert Fisk. 1996.

———. Remarks aired on the al-Jazeera television news network. 7 October 2001. Reprinted in the *Boston Globe,* 8 October 2001.

Blunt, Lady Anne. *A Pilgrimage to Nejd, the Cradle of the Arab Race: A Visit to the Court of the Arab Emir and "Our Persian Campaign."* 2 vols. London: John Murray, 1881; reprint London: Frank Cass, 1968.

Broucke, Jeanne. *L'Empire Arabe d'Ibn Seoud.* Bruxelles: Librairie Falk Fils, 1929.

Brydges, Sir Harford Jones. *An Account of the Transactions of His Majesty's Mission to the Court of Persia in the Years 1807–11, to Which Is Appended, a Brief History of the Wahauby.* 2 vols. London: J. Bohn, 1834.

Buhuth Usbu al-Shaykh Muhammad bin Abd al-Wahhab: Rahmahu Allah. 2 vols. Riyadh: Jamiat al-Imam Muhammad bin Saud al-Islamiyah, 1403H/1983.

Burckhardt, John Lewis. *Notes on the Bedouins and Wahabys Collected during His Travels in the East by the Late John Lewis Burckhardt.* 2 vols. London: Henry Colburn and Richard Bentley, 1831.

———. *Travels in Arabia Comprehending an Account of Those Territories in Hedjaz Which the Mohammedans Regard as Sacred.* London: Henry Colburn, 1829; reprint London: Frank Cass, 1968.

Burke, Edmund, III. "Islam and Social Movements: Methodological Reflections." In *Islam, Politics, and Social Movements,* ed. Edmund Burke III and Ira M. Lapidus. Berkeley: University of California Press, 1988

Burke, Edmund, III, and Ira M. Lapidus, eds. *Islam, Politics, and Social Movements.* Berkeley: University of California Press, 1988.

Burke, Jason. *Al-Qaida: In the Shadow of Terror.* London: I. B. Tauris, 2003.

Calder, Norman. "Law: Legal Thought and Jurisprudence." In *The Oxford Encyclopedia of the Modern Islamic World,* ed. John L. Esposito. Vol. 2. New York: Oxford University Press, 1995.

Commins, David. " 'Wahhabi' Doctrine in an Age of Political Expediency." Unpublished paper presented at the 36th Annual Meeting of the Middle East Studies Association, Washington, DC, 25 November 2002.

Cook, Michael. "The Expansion of the First Saudi State: The Case of Washm." In *The Islamic World from Classical to Modern Times: Essays in Honor of Bernard Lewis,* ed. C. E. Bosworth, Charles Issawi, Roger Savory, and A. L. Udovitch. Princeton : Darwin Press, 1989.

Corancez, Louis-Alexandre. *Histoire des Wahabis depuis leur origine jusqu'à la fin de 1809.* Paris: Imprimerie de Crapelet, 1810.

Coulson, N. J. *A History of Islamic Law.* Edinburgh: Edinburgh University Press, 1964.

Crichton, Andrew. *The History of Arabia: Ancient and Modern*. Vol. 1. New York: Harper & Brothers, 1834.

Didier, Charles. *Sojourn with the Grand Sharif of Makkah*. New York: Oleander Press, 1985.

Doumato, Eleanor Abdella. *Getting God's Ear: Women, Islam, and Healing in Saudi Arabia and the Gulf*. New York: Columbia University Press, 2000.

Duri, A. A. *The Rise of Historical Writing among the Arabs*. Edited and translated by Lawrence I. Conrad. Princeton: Princeton University Press, 1983.

Esposito, John L. *Islam and Politics*. 4th ed. Syracuse: Syracuse University Press, 1998.

———. *Islam: The Straight Path*. 4th ed. New York: Oxford University Press, 1998.

———. *Unholy War: Terror in the Name of Islam*. New York: Oxford University Press, 2002.

Esposito, John L., editor in chief. *The Oxford Encyclopedia of the Modern Islamic World*. 4 vols. New York: Oxford University Press, 1995.

Esposito, John L., ed. *The Oxford History of Islam*. New York: Oxford University Press, 1999+.

Esposito, John L., and François Burgat, eds. *Modernizing Islam Religion in the Public Sphere in the Middle East and Europe*. London: Hurst, 2003.

Esposito, John L., with Natana J. DeLong-Bas. "Classical Islam." In *God's Rule: The Politics of World Religions*, ed. Jacob Neusner. Washington, DC: Georgetown University Press, 2003.

———. "Modern Islam." In *God's Rule: The Politics of World Religions*, ed. Jacob Neusner. Washington, DC: Georgetown University Press, 2003.

———. *Women in Muslim Family Law*. 2d ed. Syracuse: Syracuse University Press, 2001.

Fandy, Mamoun. *Saudi Arabia and the Politics of Dissent*. New York: Palgrave, 1999.

Faroqhi, Suraiya. *Pilgrims and Sultans: The Hajj under the Ottomans, 1517–1683*. London: I. B. Tauris, 1994.

Fattah, Hala. *The Politics of Regional Trade in Iraq, Arabia, and the Gulf, 1745–1900*. Syracuse: State University of New York Press, 1997.

Fay, Mary Ann. "Women and *Waqf*: Property, Power, and the Domain of Gender in Eighteenth-Century Egypt." In *Women in the Ottoman Empire: Middle Eastern Women in the Early Modern Era*, ed. Madeline C. Zilfi. Leiden: Brill, 1997.

Finati, Giovanni. *Narrative of the Life and Adventures of Giovanni Finati, Native of Ferrara*. Translated and edited by William John Bankes. 2 vols. London: John Murray, 1830.

Firestone, Reuven. *Jihad: The Origin of Holy War in Islam*. New York: Oxford University Press, 1999.

al-Freih, Mohamed A. "The Historical Background of the Emergence of Muhammad Ibn Abd al-Wahhab and His Movement." Ph.D. diss., University of California at Los Angeles, 1990.

Goldziher, Ignaz. *An Introduction to Islamic Law and Theology*. Translated by Andras Hamori and Ruth Hamori. Princeton: Princeton University Press, 1981.

———. *Muslim Studies (Muhammedanische Studien)*. Edited by S. M. Stern and translated by C. R. Barber and S. M. Stern. Vol. 2. Chicago: Aldine, 1973.

Graham, William A. *Divine Word and Prophetic Word in Early Islam: A Reconsideration of the Sources, with Special Reference to the Divine Saying, or, Hadith Qudsi.* The Hague and Paris: Mouton, 1977.

Guillaume, A. *The Life of Muhammad: A Translation of Ibn Ishaq's Sirat Rasul Allah.* New York: Oxford University Press, 1997.

Habib, John S. *Ibn Sa'ud's Warriors of Islam: The Ikhwan of Najd and Their Role in the Creation of the Sa'udi Kingdom, 1910–1930.* Leiden: Brill, 1978.

Haddad, Yvonne Yazbeck. "Islam and Gender: Dilemmas in the Changing Arab World." In *Islam, Gender, and Social Change,* ed. Yvonne Yazbeck Haddad and John L. Esposito. New York: Oxford University Press, 1998.

Haddad, Yvonne Yazbeck, and John L. Esposito, eds. *Islam, Gender, and Social Change.* New York: Oxford University Press, 1998.

Haj, Samira. "Reordering Islamic Orthodoxy: Muhammad ibn 'Abdul Wahhab." *The Muslim World* 92, (Fall 2002): 333–71.

Hallaq, Wael. *A History of Islamic Legal Theories: An Introduction to Sunni Usul al-Fiqh.* Cambridge: Cambridge University Press, 1997.

———. "On the Origins of the Controversy about the Existence of Mujtahids and the Gate of Ijtihad." *Studia Islamica* 63 (1986): 129–41.

———. "Was the Gate of Ijtihad Closed?" *International Journal of Middle East Studies* 16 (1984): 3–41.

Hanna, Nelly. "Marriage among Merchant Families in Seventeenth-Century Cairo." In *Women, the Family, and Divorce Laws in Islamic History,* ed. Amira El Azhary Sonbol. Syracuse: Syracuse University Press, 1996.

Helms, Christine Moss. *The Cohesion of Saudi Arabia: Evolution of Political Identity.* Baltimore: Johns Hopkins University Press, 1981.

Hijab, Nadia. "Islam, Social Change, and the Reality of Arab Women's Lives." In *Islam, Gender, and Social Change,* ed. Yvonne Yazbeck Haddad and John L. Esposito. New York: Oxford University Press, 1998.

———. *Womanpower: The Arab Debate on Women at Work.* Cambridge: Cambridge University Press, 1988.

Hodgson, Marshall G. S. *The Venture of Islam: Conscience and History in a World Civilization.* 3 vols. Chicago: University of Chicago Press, 1974.

Hogarth, David George. *The Penetration of Arabia: A Record of the Development of Western Knowledge Concerning the Arabian Peninsula.* London: Lawrence and Bullet, 1904.

Hopwood, Derek. *The Arabian Peninsula: Society and Politics.* Tonowa, NJ: Rowman & Littlefield, 1972.

Huntingdon, Samuel P. "A Clash of Civilizations?" *Foreign Affairs* (Summer 1993), 22–39.

Imber, Colin. *Ebu's-su'ud: The Islamic Legal Tradition.* Stanford: Stanford University Press, 1997.

———. "Women, Marriage, and Property: *Mehr* in the *Behcetu'l-Fetava* of Yenisehirli Abdullah." In *Women in the Ottoman Empire: Middle Eastern Women in the Early Modern Era,* ed. Madeline C. Zilfi. Leiden: Brill, 1997.

Ivanova, Svetlana. "The Divorce between Zubaida Hatun and Esseid Osma Aga: Women in the Eighteenth Century Shari'a Court of Rumelia." In *Women, the Family, and Divorce Laws in Islamic History,* ed. Amira El Azhary Sonbol. Syracuse: Syracuse University Press, 1996.

Jennings, C. Ronald. "Women in the Early Seventeenth Century Ottoman Judicial Records: The Sharia Court of Anatolian Kayseri." *Journal of the Economic and Social History of the Orient* 23 (1983): 53–114.

Johansen, Baber. "Legal Literature and the Problem of Change: The Case of Land Rent." In *Islam and Public Law*, ed. Chibli Mallat. London: Graham & Trotman, 1993.

———. *The Islamic Law on Land Tax and Rent*. New York: Croom Helm, 1988.

Juhany, Uwaidah Metaireek. "The History of Najd Prior to the Wahhabis: A Study of Social, Political, and Religous Conditions in Najd during Three Centuries Preceding the Wahhabi Movement." Ph.D. diss., University of Washington, 1983.

Kamali, Mohammad Hashim. "Law and Society: The Interplay of Revelation and Reason in the Shariah." In *The Oxford History of Islam*, ed. John L. Esposito. New York: Oxford University Press, 1999.

Kandiyoti, Deniz, ed. *Gendering the Middle East: Emerging Perspectives*. London: I. B. Tauris, 1996.

Kechichian, Joseph A. "The Role of the Ulama in the Politics of an Islamic State: The Case of Saudi Arabia," *Middle East Studies* 18 (1986): 52–71.

Keppel, Gilles. *Jihad: The Trail of Political Islam*. London: I. B. Tauris, 2002.

Khalidi, Tarif. *Arabic Historical Thought in the Classical Period*. Cambridge: Cambridge University Press, 1994.

Khan, Zafarul-Islam. *Hijrah in Islam*. London: Muslim Institute, 1997.

Khouri, Dina Rizk. "Drawing Boundaries and Defining Spaces: Women and Space in Ottoman Iraq." In *Women, the Family, and Divorce Laws in Islamic History*, ed. Amira El Azhary Sonbol. Syracuse: Syracuse University Press, 1996.

Laoust, Henri. *Essai sur les doctrines sociales et politiques de Taki-d-Din Ahmad b. Taimiya*. Cairo: Institut Francais d'Archéologie Orientale, 1939.

———. "Ibn 'Abd al-Wahhab, Muhammad b." In *The Encyclopaedia of Islam*, ed. B. Lewis, V. L. Menage, Ch. Pellat, and J. Schacht. New ed. Vol. 3. Leiden: Brill, 1971.

———. *Les Schismes dans l'Islam: Introduction à une étude de la religion musulmane*. Paris: Payot, 1965.

Lapidus, Ira M. *A History of Islamic Societies*. Cambridge: Cambridge University Press, 1988.

———. "Islamic Political Movements: Patterns of Historical Change." In *Islam, Politics, and Social Movements*, ed. Edmund Burke III and Ira M. Lapidus. Berkeley: University of California Press, 1988.

"L'arroseur arrose." *Jeune Afrique*. 17 August 1996.

Levtzion, Nehemiah, and John O. Voll, eds. *Eighteenth-Century Renewal and Reform in Islam*. Syracuse: Syracuse University Press, 1987.

Lewis, Bernard. *What Went Wrong: Western Impact and Middle Eastern Response*. New York: Oxford University Press, 2001.

Lorimer, John Gordon. *Gazetteer of the Persian Gulf, Oman, and Central Arabia*. 4 vols. Calcutta: Superintendent of Government Printing, 1915.

Makdisi, George. "The Hanbali School and Sufism." In *Humaniora Islamica*. Vol. 2. The Hague and Paris: Mouton, 1974.

———. "Hanbalite Islam." In *Studies on Islam*, trans. and ed. Merlin L. Swartz. New York: Oxford University Press, 1981.

————. "Ibn Taimiya: A Sufi of the Qadiriya Order." *American Journal of Arabic Studies* 1 (1974): 118–29.

————. *L'Islam Hanbalisant*. Paris: Librairie Orientaliste Paul Geuthner, Ca. 1983.

————. "The Sunni Revival." In *Islamic Civilisation, 950–1150: A Colloquium Published under the Auspices of the Near Eastern History Group, Oxford, and the Near East Center, University of Pennsylvania*, ed. D. S. Richards. Oxford: Faber, 1977.

Margoliouth, D. S. "Wahhabiya." In *E. J. Brill's First Encyclopaedia of Islam, 1913–1936*. Vol. 8. London: Brill, 1987.

Meriwether, Margaret L. "The Rights of Children and the Responsibilities of Women: Women as Wasis in Ottoman Aleppo, 1770–1840." In *Women, the Family, and Divorce Laws in Islamic History*, ed. Amira El Azhary Sonbol. Syracuse: Syracuse University Press, 1996.

Mernissi, Fatima. *The Veil and the Male Elite: A Feminist Interpretation of Women's Rights in Islam*. Translated by Mary Jo Lakeland. Reading, MA: Addison-Wesley, 1991.

Nadwi, Masood Alam. *Mohammad bin Abdul Wahab: A Slandered Reformer*. Translated by M. Rafiq Khan. Jamia Alafia, Varanasi, India: Idaratul Buhoosil Islamia, 1983.

Nashat, Guity, and Judith E. Tucker. *Women in the Middle East and North Africa: Restoring Women to History*. Bloomington: Indiana University Press, 1999.

Niebuhr, Carsten M. *Travels through Arabia and Other Countries in the East*. Vols. 1–2. Edinburgh: R. Morison and Son, 1792.

Ochsenwald, William. *Religion, Society, and the State in Arabia: The Hijaz under Ottoman Control, 1840–1908*. Columbus: Ohio University Press, 1984.

d'Ohsson Ignatius, Mouradjea Ignatius. *Tableau Général de l'Empire Ottoman*. 3 vols. Paris: Imprimerie de M. Firman Didot, 1790.

Palgrave, William Gifford. *Narrative of a Year's Journey through Central and Eastern Arabia (1862–3)*. Vols. 1–2. London and Cambridge: Macmillan, 1865.

Pannier, Bruce. "Wahhabism and the CIS (from Fergana to Chechnya)." RFE/RL, Internet document, 19 May 1997.

Pearl, David. *A Text on Muslim Personal Law*. London: Croom Helm, 1979.

Peters, Rudolph. "Idjtihad and Taqlid in 18th and 19th Century Islam." *Die Welt des Islams*. 20, nos. 3–4 (1980): 131–45.

————. *Jihad in Classical and Modern Islam: A Reader*. Princeton: Markus Wiener, 1996.

Philby, H. St. John. *Saudi Arabia*. London: Ernest Benn, 1955.

Powers, David S. *Studies in Qur'an and Hadith: The Formation of the Islamic Law of Inheritance*. Berkeley: University of California Press, 1986.

Qamar, Zubair. "Who Are the Wahhabees ('Salafis')?" Internet document, 31 March 1988.

Qutb, Sayyid. *Milestones*. Karachi: International Islamic Publishers, 1988.

al-Rasheed, Madawi. *A History of Saudi Arabia*. New York: Cambridge University Press, 2002.

Rashid, Ahmed. *Jihad: The Rise of Militant Islam in Central Asia*. New Haven: Yale University Press, 2002.

————. *Taliban: Militant Islam, Oil, and Fundamentalism in Central Asia*. London: I. B. Tauris, 2000.

Raymond, Jean. *Mémoire sur l'origine des Wahabys sur la naissance de leur puissance et*

sur l'influence dont ils jouissent comme nation: Rapport de J. R. date de 1806, docu-
ment inédit extrait des archives du ministère des affaires étrangères de France. Cairo:
Imprimerie de l'Institut Français d'Archéologie Orientale, 1925.

Rentz, George Snavely, Jr. "Muhammad Ibn 'Abd al-Wahhab (1703/4–1792) and the
Beginnings of the Unitarian Empire in Arabia." Ph.D. diss., University of California, Berkeley, 1948.

———. "Wahhabism and Saudi Arabia." In *The Arabian Peninsula: Society and Politics,* ed. Derek Hopwood. Tonowa, NJ: Rowman & Littlefield, 1972.

Rousseau, Jean Baptiste Louis Jacques. *Description of the Pashalik of Baghdad, suivie
d'une Notice sur les Wahabis, et de quelques autres pièces historiques relatives à
l'histoire et à la litterature de l'Orient.* Paris: Treuttel et Wurtz, 1809.

Sadleir, George Forster. *Diary of a Journey Across Arabia, 1819.* Naples: Oleander, 1977.

Safran, Nadav. *Saudi Arabia: The Ceaseless Quest for Security.* Ithaca and London: Cor-
nell University Press, 1985.

Samuel, Oloche. "Appeal to Stop Stoning Rejected." *Boston Globe,* 20 August 2002.

Sasson, Jean. *Princess: A True Story of Life behind the Veil in Saudi Arabia.* New York:
Morrow, 1992.

Saunders, Daniel. *A Journal of the Travels and Sufferings of Daniel Saunders, Jun.: A
Matter on Board the Ship Commerce, of Boston, Samuel Johnson, Commander,
Which Was Cast Away Near Cape Morebet, on the Coast of Arabia, July 10, 1792.*
Hudson, NY: Ashbel Stoddard, 1805.

Schacht, Joseph. *An Introduction to Islamic Law.* New York: Oxford University Press,
1964.

———. *The Origins of Muhammadan Jurisprudence.* 4th ed. Oxford: Oxford University
Press, 1964.

Schwartz, Stephen. *The Two Faces of Islam: The House of Sa'ud from Tradition to Terror.*
New York: Doubleday, 2002.

Semerdjian, Elyse. "Qadi Justice or Community Interest? Gender, Public Morality,
and Legal Administration in Nineteenth Century Aleppo, Syria." Ph.D. diss.,
Georgetown University, 2002.

al-Shaikh Muhammad b. 'Abd al-Wahhab, Shaikh Sulaiman b. Abdullah b., *Majmu'at
al-Tawhid.* Edited by Rashid Rida. Vol. 1. Cairo: Al-Manar, 1346H/1927.

Sisters-in-Islam. *Are Muslim Men Allowed to Beat Their Wives?* Selangor, Malaysia:
Sisters-in-Islam, 1991.

Sonbol, Amira El Azhary. "Adults and Minors in Ottoman Shari'a Courts and Modern Law." In *Women, the Family, and Divorce Laws in Islamic History,* ed. Amira El
Azhary Sonbol. Syracuse: Syracuse University Press, 1996.

———. "Law and Gender Violence in Ottoman and Modern Egypt." In *Women, the
Family, and Divorce Laws in Islamic History,* ed. Amira El Azhary Sonbol. Syracuse: Syracuse University Press, 1996.

———. "Rape and Law in Ottoman and Modern Egypt." In *Women in the Ottoman
Empire: Middle Eastern Women in the Early Modern Era,* ed. Madeline C. Zilfi. Leiden: Brill, 1997.

Sonbol, Amira El Azhary, ed. *Women, the Family, and Divorce Laws in Islamic History.*
Syracuse: Syracuse University Press, 1996.

Spectorsky, Susan. *Chapters on Marriage and Divorce: Responses of Ibn Hanbal and Ibn
Rahwayh.* Austin: University of Texas Press, 1993.

Speight, R. Marston. "Hadith." In *The Oxford Encyclopedia of the Modern Islamic World*, ed. John L. Esposito. Vol. 2. New York: Oxford University Press, 1995.

Spellberg, D. A. *Politics, Gender, and the Islamic Past: The Legacy of A'isha bint Abi Bakr*. New York: Columbia University Press, 1994.

Stephens, John Lloyd. *Incidents of Travel in Egypt, Arabia Petraea, and the Holy Land*. 11th ed. 2 vols. New York: Harper & Brothers, 1860.

Taha, Mahmoud Mohamed. *The Second Message of Islam*. Translated and introduced by Abdullahi Ahmed An-Na'im. Syracuse: Syracuse University Press, 1987.

Tamisier, Maurice. *Voyage en Arabie*. Graz: Akademische Druck, 1976.

Thompson, Charles. *Travels through Turkey in Asia, the Holy Land, Arabia, Egypt, and Other Parts of the World*. Carlisle, PA: Archibald London, 1813.

Tucker, Judith E. "The Fullness of Affection: Mothering in the Islamic Law of Ottoman Syria and Palestine." In *Women in the Ottoman Empire: Middle Eastern Women in the Early Modern Era*, ed. Madeline C. Zilfi. Leiden: Brill, 1997.

———. " 'And God Knows Best': Fatawa as a Source for the History of Gender in the Arab World." Unpublished paper in the possession of the author.

———. *In the House of Law: Gender and Islamic Law in Ottoman Syria and Palestine*. Berkeley: University of California Press, 1998.

Tucker, Judith E., ed. *Arab Women: Old Boundaries, New Frontiers*. Bloomington: Indiana University Press, 1993.

al-Uthaymin, Abd Allah al-Salih. Interview with author, 18 November 1997, Georgetown University, Washington, DC.

———. "Muhammad Ibn 'Abd al-Wahhab: The Man and His Works." Ph.D. diss., Edinburgh University, 1972.

———. *al-Shaykh Muhammad Ibn Abd al-Wahhab: Hayatuhu wa-Fikruhu*. 2d ed. Riyadh: Dar al-Ulum lil-Tiba'ah wa-al-Nashr, 1992.

Utvik, Bjorn Olav. "The Modernising Force of Islamism." In *Modernizing Islam: Religion in the Public Sphere in the Middle East and Europe*, ed. John L. Esposito and Francois Burgat. London: Hurst, 2003.

Vassiliev, Alexei. *The History of Saudi Arabia*. London: Saqi Books, 1998.

Vogel, Frank Edward. "Islamic Law and Legal System Studies of Saudi Arabia." Ph.D. diss., Harvard University, 1993.

Vogel, Frank Edward, and Samuel L. Hayes III. *Islamic Law and Finance: Religion, Risk, and Return*. The Hague: Kluwer Law International, 1998.

Voll. John O. "Foundations for Renewal and Reform: Islamic Movements in the Eighteenth and Nineteenth Centuries." In *The Oxford History of Islam*, ed. John L. Esposito. New York: Oxford University Press, 1999.

———. "Hadith Scholars and Tariqahs: An 'Ulema Group," *Journal of Asian and African Studies* 15 (July–Oct. 1980): 264–73.

———. *Islam: Continuity and Change in the Modern World*. 2d ed. Syracuse: Syracuse University Press, 1994.

———. "Muhammad Hayat al-Sindi and Muhammad Ibn 'Abd al-Wahhab: An Analysis of an Intellectual Group in Eighteenth Century Medina." *Bulletin of the School of Oriental and African Studies* 38, no. 1 (1975): 32–39.

Wahba, Shaykh Hafiz. "Wahhabism in Arabia: Past and Present." *Journal of the Central Asian Society* 26, no. 4 (1929): 458–67.

Wallin, G. A. *Travels in Arabia (1845 and 1848)*. England: Falcon-Oleander, 1979.

Wellsted, J. R. *Travels in Arabia*. Graz: Akademische Druck, 1978.

Western Arabia and the Red Sea: B.R. 527 (Restricted) Geographical Handbook Series. Naval Intelligence Division of the British Armed Forces, June 1946.

al-Yassini, Ayman. "Ibn 'Abd al-Wahhab, Muhammad." In *The Oxford Encyclopedia of the Modern Islamic World*, ed. John L. Esposito. Vol. 2. New York: Oxford University Press, 1995.

Zarinebaf-Shahr, Fariba. "Women, Law, and Imperial Justice in Ottoman Istanbul in the Late Seventeenth Century." In *Women, the Family, and Divorce Laws in Islamic History*, ed. Amira El Azhary Sonbol. Syracuse: Syracuse University Press, 1996.

Ziadeh, Farhat. "Law: Sunni Schools of Law." In *The Oxford Encyclopedia of the Modern Islamic World*, ed. John L. Esposito. Vol. 2. New York: Oxford University Press, 1995.

Zilfi, Madeline C. " 'We Don't Get Along': Women and *Hul* Divorce in the Eighteenth Century." In *Women in the Ottoman Empire: Middle Eastern Women in the Early Modern Era*, ed. Madeline C. Zilfi. Leiden: Brill, 1997.

Zilfi, Madeline C., ed. *Women in the Ottoman Empire: Middle Eastern Women in the Early Modern Era*. Leiden: Brill, 1997.

Index

bin Laden, Osama (*continued*)
on martyrdom, 275
religious ideology of, 4, 256
as Saudi dissident, 266, 268–71, 272
on Soviet Union, 267
as Sufi, 274
and Taliban, 266
as terrorist, 5, 193
Bosnia, 4
Brydges, Harford Jones, 245–46
al-Bukhari, 52, 104
Buraydah, 233
burqa', 123
Bush, George W., 275

Caliphs, Rightly Guided, 42, 43, 47, 54–
56, 107, 118
Central Asia, 266, 268, 290
Chechnya, 268
Christian fundamentalists, 9
Christianity, 56, 77
Christians, 56, 60–61, 65, 71, 85, 98,
100, 133, 205, 211, 239, 256, 261–62,
274, 275
Cold War, 257, 266
Companions of Muhammad, 10, 31, 32,
47, 50, 52, 53–54, 55, 66, 67, 85, 88,
94, 95, 96, 98, 105, 106, 107, 112,
118, 119, 126, 140, 155, 199, 209,
214, 233
concubines, 125
Crusaders, 262, 274, 275
Crusades, 247–48
custody issues, 188–89

Damascus, 247
dar al-harb, 230, 249
dar al-Islam, 230, 243, 248, 249, 250,
256, 289
dar al-jahiliyyah, 261
dar al-kufr, 230, 243, 248, 256, 289
da'wah, 194, 198–201, 225
Deuteronomy, 12
dhikr, 45
dhimmi, 98, 155, 207, 211, 213, 220, 222,
233–34, 239, 274, 288
al-Diri'yah, 34, 37, 38, 66
divorce. See *khul'*; *talaq*
domestic violence, 170–71

Eastern Province, 83
Egypt, 256–58, 264, 265, 276
engagement, 153
European colonialism, 7, 8, 234–35, 238,
239, 256

fai, 212
Faisal, King of Saudi Arabia, 270
al-Faruqi, Ismail Raji, 3
fatawa, 94, 114, 158, 223–24
of Muhammad Ibn Abd al-Wahhab, 5,
32, 59, 67, 93, 116, 157–58, 223–24
of Osama bin Laden, 275–76
Fatima, 49, 86, 127
Fatima bint Qays, 138
fiqh, 94, 96, 107, 113–15, 121
Firestone, Reuven, 228–32
fitnah, 54, 156, 286
Fi Zilal al-Quran, 259
Free Officers, 257

ghanimah, 212–17
ghazw, 202–3, 213
Goldziher, Ignaz, 108
Gospel, 45
Great Britain, 257
Gulf War, 269, 276

hadith, 27, 28, 29, 62, 63, 68, 144, 164–
65, 195–97, 221–23
authentication of, 10–11
as interpreted by Muhammad Ibn Abd
al-Wahhab, 11, 13, 25, 30, 31, 32, 40,
42, 45–56, 63, 67–68, 69–70, 73,
74, 77–78, 85, 86–90, 91, 94, 95–
101, 103, 104, 105, 106, 107–8, 109–
18, 120–21, 124, 125–27, 129, 134–35,
136–37, 140, 143, 144, 155, 161, 162–
63, 164–65, 173, 174, 195–97, 199–
200, 207, 218, 219, 221–23, 229,
232–33, 240, 253–54, 259, 281–83,
288
and Quran, 51–54
as source of Islamic law, 95–101, 103,
104, 105, 109–18, 120–21, 174
as source of scripture, 9–10, 45–51, 58
study of, 10–11, 20–21, 30
Hamzah, Shaykh Mir, 275
Hanafi law school, 94, 96, 106, 140, 179